PRAISE FOR DAVID KENYON WEBSTER'S
CLASSIC WORLD WAR II MEMOIR
PARACHUTE INFANTRY

"I never had the privilege of meeting David Kenyon Webster, but I admire him without stint. He was a good soldier and a wonderful writer, one of the brave thousands of American combat infantrymen who helped win the war and thus preserve our freedom, and one of those very few with the talent and energy to write about the war in a way to help those of us who came later to understand it."

—Stephen Ambrose (*from the Introduction*)

"I join Stephen Ambrose in recommending this book to anyone of any age with an interest in the exploits of the airborne forces and ground combat in the European Theater of Operations, as told by a truly gifted narrator."

—Clay Blair, *The Washington Post Book World*

"[*PARACHUTE INFANTRY*] merits a place among the classic accounts of men in battle."

—Page Smith

"In this first-rate, skillfully written soldier's story, Webster achieves a perfectly pitched sad sack sarcasm that is an authentic witness to the combat experience. The best of 1994's D-Day anniversary books."

—*Booklist*

PARACHUTE INFANTRY

An American Paratrooper's Memoir of D-Day and the Fall of the Third Reich

DAVID KENYON WEBSTER

Delta Trade Paperbacks

A Delta Book
Published by
Dell Publishing
a division of
Random House, Inc.
1540 Broadway
New York, New York 10036

Cover design by Roberto de Vicq de Cumptich
Cover photograph by Carl Rosenstein

Book design by Virginia Norey

Unless otherwise noted, all illustrations are from the author's personal collection, now in possession of Mrs. Charles B. Embree, Jr.

Photograph on page v, *The American Cemetery in Normandy* by Virginia Norey.

Portions of Chapter 1 first appeared in somewhat different form as "The Night Before D Day," *Saga* (October, 1959). Portions of Chapter 4 first appeared in somewhat different form as "We Drank Hitler's Champagne," *Saturday Evening Post*, May 3, 1952, and are reprinted with permission.

Delta® is a registered trademark of Random House, Inc., and
the colophon is a trademark of Random House, Inc.

LIBRARY OF CONGRESS CATALOGING-IN-PUBLICATION DATA
Webster, David Kenyon, d. 1961.
    Parachute infantry : an American paratrooper's memoir of D-Day and the fall of the Third Reich / David Kenyon Webster.—Rev. ed.
        p. cm.
    "A Delta book."
    Contains letters home from the author.
    ISBN 0-385-33649-7
    1. Webster, David Kenyon, d. 1961.   2. World War, 1939–1945—Campaigns—France—Normandy.   3. United States. Army. Parachute Infantry Regiment, 506th. Company E—History.   4. World War, 1939–1945—Personal narratives, American.   5. Soldiers—United States—Biography.   6. Normandy (France)—History, Military.   I. Title.
D762.N6 W43 2002
940.54'2142—dc21   2002067265

Reprinted by arrangement with Louisiana State University Press
Manufactured in the United States of America
Published simultaneously in Canada
November 2002

BVG   10 9 8

To my wife, Barbara, who was 15 years old
at the time and not aware of D-Day,
and to the friends left in the green fields of Europe,
who never came home to tell about it.

ACKNOWLEDGMENTS

MOST OF THIS BOOK is based on letters written during the war and on recollections put down at length right after the war. Whenever possible, the facts were verified in histories of the period, especially Leonard Rapport and Arthur Northwood, Jr.'s *Rendezvous with Destiny: A History of the 101st Airborne Division* (New York, 1948). The United States Army was quite helpful, providing maps, photographs, and historical works. Special thanks are due Pat Christenson, Bob Rader, Virginia and Leonard Rapport, Burr Smith, and Hans Wesenhagen.

INTRODUCTION

Stephen E. Ambrose

DAVID KENYON WEBSTER MAY HAVE BEEN THE ONLY HARVARD "English lit" major who volunteered for the parachute infantry and who then fought through the campaign in northwest Europe as a combat infantryman. He didn't have to do it. His family was moderately wealthy and had influence, so he could have had a commission if he had wanted one, or a cushy job far behind the front lines. But he wanted to see the war firsthand, to be a participant, to do his part in crushing Hitler and the Nazis. He insisted on fighting from a foxhole rather than typing up reports at Company Headquarters or handing out footballs and baseballs at a rest area in the rear.

His motives for insisting on being a member of a parachute infantry regiment went beyond patriotism. Webster wanted to be a writer. Heavily influenced by the literature of World War I, he wanted to experience and then describe combat. He had a flair for writing, a keen sensitivity, and a well-developed ability to observe and comment. With those talents, and using the perspective of a paratrooper, he produced an outstanding memoir of the war. It is rich in detail and rewarding in its revealing anecdotes about men at war. Webster is scathing in his denunciation of officers who were "chickenshit," whether in barracks or on the front lines. He is full of heartfelt praise for noncoms and enlisted men who did their jobs. He is honest about the actions of his fellow soldiers, in camp, in combat, as conquerors.

Webster's book has all the features that make for a classic wartime memoir. He describes training; the relationships that develop within a squad, platoon, and company; the first combat jump into Normandy; the experience of killing and getting shot at (and hit); attitudes toward civilians, whether friendly as in France and Holland or unfriendly as in Germany; grousing about the army and its ways; and more. Webster manages to show us the general and the particular, the universal experience and the unique detail, in a flow of words that the most professional writer would envy.

Overall, I recommend this memoir to anyone who wants to know more about World War II, about combat, about being a paratrooper, about discovering oneself and being involved when the whole world was being tested and threatened. It brings back a place and a time, a sense of commitment, the feeling of "we are all in this together" as the United States and her allies fought for freedom.

MOST GIS IN WORLD WAR II found that their service in the army was a broadening experience. Webster was no exception. The soldiers met men they never would have known otherwise, men from all over America, men from different economic, social, and ethnic backgrounds. In the novels about the war, the typical squad is made up of a Jew from New York, an Indian from Montana, a Swede from Minnesota, a Pole from Chicago, a Cajun from New Orleans, and so on. At the beginning of the novel, they hate one another. The shared misery of training pulls them together, as does the common hatred of their drill instructors and junior officers. Combat strengthens the bond, to the point that they become a band of brothers, trusting and loving one another as they had never before trusted or loved anyone. And the truth is that this happened in fact before it was written up as fiction—in this case at least art truly imitated life.

Webster was a man of books and libraries, a reader and a writer, thrown into an intimate and life-dependent relationship with ill-educated hillbillies, southern farmers, coal miners, lumbermen, fishermen, and other typical paratrooper enlisted men—in short, with a group of men with whom he had nothing in common. He would not have particularly liked or disliked them in civilian life—he just would not have known them. Yet it was among this unlikely group of men that Webster found his closest friendships and enjoyed most thoroughly the sense of identification with others.

He was wounded in Holland, in October, 1944. He rejoined his squad in January, 1945, and later he recalled his feelings: "It was good to be back with fellows I knew and could trust. Listening to the chatter, I felt warm and relaxed inside, like a lost child who has returned to a bright home full of love after wandering in a cold black forest." He went on: "You felt like part of a big family. You are closer to these men than you will ever be to any civilians."

Webster and his fellow squad members had developed a bond that is unique to combat infantrymen. Just as there is no human experience to equal that of combat, so there is no human relationship to equal that of comrades-in-arms. Their relationships are closer than those of brothers, different from those of lovers, stronger and deeper than those of friends.

Philosopher J. Glenn Gray, himself a frontline soldier in World War II, got it exactly right in his classic work *The Warriors*: "Organization for a common and concrete goal in peacetime organizations does not evoke anything like the degree of comradeship commonly known in war. . . . At its height, this sense of comradeship is an ecstasy. . . . Men are truly comrades only when each is ready to give up his life for the other, without reflection and without thought of his personal loss."[1]

Private Kurt Gabel of the 513th Parachute Infantry Regiment described his experience in words that Webster might have written: "The three of us, Jake, Joe, and I, became . . . an entity. There were many entities in our close-knit organizations . . . core elements within the families. . . . This sharing evolved never to be relinquished, never to be repeated. [It produced] incredible results in combat. [Men] would literally insist on going hungry for one another, freezing for one another, dying for one another. And the squad would try to protect them or bail them out without the slightest regard to consequences, cussing them all the way for making it necessary. Such a rifle squad . . . was a mystical concoction."[2]

I have interviewed hundreds of soldiers from World War II—American, British, Canadian, German, French—ranging from the supreme commander of the Allied Expeditionary Force to the lowest privates. Virtually without exception, they tell me that their closest friends, the men from whom they have no secrets, the men with whom they would gladly share their last piece of bread, the men they call on the phone when they get drunk on New Year's Eve, the men they name their children af-

---

1. J. Glenn Gray, *The Warriors: Reflections on Men in Battle* (New York, 1959), 43, 45, 46.
2. Kurt Gabel, *The Making of a Paratrooper Airborne Training and Combat in World War II* (Lawrence, Kans., 1990), 142.

ter, are the men with whom they served in the war. No one could ever envy the combat experience—it is truly hell—but everyone has to envy the comradeship that is unique to the combat experience.

All armies, through the ages, have attempted to create that bonding that becomes an "ecstasy," a "mystical concoction," but few succeeded as well as the paratroop infantry of the U.S. Army in World War II, and none better than was done in Webster's rifle company, Company E of the 506th Parachute Infantry.

PROFESSOR PAUL FUSSELL, a junior officer in a rifle company in the war, wrote in his book *Wartime* that the soldier going into combat the first time thinks to himself: "It *can't* happen to me. I am too clever/agile/well-trained/good-looking/beloved/tightly laced, etc.," to ever get hit. After a few hours or days or weeks of combat, that attitude gives way to: "It *can* happen to me, and I'd better be more careful. I can avoid the danger by watching more prudently the way I take cover/dig in/expose my position by firing my weapon/keep extra alert at all times, etc." Then comes the realization that "It *is going to* happen to me, and only my not being there [on the front lines] is going to prevent it."[3]

Webster could attest to the truth of Fussell's insight. After his combat jump into Normandy, when he had returned to England to prepare for the next jump, Webster wrote his parents: "I am living on borrowed time. I do not think I shall live through the next jump. If I don't come back, try not to take it too hard. I wish I could persuade you to regard death as casually as we do over here. In the heat of battle you expect casualties, you expect somebody to be killed and you are not surprised when a friend is machine-gunned in the face. You have to keep going. It's not like civilian life, where sudden death is so unexpected."

When his mother wrote to express her considerable alarm at this attitude (and her worries about her youngest son, John, who had just joined the paratroopers), Webster was blunt in his reply: "Would you prefer for somebody else's son to die in the mud? You want us to win the war, but you apparently don't want to have your sons involved in the actual bloodshed. That's a strangely contradictory attitude. Somebody has

---

3. Paul Fussell, *Wartime: Understanding and Behavior in the Second World War* (New York, 1989), 282.

to get in and kill the enemy. Somebody has to be in the infantry and the paratroopers. If the country all had your attitude, nobody would fight, everybody would be in the Quartermaster. And what kind of country would that be?"

For the combat infantryman, there is no way out short of the end of the war or the loss of a limb. Any other wound would be patched up and the soldier sent back to the front lines. So it was with Webster. In Holland, in October, during an attack on a German position, "what felt like a baseball bat slugged my right leg." Webster recalled that it "spun me around and knocked me down." All he could think to say was, "They got me!" which even then seemed to him "an inadequate and unimaginative cliché." (Like all writers, he was composing his description of the event as it happened.)

It was a clean wound. The bullet went in and out of Webster's calf, hitting no bone. A million-dollar wound. I got it made, he thought to himself. When the medic got to him, Webster had a big grin on his face.

The grin didn't stay. Webster was patched up, sent to a replacement depot, and listed as fit for combat. He insisted on rejoining his unit: If he had to fight, he wanted to be with the best, and E Company of the 506th PIR had no superior. "If I had my choice," he wrote his parents, "I'd never fight again. Having no choice, I'll go back to E Company and prepare for another jump. If I die, I hope it'll be fast." In another letter, he wrote, "The realization that there is no escape, that we shall jump on Germany, then ride transports straight to the Pacific for the battle in China, does not leave much room for optimism."

He wasn't volunteering. He never volunteered. He made it a rule of his army life never to do anything voluntarily. He was an intellectual, as much an observer and chronicler of the phenomenon of soldiering as a practitioner. He was there to do his duty, and he did it, but he never volunteered.

He also never let a buddy down in combat and was ready to go above and beyond the call of duty if necessary. In February, 1945, at Haguenau in western Germany, he and Private Bob Marsh got orders to set up a machine gun to provide covering fire for a patrol if needed. They were exposed in such a way that if they fired, a German self-propelled gun directly across the river would spot them without the aid of observers. But they decided that if the patrol was fired upon, they would open up with everything they had, "because the lives of some twenty men might depend on us." Webster, the usually cool observer, commented, "This was one of those times where I could see playing the hero even if it meant death."

ONE CHARACTERISTIC OF LIFE on the front lines is that there is no past or future, only the present. Glenn Gray calls it "the tyranny of the present." He speculates that this is why soldiers will go to such extraordinary lengths to get souvenirs. In Holland, as he was crawling and limping his way to the rear after suffering his leg wound, under fire from a German 88mm cannon, Webster spotted a German camouflaged poncho and decided it would make "an ideal souvenir." He stopped to "scoop it up." Gray explains why Webster, and so many others, would take such chances for a worthless piece of uniform: "Primarily, souvenirs appeared to give the soldier some assurance of his future beyond the destructive environment of the present. They represented a promise that he might survive."[4]

WEBSTER LOVED the Dutch people, thought the British people were quaint but dull, had serious reservations about the French, and began the war hating the Germans. He wanted them taught a lesson, so that they would never again try to conquer Europe. In July, 1944, he wrote his parents, "I cannot understand why you hope for a quick end of the war. Unless we take the horror of battle to Germany itself, unless we fight in their villages, blowing up their houses, smashing open their wine cellars, killing some of their livestock for food, unless we litter their streets with horribly rotten German corpses as was done in France, the Germans will prepare for war, unmindful of its horrors. Defeat must be brought into Germany itself before this mess can come to a proper end; a quick victory now, a sudden collapse, will leave the countryside relatively intact and the people thirsty for revenge. I want the war to end as quickly as anybody wishes, but I don't want the nucleus of another war left whole."

In April, 1945, after seeing his first slave labor camp, Webster was furious. "There was Germany and all it stood for," he wrote. "The Germans had taken these people from their homes and sentenced them to work for life in a factory in the Third Reich. With cold deliberation the Ger-

4. Gray, *The Warriors*, 82.

mans had enslaved the populace of Europe." So far as Webster was concerned, "The German people were guilty, every one of them."

But after living in Germany for a few weeks, Webster found that despite himself he was drawn to the people. "The Germans I have seen so far have impressed me as clean, efficient, law-abiding people," he wrote his parents. They were churchgoers. "In Germany everybody goes out and works and, unlike the French, who do not seem inclined to lift a finger to help themselves, the Germans fill up the trenches soldiers have dug in their fields. They are cleaner, more progressive, and more ambitious than either the English or the French." Like other GIs, Webster identified with the clean, hard-working, disciplined, educated, middle-class Germans. Right here was laid the basis for the German-American alliance that flourished during the Cold War.

WEBSTER HATED THE ARMY. He hated its chickenshit ways, its bumbling bureaucracy, its privileges for officers and contempt for enlisted men. He wouldn't have done it again for one million dollars—but he wouldn't have taken a million dollars for the experience, either.

He got out of the army in 1945, thankful beyond words that he didn't have to make that "big jump" into Japan. He moved to California and worked at a variety of jobs as he wrote and submitted articles and the manuscript of his memoirs to various publishers. He placed many articles, the top being in the *Saturday Evening Post* on the taking of Hitler's Eagle's Nest in the Alps, but he could not find a publisher for his memoirs. (The publishers right after the war wanted novels with lots of sex, not authentic memoirs.) He became a reporter, first with the Los Angeles *Daily News*, then with the *Wall Street Journal*. In 1951 he married Barbara Stoessel, an artist and sister of Walter J. Stoessel, Jr., who later became American ambassador to Poland, the Soviet Union, and West Germany.

Webster had always been fascinated by sharks. Barbara explained: "The shark, for him, became a symbol of everything that is mysterious and fierce about the sea. He began gathering material for a book of his own. His research went on for years. He studied sharks firsthand, underwater, swimming among them; and caught many, fishing with a handline from his eleven-foot sailing dinghy, which he had named *Tusitala*, which means 'Teller of Tales.' "

Webster wrote his book and submitted it twenty-nine times, but could not convince a publisher that anyone wanted to read about sharks.

On September 9, 1961, Webster set sail from Santa Monica with squid bait, a heavy line, and hook for shark fishing. He never came back. A search the next day discovered the *Tusitala* awash five miles offshore. One oar and the tiller were missing. His body was never found.

Barbara was able to get his book on sharks published in 1963, by W. W. Norton and Company, under the title *Myth and Maneater.* There was a British edition and a paperback edition in Australia. When *Jaws* was released in 1975, Dell issued *Myth and Maneater* in a mass-market paperback.

For my part, I never had the privilege of meeting David Kenyon Webster, but I admire him without stint. He was a good soldier and a wonderful writer, one of those brave thousands of American combat infantrymen who helped win the war and thus preserve our freedom, and one of those very few with the talent and energy to write about the war in a way to help those of us who came later to understand it.

PARACHUTE INFANTRY

FOREWORD

ALL MY LIFE I WANTED TO GO TO ENGLAND. I WANTED TO RIDE A big, black boat with white cabins and red funnels across the Atlantic and bicycle through the British Isles to the places that I had read about in *Ivanhoe, Kidnapped, Robin Hood, Lorna Doone,* and *The Black Arrow.*

My poets were the English poets, and when I played with toy soldiers, they, too, were English: sturdy, kilted Scotchmen running with fixed bayonets; tall, bright-red Guardsmen on parade in great black busbies. As a small child, I was dressed by my parents, who are of English and Scotch descent, like Christopher Robin in button shoes, leggins that buttoned up the side, and a dashing little Black Watch cap with a checkered red-and-white band around its sides and two twirling black ribbons in back.

Finally, in September, 1943, I did go to England. I was a little boy no longer. The toy soldiers had come to life. Instead of a Black Watch cap with ribbons, I wore a steel helmet with a parachutist's chin strap. Jump boots were my leggins now, an M-1 rifle my steamer basket.

We came down from Camp Shanks and crossed the black Hudson at midnight on a ferry from West New York. Welders were cutting up the capsized hull of the *Normandie* nearby, but there was no time for sight-seeing, for all too soon the ferry banged into the river end of the Cunard Line pier and dropped its ramp and up we went.

Gone were the stevedores and the taxis out front, gone the white-jacketed porters, the hurrying peacetime voyagers and their friends and relations. In their place we filed, a lone Battalion bent under its barracks bags. Half a dozen Red Cross women handed us coffee and dough-nuts and little green sewing kits, but we could not linger to chat with them. We marched quickly by with a faraway look in our eyes, snatched cards marked with our sleeping quarters and eating time from an officer at the foot of the gangplank, and without stopping, clutched our steep, sweaty way onto the old gray *Samaria* and went aft to the sheets of canvas stretched between iron pipes that were our bunks.

We left in the morning. There were no steamer baskets, there was no confetti. There was no "All ashore who are going ashore!" because *nobody* was going ashore. Our sole audience was a handful of bored stevedores standing by the hawsers. They cast us off, and the hawsers splashed and wriggled back up into the ship. Then the tugs pushed us out and left us, and we turned slowly, without a band or a wave of good-bye, and went down the river with the tide.

I was going to England at last, but not quite as I had envisioned.

The Jump into
Normandy

IT WAS THE END OF MAY, 1944. WE HAD BEEN IN ENGLAND EIGHT months while others fought, and now our time had come. A last inspection, a last short-arm; clean the barracks and police the area. Every man gets a new jumpsuit and an orange smoke grenade. We move out at noon.

O.K., let's go. Mount the buses and say goodbye to the village of Aldbourne, to its green hills and mossy barns and thatched cottages, to the white pubs, the brown cow-pond, the old gray church. A V sign, a wave of the hand, a friendly smile for the two bakers and Barney and Ma and the crippled man who drags a child's cart, collecting cans for the scrap-metal drive. No more London, no more mild-and-bitter, no more field problems or playground jumps.

We were hot and crowded on the ride south but not unaware of the beauty around us, a beauty made more lovely by the knowledge that many of us would never see it again. Loaded with gear and ammunition and sweating terribly in woolen winter uniforms, we drove under the tall green trees south of camp, past Wittenditch and the back hill to Ramsbury, past the cozy tea room at Chilton Foliat and the water meadow and cattail bog that fronted on the pink, Elizabethan magnificence of Littlecote Manor, home of the legendary wild Darrells and more recently of our regimental commander, Colonel Robert F. Sink.

We crossed the Kennet River on an arched stone bridge, made a sharp left turn at the Froxfield-Littlecote intersection, and rolled through Hungerford to the Great Western Railroad station on the outskirts, where we must have waited for hours. At least it seemed like hours, for the sun was so hot, our gear so tight, our clothes so airless and itchy. Gradually the talk died down and more and more men lay back on their musette bags and fell asleep. Tension passed into boredom.

It was supposed to be a secret that we were setting off for the Invasion of Europe, but the secret was hard to keep from passersby. Our fresh

bandoleers, new ammunition pouches, and full musette bags; the camouflage netting on our helmets; the bundles of orange cloth and identification panels that almost every man carried; the trench knives sewn on
our boots; the tense, excited way we talked.

I, however, was still skeptical, for I had imagined that our last move
would be at least as well disguised as our arrival in Aldbourne. It would
be proper, correct, and traditional, I thought, to fade away from Aldbourne on a cold, dark night in a sealed convoy. After all we had been
told about security, it seemed foolish to move us out so openly for
D-Day at hot high noon. I looked at the orange cloth and the orange
smoke grenades and loudly proclaimed, "Hell, this is just another goddamn maneuver. This time we're the orange team."

Our train slid in and stopped. We piled aboard, a squad of twelve to
each compartment designed for six civilians, threw our excess gear on
the floor, and put the machine guns and mortars in the luggage racks
overhead and the musette bags under the seats. Down came the broad
leather window straps and with them the windows, and soon everybody
had settled back quietly with his thoughts and his memories and forebodings to rest awhile and enjoy the trip.

Fast and smooth we rode, shot through the green landscape in our
sealed tube, as if we were trying to make up for all our waiting. We rattled south and west, through pocket villages and little towns we'd never
heard of before. Through Pewsey and Westbury and Bruton and Cas
Cory, Yeovil and Axminster. Through tunnels and across rivers that
would be brooks and creeks in our own land (the Avon, the Wylye, the
Stour, the Frome, the Axe). As we got sleepier and sleepier, we came
nearer the Channel and saw scores of overgrown 1940 pillboxes, their
sagging barbed wire draped with wild vines.

"Tweet, tweet!" our engine shrilled as we rattled through the stations
without a pause. "D-Day calling," the wheels replied, "D-Day calling,
D-Day calling, D-Day calling."

We dozed or talked softly, smoked or looked out the windows, opened
our K rations and ate them. The hills got bigger and greener, with great,
shadowy belts of trees on their tops, and the train increased its speed.
Whistling shrilly at tunnels that blew soot back at us through the open
windows, it carried us like a tidal wave toward the dark shore of combat
for which we had been so long preparing. On and on, "D-Day calling,
D-Day calling, D-Day calling."

At twilight time, we rattled into a village way station and stopped. Men got out of the forward cars, cursing and banging their gear, and soon an officer shouted in our window, "Everybody outside! This is it."

We untangled our harness and twisted into it and fell out on the platform, rubbing our eyes in the sudden glare. HONITON, a sign said.

We looked around and saw a little brown hamlet poured unevenly down steep cobblestone streets. Not a civilian was in sight. It was so utterly deserted that it reminded me of Las Vegas at nine in the morning.

Machine guns and mortars on our shoulders, we staggered up a steep incline, turned a corner, climbed aboard a column of trucks waiting for us with tailgates down and motors running, and drove slowly out of town.

"Where are we going?" someone asked our driver.

"To this airfield five miles out."

"Oh . . ."

And that was that.

The long brown convoy snaked and whined and grated uphill with dryly shifting gears on a narrow, dusty road. Higher and higher we went, until at last we reached the topmost plateau, a man-made butte for runways. We stopped in a country lane bordered by stout hedgerows sweet with honeysuckle.

I looked over the tailgate and saw a half-timbered cottage down the way and a line of green pyramidal tents on the other side of the north hedge and suddenly recognized the place. We had bivouacked here before the last night jump a few weeks ago. It was simply a bivouac area then and a very good one, but nothing more. Now it was the marshaling area.

ENTERTAINERS AND NEWSMEN on deadline can talk all they want to about tension, but they wouldn't know tension if you dipped it in a bucket of water and hit them in the face with it—unless they had spent five days in a marshaling area, waiting to start the Invasion of Europe.

The only comparable sensation would be those last five days in the death house, when everybody is quiet and considerate and they feed you well and let you sleep late and write letters and give you little favors and comforts. The chaplain comes around to see you, the warden makes a speech, and maybe you write a letter to your mother.

If you have a mother and she still cares.

Or you write your girlfriend, who is probably going steady with somebody else by now, as ours were.

Finally there isn't anything more to do. You eat your last meal and put on your clothes and walk down the corridor to the big flash. You go out of the world the way you came in: surrounded by people and utterly alone.

That's the way it was in the marshaling area.

Ours included both the runways from which the C-47s and gliders were to take off and the tent cities pitched on their outskirts for the accommodation of waiting parachutists and glidermen. Troops were assembled here for greater control, absolute secrecy, and more intimate instruction in the tasks before them. They were briefed and issued maps and whatever special equipment or ammunition was necessary to complete their wardrobe. They loaded the bellies and doorways of C-47s with parapaks of bandoleers, mortar shells, and machine-gun ammunition, with K rations and D rations, medical supplies, and 75mm pack howitzers. Jeeps, trailers, and fully assembled 105s were lashed down in British Horsa and American CG4A gliders. Nobody visited other companies, nobody left the area for a mild-and-bitter. We walked in the shadows of the hedgerows and amused ourselves without the Red Cross or the U.S.O.

Since S.H.A.E.F., or something equally academic and Olympian, feared the consequences of German observation planes noticing new paths beaten across the meadows to the slit trenches, we were ordered to follow the U-shape of the hedges to the latrine, instead of cutting straight across. S.H.A.E.F. never explained how the Luftwaffe could miss hundreds of planes and gliders and scores of tents and still pick up a threadlike Indian trail through foot-long grass. But then, S.H.A.E.F. never explained a lot of things.

THE TRUCKS DROVE AWAY and left us in the peaceful silence of a country twilight. The sun was fading, swallows glided home, and still we stood, hot, tired, sooty, and churlish. Our O.D.s itched. We were bleary from naps on the train and dusty from the truck ride. The snaps on our musette bags bit and twisted into our collarbones. Be done with it, be done with it! our patience cried. We've hurried up and waited for two long years. Now let's *go!*

"Is the coffee ready yet?" someone called in a loud voice to our right. A cuckoo whispered down the lane by the timbered cottage, and there was a clatter of pans out of sight behind the north hedge. Its wings and fuselage marked with broad white identification bands, a great, brown C-47 rustled over us with its flaps down and glided to a landing out of sight several hundred yards away.

Our captain, who had disappeared through an opening in the hedge, popped up again and took a stand on a mound in the opening. "On your feet, Headquarters Company!" he shouted. "Let's go!"

THE FOOD SITUATION was incredible. No sooner had we relaxed on our camp cots in squad tents as close and hot as New York in August than a shrill cry of "Chow!" brought us out on the path with a clatter of utensils. Friendly, obliging Air Corps K.P.s loaded our tin dishes like garbage scows. It was a beautiful load: white bread (our first overseas), great gobs of melting butter, marmalade from an open keg swarming with yellow-jackets, rice pudding and cream, all the coffee you can drink.

"Seconds? Why sure, help yourself, buddy."

"You're kidding?"

"No, no, we got orders to give you guys all you want."

The millennium had arrived.

While we were smoking and chatting and thinking about thirds in the hushed, drowsy lull afterward, the C.Q. put his head in the tent flaps and shouted something about a movie in fifteen minutes.

A rumor, we said. White bread and movies on the same day? Impossible.

But this was the marshaling area, where Air Corps engineers did all the chores and nothing was too good for paratroopers, so movies it was.

They were held in the base theater near the runways half a mile away, with the whole Regiment in attendance. The atmosphere was more like a cruise to Bermuda or a high-school graduation party than a prelude to Invasion. Friends shouted to friends in other companies and battalions; officers visited back and forth; Colonel Sink stood benignly up front like a headmaster, smiling at his boys, or people, as he called us.

The movie started with a Gothic title starkly emblazoned on a gigantic swastika. This was soundly hissed. The camera lowered its focus to a battalion commander below the swastika who was addressing his men in frantic, Hitlerian fashion from a platform in a hangar. He wore a parachutist's rimless bowl helmet and a long, spotted jump jacket. His pants were perfectly bloused over his boots. The sound track, which was in German, carried his guttural ravings to us. We hissed again and again.

When his speech was over, his men leaped to their feet, shot their right arms in the air, and shouted, "Heil Hitler!" Then they turned and trotted out to the planes.

Their mission, a narrator explained in English, was to seize and hold a bridge at Moerdyk, Holland, until an S.S. panzer division broke through and relieved them. We followed their progress closely, for the picture, like everything that had to do with foreign paratroopers, was fascinating.

The Germans adjusted their chutes and piled into their corrugated-iron JU-187s, which resembled the old Ford trimotors. As they climbed through the door, they waved to the cameraman and smiled with bravado, but they weren't fooling anybody. They were scared. We could see the fear in their eyes.

We saw it in their faces, too, when they stood up and hooked up, and in the jumpmaster's mouth as he leaned out the door and checked the country below for landmarks.

Suddenly he nudged the second man and pointed down. "There it is! There it is!" he seemed to say.

A wide river and a long black bridge rode slowly into view far below.

The Germans started jumping when the plane was on the other side of the river. Jumping, did I say? They swan-dived, spread their arms and sailed out like divers off a high board. We roared with laughter. It was a ludicrous sight.

They were less amusing on the ground. As the chutes floated down so soft and white and pretty, the Germans went into action. They ripped off their harness and ran fast across the flat meadows toward a village near the bridge. They were determined men who carried their machine pistols and machine guns as if they fully intended to use them. Dodging into holes and ditches and running madly from tree to tree and house to house, they showed a perfect knowledge of the theory of war and its practical application.

Soon the Germans had cleared the village, blasted the pillboxes at the bridge approaches, and captured some rather sheepish, obviously rehearsed Dutch soldiers in medieval black helmets. Then they dug in.

The Dutch counterattacked. Mortars burst on the houses and around the Germans' holes and thundered black and heavy on the bridge, but the invaders held. Finally the S.S. rattled across the river in black tanks. The paratroopers jumped wildly out of their holes and hugged them, and the picture was over. It ended as it had begun: with a swastika.

We thought of those burly German paratroopers in the long silence before the lights came on again and wondered if they would be waiting for us wherever we were going. Sensing our subdued mood, Colonel Sink got up and made a little speech that I will reproduce as best I can.

"Men," he said, wiping his face with his hand, "we've shown you this picture because we wanted you to see how the Germans fight.

"Did you watch them closely? Did you see how fast they moved? How they used every bit of the available cover and concealment? Remember those things when you go into combat.

"You remember what General Montgomery told you. He said he'd seen the German troopers and he'd seen you, and by God, he said he felt sorry for the Germans. You're bigger than they are and a hell of a lot better. You *can* whip 'em, and by God, you *will*!

"Now go get a good night's sleep. We have a lot of things to do in the next couple of days."

THERE WAS NO REVEILLE in the marshaling area. With a whistle for a mouth, the C.Q. stuck his head in the tent and screamed, "Breakfast!" and either you got up or you didn't. Nobody cared; only your stomach knew the difference. Those who ate got seconds and thirds on fried eggs (a monthly treat in Aldbourne) while those who didn't slept on, with less time to worry.

When the mess kits were washed and the late sleepers roused, we folded our blankets at the foot of the cots, rolled up the sides of the tents, and waited passively for the first formation. No word came, and as the sun rose higher and the tent got hot, more and more men fell asleep again. The only sound was the buzzing of the flies.

That's when the rumor blew through the tents. "The news is out!" men called from field to field and hedgerow to hedgerow. "They've chosen the drop zone."

The C.Q. came around shortly afterward, and we left the area in formation and assembled, one platoon at a time, in the closely guarded battalion briefing tent. Our platoon leader told us that a real beauty was waiting for us here.

Two large sandtables stood on yard-high legs in the center of the tent. Maps and diagrams hung from the rear wall. Our instructor, the S-2 captain, watched us come in and look around. Yale men, his face seemed to say as he stared at us dully with a studied air of unshaven indifference, must remain poised and blasé in the presence of the unwashed. When the last man had ducked in, the guard secured the door flap and the captain started to talk.

"I have something here," he said, "that may interest you: a sort of field problem . . . These are sandtables, one for the big picture and one our own size. You've seen other sandtables before at other airfields before other jumps, but these are different.

"We're jumping behind the enemy lines on the peninsula of Normandy. Don't look blank. Surely you've heard of Normandy? It's a large peninsula on the coast of central France about a hundred miles southeast of here."

He stepped to the back wall, unrolled a map of southern England and central France, and taking a pointer, indicated Normandy.

"Here's where we are, and here's where we're going. Normandy's rather a large peninsula, but we're not going to take it all—at first.

"We're going to jump behind the beaches ahead of the infantry. We'll go in about midnight, they'll hit the beach at six A.M. So we'll be all alone that night.

"There are two beaches: Utah, here, and Omaha, here. We drop behind Utah. The 4th Division is supposed to pass through us on D-Day.

"If they take the beach.

"The 82nd's jumping up here around St. Mere Eglise, and the British 6th Airborne Division will go in ahead of their infantry here. But let's not worry about those people. We'll have enough worries of our own."

The captain stepped from the map to one of the sandtables. Nobody breathed. Normandy? Normandy? I said to myself. All I know about Normandy is William the Conqueror, and that was 1066.

"Gather around me here, so everybody can see. If I point it out to you on the sandtable, then perhaps you will be better able to visualize the operation.

"See this bend, where Normandy joins the mainland? See the flat green land at the bend? That's the estuary of the Douve River. It divides the two beachheads. Carentan is the key city. We have to take the bridges to it and the high ground along the Douve, but we'll land north of the river behind Utah Beach, here.

"The main purpose of jumping at night, aside from the obvious ones of dodging flak and surprising the Germans, is to give us plenty of time to clear the roads to the beach, so the 4th Division can get in. The 101st has to take the four southern causeways from Utah Beach to the high ground and hold them open at all costs. We'll also have to take the key villages and strongpoints and knock out a couple of gun batteries and any odd Jerrys who get in our way.

"Our Regiment must take the two causeways, Exits One and Two, here. The Germans may flood the low ground behind the beach and confine the infantry to these causeways so they are *A* Number One on our list of objectives. They have to be taken and *held.*

"Those gun batteries I just mentioned have to be wiped out. If they're not fully destroyed, we may be all alone in Normandy, because they can stop the infantry right in the water. Somebody will also have to blow up the communications lines to the beach and somebody else will have to take these little villages: St. Marie du Mont, St. Martin de Varreville, Foucarville, St. Germain de Varreville, Audouville, La Hubert, Pouppeville, and a couple of others you needn't worry about.

"As far as we know, not too many Germans are waiting for us down there. We have information coming in from the Underground every day and photo-reconnaissance planes over the area right now, and we don't think the Germans are expecting us. There's a tank school in Carentan, which is the biggest city in our sector and one that we'll probably have to take later, but they're training with beat-up old 1939 Renault tanks and shouldn't cause us too much trouble.

"The other Germans are mostly static-defense troops, low-grade Poles and White Russians with German officers and noncoms. Most of them were forced into the Wehrmacht after they were captured on the eastern front, so they shouldn't put up a very enthusiastic fight. They're formed into two divisions: the 709th and the 243rd. The 243rd has a lot of veterans who were transferred from the Russian front to Normandy for a rest. We won't give them much rest, I can assure you. Oh yes, G-2 says that elements of the 716th Infantry Division are also roaming around down there. But don't worry about those three divisions. A German division is lucky nowadays if it has three thousand men in it.

"Just a few more words before you go. Our mission, as I said before, is to jump behind the enemy lines on the peninsula of Normandy. Now for the timing.

"We'll leave at 11:30 P.M. The 2nd Battalion will drop and assemble on radar and a string of three white lights set up by the Pathfinders in an orchard near a crossroads village named Hébert. We'll march to and hold the two southern causeways from Utah Beach. We'll kill any Germans who get in our way.

"And don't forget that word *kill*! Hitler has ordered the Wehrmacht to treat all Allied parachutists as spies and shoot them on the spot. So you know what to do with the Germans. We're not playing with flags and umpires anymore."

Glancing disdainfully at his wristwatch, the captain ended his monologue and looked around the tent, dull-eyed and absolutely uninterested.

IT SCARED ME, it seemed like a dream, I kept hoping I'd wake up and find myself in Aldbourne. We were jumping behind the enemy lines at midnight and meeting three divisions of Germans.

Good God.

It was typical of the Regiment, though, and in keeping with everything that we had done before—perhaps that was why we had done them. In basic training, we had run seven miles up and down a north Georgia mountain, Currahee by name (a translation of which furnished our regimental motto, "We Stand Alone"), and did it in forty-five minutes. We had made a record forced march of 115 miles in three days from Toccoa, Georgia, to Atlanta. We had had only 1 percent refusals at the Parachute School, as compared with the usual average of 20 percent. Now they told us that we (and the 501 and 502) were to fight three divisions of Germans. It was fitting and proper.

But I didn't like it a bit.

The war for me, as for most men, was not a career or a chance for advancement—those things were for generals only—but a trap in which I might well be killed or maimed for life.

It came over me now, as I dozed in the warm sunshine and thought of summers when my life was my own, when I sirred nobody and wore what I pleased. I closed my eyes and dreamt of fishing from an old gray rowboat tied to a bell buoy a mile off Wickford harbor, of sailing to fallow islands in Narragansett Bay and exploring deserted farmhouses, of canoeing through dark pine woods on a cold Adirondack stream, of hiking down the Grand Canyon and across the Colorado River for a dip in Bright Angel Creek and then hiking out again. In those days I could decide a certain amount of my fate. This was now in other hands, hands guided by brains that regarded me not as a person who liked boats and travel and the wet wind on a ruffled sea, but as a number.

EISENHOWER ARGUED for our mission with timid British airmen and insisted on dropping paratroopers behind the beaches and finally had his way even with that grand amateur strategist Winston Churchill. Nothing, he told them in secret conferences, would be left to chance. The planes would be clearly marked and heavily escorted, the Navy alerted for their passage, the pilots and parachutists intensively briefed. Give the airborne and the assault infantry the best possible equipment, he said, and the most comprehensive physical and psychological preparation. Allow them no time for daydreaming or self-pity.

Issue maps, beautiful maps, maps so complicated that they would baffle the world's cartographers, maps so delightfully simple and explicit that they showed the individual houses in St. Marie du Mont. The officers get silken souvenir getaway maps that are to be hidden on their person for use in case of capture. All ranks draw three yard-square maps of Normandy, two for the base and one for Cherbourg and the tip. A distorted photo-map of the drop zone is given each man to play with as with a picture puzzle.

The maps led to our parachutes, which were stored in a huge hangar on the edge of the airfield. We marched cheerfully down the lane and passed an old woman in a Hansel-and-Gretel cottage who came to the gate to smile and wave to us.

The regimental riggers who always packed our chutes were waiting for us at the hangar's mouth with a mountain of green canvas kit bags containing our main and reserve parachutes. We threw our bags on our shoulders and staggered indoors, where our company commander lined us up and bade us fit on our harness.

And so we sweated with leg straps, main lift webs, bellybands, and chest buckles, loosening here, tightening there, until all were evenly secured and so tight that we were bent over like arthritic old men. We checked the fish-line lacing on the outer cover of our backpacks, for this alone held the canopy in until our falling body weight ripped off the cover, and made sure that our anchor line was tucked securely into its rubber bands on the top of the cover. Click, snap; click, snap: Make sure the anchor line snap fastener works smoothly. We are jumping at midnight. There will not be time or light enough to check these things then. So check and recheck and check again and again.

When the chutes had been adjusted, we put them back in the kit bags, zipped them shut, marked the bags with our names and Company, and lined them up in a company file, so that we could march in at departure time, pick them up without delay or confusion, and go straight to the planes.

We were next assembled on a glaring white runway to listen to an Air Corps captain discuss Mae Wests and life rafts. Every plane will have a collapsible rubber raft near the door for the trip across, he said, and every man must know how to assemble it. Pull this, shove that, paddles here, this is a signal lamp, a flutter valve. Here's the drinking water, the Very pistol, a package of colored dye, the emergency rations. Remember when the 504 was knocked down by the Navy going into Sicily and be prepared to abandon ship.

And the Mae Wests. This is a Mae West: a flat, two-foot-long, yellow rubber object rounded at one end, with a hole for the head and a square bottom. Blow it up with this little tube on the right front near the aperture or pull this little cord at the bottom. It releases a vial of carbon dioxide that will immediately inflate your jacket.

The Mae West is worn under your parachute, but for God's sake, get out of your harness before you inflate it or you'll be strangled.

Twelve years ago, when I was 10, I played at being a soldier. I walked up the brook behind our house in Bronxville to a junglelike, overgrown field and dug trenches down to water level with my friends. Then, pretending that we were doughboys in France, we assaulted one another with clods of clay and long, dry reeds. We went to the village hall and studied the rusty rifles and machine guns that the Legion post had brought home from the First World War and imagined ourselves using them to fight Germans.

But we never seriously thought that we would ever have to do it. The stories we heard later; the Depression veterans with their apple stands on sleety New York street corners; the horrible photographs of dead bodies and mutilated survivors; "Johnny Got His Gun" and the shrill college cries of the Veterans of Future Wars drove the small-boy craving for war so far from our minds that when it finally happened, it seemed absolutely unbelievable. If someone had told a small boy hurling mud balls that he would be throwing hand grenades twelve years later, he would probably have been laughed at. I have always been glad that I could not look into the future.

High overhead, a 24-hour cover of P-47 fighter planes crossed and recrossed the blue sky, lacing it with cottony vapor trails. Nine C-47s circled the airdrome, peeled off, and landed one by one. They were coming in from all the Troop Carrier bases in southern England; a great, brown plane stood silent and ready for us now at almost every parking space along the runways.

OUR GENERAL WAS INTELLECTUAL, fervent, believing, but he was not one of the boys, like slim Jim Gavin of the 82nd, who carried a rifle and bore the nickname of "The Two-Star Platoon Leader." Our general spoke as he thought and acted, and I will do my best to reproduce his speech as it was given. It was a good speech of its kind. I only regret to say that it left his audience quite unmoved.

"Men," he said to the Regiment assembled above him on a grassy slope west of our tents, "we have ahead of us the biggest job of the Invasion. The 101st has been chosen to kick off. We're the first team, the best division in the Army, so we've been chosen to go in first.

"The Germans are good, but you are better. You're fighting for a good cause; his is rotten. As soon as you've gotten the upper hand, he'll come running to you with his arms in the air, crying, 'Kamerad!' I've seen it happen.

"But don't think it happens easily. Don't think you're going to walk in and take over. You're going to have to fight for every yard of ground and fight night and day to hold it.

"The Germans will counterattack again and again, because that's their specialty. As soon as they lose a position or a battle, they re-form and counterattack while you're still digging in. They try to catch you off balance. I want you to throw them back every time.

"We're jumping between 12:30 and one in the morning. H Hour for the infantry is six. That gives us approximately five hours to clear the causeways and destroy the gun batteries. We've *got* to clear those causeways and hold them open! The 4th Division is counting on us. We *can't* let them down!

"I've just seen General Eisenhower. He says it will be two days before we'll know for sure whether the Invasion will succeed or fail. After two days, the balance will be in our favor.

"So what I want from you men is *two days*! Two days and nights of violent effort, two days and nights of ceaseless, savage fighting. *Drive* yourselves! You've done it before. *Force* yourselves! Hold on and *fight* like the world's best soldiers. American paratroopers! The whole Invasion depends on you.

"I have one last request to make of you: I want every man who jumps on D-Day to go out the door shouting, 'Bill Lee!'

"General Lee is sitting at home by the radio now, waiting for the Invasion to begin. As a tribute to a great parachutist and a great leader, I want every man to shout 'Bill Lee!' when he jumps. Don't count one-thousand, two-thousand, three-thousand. Yell 'Bill Lee!' instead."

THEY WERE BEATING an AWOL in another company. It was June 4th. D-Day was scheduled for tomorrow.

The 1st sergeant, a surly Tennessee Regular said to have been the middleweight boxing champion of Panama with the old 503, lined the Company up in two parallel columns and made the AWOL run the gantlet.

"This sonofa*bitch*," he shouted, "will get us *all* killed!"

The AWOL put his hands over his face and cried and staggered bloody down the line as some of the men (but not all, for most found the sport brutal and degrading) struck at him savagely.

They had found him in a local pub the night before. He was drunk. He was telling the civilians about the Invasion. He was giving the Regiment to the Germans. The civilians called the authorities.

So they dragged him back to his own Company and beat him till he could hardly walk. They kept him under guard till the time came and then marched him at the point of a gun to the planes with the rest of the Company. He was killed in action the next day.

(By way of contrast, a major general who revealed the Invasion date at a cocktail party in London was slapped on the wrist and sent home first class to a service command. It all depended on your rank and your perspective and how close you were to the Germans.)

Now it was certain, now the day was set. Of all the planes that had landed on the runways, not one had left. The 1st, the 4th, and the 29th Infantry Divisions were seaborne in vast gray fleets, and the Germans had already started parachute and panzer reinforcements from Brittany and northern France to meet them. Savernake Forest and all the roads in southern England were lined with green wooden cases of mortar and artillery ammunition, and the later waves of Bradley's 1st Army clattered and clanked their dusty way south through the ancient Devonshire villages to the medieval ports that held their barges. London was empty. There were no troops on pass in Edinburgh and Birmingham. Half the trains suddenly disappeared from the British timetables. The wave of the future swelled up in the green country to sweep across the narrow sea and smash the hateful race that worshiped war. D-Day was scheduled for tomorrow. It blew icy fumes of fear in our faces as we gathered in the S-2 tent for the final briefing.

"At ease, men," the captain snapped, all indifference gone from his voice and attitude. "I have something important to tell you that you may already know: We're leaving tonight. This is final.

"The Pathfinders take off at 9:50, the 1st Battalion at 11:05, we go at 11:15. The whole Regiment will be airborne by 11:30.

"The Pathfinders will land half an hour before anybody else and set up radar as three sets of assembly lights, red for the 1st Battalion, white for the 2nd Battalion, and blue for the 3rd.

"Each battalion will also assemble on a bugle call. So if you can't see the white lights in the orchard, listen for the bugle. Our call will be two blasts, tata. Remember, two for the 2nd Battalion: tata!

"We jump at one o'clock. As I told you before, we'll assemble in an orchard near Hébert, pronounced *Aybare*. If you're lost and run across a Frenchman, ask the way to Hébert, not Herbert, as I've heard some of you pronounce it.

"If you've studied your maps and listened to your officers, you'll know that Hébert isn't even a town. It's a couple of houses and a crossroads surrounded by apple orchards. The Germans have planted antiairborne poles and mines in most of the other jumpfields in our sector, but as far as we know, our fields and orchards are clear. I guess they didn't think we'd be crazy enough to jump near orchards, but they don't know how crazy we are. If we were sane, we wouldn't be here.

"As soon as the Battalion is assembled—we'll allow an hour for all the strays to come in—we'll move out and secure the two southern causeways.

"That's the big picture. You men know your platoon and squad assignments, so I won't go into smaller details. I'd rather discuss the route we're flying and our means of identification at night.

"Once each battalion is airborne and formed in a V of Vs, it has sixty minutes' flight time to reach the drop zone. Follow me closely on this map.

"Here we are, about ten miles north of the Channel. We fly due south. As soon as we're over the Channel, the planes will drop down to five hundred feet. We'll fly at that elevation till we hit the coast.

"We'll make a turn over water, pass between the Channel Islands of Guernsey and Jersey, and go straight across Normandy to the east side.

"The Air Corps will give us the red light when we reach the Channel Islands. We'll stand up and hook up and remain standing for twenty minutes before we jump. This will minimize the area of our bodies exposed to flak and put us in jumping position in case the plane is hit.

"We'll cross the Channel at 150 miles an hour. When we reach the coast of Normandy, we'll rise from 500 feet to 1,500, fly across the peninsula at that height, and drop down to 700 feet for the jump. The planes will then slow down to 110 miles an hour.

"Seven hundred feet at 110 miles an hour: Those are the Air Corps' orders. Our pilots have been ordered not to break formation or they'll be court-martialed. They will use absolutely no evasive action; they must hold formation regardless of flak and make an accurate, concentrated drop at all costs. Big white and black identification stripes have been painted on all the planes and gliders so the Invasion fleet won't open up on us as we pass overhead.

"This is a combat mission—everybody jumps! Nobody, but nobody, goes back to England. The pilots have orders to jump every man in their planes. If they miss the drop zone, and it's happened before, in broad daylight, they'll drop us on the Douve bridges. These are second only in importance to the causeways.

"There will be forty planes in a serial, each serial a battalion, and six minutes between serials over the D.Z. So wherever you land, clear that jumpfield *fast*! Get out of the way of the next serial because they're dropping pack 75s and a lot of other heavy equipment with the men.

"You'll have two means of identification: the password and this dime-store metal cricket. The password is 'Flash . . . Thunder.' If you hear somebody coming toward you, cover him and challenge him with 'Flash.' He should reply 'Thunder.' If he doesn't answer your 'Flash' and doesn't use his cricket, then you'd better speed him on his way with a bayonet or a hand grenade.

"This cricket is an ingenious idea. Sometimes I'm convinced that the Army thinks of everything. Who else could conceivably have thought of using a child's toy for combat identification? This cricket will probably surprise the Germans as much as our presence in his beloved West Wall. One click, like this, to be answered by two. Simple, isn't it? You hear somebody coming and click-clack, and he'll answer, click-clack, click-clack. Hold on to these crickets; they're lifesavers. Get some string and tie them around your necks, so you won't lose them.

"Remember, your life depends on two things, this cricket (click-clack . . . click-clack, click-clack) and the password, 'Flash . . . Thunder.'

"We want to take the Germans by surprise. In order to do so, we'll have to move as quietly as possible. Nobody jumps with a loaded rifle. Nobody shoots if he can possibly avoid it. Use your bayonet! Use your hand grenades!

"This will be night work, silent and deadly. Once you get free of your chute, whip out your bayonet and ram it on your rifle. Don't give away your position by shooting at strange noises.

"Sneak up on 'em! You have the psychological advantage; you're attacking. They're sitting passive in their holes and billets, scared to death. They don't know where you are or who you are or how many of you are after them. Crawl up on 'em in the long grass and kill 'em with your trench knives. Cut their throats. Strangle 'em if you can. But don't shoot!

"Above all, *kill* 'em! We can't be dragging a lot of prisoners around with us at night.

"You know where they are and what to do with them: the officers' mess and billets and Company of infantry at St. Marie du Mont, the platoon on the gun batteries at St. Martin de Varreville, and all the others.

"Go down there and get 'em and kill every last sonofabitching German you find."

THE COLONEL WAS our last speaker and our best, and when he finished talking, I felt better about going. I knew we would make it all right.

In fact, he was about the only officer in the Regiment who was never goddamned. He could be direct and forceful and hard and still make us laugh and do his bidding. Take the case of the wool-knit caps.

For some strange, unaccountable reason, the wearing of wool-knit caps in the 101st Airborne Division was apparently considered a crime more heinous than rape. If the general caught a man taking a break in one of these knitted affairs with stiff little visors, he stopped the problem and personally scolded the bewildered miscreant and his immediate superiors. British commandos might raid Dieppe in socklike caps and British parachutists wear red berets to Sicily, but we slept in our helmets and hid our wool-knit caps under their iron lids. This was a source of constant friction, with men continually trying to wear them and the officers, goaded from on high, on the lookout to snatch them off. Wool-knit caps became a command phobia of such proportions that the colonel had to devote a large portion of his firm talk to this tender subject. D-Day was tomorrow, and he was talking about wool-knit caps. The thought of it made me laugh.

"Now, men," the colonel said, rubbing his hand over his face and moving his overseas cap back and forth, "I don't care what else you do, but for God's sake, don't let the general catch you in a wool-knit cap! Steal a tank, rob a German payroll—anything but a wool-knit cap. He caught one of you wearing one on the last jump and gave me hell for it.

"Now, I don't like to catch hell, and I know you don't, so if you have to wear a wool-knit cap, keep it under your helmet all the time. The general's hell on wool-knit caps."

Master of the equivocal statement, he nevertheless talked our language, and when he gathered the Regiment around him after lunch for a last conclave, he didn't discuss the Allies or the Four Freedoms, Nazi tyranny or a Crusade in Europe. He talked of war as it is to soldiers: Kill or be killed. He talked of fire and movement, of the 82nd and the 101st, of the 501 and the 502, our brother regiments, and of the 327th Glider Infantry Regiment, which would come in by barge.

Weaving slightly back and forth, he smiled at his men, moved his hat around his head, wiped his face a few more times. He spoke of the enemy's avowed intention of killing every paratrooper they caught where they caught him and of our reciprocal intentions toward his infantry. He spoke of the need for silence, of bayonets and hand grenades, of the flak expected above and the Germans below. He dwelt at such length on the general's demand for two days' violent effort that he left the impression in our minds that this was the limit expected of us. Gas might be used in a desperate attempt to stop the Invasion, so keep your masks handy. Don't drink the water; the Frenchmen don't. Keep your wool-knit caps under cover. Watch out for mines and booby traps. Don't jump with any identification but your dog tags. We want to keep this thing secret, so they won't know how many of us there are, and if you're captured and interrogated, just tell them your name, rank, and serial number—nothing else. There will be no saluting in Normandy, and officers are not to be sirred. When he had covered all possible contingencies, the colonel looked around, relaxed his stance, and reminisced.

"Men," he said, shoving his cap to the back of his head, "we've been together a long time. You're probably as sick of it all as I am. You're sick of field problems, and so am I. We're ready to go to combat.

"Two years ago almost to this day I started this Regiment. It was the sixth parachute regiment formed and the first to take its basic as a unit, the first to go through jump school as a unit.

"We were an experimental regiment then. The Army was watching us. It's *still* watching us. We proved ourselves then, we'll prove ourselves now. We outmarched the Japs, we had the lowest percentage of refusals at Benning. Now we're going to show 'em again: The 506th is the best goddamn regiment in the Army.

"I promised you people in Toccoa that we'd go to combat. We've been stalled and put off for two years, but now we're finally going. This is a combat outfit. You joined the 506th to fight. You were trained to fight. And tonight we're fighting.

"Anybody who doesn't want to fight can get up and leave now. This is your last chance. Anybody want out? We won't hold it against you. Anybody want to quit?"

He stared at his audience with a smile on his face.

"Nobody? Not a hand raised? I knew it. O.K., then, everybody jumps! That's a direct order. From now on it's twenty years. Refusal to jump in combat is desertion under fire.

"But I don't think any of you men will refuse on this one. You've come too far, you've done too much, you're too good to quit now. We dropped the quitters a long time ago."

The colonel paused and smiled again, a smile of pride. His confidence in us gave us confidence in ourselves. He put his hands on his hips, leaned back, and said, "I feel sorry. I feel mighty sorry for those Germans. God help 'em all when we get to Normandy."

The audience laughed, and he raised his hand and shouted, "I want you men to go over there and *kill* those people and get us a Presidential Citation! You can *do* it. Good luck and *God* bless you!"

CLICK-CLACK, SNAP . . . Click-clack, snap . . . Click-clack, snap. Someone in the next tent was working a .45's barrel cover back and forth, back and forth, snapping the trigger at imaginary Germans. The noise was maddening.

I lay on my cot in the late afternoon. My clothes were wet with sweat, and I felt weak all over.

Click-clack, snap . . . Click-clack, snap . . . Click-clack, snap.

The 2nd Battalion jumps at one. . . . Everybody jumps. . . . Kill 'em all. . . . We been together a long time.

Click-clack, snap. "Anybody got a boxa .45 ammo?"

I wanted to scream. I tossed and rolled and couldn't sleep.

The wind had started after lunch. It blew strong and sullen from the west, rattling the tent and flapping the canvas up and down. The trees bent and whistled and the hedges rustled and hummed ominously. The wind blew, and the paratroopers held their breath, for a strong wind was worse than a bad jumpfield.

"That's a gale," I said to myself, "a goddamn gale. I hope this isn't another Sicily."

The 504 and the 505 had jumped at night in a high wind in Sicily. They had been scattered all over the island; blown up and down the beachhead, they were almost completely disorganized. One battalion of the 504 was blown off its course and over the invasion fleet, which the

Air Corps had orders to avoid. Thinking it was a German air raid, the fleet opened fire on them and knocked them into the sea; the Battalion was lost to all effective action. Gliders with artillery and 57mm antitank guns were blown down and dispersed over a huge area. It was a brutal jump—in a high wind.

The wind blew and blew and blew. It bent the hedges and rattled the tent ropes. It knocked down the canvas screen around the officers' slit trench and ballooned up tents till they strained to rise and fly away. It clanked the pots in the mess hall, coated the tables with dust, flapped and ripped at the maps in the S-2 tent. I could barely hear my tentmates talking.

The wind almost blew us down on our way to supper. We braced ourselves and leaned against it, and each man's eyes said what his heart felt: We can't jump in a wind like this. They won't do it; they can't do it. They'll lose us all. We'll be scattered all over Normandy. We'll break our legs and our backs. We'll get concussions. We'll lose our equipment. The gliders will be smashed to pieces.

Steak, they gave us, and mashed potatoes. Fresh peas and white bread and our first ice cream overseas. Seconds for everybody. Eat hearty, lads, we're jumping tonight.

West of our tents, where the wind came from, a mighty shouting filled the air. Men whooped and hollered and gave the Rebel yell. The joyous sound swept over the marshaling area like a tidal wave.

I sat bolt upright. Could it be? Can it be? Oh God, I hope so.

The C.Q. stuck his head in the air and screamed deliriously, "They called it off! They called it off! No jump tonight! Too much wind. Yippee!"

Yelling and laughing like idiots, we leaped from our cots, incoherent with joy, and danced wildly on the sod floor. Men ran from tent to tent shaking hands and slapping backs and screaming at the top of their lungs. The reprieve had come to the death house.

YOU CAN PUT OFF A SHAVE for a week or more. You can break a date and postpone a wedding. Doctors can even delay death.

But you can't put off an invasion—not for more than a day. Not when three airborne divisions are waiting in marshaling areas and six infantry divisions are already at sea. You can't delay the Invasion of Europe more than a day when the landing depends so much on a full moon and a minus tide that comes only three or four times a year.

Now it was final and irrevocable: We were jumping tonight, wind or no wind, one German or ten thousand. The S-2 captain said that the enemy had just moved his 91st Infantry Division into the area behind Utah Beach and that we were going there regardless.

The wind had blown itself out while we slept. We woke up, late and rested, on a still summer morn, noted the lack of wind, and immediately knew that our reprieve had been good for only one day.

In the little, hundred-yard-square meadows bounded by dense walls of intertwined earth and stone and hedge and tree, the separate companies, hushed by the finality of departure, lay silent in their tents and waited to go. Men who had celebrated so loudly the night before could barely talk today. They bit their lips and worked their bolts and spent the longest day of their lives in semi-idleness, waiting, waiting, waiting. There was no laughter, no singing or shouting; the most inveterate gambler couldn't get a crap game started. A deadening stillness hung in the warm, sweet air.

Late in the afternoon, the supply sergeants began to circulate cans of camouflage greasepaint and handsful of burnt cork, and we streaked our faces and darkened the backs of our hands for the night ahead.

They gave us stew before we left. The Air Corps said we were lucky to get that, for it was all that was left. "We hadn't counted on feeding you another day," they explained. We filed through the chow line at four o'clock in blackface and listened dully to the K.P.s apologize for the fare—C rations, leftover scraps of bread, and coffee—and cursed the Army for sending us over on such a meal.

At five o'clock, the C.Q. went from tent to tent and warned us that we were moving out in half an hour. Put on your gear and stand by.

First you put on your cotton underwear. Then you wriggled into your woolen long johns. O.D. shirt and trousers were next, and over all, a shrunken, impregnated jumpsuit. It was a stifling ensemble for seersucker weather, and I prayed, as I buckled on my musette bag and hung my cartridge belt with a canteen, a bayonet, a trench knife, a first-aid packet, and a pair of stolen wire cutters, that I would not have to make a water landing. I zipped my jump jacket up to the collar and could barely breathe.

Hot, itchy, stiff, and extremely confined, I broke my rifle down with trembling fingers and put its three pieces into the padded canvas case that would be buckled under my reserve chute. Then I lay down stiffly, like a knight on a sarcophagus, and closed my eyes and tried to think of other things. But I couldn't.

There was no way out, no escape. The miracle happened yesterday; it won't happen again. We're going regardless. . . . Ten thousand Germans . . . This is fantastic; I must be having nightmares. . . . Summer is vacation time. . . . God, it's quiet. . . . What a lousy way to leave the world. Nobody to say goodbye. Nobody who loves you waving from the door. No friends or relatives at the bedside . . . How quiet it is— and godforsaken lonely. In the old days the soldiers had drums and bugles. The English still have bagpipers. . . . Nobody gives a damn for us, nobody cares. We'll fight their war, they'll all make money and get good jobs and gripe about the butter shortage and chisel on the gas ration.

WE STARTED OFF AT route step, four abreast, filling the sunken lane with our bulging bodies and the heavy tramp-tramp of our boots. Nobody joked or sang or whistled, nobody laughed or counted cadence. Our gear made the only sound—a muffled clatter of shovel, gas mask, and bayonet against moving legs—our gear and our heavy boots, tramping, tramping, tramping. A hundred and twenty men, no shouting or cries, nothing but a dull tramp and a muffled clatter.

We came to the old white cottage with the thatched roof and a sagging fence out front that we had passed before, on our way to fit on our chutes. The cottage faced the road and bordered on the airfield near the shed where the civilians had been working. Beyond it, black and ominous, loomed the giant maw of the hangar where we had stored our chutes. The old woman came out again, with her sunken face and bent back, and stood by a row of hollyhocks and watched the long, bobbing line of blackfaced men come up a dip in the road and go by. She burst into tears and pulled out a small lace handkerchief and waved it. "God bless you," she called softly, "God bless you all."

Nobody called to her or waved back. Other things were on our minds now: the big ground, the gun batteries, the villages and causeways. For half an hour, the entire Regiment bobbed past her in the thin light of late afternoon, as company after company funneled onto the one road that led to the kit bags, and for half an hour she stood at the fence and cried and called and waved goodbye.

We crossed the parking strip where we had tried on our chutes and went in the hangar, now become a seething, dark hell of shouting, wild-eyed men in blackface. Soldiers who had lost their chutes scrambled among the rows of bags, seeking their own while officers shouted directions and noncoms ran up and down the line in an effort to organize the chaos. The hue and cry rang and echoed in the girders overhead, changing our mood from sullen quiet to noisy excitement.

The line ahead of us started to move. As we followed them inside, Apache-faced savages ripped open lead-lined cases of hand grenades and rifle bullets and offered extra ammunition to passersby. G.I. trucks backed into the far end, which opened on the airfield, and hauled load after load of parachutists off to their planes. Headquarters Company lined up on its bags.

A rigger who was helping with the chutes and the movement went down the column talking to the men. He was cursing the outfit for not letting him go over with a line company.

"I told the colonel I wanted to go," he said. "The hell with flying re-supply! I didn't join this goddamn outfit to be a messenger boy; I want to jump. Colonel said I had to stay here and fly the ammo over. Piss on that! Fuck the ammo! Fuck resupply! If I can get a chute, I'm going."

You jerk, I thought. You goddamn jerk.

"Headquarters Company, on your feet!"

We went to the far door, where two men were passing out more ban-doleers and hand grenades and where a third man stood beside a pile of mimeographed sheets of paper. "Here, buddy," he said as we went by, "take one of these. They're from Eisenhower."

Angered by the boyish eagerness of the rigger and irritated by the wild strangeness and tumult of the hangar, I snatched the paper from him and rammed it into my pocket. Eisenhower! What's he got to do with me now?

A G.I. truck picked us up and took us to our plane. Both sides of the runway on which we drove were lined for half a mile with full-bellied C-47s with clinging loads of equipment bundles and armed crews lolling in the doorways. The truck turned left a quarter of a mile from the hangar and stopped beside one of the planes. "Everybody out!" our lieutenant cried.

While we were unloading, another truck drove up with a three-man naval fire-control party from division headquarters, a runner from company headquarters, and two demolitions men whose waists were encircled with primacord and whose pockets bulged with blocks of T.N.T.

Our lieutenant lined us up in jumping order and made us count off. There were twenty-one of us altogether. He placed Sergeant Graham, a calm, stocky Middle Westerner, at the rear and himself first as jumpmaster. We counted off again, and then he gave us a direct order to jump and bade us refit our chutes.

This took about fifteen minutes, for almost every strap and buckle had to be readjusted for a girth increased by clothing, gear, and supplies. When we were finally satisfied with the fit, we put the main chute on the ground, tilted with the top rest on the reserve, and using it as a backrest, lay down to wait for darkness.

THE DARKNESS WAS a long time coming, for with double daylight savings time in effect, the sun hung in the sky till nine or ten at night. We could lean against our chutes for hours yet, watching the birds glide home and the big, green Devonshire hills change color.

Porter, the medic, who had been put in our plane and who always joshed me about being a Groton man (which I was not), got up with me and walked to the edge of the strip, where we relieved ourselves. The splash of urine sounded by every plane.

"Must have been the coffee," Porter said. Usually bouncy and noisy, he seemed rather subdued tonight.

"Yes," I replied. I did not feel like talking. The enthusiasm that had stirred me to join the paratroops and the challenge that had kept me going were gone forever. In their place I felt a numbness, a blank, heavy, all-filling numbness. "Beautiful country," I said at last, zipping my fly.

Porter nodded, and we stood together and stared in silence at the hills.

We were on the rim of the parking strip, where the airfield's butte dropped off steeply into fallow green fields, and we could look down a long slope of high grass and waving buttercups to a wide and winding valley that followed the course of a dark brook three or four miles through strips of forest. There were light-green patches of meadowland and pale-brown fields of grain on the slopes on both sides of the valley, with here and there an isolated farmhouse.

"It's another world, isn't it?" Porter murmured. "I mean, it's one that has no connection with ours."

I nodded and turned away and went back to my chute.

Wonder what Eisenhower has to say? A pep talk probably. These big generals all talk about war as if it were a football game, and maybe it is to them, with their charts and maps and secret codes. I never heard of anybody getting killed in a football game.

I pulled out the mimeographed sheet and read it.

Eight o'clock.

"It won't be long now," said little Ash, an ammo bearer sitting nearby.

My head bobbed up and down, half hearing, as I frowned at the clichés that covered the page. "Christ," I muttered. I crumpled the paper and threw it away. Oh hell, I said to myself, why throw away a souvenir? I retrieved it, smoothed it on the concrete, and put it in my breast pocket. "Crusade," I thought. "Liberty-loving." "Home front." "Victory." This was written by a Prince of Platitudes.

"It's from Eisenhower," Ash said defensively. He had been watching me.

"Oh God, those generals . . . They don't talk our language. There isn't a one of them knows why we are here. Do you know why we are here?"

Ash shrugged his shoulders. How could a man desecrate a letter from Eisenhower?

"We're here because the outfit's here. That crap has nothing to do with it. If we fight, it's because the outfit's fighting, it doesn't matter who, not because we're a bunch of knights on a goddamned Crusade. This war doesn't mean a thing to me beyond this outfit. I never met a G.I. who knew what the war was about or who believed in it, did you?"

Ash sighed. This was no time to admit that the war and the jump to come had no meaning.

"Piss on S.H.A.E.F.!" I yanked out my trench knife and began to strop it on my boot.

8:30.

"Hurry up and wait." Porter sighed. He was lying on my left. "God-damn Army'd rather be four hours early than two seconds late." He flipped his cigarette butt down the runway and lit another.

I grunted, got to my feet, and relieved myself again. Ash sat huddled up, his arms around his knees, and watched me. When I returned, he shifted his stare to the cold yellow sun, which was sinking rapidly toward the horizon. He wanted to stop it, to reach out with me and all the others and hold it up in the sky. Only a dish-edged distance separated us from darkness.

Nine o'clock.

All over the airfield, the quiet groups of men by each plane turned their eyes to the west and watched the sun bulge suddenly large and then drop out of sight.

I went to the edge of the strip and relieved myself for the third time. Four other men followed suit. A few planes started to roar, then died out. "Just checking their motors," one of the men said. His face was dripping with sweat.

9:30.

"It won't be long now," Porter said. "Are you ready to go?"

"Ready as I'll ever be."

I shiver and sweat at the same time. My head is shaved, my face darkened with charcoal, my jumpsuit impregnated for gas. I am carrying over a hundred pounds of equipment. I have two bandoleers and three hand grenades for ten thousand Germans, and yes, I am ready.

Ten o'clock.

More and more men got up and relieved themselves. Someone said it was the coffee we had for dinner, but that didn't get a laugh anymore. The smokers lit one cigarette off another and lost themselves in the smoke, but there was no escape for the nonsmokers. They could only think.

My mind whirred and clattered with all the things I had learned in the briefing tent. The password, "Flash . . . Thunder." One click of the cricket in challenge, two in reply. Check your sleeve detector for poison gas. Loosen your trench knife in its sheath. Take the villages, the causeways, the Douve bridges, the high ground. White for the 2nd Battalion. If the lights don't go up, listen for the bugle call, tata, two for the 2nd Battalion. Tatatatatatatata. I'm going nuts. Hébert is the drop zone, pronounced *Aybare*. A crossroads village surrounded by apple orchards. Kill 'em all; they're not going to be taking *us* prisoner at night. Use your bayonet and your trench knife and creep up on 'em in the long grass. We'll be stood up and hooked up for twenty minutes. Everybody jumps, nobody goes back to England; we need all the firepower we can get. No, the Air Corps says the Germans haven't flooded the low ground behind Utah Beach. The 2nd Battalion jumps at one. There are ten thousand Germans waiting for you down there. Go get 'em!

10:45.

The crew chief climbed down the short metal ladder from the plane and stopped at its foot. "Let's go, men," he said. "It's time to load up."

WE PUT ON OUR CHUTES and snapped the buckles and with our rock-heavy musette bags banging against our knees, shuffled to the ladder and were helped up by our lieutenant and the crew chief. Once aboard, we groped our way through the close darkness to the cold aluminum bucket seats that lined both walls and sat down.

I waddled forward to a spot between Porter and Ash. My body was steaming hot. I sat down and closed my eyes and tried to go to sleep, but the weight of my chute and my equipment was too oppressive. I began to think of the water we would pass over and of my chances of getting free of my harness in time to prepare for a water landing. I hope I don't land in the Channel or the Douve River, I thought. I'd drown before I could get free of my chute.

The plane filled up, the crew chief took in the ladder and lashed it beside the door. Some men smoked, others went to sleep, the majority sat and blinked at the darkness. The crew chief, a heavy man with a bald head and a fatherly air, came up the aisle with packets of airsickness pills and quart ice-cream cartons for vomit, then returned to his stand by the door.

Our lieutenant joined him. He glanced nervously at his watch and then looked outside. The darkness for which we had been waiting two years had finally come. He turned away from it and said, "Remember what Colonel Sink told you: Everybody jumps! Sergeant Graham will enforce this order. He's the last man out of the plane. If the man ahead of you falls, grab him and push him out! If we get knocked down in the Channel be sure to take off your chute before you inflate your Mae West, otherwise you'll be strangled. Good luck, men, good luck to everybody!"

10:55.

All the planes warmed up at once. The thunder was deafening. I opened my packet of airsickness pills and downed the contents in one gulp, hoping that their sedative would numb me completely.

Ash grabbed my forearm. "Jesus, Webster," he said, "we're going."

Sergeant Graham, who was next to the bulkhead by the radio room, raised his voice and yelled, "Say goodbye to England!" I nodded and tried to smile.

The motors died down to a throbbing rumble. The crew chief leaned out the door and quickly pulled his head in as a plane went by. "There they go, there they go!" he shouted. "They're *off!*"

Eleven o'clock.

The tail swung around in a dizzy arc, almost throwing us from our seats. "This is it," the crew chief said, buckling on his flak vest. The C-47 trundled up the runway with squeaking wheels and a heavy, coughing, all-powerful rumble until it reached the line of departure, where it stopped and waited for the signal to take off. The pilot gunned the motors and then let them idle.

11:15.

The signal flashed from the control tower. Go! Go! it blinked. Kill 'em all!

There was a last, terrible, rattling, all-pervading roar, and the plane began to move ahead. Then, gaining speed, it raced down the runway, faster, faster, faster. We held our breath and clung to our seat belts. The tail rose slowly until the cabin floor, which had been aslant, was level with the ground. When it seemed as if we would never leave the runway, the plane's nose lifted and we were airborne.

The motors' roar faded to a steady drone. With a collective sigh of relief, we relaxed and undid our seat belts. We were committed at last: The Invasion had begun.

"CIGARETTE?" Porter said, on my left.

"No thanks." I smiled. With the lift from the ground, I had experienced a sudden total change of feeling. The load of brooding worry had dropped off, leaving me light, reckless, resigned, and almost detached. Part of this feeling was due to the drowsy effect of the sleeping tablets, but most of it was sheer relief at the end of all the waiting.

I looked around to see how the others were reacting to the takeoff.

Only the smokers, who were faintly lighted by the firefly glow of their cigarettes, were visible. When they inhaled, the flaring tips lit up their shadowy, blackened faces. They did not look happy.

The engines roared louder, as if for a grip on the sky. We were bucking and slamming around now in the rough air currents above the big Devonshire hills that had once seemed so lovely.

I turned stiffly, and staring out the window, saw, far below in the shifting moonlight, the dotted white perimeter lights of the field and the tiny red-and-green wingtip lights of other C-47s taxiing and taking off and getting into formation. My God, I thought impatiently, we're still circling the airfield.

We banked again and continued round and round in a great, droning loop until the whole 2nd Battalion was formed in a long V of Vs, nine planes wide.

While I watched, a red light crept up on us in the darkness outside. It was our wing plane moving into position. When it was almost abreast, it throttled down and rode alongside with a bouncing, yawing motion.

It's too close, I said to myself, my eyes fixed on the light. One dip, one twist, and we'll come together and both go down. Oh hell, why worry? There's nothing I can do about it now.

The moon went behind a cloud, and I twisted back into position. Suspended in a rackety darkness lit only by cigarettes and a tiny blue ceiling light in the pilot's passageway, I felt as if I were in the wildest of bad dreams, riding a nightmare to a Goya hell. A night jump was always eerie, but this one seemed so utterly unreal and incredible and yet so final that it wrung the feeling out of me and left me passive, indifferent. Impatience was now my greatest emotion.

"Come on!" I whispered to myself. Let's get it over with. Let's ride this buck to the end of the line, bail out, and start shooting people. That's what I joined the paratroops for—to fight—not to train, train, train. I'm stuck with the Army and sick of it and tired of training. Let's get it over with. The hell with it!

The Battalion made one last banking turn and headed south for the English Channel. The bouncing lessened, but not the noise. A cold wind came in the open door, strong and quite forbidding.

The crew chief left his stand near the door and, stopping here and there to chat with the men, slowly worked his way back toward the bulkhead where Sergeant Graham was sitting.

"How's it going, buddy?" he said to Porter. "Everything O.K.?" He was wearing a steel helmet, a Mae West, a flak vest, a seat parachute, and a .45 in a shoulder holster, and he was trying hard to be friendly and helpful.

"You call this O.K.?" Porter replied. He grinned, and the crew chief went on.

Someone vomited near the door. The smell mingled with the oily engine odors and the smoke of the cigarettes and made another man vomit.

"I should have walked," Sergeant Graham remarked. "Only I would have gotten my feet wet."

The crew chief laughed and went up to visit with the pilot.

The plane lurched and plunged, bounced from side to side, racketed back into position with a tearing, straining sound in its motors. I thought again of the wingtip light only a few feet away and of the possibility of a midair collision and a crash in the Channel, then shrugged my shoulders and dismissed the thought.

Death was no longer a mystery or an old man's prospect, but an immediate likelihood. Whatever happened now, I would simply be carried into it. The Air Corps did the worrying en route and we did the jumping at the end of the line. After that we might be able to determine a certain amount of our fate. But now we were simply passive passengers on a one-way ride, live cargo being shipped across the Channel for dumping behind the beaches.

The crew chief made a return trip to the tail, clutching the anchor line that ran down the plane's ceiling, and stood by the open door. He beckoned to our lieutenant, who rose clumsily from a seat nearby and looked out, then nodded and smiled. Facing down the aisle, the lieutenant yelled, "Look, men, look! It's the fleet."

I turned stiffly to the window again, like a rusty robot, and gasped, "Man, oh man."

Five hundred feet below, spread out for miles on the moonlit sea, were scores and scores of landing barges, destroyers, cruisers, and attack transports. They were bearing the infantry slowly east, like a flood of lava, to a dawn assault on the shingle shore of Normandy.

As the Battalion passed overhead, a lamp blinked up at us from a command ship. All the planes' wingtip lights flashed off. The blue lights went out in the pilots' passageways.

My shoulders swung away from the window. I stared at the men opposite me in the racketing, vibrating, oil-reeking, vomit-scented darkness. "Isn't it great?" I said to Ash. "Those guys are going *in!*"

There was no reply, so I turned and looked at Ash, who had said for months that he was going to die on D-Day and who by comparison made me seem like an optimist, and saw that he had not heard me. He looked very scared.

I started to tell him that everything was going to be all right, but as I shouted the first words, my ears tingled and the engines' pitch changed as they strained for altitude. It wouldn't be long now, I knew, and suddenly lost interest in Ash. My stomach tightened and filled with ice, and a voice told me to get ready. "It's coming," the voice said, "it's coming."

The red light flashed on in the jump panel beside the door.

The plane lurched and roared as if in answer, and our lieutenant staggered erect, grabbed the anchor line with one hand, and snapped his static line to it. "Stand up and hook up!" he shouted.

These were the Channel Islands Guernsey and Jersey, between which we now were flying. We knew they were the Channel Islands because we had been told that we would stand up and hook up when we reached them. Only twenty minutes to go, we stood up and hooked up over a hostile land of flak batteries and antiaircraft machine guns. As we passed between the islands, tiny red dashes of tracer fire floated up at us lazily from both sides.

The men rose woodenly from their seats, felt blindly for the anchor line, clicked their static-line snap fasteners to it, and held on. How did I ever get into this?

Now we stood in one line, facing the tail, so crowded together that we could scarcely breathe. This was the line of departure: the Channel Islands.

"Push me," Ash said. "Push me when we go." He was clinging to the static line with both hands.

The plane went slower and slower, the motors got louder and louder. From the strain on them, I could tell that we were still climbing, gaining altitude for the run to the drop zone.

A stream of tracer bullets floated up at us, speeded up as they passed the windows, and disappeared with a rattling burrat.

We had reached the mainland. It was a little after midnight. The infantry was due at six . . . "if they take the beach."

Someone threw up and cursed, and Porter had to catch me to keep me from falling in a sudden lurch as the pilot took evasive action to avoid another flak nest that had opened fire on the planes ahead.

Ten thousand Germans.

Oh God, I prayed, get me out of here. I don't want to blow up in the sky and burn to death. I don't want to die like a mouse in a can on a garbage-dump fire. I want to die fighting. Let's jump, let's jump, let's go, go, go!

"Check your equipment!" the lieutenant shouted.

I felt the snap fasteners on my leg straps. They were closed tightly and in place. How about the reserve snaps? Also good. And the bellyband? In place. I knew the chest buckle was snapped, for it had dug into my ribs ever since I had put on my chute.

Now I checked Ash, who stood in front of me, while Porter checked my back, for each man was responsible for himself and the man ahead. Yes, Ash's backpack was all right; the chute was in its cover, the rubber bands still held most of the static line in position.

Burrrrat, another machine-gun burst crackled around the plane.

"Sound off for equipment check!"

Up by the pilot's passageway, where Graham had been crowded into the entrance, the lieutenant's command sounded like a child's whisper. The pilot gunned the engine and threw the craft from side to side.

An 88mm shell burst outside with a quick flash and a metallic bang. The blast tilted the plane, throwing men onto the seats. They clutched their way back up again.

"Sound off for equipment check!" the lieutenant shouted again.

"Number twenty O.K.!" Graham roared. "Like hell, I'm O.K.," he confided. "I'm scared speechless." He slapped Porter's shoulder.

"Number nineteen O.K.," cried Porter, slapping my shoulder as a signal for me to shout.

I yelled that I was O.K. and then Ash took up the cry and passed it on.

The plane dove toward the ground, passing under a string of three white flares that hung malevolently motionless in the sky. The pilot twisted and yawed and raced back up again.

I smelled the smoke and oil and puke and gagged on my supper as it rose in my throat. Ash whispered the Lord's prayer, and Graham goddamned the pilot for using evasive action.

"Number fourteen O.K.!"

"Number thirteen O.K.!"

I shook my head and clamped my teeth shut. I was beyond all hope. If you have to die, you have to die—and what a way this is! If you have to jump, you have to jump. A man's life and death are decided by forces that he cannot fight. He can only question them and rebel against them, but in the end, he has to go with them. For Chrissake, let's get out of this firetrap!

The plane slammed up and down, zigzagged, rattled and roared, threw us from side to side with such violence that several of us fell down again, cursing the pilot.

The muscle and fiber melted from my legs. It was all I could do to remain upright and not dissolve into a gibbering, gutless blob of fear. Too weak to stand, I clung to my static line with both hands. I felt like crying, screaming, killing myself.

A flash of light came in the window, and I glanced outside and saw wisps of cloud streaking by. Now and then a pale, full moon, mocking in its serenity, appeared briefly among the long, thin, scudding black clouds. This is a night for murder, I thought. God must have planned it that way.

"Close up and *stand* in the door!" the lieutenant yelled.

Left foot forward in a lock step, each man pushed hard against the man before him. The plane bounced up and down and gasped for altitude.

I could feel Graham crowding Porter and Porter crowding me, but I had forgotten all about them. I had forgotten all about everything and everybody but Pvt. David K. Webster, who wanted to get out of this plane more than anything else in the world.

The motors faded out somewhat and the plane rustled through the air more slowly.

We're over the drop zone, we're over the drop zone! Let's *go!* I had an insane urge to jump.

"GO!" the lieutenant shouted. He bent over and lifted the ends of the parapaks, slid them out the door, and jumped after them. The line of men surged forward.

Two men fell down on the threshold. There was a wild, cursing tangle as others fought to lift them and push them out, and then the line moved again, sucked out the door like a stream of water. I shuffled up, glanced down, and stopped, dumbfounded.

All I could see was water, miles and miles of water.

But this was D-Day and nobody went back to England and a lot of infantry riding open barges seasick to the low-tide beaches were depending on us to draw the Germans off the causeways and gun batteries, and so, as Porter hurled himself against me, I grabbed both sides of the door and threw myself at the water.

I FELL A HUNDRED FEET in three seconds, straight toward a huge flooded area shining in the moonlight. I thought I was going to fall all the way, but there was nothing I could do about it except dig my fingers into my reserve and wait to be smashed flat. I should have counted one-thousand, two-thousand, three-thousand—the general would have had me shout, "Bill Lee," but that was expecting too much—and yet all I could do was gape at the water.

Suddenly a giant snapped a whip, with me on the end, my chute popped open, and I found myself swinging wildly in the wind. Twisted in the fall, my risers were unwinding and spinning me around. They pinned my head down with my chin on the top of my rifle case and prevented me from looking up and checking my canopy. I figured that everything was all right, because at least I was floating free in the great silence that always followed the opening shock.

For several seconds, I seemed to be suspended in the sky, with no downward motion, and then all at once, the whole body of water whirled and rushed up at me.

Jesus, I thought, I'm going to drown.

I wrenched desperately at my reserve-chute's snap fasteners as the first step in preparing for a water landing. I also had to undo two leg snaps, my chest buckle, and the bellyband. The next step would have been to drop the reserve and work myself into the seat of my harness, so that I could fling my arms straight up and drop from the chute when I was ten feet above the water. I didn't even have time to begin the procedure.

We had jumped so low—about three hundred feet, instead of the scheduled seven hundred—that while I was still wrenching at the first reserve snap, I saw the whole immense sheet of water rushing up at me twenty feet below. I've had it, I thought. That goddamn Air Corps. I reached up, grasped all four risers, and yanked down hard, to fill the canopy with air and slow my descent. Just before I hit, I closed my eyes and took a deep breath of air. My feet splashed into the water.

I held my breath, expecting to sink over my head and wondering how I was going to escape from my harness underwater—and hit bottom three feet down. My chute billowed away from me in the light wind and collapsed on the surface. I went to work to free myself from my gear. Immensely relieved at the safe landing, I undid the reserve and discarded it, yanked loose the bellyband, unsnapped the leg straps and chest buckle, detached my rifle case, and let the harness sink into the swamp. I was on my own at last.

The silence ended abruptly with a long, ripping burst, burrrrrrrp, that made me look around in fright.

That's a German machine gun, I told myself. They've seen me. The bullets cracked and popped in the air above, and as I stared open-mouthed and paralyzed with fright, I saw whiplike tracers darting at me from some far-off place. I dropped to my knees in the cold, black water, which tasted old and brackish, as if it had lain still for a long time, and passively waited to be killed.

Somebody wants to kill me, I thought. So this is what war is really like? I couldn't believe that somebody wanted to kill me. What had I done to them?

I wanted to go up to them and tell them that I didn't want to kill anybody, that I thought the whole war was a lot of malarkey. I don't want to hurt anybody, I would say. All I ask of the world is to be left alone.

The machine gun fired again, a longer burst that held me motionless. It was like a bad dream.

I shook my head to make sure it was true, and it was. The bullets were not in my imagination; they were real, and they were seeking me out to kill me. The gunners wouldn't even let me get close enough to talk it over with them. They wanted to kill me right here in the swamp.

The machine gun searched the area again. Far off in the night, others burped and spluttered. Enemy rifles added their popop . . . pop . . . popopop.

I waited about five minutes for someone to walk up and kill me, then my courage returned when I noticed that the shooting was all quite far away. I rose from the water, assembled my rifle, and loaded it and rammed on my bayonet. I was ready to go.

Burp . . . burrrrp . . . burrp . . . cracklecracklecrackle . . . popop   . . .
burp . . . popopop.

Lost and lonely, wrestling with the greatest fear of my life, I stood bewildered in the middle of a vast lake and looked for help.

I shivered convulsively and started to cry, then thought better of it.
The hell with everything! I'm here for keeps; make the best of it. At least
I can try to get out of this swamp before sunrise.

I took the little brass compass from my pocket and looked at it in the
next spell of moonlight. The needle was frozen in position. I shook the
compass and cursed and, holding it close, saw that it was filled with water. "Sonofabitch," I hissed, throwing it away. A wiseguy probably made a
fortune off those compasses in the States. And now men will die because
somebody gypped the government and made a fortune. Sonsofbitches.

A flare burst over the water several hundred yards away. I bowed my
head and waited for the bullets to hit me like a baseball bat, but there
were no bullets. The flare died out with the afterglow of a burnt match,
and I looked around in the moonlight. I sought an orchard, three white
lights, a crossroads village named Hébert, five hundred men from the
2nd Battalion, and all I saw was water and flares and tracers. I listened
for our bugle call, and all I heard was enemy rifle and machine-gun fire.

Suddenly the whole thing struck me as ludicrous: the preparations
and briefings, all the maps and sandtables. For all the good they did, the
Army might as well have yanked us out of a pub and dumped us off
helter-skelter to find our own way to the Germans. Instead of a regiment
of over 1,500 men carefully assembled on a well-defined drop zone,
D-Day was one man alone in an old swamp that the Air Corps said didn't
even exist.

The angry clatter of a plan gone wrong filled the air. Zigzag tracers
arched through the sky, and there were red flares, green flares, white
flares. Grenades and mortars thumped and blammed, while small arms
continued their serenade to liberation. From inland came the strange
tolling of a church bell. "Invasion, Invasion," it seemed to clang to the
Germans still in their billets. "Kill them in their chutes." I stood trans-
fixed, as at a great natural spectacle. The uneasy moon shifted behind
some dark, racing clouds, and black night fell again, but there was no
peace.

My courage, which had flared up briefly, died down again. My God, I thought, only the Germans are shooting. They must have been expecting us. We're done for; the Invasion will fail; we'll be rounded up and butchered by the S.S.

Now a new noise came to me—the distant rumble of a massed flight of planes—and my spirits rose. The planes were coming toward me: I followed their progress by the fountains of tracer that splashed up at them. It's the 501, I thought excitedly. They're due now. Come on down and we'll get 'em together!

They jumped in a moonlit moment in a 4th of July sky laced with great fans of tracer bullets. The bullets lit the planes and the shadowy parachutes of the men tumbling out of them like strings of ball bearings and followed the men to the ground, fanning back and forth with a ferocious rattling. Sick in the stomach, I watched the men swing helpless in the heavy fire. I wanted to help them, but there was nothing I could do but watch with mounting anger and hate.

"Those freaking Krauts!" I whispered. I wanted to kill them all.

I threw away my gas mask and adjusted my musette bag on my back. The box of 30-caliber ammunition I had carried on the jump was dropped at my feet—where was the machine gun that would use it now? I took my Hawkins mine from a big pants pocket and threw that away, too, for there were no tanks in the flooded area. I had to travel light to reach the Germans before dawn.

Swish . . . Swish . . . Swishswish: a sound of wading came to me.

I held my breath and sank slowly into the water with my rifle ready. A flare rose in the distance, but it was no help, for all I could see was black night and black water. The swishing came closer.

With my finger tight on the trigger of my M-1, I reached for the cricket hanging from a string around my neck. The wader was very close now, but I still couldn't see him. I had a slight advantage, however, in that a person at night can see better looking up from ground level than looking down from a walking height. I squeezed the cricket, click-clack, and waited.

The wader stopped. I held my breath until it was ready to burst from my chest in a gigantic pop. Bayonet, hell! I'm going to shoot this sonofabitch. One more step and I'm shooting.

Click-clack, click-clack.

"Who is it? Jesus Christ, who is it?"

"Lachute, Headquarters Company."

"Polecat! It's me, Webster." I jumped up with a splash, walked to him, and hugged him and pounded his back and told him how glad I was to see him. "I thought there were only Krauts down here," I remarked.

"Sure sounds like it, doesn't it, buddy?" He was as glad to see me as I was to see him. "Looks like they got us by the ass. Seen anybody else from the plane?"

"No. I've only been out of my chute ten or fifteen minutes. One more step and I would have shot you."

A small, slender young man from New Orleans, with liquid black eyes and a lively sense of humor, Lachute said that he hadn't even seen me, not even after he had heard my cricket. "What'll we do now?" he inquired.

"Go to the high ground; there's no cover here. We have to get out of this swamp before daylight. . . . Freaking Air Corps sure made a mess of this one, didn't they? How's your compass?"

Lachute searched his pockets and handed me his compass. It, too, was waterlogged. I threw it away with a curse.

We had to orient ourselves before we could go anywhere, and so I crouched at water level and waited for the moon to reappear. In its light, I looked around slowly in a complete circle. There was a big, dark ridge about a mile away that was dotted with flares and gun flashes. Parallel to it, on the other side of the flooded area, was a lesser ridge. The flooded area was about a mile and a half wide. There was no action on the lesser ridge. "That must be the sand dunes behind the beach," I said.

I closed my eyes and tried to re-create the sandtable in the S-2 tent at Honiton. Evidently we had been dropped between Utah Beach and the mainland, in the low ground spreading out from the estuary of the Douve River. The thing to do now was to head for the big ridge and help shoot the Germans off it. The infantry was due at six. They couldn't cross the flooded area with Germans still on that ridge.

"Let's go," I whispered, standing up and starting off.

"Where to?"

"The high ground. That big ridge where all the shooting is. See those flares? See the trees? Man, they're killing troopers up there. What a sound those church bells make! It gives me the creeps."

"Yeah, it sounds like a funeral. Our funeral." Lachute laughed.

We waded fifty yards, then stopped abruptly when we heard a number of men talking in the loud tones of irritated soldiers on a tedious field problem. "Oh Christ," one said. "Let's get out of here." "Nah, nah," another replied. "Stick around till morning, then we'll see where to go."

I clicked my cricket. The talking stopped, but there was no answer to the challenge, so I clicked again. "Flash," someone whispered. "Thunder," I replied. We walked up to a grassy hummock twenty yards long and almost a yard high.

Six men squatted there like chickens flooded out of their roost and clacked noisily at the deceiving Germans. There was a 1st sergeant from a 2nd Battalion line company, a Headquarters Company machine gunner who had lost an older brother with the 504 at Anzio and who had joined the paratroops to avenge him, two men from the 501, one from the 502, and an 82nd Airborne man from the 508; four of the six regiments that had jumped were represented. Nobody knew where they were or what to do next. They had been debating the issue for almost half an hour, according to the machine gunner, a hotheaded 18-year-old from a large Italian family in Trenton, New Jersey. He told me that he was sick and tired of the whole goddamn bunch.

I went to the 1st sergeant, who was the senior noncom and theoretical leader, said hello, and asked if he knew where we were.

"Beats the hell out of me," he said cheerfully. "Nobody's compass works. I'm going to stay here till daylight, then take off."

I gaped at him. "You're crazy," I said. I had never liked him before, and now I wanted to spit on him. "They're killing troopers up there. We have to get those Krauts."

"Oh hell . . ."

"On top of that, if you wait till daylight, the Krauts on the high ground will nail you before you go a hundred yards. There's no cover in this swamp. I'm going up to that big ridge. You can come if you want to, but I don't really give a damn, because I'm going anyway. But first I'm going to junk these O.D.s. They weigh a ton."

I removed my webbing and spread it carefully on the ground. A flare arched through the sky and burst almost directly over the hummock, lighting us all in its fierce glow. A machine gun followed the flare, and once again I had the sensation of being watched. "Jesus," somebody gasped, "they seen us." The flare died out, and the machine gun, which had been shooting high, stopped firing. Everybody commenced arguing again, louder than before, over whether they should leave the island or stay, and what direction they should take when and if they left and what they should do when they arrived wherever they were going.

Group action, I thought, undressing quickly and throwing away my water-soaked woolen shirt and pants. I do better on my own.

I took off my wool underwear, wrung it out, rolled it up, and put it in my musette bag. I cut off the bottoms of my jump pants to keep them from holding water. Then I put my jumpsuit and webbing back on again. I threw away my jump rope and two cartons of cigarettes that I had brought along to trade with the friendly natives.

"Let's go," I said to Lachute. "The hell with these guys."

"O.K., buddy."

"I'm with you too," the young machine gunner said. He turned to the others and asked if they wanted to come along. Most of them rose—all but the 1st sergeant, who remained seated. He cautioned us to be careful and not get hurt. As we moved off he rose uncertainly and watched us go, then sat down again.

A flare rose over the big ridge, and the Germans started shooting under it. A Thompson submachine gun pututted, and an M-1 joined its solid bamming in reply.

I smiled. The troopers on the high ground were coming out of it. There was hope for us all.

Listening intently, freezing under flares, crouching, and eyeing the night with distrust, our little column waded slowly across the flooded area. The lone M-1 and Thompson died out, the enemy firing increased, the hope that had flared in us flickered low again. We all felt tired and depressed and discouraged, the usual reaction that set in an hour or so after every jump. I wanted to lie down and go to sleep, but there was no place to lie down.

Wading slowly across a field two feet in water, I pushed through a line of reeds and suddenly stumbled headlong into a hidden ditch six feet deep. Throwing my arms high to keep my rifle dry, I held my breath and drove forward underwater. After ten feet, I staggered up a steep bank and back into the air again. Lachute, who had stopped bewildered when I had vanished, stood on the far shore, awaiting developments.

"Watch it!" I whispered, as the other men came up. "That ditch is six feet deep."

"I can't swim," Lachute said.

"I'll help you," I replied. "Be right over." I took a deep breath and held it and went back underwater. He climbed on my shoulders, holding both our rifles, kicked his heels in my side, and yelled, "Giddyap!" I walked down into the deep ditch, staggered across, and forced my way up the other bank, where we waited shivering for the rest of the men to join us. When everybody was over, we set out again, hoping that our ammunition had not been dampened.

There was a deep drainage ditch like this on the edge of almost every field; we had to make such a crossing every hundred yards or so. The process exhausted us and we had to stop more and more frequently to lean on our rifles and gasp for air.

The sound of American firing grew more widespread, as scattered paratroopers on the high ground gradually came together and sought out the Germans in the fields and villages. The church bell rang no more, the flares diminished, and slowly the moon, which saw it all begin, dropped down in the west.

Two men from the 82nd waded up on us quickly from the right, accompanied us for several hundred yards, then drifted off as casually as they had come. Lachute threw away his gas mask, and the others discarded all their superfluous equipment. The ridge got bigger and longer and higher, the air turned suddenly very cold, and finally the sky lightened and dawn came with a gray drizzle.

Our group began to break up. The two 501 men, who were carrying all their company-headquarters maps, said goodbye and went off to seek their captain, while the others went to the side or continued forward. Lachute and I headed for a patch of young trees that offered some concealment in the final approach to the ridge. Finally we were the only ones left. We stopped and ate breakfast among the trees.

While we were eating, a massive group of A-20 light bombers came up behind us, following the coastline, and laid a string of bombs a mile long on the sand dunes behind Utah Beach. This was the preliminary bombardment; the Infantry was ready to come ashore. The smoke rose a thousand feet into the air. We stood up and cheered as the kettledrum booming of the bombing came to us.

Lachute noticed a column of men wading parallel to the big ridge and decided to join them, even though they were dangerously exposed and appeared to be going into a firefight. I decided to follow the little trees closely then cut across a tree-covered mound about fifty yards from the base of the ridge. We wished each other luck and set off on our separate ways.

As I came up to the tree-covered mound, I heard someone call my name, "Webster! Webster!" I looked around and saw little Ash lying on the ground.

"What's the matter?" I inquired, kneeling beside him. He appeared to be hurt and in shock. "Are you wounded?"

"No, I wrenched my ankle on the jump. I can't move. God, it hurts."

I looked around at the ridge. It was only about fifty yards away. A channel of deep, black water about twenty yards wide lay at its base.

"Come on," I said. "I'll help you reach dry ground."

"No," he replied. "I'm going to die here. I'm hurt, I can't go any farther."

I looked at him, and I thought of what fun he had been in Aldbourne and of the time I had met him in London and of the raucous little songs he used to sing, and I felt like crying.

"Come *on!*" I said. "For Chrissake."

He shook his head. "I said this jump was going to be my last, Web, and it was. You go on. I'm staying here."

"They'll kill you. Better get out of here while the coast is clear."

"So long, buddy." He gave me his hand, and I shook it hard. I could not understand what had come over him.

I left the mound and, slinging my rifle over my back, swam to the edge of the big ridge. Ash waved to me when I got out, and I waved back and started off on a forest path with the safety catch off my rifle and my eyes scanning everything ahead. A hundred yards later, I came to a road that led out of the swamp. A band of men was milling about on its edge, near a little stone stable. They had just cleaned out a pocket of Germans, they said, and were about to follow after another group of paratroopers who had gone over the ridge. I sat down in the stable and fell asleep. An officer roused me in a few minutes and told me to go up the road with the rest of the men.

The road passed through a dense forest of trees so thick and lush with undergrowth that it looked like a jungle. After a while, it topped the ridge and came out in a little village. No civilians were on hand, but the place was full of life, as dozens of wild-eyed paratroopers in black-face ran about in the streets. One group found a German truck and piled into it. They immediately drove down a side street in search of the enemy. An E Company man passed by on a captured motorcycle, while two others from the 506th came up in a farm cart drawn by a fine brown horse. A lone paratrooper stood in the center of the village square, firing his rifle at the bronze rooster weather vane atop a very old church.

Stopping to watch the fun, I noticed men running up a side street with bottles in their hands. "Where'd you get the liquor?" I inquired, as the men came together and began to move out of the village in parallel columns.

"Third house down there, buddy," one of them replied. "Door's open. Help yourself."

I ran down and went in. The liquor cabinet, which had been broken open by an earlier liberator, stood in one corner of a dark living room with lots of lace and old, dark furniture. Ashamed of myself for house-breaking and yet chilled through by the night's immersion, I selected a fifth of Hennessy Cognac and ran back to join the column.

I tried to dig the cork out with my bayonet, then smashed the top of the bottle against a rock and began to drink. The column I had joined was mostly 2nd Battalion; I was home again. Glad to be back with the outfit and bound I knew not where, I swallowed a huge mouthful of the liquor. It seared its way down my throat and whirled around in my stomach like a blowtorch.

The warmth spread through my body, making me smile with pleasure. I was alive, and I intended to stay that way.

[Editor's note: A few days later, David Webster was wounded—as he later wrote, "nicked by a tiny piece of shrapnel." He was evacuated to England.]

MEMORIAL SERVICES, I mused as our bus left Aldbourne, are usually civilian affairs. The hometown turns out, the American Legion marches, a handful of graying mothers lay wreathes on scattered graves while a high-school bugler blows "Taps." Very seldom does a fighting outfit hold formal services for its dead in wartime. And yet that is what we are going to do this August 28th.

We had returned to England after 31 days in Normandy, and we could look forward to a long memorial service, for the losses on the jump had been heavy—dead paratroopers scattered like blown leaves over all the roads, fields, hedges, and villages—and they had been followed by equally heavy losses in later fighting for places like Carentan, St. Marie du Mont, and St. Come du Mont.

In the end, and with the assistance of men from other units, the Regiment's D-Day objectives had been taken and consolidated. On June 11th, after fighting farther and farther in from the beaches, we moved at night down a long causeway strewn with the bodies of 502 men lost in a frontal attack and in the flickering light of a burning factory, cut cross-country to flank the key city of Carentan, juncture of the Omaha and Utah beachheads.

Now we were back in the soft-green hills near Aldbourne, where our overseas story had begun. Our ranks had been filled with replacements in whom nobody was interested; we had received a week's furlough, new green jumpsuits, and machine guns with bipods for hedgerow fighting; and our training schedule had been jammed night and day for more than a month with infuriating field problems. We were ready to go again, but we did not look forward to it, for the adventure was over, the battle was joined, the rest would be brutal.

The Allied armies were running wild in northern France, moving so fast through the disorganized Germans that S.H.A.E.F. had already canceled a jump on the St. Arnault Forest for which we had been alerted and moved to the marshaling area ten days earlier. An armored division had taken the forest before we could leave, and so we had returned to our barracks. It was a lucky break, greeted with great cheering.

We knew, though, that our luck couldn't last indefinitely, and as we drove toward Littlecote, where the service was to be held for the men lost in Normandy, we looked at England with loving eyes, knowing full well that our time was running out.

England was our home now, while the States, with their huge, raw camps and southern garrison towns, were only a faraway memory. Civilian life was so remote and unthinkable that it had simply ceased to exist.

We rode down the narrow, winding Hungerford road and savored the old, familiar landscape. Here was the back route to Ramsbury, the 10th-century seat of the Bishops of Wiltshire, "a place of great antiquity and considerable historical and antiquarial interest," according to the guidebooks. We had practiced farcical river crossings near Ramsbury on cockles made of shelter halves and tent poles. It was summer and a

chance to swim and cool off in the River Kennet in front of a graceful
brick manor house built in 1676 by a nephew of the famous architect
Inigo Jones, and we had enjoyed ourselves thoroughly.

The bus rolled on. As I looked out the window, so glad to be alive and
back in England, I got more and more homesick for the old outfit with
each succeeding landmark. Every crossroads, every field had a meaning
and a story for someone who had died in the Invasion. I watched the ancient lands go by, then I closed my eyes and saw the Regiment as it once
was, tramping down the shining wet roads in the old, tan jumpsuits,
weapons clattering and sergeants shouting cadence. I heard them
whistling "She Wears a Yellow Ribbon" ("for a trooper who is far, far
away") and watched them turn off and go cross-country, breaking fences
and stealing rutabagas, to flank a simulated strongpoint. They had been
together two years, closer than brothers, and their average age was 21,
but now it was over, the close of old days when we were all Toccoa men
who had started with the outfit in the summer of 1942.

We're almost there now, I thought, as we turned onto a mossy, arched
stone bridge. I looked down into the River Kennet, where demolitions
men had once dynamited fish with T.N.T. and Gamon grenades, and saw
trout still nervously finning in the bottom reeds, just as they had before
D-Day. Somehow or other, because I felt changed and different, I expected everything else to be changed, but the trout were the same as
ever. They would be under the bridge long after we had left this green
and pleasant land.

The bus turned right and passed between two tall brick gateposts
near a vine-covered gatehouse. We went slowly up a graveled drive lined
with stately poplars and stopped behind a row of buses that had
brought the 1st Battalion. We unloaded and formed up.

It was mid-morning, August 28, 1944, two months and twenty-two
days after D-Day, and the sky, which had been surly gray at reveille, was
blue and clear and filled with hope. After a long wait, we began to move
slowly onto a soft green field behind Littlecote.

A reviewing platform had been erected in the center of the field.
Colonel Sink, his staff, and several civilians (probably the owners of Littlecote) stood on the stand and watched us pass. A band from a parachute artillery battalion played us into position with the strains of the
death march that goes, "Once in the dear, dead days beyond recall."

When the Regiment was formed, Chaplain McGee stepped to the front of the stand and made a short speech to the effect that the dead had not died in vain, that they were really heroic, that we should be inspired by them, etc.

The general was the next speaker, but he didn't come through very clearly, for a flight of C-47s chose this moment to circle overhead in memory of the men they had carried to their death. They circled and roared at a low altitude, dipping their wings in salute, and shout as he would, the general could not be heard.

The planes left the area just before he finished. A lieutenant from regimental headquarters stepped forward and began to read the roster of men killed in action. He called the roll in a loud, clear voice and paused between each name, so that every man would be remembered.

The list was very long—231 names—and aroused a flood of memories. As it went on and on, I looked at the pink Elizabethan magnificence of Littlecote, stretched out on the site of a Roman villa, at the mullioned windows and scores of picturesque gables, the beautiful rose garden and ivy-covered brick walls, and I thought of all the fine young men who were no longer alive to enjoy the beauty of a great, 16th-century home.

"Lt. Col. Robert L. Wolverton," the lieutenant read aloud.

A wonderful man, I mused, everything an officer should be: rugged, aggressive, competent, cheerful, informal, understanding. He'd played on the regimental football team the day the 506th beat the Air Corps "E.T.C. champs" 40 to 0 in the soccer stadium at Reading. A private had been the captain of the team and Col. Wolverton, commander of the 3rd Battalion, a substitute linesman. Whether he even got into the game I did not know, for there were lots of substitutes.

"Capt. Jerre S. Gross."

Always looking out for D Company. They were his boys, he said, and they came first.

Captain Gross stood up for his Company and his men; he was the ideal company commander. They knew it and liked him for it and stood up for him in turn.

"First Lt. Freeling T. Colt."

They said he had been a lawyer in civilian life, that he had once gotten a man out of a court-martial on a legal technicality, but this was hearsay. All I knew was that he came from Westchester County, New

York, where I grew up, and that he could carry on an intelligent conversation. Big, smiling, with a rather boyish face, he treated his platoon in F Company with more reason than severity and still got good results.

That was the way he had treated me. I had been clumsy and foolish when I came in the Army, dragging around an overnight bag with Harvard stickers on it and fumbling my rifle at inspections, but Lieutenant Colt had been kind and understanding, and I had always liked him for it. He was the only officer I felt at ease with and could talk to, but now he was gone, drowned in his chute in the black swamp behind Utah Beach. A lot of men drowned in that swamp; I was lucky to have landed in shallow water.

"Private William E. Ash," the lieutenant shouted.

Ash was many things: a voice (sort of Southern); a song, "Galway Bay," which he sang soft and sentimental, with tears in his eyes; and a favorite saying ("We's goin' tuh coombat, and we ain't *never* comin' back").

He was right about that, for in the end, and as I had feared when I left him behind in the swamp, Ash stayed in Normandy, Ash and 230 others.

I looked for him the first night, when the 2nd Battalion, which was the first to be organized—150 men out of more than 500—set up a defensive position and dug in, but he was nowhere. He still hadn't shown up a week later. Well, I thought, maybe he made it back to England on a hospital ship.

But when I asked the men returning from Normandy a month afterward what had happened to him, I learned that his luck had run out only a few yards from the place where we had met. Apparently he had changed his mind about staying on the hummock and had forced himself to swim to the big ridge.

The move was his undoing, for there were still plenty of Germans left in the woods after the rest of us had gone on. Ash went to the stone stable where I had rested briefly and lay down with the wounded men collected there in an impromptu aid station. Here the Germans found him and the others, and swarming in without mercy, killed them all.

Ash had a small, sad, prematurely wizened face to match his small body. He was one of the few men who knew that they were going to die on D-Day, knew it just as we all know that we are going to die but not exactly when. He said his first combat jump would be his last, and so it was. I missed him very much; the machine-gun platoon was not the same without him.

"P.F.C. Richard K. Buchter."

If life were measured on the basis of energy, then Peppy Buchter should have lived forever, because he had more energy than any *two* men in F Company. A Pennsylvania farm boy, shy with women, he talked as if he had a quid in his mouth, and spent all his spare time playing touch football or softball on the sloping, rutted meadow that was our parade ground. Others might beer up at the Gross Keys; Buchter preferred athletics. A chunky, stooped young man with a rough-hewn brown face and country manners and a good heart, he never missed a day's duty. His reward was the good soldier's reward: a long burst in the chest from a German machine gun as he floated down on St. Mere Eglise.

It was a long list with many unfamiliar names and a wrenching inside for every one you knew, and the lieutenant read so slowly and the sun grew so hot that I began to feel sick and dizzy. I wished that I had not come, that I had not joined the Army and volunteered for the paratroops and gotten to know so many men who had died and so many others who might die later.

My feelings were shared by many others; every now and then, someone else would sniffle or blow his nose.

I recalled a movie I had once seen. It was one of those terrible John Agar war movies, but one of the characters, a company commander, had expressed a thought that had stuck in my mind: Don't get to know your men personally. This was a fine, theoretical idea for the back lot at R.K.O., but how, in practice, could an officer or anybody else help knowing men lived with as intimately as we lived in the Army? Only Himmler could be that objective, and who wants to be Himmler?

"T-5 Howard R. Porter."

How, for example, could you help knowing Porter, the medic? He made all the jumps with you, went on all the field problems. You bumped into him in town on pass or furlough. You got to know Porter whether you liked him or not.

Porter was of medium build, with a round head, shining brown eyes, and a very short crew cut, and he walked bouncy on his heels with his toes out. The son of a Middle Western railroad man, he had emigrated to California when war broke out. He had gotten a job at Douglas, where he claimed to have risen to lead man, whatever that is, and had shared an apartment and a gay bachelor life with some friends in Santa Monica. Drafted into the Army when General Hersey shook down the defense plan for eligible youths, he volunteered for the paratroops and joined the 506th at Toccoa, Georgia, where the Regiment was formed for basic training. He was assigned to the medics and learned in time how to treat the clap (with sulfa pills) and syphilis (with penicillin shots) and what proportion of medicinal alcohol to add to a #10 can of pineapple juice to make a socially acceptable cocktail.

Now, as I stood at Littlecote, I thought of how subdued he had been in the plane on the way to Normandy and of how strange it was that we should ride side by side and yet never see each other again. Was there any meaning to life or to war, that two men should sit together and jump within seconds of each other and yet never meet on the ground below? I was a goldbrick and had been spared, while the medic, who could have saved so many lives, had been killed—right on the edge of the flooded area, by the same machine gun, they said, that had killed John D. Halls. I guess the Germans couldn't see his Red Cross armband or the red cross on his helmet or the big red cross on the first-aid kit on his hip.

The Rs—Radeka, Radovich, Ramirez, Repine, Rigaux, Riggs, Riley, Risner, Robbins, Roberts, Ronzani—and now the Ss. This is a very long list, and it takes a very long time. The sun is so hot that two men have fainted already.

"T-4 Benjamin J. Stoney."

I wanted a drink of hard cider. The bottle of Hennessy that I had acquired in the first village up from the swamp had long since evaporated, and I was tired of water. So I got up from the ditch and started back to a farmhouse where an old man (for the old men were always good to us) was giving away his homemade stock of wonderful, tingling Normandy cider. I never reached the farmhouse.

This was Vierville, about June 8th, on the road to Carentan. Two rifle companies had already passed through town without opposition. Headquarters Company was diverting itself for some brief, ecstatic moments, shooting every weapon it had at a lone sniper in the church steeple. I had lain in the gutter, watching the marksmen, until a bullet from the belfry spatted the dust in front of my nose, then I had moved across the road to a deeper ditch in the shade of a thick stone wall. Shortly after this, our lieutenant had shifted us forward to some other ditches just beyond town and a rumor spread that there was free cider in the farmhouse at the last crossroads.

Always the conservative soldier, I waited until the rumor was confirmed by the sight of men with full canteen cups coming from there before I buckled my gear, slung my rifle, and strolled leisurely toward the farmhouse courtyard, where Sergeant Hoagy and other machine gunners were sunning and sipping.

"Krauts!" someone yelled.

I stopped in my tracks and whipped my rifle off my shoulder, clicking it off safety.

Pututut . . . Pututututututut, an M-3 "greasegun" submachine gun spat angrily near the intersection, twenty yards ahead of me. Sergeant Hoagy's sunbathers vanished into the courtyard, while Captain Cox, our company commander, leaped back from the corner of the nearest hedgerow, cursing and yanking at his M-3 in an effort to clear a stoppage.

"Kraut troopers!" he shouted. "They're dug in along the road here. Kill 'em, kill the sonsabitches!"

Tech Sergeant Stoney, from Battalion S-2, ran up the ditch and took the captain's place at the corner with another M-3. Just as he leaned out to fire, a German leveled a machine gun on him and caught him in the face with a short burst. He spun around and lay still, his gun clattering to the pavement behind him.

Sergeant Hoagy's men took up firing positions at the courtyard gateposts and began to shoot back at the Germans. A rifle grenade tumbled through the air end over end toward them and exploded in the courtyard. Sergeant Hoagy reeled out of the cloud of oily black smoke, blood streaming down his face, and staggered up the road to the medics.

Its cider siesta over, Headquarters Company abruptly came to life. Everybody who had been relaxing in the ditches took up firing positions behind the hedges. A cloud of white smoke began to drift toward us from the other end of town, and when I looked over my hedgetop, I saw dozens of Germans running through some woods in the low ground three hundred yards to my direct front. They were working their way up a wall to my right, evidently planning to cut us off from the rest of the Battalion. I started shooting like mad.

Colonel Strayer ran down the ditch, took a quick look at the low ground, and shouted, "Get those goddamn tanks back up here!" A runner departed at high speed to overtake a column of 2nd Armored Division tanks that had passed through us shortly before.

"Krauts in the graveyard!" someone yelled near the church. The cry kindled a spluttering, banging firefight.

At the far end of town, from which we had come half an hour before, the white smoke rolled closer and closer. I imagined a Tiger tank creeping up on wide, clanking treads to blast us with its 88 and hose the ditches with machine guns.

While I watched the smoke, a German jeep popped out of it and whirled boldly through the village. It was flying a big Red Cross flag and carried two wounded Germans on stretchers in back, and it was such a startling phenomenon, with a big, husky German paratrooper at the wheel, that nobody made a move to stop it. It drove boldly down the middle of the road until it was finally stopped by an officer with more presence of mind than the rest of us. The jeep was commandeered; the driver, a medic, was shot for carrying a pistol; and the two wounded men were left by the side of the road to die.

Now a big, blond private from the communications platoon shoved a tall, terrified young German parachutist along the road at the point of his carbine. The German walked quivering, his hands folded on top of his bowl helmet. His eyes rolled from side to side in fear and curiosity as he blinked down at the men watching him from the ditch. When the shooting flared up, his captor halted him and tried to make him lie down, but the German, who was afraid he was going to be shot, pretended not to understand the order. Eddie Weeks, a Brooklynite ex-boxer and a character in his own right who had drifted back from D Company, jumped up, ran over to the prisoner, and slammed him savagely down on his face.

"Cut it out, Weeks!" someone yelled. "Lay off the sonofabitch!"

Weeks returned sulkily to his ditch, and a G.I. who spoke the language told the German to lie flat till the shooting was over.

Cheered on by the riflemen, three dusty tanks clattered back down the road. Their commanders studied the situation in a maddeningly leisurely fashion and then went into action. I was so absorbed in my own shooting that I didn't notice one of the tanks move up behind me, stop, and swing its 75 across the hedge near my ear. It fired, and the blast almost blew me off my perch. I jumped down with a curse and took up a more distant position.

That was Vierville, a town nobody ever heard of. The skirmish there was typical of the early fighting in Normandy. Groups of paratroopers would inadvertently bump into wandering bands of Supermen; there would be a brief firefight; and one side would get fire superiority and move in for the kill.

As it was, the tanks won Vierville for us with their high-explosive shells and 50-caliber machine guns. The main body of Germans, which I had seen running through the woods, bogged down in a swamp there and were piled up dead two and three deep by the tanks' cannon. It was a battalion of our enemy counterpart, the 6th Parachute Regiment, and this was its first time in action. When he surrendered, the battalion commander crawled out of his C.P. on his hands and knees with tears in his eyes, begging not to be shot, for a particularly vicious and not overly brave person in our Company was killing some wounded prisoners nearby. It was reported that the German commander lost more than two-thirds of his men in that one, short action.

Stoney was our only casualty, Stoney, the quiet, stocky Indian from S-2. But every village had a Stoney—or two Stoneys—or many more, because that is how wars are finally fought and won, not by rich factories and the coddled Air Force, but by the infantry, who take the ground and kill the enemy, and the infantry is Stoneys.

I RETURNED TO LITTLECOTE with a start when the lieutenant ended his list abruptly with a private named Zoltz. For a few seconds the Regiment stood sad and silent in the lovely Wiltshire dale under the big, white, summer clouds that were so peaceful and eternal, and then, before we could start coughing and shifting our feet, Chaplain McGee stepped to the front of the reviewing stand and said, "Let us pray. We will read aloud the 506th Parachute Infantry prayer that is printed on your program sheets."

We had been handed these programs as we marched onto the field. The prayer, a fine example of the Gott mit Uns spirit of the paratroops, was written by Lt. James G. Morton.

"Almighty God," we began, "we kneel to Thee and ask to be the instrument of Thy fury in smiting the evil forces that have visited death, misery, and debasement on the people of the earth. We humbly face Thee with true penitence for all our sins, for which we do most earnestly seek Thy forgiveness. Help us to dedicate ourselves completely to Thee. Be with us, God, when we leap from our planes in the dark abyss and descend in parachutes into the midst of enemy fire. Give us iron will and stark courage as we spring from the harnesses of our parachutes to seize arms for battle.

"The legions of evil are many, Father; grace our arms to meet and defeat them in Thy name and in the name of the freedom and dignity of man. Keep us firm in our faith and resolution, and guide us that we may not dishonor our high mission or fail in our sacred duties. Let our enemies who have lived by the sword turn from their violence lest they perish by the sword. Help us to serve Thee gallantly and to be humble in victory."

There was a pause and then through the still, warm air came the clear notes of a lone bugle playing "Taps":

> *When your last*
> *Day is past,*
> *Some bright star*
> *From afar*
> *O'er your grave,*
> *Watch will keep.*
> *While you sleep*
> *With the brave.*

The Regiment said, "Amen," and lifted their heads. "Call your battalions to attention!" the adjutant shouted.

Colonel Strayer spun on his heel and threw back his shoulders. "BaTALLYOWN . . . tenSHUN!"

We straightened our backs, raised our heads, clicked our boots together, slapped our hands to our sides. The band began to play "Onward, Christian Soldiers," and the 1st Battalion went by. We wheeled about and followed them off the field.

The Invasion was over, the memorial service had ended. In Normandy, the dead lay forever silent in the dappled-green parachutes that had carried them to earth. We were ready to go again, because we could only go forward, never back.

Somebody had to do it. We were not ashamed of the task. We were the infantry, the Queen of Battles. The truck drivers could do their part and get our battle stars, the manufacturers could get rich on cost-plus-10-percent and shout that wars are won by production, but we knew that nothing was solved and nothing accomplished until the infantry had killed the enemy and driven him from his ground.

And so we went forward, one regiment, filled up with replacements, the dead as fine and strong a part of us as the living men, so fresh and new, who had come to take their place.

The Windmills
Were Wonderful

I WAS READING A BOOK. IT WAS NOT A VERY WELL-WRITTEN BOOK, BUT it interested me at the time because I was the first scout in a rifle squad and the book was about my trade. I wanted to finish it before we jumped.

It was September 17, 1944, a beautifully clear Indian Summer day, and we were circling Membury Airdrome, forming up for the flight. The time was noon, our destination Holland.

I glanced out the window and saw Aldbourne off to our right; we were still circling. Nobody had said goodbye to us in Aldbourne when we marched out this time, because we had already marched out twice since our return from Normandy, and the villagers thought this was just another dry run. But it was final, very final. I didn't particularly mind, for I was fed up with training and ready to go in again and take my chances. In fact, I was so bored that I had transferred from Headquarters Company, 2nd Battalion, to E Company in search of the action that I had missed in Normandy.

I tried to read some more of my book, but it failed to hold my interest. My mind wandered to the jump ahead.

This was the largest airborne mission in history, the three-division jump of the 1st Allied Airborne Army. The 101st Airborne Division was leaving England simultaneously with the 82nd and the British 1st. We would all land astride a highway in southern Holland that ran fifty miles from Eindhoven in the south to Arnhem in the north, capture the canal and river bridges, and hold the road open for tanks of the British 2nd Army to burst through the enemy into the broad plains of north Germany and flank the Siegfried Line.

Everything depended on the bridges. If they were taken and held, the armor could go north. If even one bridge was lost, the whole operation would be delayed and might even fail. Many men would die, because we were very deep in enemy territory, and there was no way out for us but on the British tanks.

The British 1st Airborne Division ran the greatest risk, for they were farthest north, over seventy miles from the present battle lines in Belgium near the Albert Canal. A fine, spirited outfit with whom we had become acquainted in joint maneuvers in England, the 1st had never been in action before as a unit. Its cadre, however, was composed of quiet, older men who were veterans of Africa, Sicily, and Italy, and so it would not go in wholly green. We had watched a battalion of the 1st start back for their barracks on a fifteen-mile hike in a driving rain that would have had us all cursing aloud and had marveled at their snap and spirit as they had moved off briskly in step, whistling "I've Got Sixpence." Now their spirit would be tested on the bridges at Arnhem, where the Lower Rhine formed the last obstacle to the armor heading north. A pretty resort city of about ninety thousand population, Arnhem was said to be near a large German panzer training area; enemy tanks were expected.

Veterans of Sicily, Italy, Normandy—and of great bar brawls with the 101st—the 82nd Airborne Division would land ten miles south of Arnhem at Nijmegen, a city of about 94,000 inhabitants, and seize its bridges, which spanned the Waal River. Another branch of the Rhine, the Waal was a formidable obstacle with two giant bridges, one for cars and another for railway trains. The 82nd also had to capture the Maas-Waal Canal bridge at Grave, a long, curving highway bridge over the Maas River, and the pine-covered hills at the edge of the Reichswald, about five miles east-southeast of Nijmegen. This was the highest ground in Holland.

The 101st had three main canal bridges along the road to Arnhem. They were located at Veghel, Zon, and Eindhoven, a city slightly larger than Nijmegen, which the 1st and 2nd Battalions of the 506th had been ordered to capture the day of the jump. In a sense, we were the luckiest of the three divisions, because we were the farthest south and would be the first to meet the British tanks—if they broke through to us. There was always the question of whether the tanks would or would not break through.

Trying to forget what lay ahead—the German tanks operating in perfect tank country; a drop zone that could be flooded; the British armor held up far away; our extreme vulnerability on a daylight drop—I returned to my book.

Only a few pages were left now. I wanted very much to finish them before I left the plane, so that I wouldn't have to carry the volume with me.

It was not the kind of book that I cared to keep. In fact, it was quite disappointing, for it lacked the color and spirit that I had hoped for in a tale of its kind.

Oh hell, I thought as the plane leveled out and began a steady drone, I can't concentrate on this today. It was easy to concentrate in the marshaling area, where there was nothing but mud and tedium, but too much is on my mind now. I looked out the window again.

The 2nd Battalion was formed in a long column, nine planes wide. Headed due east, we were rapidly approaching the north suburbs of London.

I was calm and almost unworried, for the daylight was considerably more reassuring than the night had been on the way to Normandy. I could see P-47 and P-51 fighter planes swarming all around and above us. They would escort us to the drop zone to beat off enemy fighters and strafe any flak batteries that opened fire on us from the ground.

All in all, it was a good plan, proceeding smoothly.

Colonel Sink had said that it would. In the best form yet, he had given us a colorful farewell the day before.

"You'll meet British tanks," he had said, "some of them Cromwells, others Shermans. The Cromwells look like a cheesebox on a raft. They mount a 76mm cannon with a muzzle brake that makes them look like Kraut tanks, but for God's sake, don't shoot 'em, because they're there to help you.

"And these Guards divisions," the colonel had continued, wiping his face and moving his hat back and forth across his head, "they're goddamn good outfits. Hell, you can't get in 'em unless you have a Sir in front of your name and a pedigree a yard long. You'll see the Royal Household Cavalry and the 17-21st Lancers, fighting mad 'cause they're not on horses.

"But don't laugh at 'em. They're good outfits.

"This time take *lots* of prisoners!" the colonel had shouted. "With luck, we might even be out of there in ten days."

A laugh had rocked the marshaling area. Too many of us remembered the "two days' effort" asked of us before Normandy—two days that had somehow stretched into thirty-one. We weren't buying that again.

Colonel Sink had smiled and held up his hand for silence. After the cries of "Oh Christ" and "Shit" had died down, he had given us a direct order to hide our wool-knit caps in Holland. "General Taylor spotted one of you people in a wool-knit cap in Normandy, and men, he really raised hell about it. Now, I don't want to catch hell, see, and I know you don't, so for God's sake, if you *have* to wear a wool-knit cap, hide the damned thing under your helmet and don't let the general catch you with that helmet off! That's an order, men, goddammit. The general can't stand those little hats."

Delightful as ever, the colonel had rambled on, carrying the Regiment with him on waves of laughter. "This is a good outfit," he had concluded, "good enough to win a Presidential Citation in Normandy. I know you people can do all right, so I don't have to talk about fighting. You old men look after the replacements, and we'll all get along fine together."

The colonel, I mused with a smile. If only all the officers were Colonel Sink. Someday I hope to meet him and shake his hand and tell him how much we liked him.

I tried to read, but the book was too dull, and so I skipped some pages and then checked the landscape below.

We were over London now. It was Sunday morning, and the streets were quite empty. Here and there, a few people stood on the sidewalks and waved up at us.

London clutched my heart and tried to pull me down. I wanted to relax, to go with it all the way to the nearest Underground station, but I couldn't move. Jammed in with twenty other men, I could only watch the familiar streets fade slowly away from us far below and wish that I were walking on their hard surface, instead of riding a noisy, bouncing airplane to combat and possibly my death.

It was too pretty a day to go to war. Those civilians, I thought, how lucky they are! They'll go to church and then have a big Sunday dinner. And tonight in the pubs, they will wonder where we went and what larger battles we are a part of. Safe and warm, they will discuss the war till closing time, then drift home to soft beds in quiet houses. We'll be crawling up a ditch by then, with dry throats and sweaty foreheads, or else we'll be dug in, waiting for the enemy to come out of the night. How much better it will be tonight in London!

"See the water?" somebody remarked. "We're over water already."

God, I thought, looking down.

The city had disintegrated into scattered houses on large lots that ended at the banks of a yellow-brown body of water. As we crept slowly overhead, the water deepened to pale green, turquoise, and then midnight blue.

We're done for, I thought in despair. Goodbye, England.

My stomach tightened. I hoped that our plane would break down, that we would have to turn back, but the engines' roar was as steady as ever. The white cliffs faded away. I tried to find distraction in my book, but I couldn't resist looking out the window.

Down below, miniature waves molded on a deep-blue sea slapped against motionless model boats anchored at regular intervals to mark our course. The sea, which reflected the sky, seemed very strong and deep, a Maxfield Parrish blue.

I returned to my book, but before I could really concentrate, we were over land again, roaring with gathering speed above the high, white cliffs of the French coast.

There was rolling farmland behind the cliffs. Soon the country flattened out. We passed many wrecked villages and came to a huge flooded area so still and motionless that it seemed as if life had been suspended there. Nothing moved in the trees or among the houses or in the little Flemish villages where the water stood six feet deep. I hoped that the Germans had not flooded our drop zone.

We dipped lower. The final run would be made in at six hundred feet, to minimize the danger of flak; this was the start of it. The knowledge twisted my stomach and turned it cold.

I was through with the book at last. Before I could put it down, someone jostled my elbow and pointed ahead. "Looks like the front," he said.

A big canal lay across our path. A column of tanks and trucks a quarter of a mile long inched forward on a highway almost directly below us to a Bailey bridge partially obscured by clouds of white smoke. Orange smoke pots burned nearby as identification of friendly forces. This was the front: the Albert Canal. The Guards Armored Division had forced a crossing and were fighting to widen the bridgehead. They were supposed to break out of the crossing today and drive north to Holland. A handful of British soldiers waved to us from the banks of the canal and then disappeared in the smoke.

We swooped over the German lines in a brief rattle of small-arms fire. This was enemy country now, and a beautiful day for flak.

"Stand up and hook up!"

I lunged at the anchor line and snapped the end of my static line to it. The book was still in my hand. There was no flak yet. I dropped the book on a seat so the Air Corps could read it and smiled at the title— *We Jumped to Fight*. Written by Lt. Col. Edson D. Raff, a pioneer parachutist, it was the story of the 503 in Africa. I was very disappointed in both the writing and the story, but the title was appropriate.

"Check your equipment!"

My chest and leg straps were properly centered in the new, British quick-release fastener in the middle of my chest. My reserve-chute snaps were snug. I moved the .45 I had bought from a crew chief after Normandy for $50 close to my front, where I could reach it quickly. A bullet was already in the chamber. No German was going to bayonet me or cut my throat on *this* jumpfield.

"Sound off for equipment check!"

The door was open and the motors so loud that I could barely hear the men behind me shout their numbers. Someone prodded me, and I yelled and slapped the shoulder of the man ahead of me. As the lead scout, I was closer to the door than I had been in Normandy, but my impatience to leave was not less. All I wanted now was out. My legs were weak, and I swallowed again and again. There was no flak.

"Close up and stand in the door!"

The flat green fields of Holland flashed by a few hundred feet below. I saw a windmill, a small pine forest, a canal crossing. In the distance, the spire of an immense church rose from a cluster of tile-roofed houses.

No flak, I said to myself, no flak. Maybe this won't be so bad after all.

We were jammed together so tightly that I could hardly breathe. Our left legs were all forward in a lock step, ready to go. The jumpmaster was crouched by the equipment bundles in the door.

The pilot lowered the flaps, and the plane slowed down.

Still no flak. Come on, let's go! No flak.

"GO!"

Rattle, rattle, blam, crash! the line of men surged forward, flinging their static lines at the tail as they jumped. I followed them. Stopping all thought, my mind went blank, and I ran out the door without taking the proper stance.

I fell without knowing that I was falling, without even seeing where I was headed. Suddenly the opening shock unsnapped me.

I was spinning furiously, for my poor exit, combined with a badly packed chute, had twisted my risers and suspension lines so much that my head was pinned down hard with my chin touching the top of my rifle case. I couldn't look up to check my canopy, but I didn't particularly care. Why worry? I thought, glad to be out of the plane and on my own, I'm alive and floating free.

Everything looked fine on the ground. There were no trees, rocks, roads, or houses on the mile-square, brownish-green field that was our drop zone. Flat and smooth, the field was cut here and there by low barbed-wire fences and shallow drainage ditches. No enemy was in sight; there appeared to be no hostile ground-fire.

The drop zone was alive with men. Hundreds of spotted-green parachutes dotted the grass, while still more floated down in a beautiful spectacle alive with shouting. This was a big jump—a regimental combat team on one field—and we were all landing together. It was a thrilling sight to see.

My risers had untwisted by the time I was ready to land. I reached up, grasped all four, pulled down hard, and landed standing up. This was a sin in combat, but I couldn't resist the temptation, for the jump was so perfect. My chute collapsed, and I lay down quickly and got free of my harness. With amazing swiftness, the other men were already clearing off the field. I did not want to be left behind.

A C-47 came over low, streaming fire from a wing. I watched with gritted teeth as the men tried to get out. One, two, three, four, five, six, seven, eight. They were still jumping when the plane slammed into the ground and blew up half a mile away. God, I thought, that could have been me.

But it wasn't. I'm still alive, and as long as things are so quiet, I think I'll get a souvenir.

I had always wanted a piece of parachute silk for a scarf but had never dared cut a chute on a training jump. Now was my chance. I pulled out my trench knife and went to the canopy.

Ku-rump.

I dropped the chute and looked up with a frown. A puff of black smoke hung over the jumpfield several hundred yards south. Airburst.

Ku-Rump!

Another shell burst considerably closer.

Eighty-eights. Time to leave.

I put my trench knife back in its sheath, picked up my rifle, and began to run toward a column of white smoke that was rising from a pine forest a quarter of a mile east. This was the assembly point for the 2nd Battalion. Another shell went off, and I increased my speed. Of the hundreds of men who had been on the field five minutes before, only a handful were left.

"Hey, Webster, help me, will you!"

I slowed down and saw Wingate limping toward me. We had been in the machine-gun platoon together. He had hurt his ankle on the Normandy jump and had been evacuated almost immediately after daylight. Now he said that his ankle was broken.

"Medic! Medic!" I shouted, not wishing to linger in the open. "For Chrissake, medic!"

A casual individual with a Red Cross armband sauntered toward us in a drainage ditch. "Keep your shirt on, buddy," he said. "I'm coming."

"Take it easy, Wingate," I said, and ran for the cover of the pine forest.

Suddenly I came on three corpses. Two paratroopers and an Air Corps crew chief, they had evidently been killed by the same airburst, for they were within a few yards of each other and still in their chutes. The crew chief had a bloody gash three inches long and an inch wide in his temple. I looked at him closely, for he seemed vaguely familiar.

Oh, I thought, remembering him, he was such a nice guy.

We had met him one night after Normandy in the Shepherd's Rest. He had long, blond hair and an open, friendly face, and he had treated us to some beers while we talked of the Air Corps and the paratroopers, for he was stationed with a troop-carrier unit at Membury and often carried us on jumps. We had thanked him by trying to steal his jeep afterward for a ride back to Aldbourne. We were drunk, and the Air Corps was always fair game, for they were rich, spoiled, carefree, and undisciplined, but we couldn't get the motor started, and so we had had to walk back to camp. The crew chief was young, innocent, and friendly. Now he was dead on the drop zone.

Ku-RACK!

The airburst was only a hundred yards away.

Ducking low, I ran for the woods, where I could make out scores of men lying low among the young pine trees.

A man passed me on the run.

"Hey," I shouted, "is this the 2nd Battalion?"

"Goddamn if I know."

I went into the forest and found myself in the 3rd Battalion. An officer suggested that I try farther north, and so I kept going until I found E Company.

Spread out in brambly ditches beside a sandy road, they were waiting for the last stragglers to come in. I lay down with the rest of the squad and began to discuss the jump.

It was, we agreed, our best overseas. The drop zone was perfect, the planes in formation, the wind light, the field flat and soft. England had nothing like it. As far as we could tell, nobody in the Company had been killed on the landing.

Five P-51 fighter planes circled a far corner of the field, peeled off one by one, and tutututut, strafed an object on the ground there. A column of greasy black smoke rose in the sky.

"Tank," a man said who was watching them with field glasses. "They just got a Kraut tank."

The planes re-formed and flew away. I watched them go with a sinking feeling in my heart, for we needed their firepower. The thrumming sound of their engines faded into silence in the south. The ditch seemed very still and lonely.

I sighed and shrugged my shoulders. What the hell, I said to myself. We're off to a good start. Maybe Holland won't be so bad after all. I opened a K ration and began to eat lunch.

IT WAS VERY HOT and anticlimactic lying in the ditch and waiting to move out. In fact, it was almost our hottest day overseas. The sun glared down from the clear sky, and there was no wind to deflect the heat, which seemed to settle in the ditch. A few men drifted up and down the sandy road, then everything was quiet. Although the stragglers had apparently all come in, still we waited to go. Our initial excitement and enthusiasm, which had reached its highest pitch as we floated down with hundreds of other men released from the planes that had held them captive, dried up in the heat and the waiting. It would have been better psychology to have set off as soon as we were assembled, but no, the Army had to wait . . . and wait . . . and wait.

Sooner or later, I knew, the waiting would end. Eventually we would meet the Germans. How would the other men react? I had never been in action with any of them before. I began to wonder about them.

Rader and I were bound to argue; we had started already. Leader of the third squad, he was tall, thin, and rather sarcastic, but steady and not easily excited.

Hoobler was his assistant. An exuberant boy from the same part of Ohio as Rader, he was his complete opposite: raucous, hearty, laughing, disputatious. I had wrecked his Thompson on a field problem in England when I had tried to mow down a giant jackrabbit, but he had taken the accident as a joke, saying that he preferred an M-1 anyway. Hoobler was young, cocky, and sturdily built. Nobody had to fear for him in combat.

He loved to josh thin little Pace, the second scout, who had come in as a replacement after Normandy. A wild crapshooter who pulled a mighty longbow, Pace had a small paratrooper's natural cockiness that, combined with his Southern spirit, forecast a fine combat soldier. He was a good man to work with as a scout.

Two replacements, Massaconi and Lyall, manned our 30-caliber light machine-gun, which had been equipped with a bipod for the operation. More experienced gunners had also taken a tripod into Holland for greater accuracy (the bipods were meant for Normandy-type fighting, where the machine guns often had to be fired from the top of walls and hedgerows), but neither of our men had thought to take this precaution, since both were new to action. Massaconi was a worldly, talkative man from Massachusetts who had trained in the 26th, or Yankee, Division. He was full of jokes, nicknames, and comments. His assistant, Lyall, was very young, likable, and chatty. Our platoon sergeant, Talbert, looked on Lyall as a bright and eager younger brother who, with the proper guidance, would turn into a great soldier. Massaconi called him Knothead.

There were two ammo bearers, Janovec and Miller, who were also new to the outfit. Janovec, who was always humming or singing "Racing with the Moon," was dour, stubborn, and sarcastic, but generally reliable—if he liked you and thought your ideas made sense. For some reason, he and I got along well together, and I preferred to have him nearby rather than almost anybody else in the squad. How he would react under fire remained to be seen. No man could possibly predict how any other man would act in combat.

Miller had a brush haircut and a missing front tooth that gave him an engaging, boyish appearance. Less than 20 years old, he had come to the E.T.O. as an infantry replacement, then volunteered for the paratroops. So far, he had drawn only one month's jump pay. Miller was very quiet and friendly and well mannered, but he did not have the independence required for the parachute infantry, where every man, in the words of a British writer, is an emperor. Each of us had to be ready to act on our own, without the least briefing, orders, or advice, and Miller was too disciplined for this kind of action. He was an ideal soldier, quiet and obedient, and I hoped that these qualities would not work to his disadvantage in the first free-for-all.

We were lying down in marching order, with Rader at the head of our twelve-man column and the others strung out behind. Hoobler brought up the rear. I looked from Miller to the next man, Rice.

No need to worry about Rice; he did enough worrying for ten men. A stocky Southerner, Rice was our grenadier. He had started as a machine gunner in F Company in Toccoa, had transferred to the kitchen, and had joined E Company after Normandy. Rice was somewhat of a busybody, especially to the replacements, whom he was forever telling what to do and how to do it. As a soldier, however, Rice promised to be an asset.

Whytsell, Wiseman, and Meth were the remaining riflemen. Whytsell was quite young and friendly, full of talk and wisecracks and a great friend of Wiseman's, whom he called Goldie. Wiseman called him Slick, for he had a very short crew cut, and palled around with him most of the time in Aldbourne and the marshaling area. Whytsell appeared to be quite a good soldier.

I liked Wiseman the best of all. A burly miner from Colorado, he was the oldest man in the squad—about 25—and the roughest. He was strong and durable and highly independent, yet intelligent, well trained, and understanding. Nobody feared for Wiseman.

The same could not be said for Meth. He was eager—he had volunteered to come along, when he could well have stayed back in the rear—but he was not a trained, hardened, or experienced soldier. Short and plump, with a Brooklyn accent, he had spent most of his Army career as a cook. One cook had, however, jumped in Normandy and had lorded it over the other cooks on his return, so most of them, to save face, had volunteered to jump in Holland. We didn't want them—they were not trained soldiers—but they were along, and so we had to help them. I was with the other cook in Normandy, and I knew what we were in for. Meth was, however, quite likable and earnest.

"ON THE ROAD, on the road!" Rader cried. "Let's go."

I stood up, buckled my cartridge belt, and put the bayonet on my rifle.

"Five yards between men. Get a move on, Webster!"

I fell in behind some men from F Company who were moving out ahead of us. It was nice to have somebody between me and the enemy.

We walked briskly east on the sandy path through the pine trees until we reached the main road, which ran north and south from Eindhoven to Arnhem. Half a mile away, we saw the tile roofs and big steeple of the village of Zon, our initial objective. The 1st Battalion had to secure the jumpfield for glider landings and aerial resupply and hold the bridge over the Wilhelmina Canal at Zon, while the 2nd and 3rd Battalions went south to Eindhoven.

Nobody came out to greet us at Zon. Dead and deserted, the village had an ominous air about it that made me click my rifle off safety. I eyed all the windows of the houses ahead. A rustling of paper flashed through the air high above me. Ignoring it, I continued to follow close after F Company.

"Jesus Christ, Webster!" Rader exclaimed. "Don't you know what that is?"

I shook my head without taking my eyes off the houses. Something was going to happen very soon, I could tell, and I didn't like it.

"That's an 88."

"Oh? Didn't sound like one to me."

"Wise up, boy."

"Hell."

Evidently the same cannon that had sent the airbursts, killed the crew chief, and knocked down one or two planes was still in action, probably near the canal bridge. The thought of it failed to worry me, for I was intent only on staying close to F Company. As the lead scout in E Company, I was now the connecting point between the two units. I was more afraid of an ambush in the village than of the 88. I knew that the civilians wouldn't be lying low if they didn't expect a battle. They knew before any soldiers when a battle was brewing. I began to sweat freely.

We approached an intersection in the middle of town.

"Go left, go left!" my platoon leader shouted. A former noncom who had won a battlefield commission in Normandy, he was dark, sturdy, and sensible. His name was Lieutenant Hudson. "Go left!" he shouted again.

F Company went straight down the road. I turned left with nobody in front of me. Edging over close to the houses, with my rifle at my hip, ready to fire, I slowed down to an invalid's walk.

"Faster! Get a move on!"

Oh, goddamn you, I thought. Goddamn all you officers. I'm out here to draw fire, and you want me to run right into it.

I stepped out at a quicker gait and, following the road as it curved to the left and then to the right, passed beyond the village. A bridge over a small creek called the Dommel River lay ahead. I looked at it and around it and then beyond it—and stopped cold.

There, a hundred yards beyond the bridge by the side of the road, near a stone barn, were three Germans. The one in the center squatted behind a machine gun, with the others close beside him. All of them waved to me in greeting.

You'll be sorry, I thought, you sonsofbitches.

Grasping my rifle by the upper hand guard and the small of the stock, I flung it above my head parallel to the ground as a signal for the men behind me: enemy in sight.

In one second, I had made the motion, yanked the rifle down to my shoulder, and aimed at the machine gunner. I wanted to kill him first, because he was the most dangerous.

The Germans continued to wave. Evidently they thought we were German paratroopers, come to reinforce them.

My eyesight was better than theirs, for I could tell a German right away by his stance, which was utterly unlike that of an American soldier, but I was not as relaxed as they were. Tense with nervousness, I leveled on the machine gunner's chest, winced, and pulled the trigger.

The bullet cracked above the German's head, and before I could fire another round, all three men had disappeared behind the barn. I cursed myself.

An enemy machine gun fired a short burst to my left. It was not aimed at me, I knew, but my brief heroics were over. I jumped behind the bridge. Some shooting, I thought, crouching close to the earth. I am the world's worst shot. Never could shoot worth a good goddamn.

Lieutenant Hudson ran up and got me back on the road and across the bridge.

A shout rippled up the column behind us: "Hold it up! Hold it up! Hold it up!"

I stopped and sidled over to the cover of the embankment.

"Come on back," Lieutenant Hudson said.

Some men from company headquarters had already started off through a field on the right, heading toward the canal. Vastly relieved to be a follower again, I fell in with the column.

We waded a filthy ditch filled with scummy water that smelled like the distilled essence of barnyard and sewer, scrambled over some barbed-wire fences, cursed our way through patches of briars, dodged across a few backyards, and suddenly came out on the broad cobblestone embankment of the Wilhelmina Canal near a brickyard with piles of sand and a water tower on steel legs.

There had been a tremendous explosion only a few minutes before. Now we saw the result: a blown bridge. The Germans had wrecked our first objective.

We scattered out in the brickyard, taking good care to have cover between us and the enemy side of the canal, and lay down to await developments. Half a dozen empty 88 shell casings lay in the vicinity, but the cannon had evidently departed.

Now what? I wondered as time went by and nothing happened. Hurry up and wait: It never changes. I sighed, and because I was hot, removed my wool undershirt and stowed it in my musette bag, then rolled up my sleeves.

The officers made us look for logs or boats or boards to get across on, but since there was nothing suitable in the vicinity, we lay back down again. There was no sign of life in the half-dozen little houses across from us.

A German rifle popped far away, and soon a barn began to burn about six hundred yards to our direct front. Small figures ran out of the barn and tumbled down from a poplar tree close to it, where they had evidently been watching us. A Headquarters Company machine gunner on the bank of the canal ran a belt through his 30-caliber, but the bullets were high and hurt nobody. A few riflemen joined him. I held my fire. If I couldn't hit a man at a hundred yards, I certainly couldn't hit one at six hundred. Why waste the ammunition? It might come in handy later.

This is dull, I thought, yawning. It certainly can't compare with D-Day. I leaned back against a foot of the water tower and blinked my eyes. It's afternoon already, I mused, and a good five miles to Eindhoven. We were supposed to take the city today. Hope the British tanks beat us to it.

A naked figure streaked past, dove into the canal, and swam twenty yards to the other bank, where two waterlogged rowboats were moored.

"Johnny Weismuller!" Hoobler cried. "That goddamn Carson." He yipped with delight.

The whole Company laughed and yelled as Carson, a first-platoon runner, climbed into one of the rowboats and paddled it back to our side. A group of men from the first squad helped bail it out, then went over to investigate the houses.

While this drama was unfolding, a less heroic but more practical unit of the 326th Parachute Engineer Battalion, which had jumped with us, was gathering boards and building a rough footbridge over the ruins of the blown bridge. Carson put on his clothes, and after a long wait, we started over, rushing down the planks one by one, into the arms of an engineer, who caught us and steadied us for the run up the other side. A slow process, the company crossing took almost an hour.

By now it was almost twilight. We had traveled two or three miles in five hours.

Fortunately, our Company had not encountered the 88. Rumors came to us that several cannon had been posted around Zon as protection for the bridge. Dual-purpose antiaircraft, antipersonnel, the 88s had fired on the planes and gliders and then leveled on the men coming down the road, killing almost a dozen.

A 3rd Battalion captain had been shot through the head in Zon by a German rifleman. Burr Smith, a big Californian, and another man from company headquarters had carried him into a little cafe and laid his body on the bar. The German gun crews' packs were still lined up neatly along the walls of the cafe, where they had had lunch, and the Dutch family that ran the place, bewildered by the sudden fighting, had stared at the dead captain and wept and sobbed, *"Gott, Gott, Gott,"* and wrung their hands. The company headquarters' men had divided the contents of the captain's musette bag and gone on their way, leaving the body with the civilians.

The sun was down by the time we had crossed the canal. The air turned cool with surprising speed as we lay in the ditches beside the highway and waited for the rest of the Battalion to come over. A twilight hush fell on the countryside; there was no sound of war or nature. Men began to fall asleep. It was obvious to all that we would not take Eindhoven today.

Never able to nap on the bare ground, I shivered in the gathering mist and wondered what was going on. As usual, we had been elaborately briefed before the takeoff—and told nothing once we were in action. I felt better when I knew what was taking place.

Just when the stars grew bright and low and the cold twisted into my muscles and made me get up and exercise to keep warm, an officer came down the road and moved us into an adjacent field, where we posted two men as guards and settled ourselves around a haystack.

Our bivouac was so congested, however, that Janovec and I decided to seek more comfortable quarters in some nearby farm buildings. Stumbling through the darkness, we came to a little shed. It looked good, but the first squad, which was very sly and first in many things, had already taken possession. They shouted us off the premises.

As we moved through the backyard toward the main farmhouse, we heard German voices coming out of the mouth of a sod-covered underground air-raid shelter to our left. We stopped.

"Cover me," I whispered to Janovec.

He unslung his rifle, and I cocked my .45 and tiptoed to the entrance, crouching low.

"*Heraus!*" I yelled. "*Hande hoch! Mach' schnell!*"

A man crept out on his hands and knees, mumbling, "*Niederländer, Niederländer.*"

I yanked him up, frisked him, and pulled him close.

It was a Dutch civilian. Quivering with fear, he told us that he was the owner of the farm. He had taken refuge with his family in the shelter as soon as the first planes had come over and had been below ground ever since.

"*Wir sind Amerikäner,*" I told him, adding that we were paratroopers, *Fallschirmjäger.* We had come to shoot the Germans, I explained. Were there any around?

"Nein, nein," he replied. He shook our hands and told us that he was glad to be free again. Welcoming us to Holland, he invited us into his house. Hoobler, ever restless and alert, had drifted up in the meantime. "Ask him if he has any food," he said.

"Ja, ja. Komm'!"

He led us into a barn where a platoon of men from Headquarters Company had settled, passed through their jealous mutterings, and opened the door to his kitchen. We shut the door to keep out the machine gunners. Hoobler lit a candle.

Chattering away happily about how much he hated the Germans and wanted to help us, our host, who was a thin, strong, middle-aged man in a dark suit and cloth cap, went to some shelves lined with Mason jars filled with preserves, and gave us an assortment of beef, peaches, and cherries. Hoobler and Janovec offered some of their cigarettes in return, while I donated a D-ration chocolate bar.

The farmer was overwhelmed. These were the first decent cigarettes he had had in five years, he said. As for the candy, he would save it for his little boy, who had never tasted chocolate.

We thanked him again for the food, suggested that he lock the door, to keep Headquarters Company from cleaning him out, and went back to the squad. The preserves were a delicious treat, and we agreed as we passed them around in the cold starlight near the haystack that Holland was indeed a fine country.

WE SET OFF AT DAWN, two battalions of a thousand men on foot, without tanks, trucks, artillery, or air support, to capture a city of a hundred thousand. The city, Eindhoven, was supposed to be lightly held. It was presumed that the Germans could not bring in enough reinforcements to stop us. The 3rd Battalion led the way.

At first we moved swiftly down the road, which was raised, like all the other roads in southern Holland, about a yard above the surrounding farmland and lined at regular intervals with tall, stately trees. Soon, however, there were scattered shots ahead. A firefight developed, and the column came to a halt. The firing continued, then died out. We got to our feet again.

On flank guard a hundred yards out on the right and pushing hard to keep up with the column, which was moving smoothly down the highway, I came on a big, dark paratrooper lying wounded in a ditch. A thick forest of high trees lay about two hundred yards farther on, to our right, and I hated to stop and offer myself as a target to a sniper who might be hiding in the forest.

"Help me, buddy," the man said. He looked like Joe Trujillo from the mortar platoon, and so I stopped beside him with one eye on the woods. The men on the road continued to move on.

"Get going!" Rader shouted, waving at me.

"Medic!" I replied. "Medic!"

"Jesus, buddy, don't leave me. I can't move."

"Medic!"

A first-aid man left the column and ran toward us.

"Don't go."

"I have to go; I'm on flank guard. The medic's coming now."

He gave me the look of a helpless man abandoned by the one person who can aid him. Hoping desperately that I wouldn't be wounded on flank guard and left behind as he had been, I ran off, feeling like an utter heel. God help anybody who is hit now, I thought. The outcome is uncertain, and there are no ambulances or hospitals.

We passed some more wounded men, all from the 3rd Battalion, which had run into the first outposts of Eindhoven, and then stopped again.

"3rd Bat's held up," Lieutenant Hudson informed us. "Looks like they've run into the M.L.R."

We cut left into open farmland to flank the enemy positions. Under a hot summer sun, we struggled through truck gardens and freshly plowed fields toward the city, which rose abruptly from the green meadows a quarter of a mile away. A German machine gun fired a long burst at us.

"Hit it!" Rader cried.

I dropped behind a small tree and wriggled around to cover the buildings. The machine gun fired again, but I couldn't locate it.

Several guns in E Company returned the fire. Manned by veterans, they carefully sprayed the windows of a long row of two-story apartment houses that faced us. Their toomtoomtoom mixed very pleasantly with the wonderful noise of breaking glass. I smiled. Everybody liked to shoot at windows.

"In that line of houses!" Rader shouted at Massaconi and Lyall. "Spray 'em, spray 'em!"

They joined the shooting. In a few minutes, however, everybody lost enthusiasm and the firing died out.

Still safe behind my little tree, I decided to abandon my gas mask, which kept banging against my legs in an irritating fashion. It was too hot to bother with nonessentials.

"On the road! Moving out."

We started down a sandy path that paralleled the buildings. The enemy gun fired another burst.

"Hoobler, take Webster and Pace and get that guy!" cried Lieutenant Peacock, our assistant platoon leader and to me the most infuriating officer in the Regiment. "I think he's in that farmhouse out there."

The place he referred to was about two hundred yards to our right front. A small dwelling, it stood all alone in a big, bare field without any covered approach whatsoever.

I gave the box of machine-gun ammunition that I had carried ever since the jump to the man nearest me and ran after Hoobler, with Pace beside me.

It was a long run over deep, sandy furrows, but we covered the distance in about ten seconds—or so it seemed, for I have never run faster in my life. While the others covered me, I beat on the door and bade the occupants come out with their hands high.

A very old man obeyed the summons. So terrified that he could only stutter, he made no sense to us, so we pushed him aside and looked indoors. There were no Germans. We ran back to the Company.

"Lieutenant Hudson got hit," Rader informed us. "Burp gun knocked him down."

"The good officers always get hit," I remarked, dreading what this would mean to us. "Now we're stuck with Peacock."

"You know it, boy, you know it."

A right swing across the field a few minutes later brought us into the streets of Eindhoven, a bright, new city built around the giant Phillips electrical plant. The first sight that greeted us was the body of a 3rd Battalion captain who had been shot through the head by a sniper in a windmill down the street.

This is a bad country for captains, I mused, wondering why they always threw a covering over a dead man's face. I looked at the windmill. It had been liberally shot up with small arms and bazookas. I hoped that the sniper had been killed.

People came out of all the houses as we marched past the windmill. "So nice to see you," they said in perfect English, for the Dutch were extremely well educated. "We have waited so long."

The column stopped, and the civilians brought us chairs to sit on, milk and tea to drink, and fresh fruit to eat. Thoroughly enjoying the role of liberator, we chatted with them gaily, for it was wonderful to feel wanted and welcome, to meet someone (for the first time) who appreciated what you were doing. Nobody had ever welcomed us to France.

A German rifle popped down the street.

"Sniper!"

I dropped my peach and fell behind a stone gatepost. In an instant, all the soldiers were flat and the civilians indoors.

Pop. Pop. Pop.

"Get him! Get him!"

"Come on, Web," Hoobler yelled. "Better cover in the schoolhouse."

We darted across the road, climbed a high wire fence, and ran behind the sturdy brick building. After examining the premises for Germans, we sat down in the sun with the schoolhouse between us and the sniper.

Hoobler took off his helmet and sighed. "This is the way to fight a war, isn't it?"

I nodded.

Colonel Sink came into the yard with Lieutenant Colonel Chase, his quiet, friendly executive officer, and a retinue of enlisted men.

Hoobler slapped on his helmet, and we struggled to our feet and tried to look alert and eager, but Colonel Sink merely smiled at us, glanced around, and went out. We returned to our sunbath.

"Let's go, Hoobler!" Rader shouted. "Moving out."

We walked all the way through Eindhoven, from north to south. Our march quickly changed from a tactical exercise to a triumphal progress as the last Germans and their machine guns and cannon were knocked out by other platoons and companies. Orange flags and armbands appeared everywhere, and the cheering, clapping crowds soon thickened so much that we could barely move. The civilians wanted to help us, to shake our hands, to pat our backs and thank us for driving away the Germans. The applause and din of gratitude was so deafening that we had to shout to each other to be heard. It was the most sincere thanks-giving demonstration that any of us had ever witnessed, and it fixed Holland forever in our hearts.

Our objectives, several bridges over the Wilhelmina Canal in the southeastern corner of Eindhoven, were taken without resistance. Guards were posted (and almost immediately blew up a truck filled with escaping German soldiers), and Lyall, Massaconi, Janovec, and Miller set up the machine gun on the roof of a liquor warehouse, which they promptly inspected via a broken skylight. Pace and I were sent down a side street to watch for Germans approaching from the east. Heroes for the day, we posed for snapshots ("I want a picture of the first American soldier I've seen"), signed our autographs, drank cognac and wine that had been hidden away to celebrate the liberation. A Dutchman, Hans Wesenhagen, served us a splendid meal of vegetable broth, roast veal, Brussels sprouts, boiled potatoes, applesauce, and fresh milk. The girls stared at us in admiration, the small boys fingered our gear, the older civilians mobbed us as if we were movie stars. Although most of them understood my linguaphone German, they preferred to exercise their English. Our language, we were told, was a required subject in Holland, where the educational level of both young and old was far higher than in America and where almost everybody also studied German and French.

"We are so glad to see you," the people said. "The Germans were terrible."

"We have waited so long. Do you have a cigarette?"

"You are good boys."

"Holland is a wonderful country. Very good people, beautiful windmills."

"Are you English? We heard the English were coming."

"No, we are American parachutists. The English panzers will come soon. Which were worse, the German officials or the Wehrmacht men?"

"The officials. The soldiers were well behaved."

"Why is that girl's head shaved?"

"She made love to German soldiers."

"You must beware! The Germans may come back. How many of you are in the city?"

"Thousands."

"We heard you are all volunteers. You are very young."

"Yes, as paratroopers we are all volunteers. Our average age is 21. Who is that man with the short hair?"

"He is in the Underground. He has just come out of a concentration camp. It was awful."

"Your girls are very pretty. Yes, thanks! Good cognac."

Einhoven was a lovely place.

"Where are we going?" I inquired.

"Goddamn if I know," Rader replied. "Peacock told me to have the squad on the road in ten minutes."

"Oh Christ. This was such a nice deal. . . ."

We had moved into a new position early in the afternoon, after the first British scout cars had bypassed heavy resistance in the south and come into the city. Located in the eastern outskirts on the bank of the Wilhelmina Canal, our new position was tactically stupid—in an open beet field below the level of a large factory which the enemy could use as a likely avenue of approach—but it was very pleasant. The owners of a nearby house brought us soup and tea and hot buckets of water for shaving, and we scrounged rabbits and fresh fruit and vegetables from other neighbors. Our holes were deep and lined with straw, the sun was pleasant, and even the steady booming of battle farther south failed to disturb our tranquillity. Hoobler became so well-known to the civilians that he adopted the name of Count Von Hoobler, much to their delight. Now we were moving out.

We bade the civilians farewell and marched off at a hurried pace to join the rest of the 2nd Battalion, which was assembling near a large church on the main road east. Nobody knew where we were going— only that this was an emergency. The rumor said that our destination was Helmond, a city about fifteen miles northeast that was supposed to be a German strongpoint.

We marched at top speed for about three hours. The Dutchmen cheered us as we passed through their villages and hung out orange flags and offered refreshments and generally acted as if the war were over, but we were no longer enthusiastic. Our feet hurt, our clothes were wet with sweat, and the handles of the 30-caliber ammo boxes cut deeper and deeper into our hands. Carrying all our gear and ammunition by hand (company headquarters, as usual, hogging all the captured vehicles), we marched faster and with fewer breaks than in basic training. The sun started to go down after we had traveled about twelve miles. Suddenly the column stopped.

"Dig in here," Lieutenant Peacock said.

It was another bad position, dominated by a railroad embankment, but we dug in as ordered. Our front was a small, brown field and a farmhouse. Nobody liked the location or the air of mystery that surrounded the whole expedition. As we continued to dig our holes and complain of our feet and officers, a German rifle cracked beyond the embankment. A single tracer arched overhead, and Lieutenant Peacock ran back to us.

"Krauts, men! Krauts!" he cried. "We're pulling out of here. On the double! We're going back to Eindhoven."

I was livid. A single tracer and everybody turned and ran. Some outfit. As I wriggled into my harness, put away my shovel, and grabbed my rifle, I wailed aloud and wondered when the Army was going to make up its mind. "Why don't they tell us something?" I yelled at Rader as we ran away from the embankment. "What the hell is going on?" He laughed.

Back we went, as swiftly as before and in as great an ignorance. Our feet burned, our throats were dry, our patience was exhausted. Lamentations of five hundred men filled the air with four-letter words. No longer trying to be tactical, we closed ranks and slowed down in the gathering dusk. Wiseman and I kept hitching rides on a horse-drawn cart that belonged to the machine-gun platoon, and Lieutenant Peacock kept peeling us off. "Goddammit," he said, almost in tears at the disorder, "if I can't ride, nobody else can either."

Just as darkness fell, a new sound rose above the general cursing. The short throbbing brrrm, brrrm, brrrm of enemy airplane motors.

We stopped and looked up.

About eight twin-engined JU-88 bombers were circling overhead.

God, I thought, they've seen us. Now they'll come down and strafe the column. And there's no place to hide—no ditches, no houses, no nothing.

We made a perfect target. The riflemen were closed up almost in parade-ground order, and the captured vehicles—horse carts, handcarts, German jeeps, trucks, and command cars—were bumper to bumper in a wild tangle that halted all movement. As the drivers swore

and shouted at each other, a lone officer ran up and down the line, trying in vain to restore order. The only thing that saved us was the cam-
ouflaging branches of the tall trees on both sides of the road.

The airplanes continued to circle, as if getting their bearings, then
went west. In a few moments, we saw them drop flares and heard their
bombs whistle down. Great fires began to burn in Eindhoven.

Considerably chastened, we spread out and started to move again.
The villages that had greeted us so wildly on the way out quickly hid
their orange banners and closed their doors and windows when they
saw us come back. Nobody waved to us or patted our backs or offered
apples and pears. They were afraid the Germans would follow us in.

While the fires crackled and popped and flared up, we stopped east of
the city and dug into the backyards. We settled down for the night to the
sound of the flames and the British armored columns rattling north.

Though we had cursed the march to Helmond and back, we now discovered that it had been our salvation, not only from the airplanes,
which had set afire a British ammunition convoy in the streets of Eindhoven and killed several hundred people, but also from an enemy armored column from Helmond.

Mounting the railroad embankment, Captain Nixon, Battalion S-2,
had spotted a long line of German tanks and half-tracks going down a
road at right angles to our front, evidently in hopes of cutting us off. The
tracer had gone by at this moment; a withdrawal was ordered immediately. By good fortune, we had outmarched the armor. The Dutch
Underground, which was extremely conscientious and reliable, had reported, according to the rumor that we heard, that there were fifty tanks
and five thousand Germans in Helmond.

I was no longer sorry that my feet were sore.

A COLUMN OF TANKS from the Guards Armored Division came up to us
at dawn the next day and stopped on the road beyond our position with
their radios crackling and an air of readiness about them that made me
shiver. A mixture of Cromwells, with long, boat-shaped hulls, and American Shermans, the tanks mounted high-velocity 76mm cannon and
bore on their sides the desert rat insignia of General Montgomery's
North African veterans.

There was no time for briefing, no time for anything but a hurried breakfast of apples and German rations, which we cooked over a little fire near our hole, for word had come in the night that the Germans in Helmond had moved up on our flank.

The dew was heavy on the grass as we got ready to go, and the air was chilly from a ground mist that reduced the rising sun to a dull white ball. Other tanks came up and moved into a nearby field, filling the air with barks and clanks and squeaks. In jaunty black berets, the men in the turrets talked quietly to one another as we went by. We halted at the head of the column on the road.

"Ride these tanks till you're hit," an officer cried, "and then start fighting!"

Six men to a tank, the first and second squads mounted the lead vehicles. We climbed on the fifth and sixth.

I did not look forward to the ride. Tanks drew artillery fire like magnets, and the difficulty of communicating with the crews inside, once the shooting started and they had buttoned themselves in, more than outbalanced any good they might do. Blind as they were, tanks had a strong tendency to hang back in action and let the infantry go ahead, thus losing touch with them altogether.

We jolted forward, twenty yards behind the fourth tank. The sun came out, and the mist began to dissipate, but I felt cold and tense. I put my bayonet on and knelt behind the turret, where I could see everything, have some protection, and still be ready to jump off at the first shot. Aloof in his turret, the tank commander nodded to us but made no effort to chat. None of us was very talkative.

"Where are we going?" I asked Rader.

"A place called Nunen. They think the Krauts have moved in. We're going to find out."

We swung around a corner and headed east by north. The air was quite clear now, and we made a lovely target as we clattered along the raised road into the open country.

These British are pretty casual, I thought, noticing that all their guns were pointed forward. They think the war is over. They talk about Patton running wild and act as if they can coast from here on. American tankers would move out with the lead gun forward, the next pointing right, the third left, and so on down the line. Thus, if an enemy target appeared on the right, it was covered. At the same time, the column was protected against ambush by the guns pointing left.

"Take it easy, Web." Wiseman grinned, noticing my nervousness. Perfectly relaxed and self-confident, he sat beside me with his back to the turret.

I laughed without taking my eyes off the road and flat fields ahead. Pace stood nearby, and Lyall and Massaconi were ready with the machine gun. Lyall had already draped a belt of 30-caliber over his shoulders. I took two hand grenades out of my pockets and hooked them onto my suspenders. The air smelled very clean and cool and country-fresh. I loved the open country. We swung north, with the sun on our right quarter.

"Do you think we'll get hit?" Miller said. He was always curious about what might happen.

"That's what they told us: 'Ride till you're hit.' "

He nodded and gulped. The seventh man aboard, he had been put on as an ammo bearer for the machine gun, which Rader liked to have up front.

"I don't like it any more than you do," I said. "Man, we're sitting ducks; they could pick us off in a minute."

After going about four miles, we stopped abruptly by a cluster of three or four houses at a crossroads. A British armored reconnaissance car stood behind one of the houses. Two men with Sten guns were peeking around the corner at the road ahead, where a large village with the usual big church of southern Holland, which was Catholic, stood sharp and clear in the morning sun almost half a mile away.

"Where's Nunen?" I yelled.

One of the guards pointed down the road. "Straight ahead of you, mate," he replied. "Jerry!"

We moved off, and everybody on the tank stood up and got ready. Nobody said anything. The lead tanks proceeded as fast as before.

When we were halfway to the village, Jack Matthews, a lively, witty rifleman in the first squad, began to yell and point to the right.

"Hey, look over there!" he shouted. "Kraut tank, Kraut tank!"

The column stopped, and all the turrets swung right.

Less than three hundred yards away, parallel to our course, a large, yellow-brown German half-track was slithering through the brush like some evil beast.

We jumped off the tanks and ran for the roadside ditches. The British opened fire. BAM! BAM! BAM! BAM!

The first shell was short. It hit the ground in a cloud of dust, and skipping like a stone on water, smashed into the side of the half-track. The other shells hit it square.

The half-track stopped and a handful of men jumped out. Men on that side of the road began to shoot at them.

Without waiting for orders, we moved down the ditches toward Nunen. The first and third squads were on the left, the second and mortar squads on the right. The tanks stayed behind to finish off the half-track.

We were among the houses in a few minutes. Scouting for the first squad, Robert Marsh, a big, rough steelworker, and little Tom McCreary, a plump tailor who was all guts, saw a German medium tank hiding behind a house farther in. The tank eased out to see what was going on, then withdrew and eased out again. A German got out of the turret and walked toward them with his hands up. They waved him on, but someone in the rear shot at him, and he disappeared. The tank backed away.

"Bazookaman up front!" Marsh yelled. "Bazookaman up front! Kraut tank."

We passed the word along, for the bazookamen usually traveled with company headquarters, well in the rear. Marsh and McCreary ran back to the first British tank, which had crept up behind us, and told its commander to shoot through the house and knock out the German tank.

"Sorry," the Englishman replied. "We can't fire now. We're waiting for orders."

They goddamned him and ran back up the ditch. "Fucking Limeys," Marsh muttered as he went by. "Come on, let's go in without them."

No orange banners greeted us in Nunen, nobody came out to wave or give us a glass of milk. We broke into the houses and went upstairs to look ahead for Germans, but none was visible.

I was so scared I could hardly talk. Crouching low, I ran through the backyards and the empty rooms in search of the enemy. A movement caught my eye, and glancing across the street, I saw a middle-aged man and his wife watching us from a second-story window.

"*Wo sind die deutsche Soldaten?*" I shouted. "Where are the German soldiers?"

"*Weg,*" the man replied. "Away."

They shut the window and disappeared.

The bazookaman still hadn't arrived.

Wiseman, Pace, Janovec, and I kept close together, then separated. I found myself alone in a backyard. An old man watched me from a home-made air-raid shelter.

"*Wo sind die deutsche Soldaten?*" I inquired.

"*Nah,*" he whispered, "*sehr nah.*" He shook his head at me, as if to say, Get out while you can, the Germans are very near.

I bent over with my rifle pointing forward and ran to the next house. Burrrrrrrrrrrrrrrp, a German machine gun fired a long burst. The bullets popped very close overhead.

"Kraut tank!" Marsh yelled. "Machine gun, Cobb. Get over here!"

Still in the ditch beside the road, Marsh and McCreary kept shouting at Cobb, who was their machine gunner, to climb the hedge that sepa-rated them from him, but he said he couldn't. They cursed him and told him to throw the gun over with some ammunition.

The enemy machine gun fired another burst. Suddenly a number of German machine guns and rifles opened fire on both sides of the road. A half-track mounting a 20mm cannon edged out from behind a house. Marsh and McCreary poured a belt of 30-caliber at its front. The half-track backed off. I began to fire at the houses ahead.

Now there was a spontaneous movement forward, for the enemy fire was still high and apparently unaimed. We crossed a small park cut with air-raid dugouts and stopped among the houses on the other side. Three or four of us were together in what was now the front. The British tanks were nowhere near, and there were no officers to tell us what to do. Wiseman, Janovec, and I went upstairs and began to shoot in all the windows, ditches, and hedges ahead. Wiseman left, and I went out in the backyard.

A bald-headed young Dutchman in a black suit ran up. "Give me a hand grenade," he pleaded. "I know where the Germans are. Let me kill them."

"O.K.," I said. "Here you are. Good luck."

He thanked me and ran crouching down a ditch that led out into the fields on our left. I watched him crawl up another ditch that paralleled the road.

The German fire continued to build up.

"Shoot, shoot!" I yelled, fanning the area ahead.

"I can't see 'em," Janovec replied.

"You *never* see 'em. Shoot where you think they are!"

KuBLAM! A mortar shell landed in the next yard.

"Mortars!" I yelled. "Let's get out of here."

Firing back as we went, we began to leave. Another shell landed across the street, then one came into the yard we had just left. I lingered a moment on the edge of the park and suddenly found myself alone. I got up and ran through the park. A mortar shell burst in a tree behind me, and I dove for the narrow opening in a thick hedge that formed the south border of the park. A man's body was blocking the opening.

It was Meth, the cook. He was moaning and clutching his right hand, which was wet with blood and looked as if it had been shot off at the wrist.

"Help me," he moaned. "Somebody help me."

I knelt beside him. A burst of German bullets crackled in the hedge above us.

"What's wrong?" I asked. "Are you hit anywhere else?"

"No. It hurts."

"Get up and run! For Chrissake, get out of here! The Krauts are coming."

"No, no, I can't move."

"You've got a ticket to England. Get up and run to the rear."

He shook his head and moaned.

I gritted my teeth. To me, a wound was a blessing, a chance to get out of action; I would have been back with the medics by now. Meth, however, was not a man who had been in action before, and so he looked on things differently. A wound to him was apparently a terrible shock, not a golden opportunity.

"Medic, medic!" I yelled.

The Germans answered with a rattling, popping salvo.

Impatient to be on my way, I loosened his collar and bandaged his wrist, which was bleeding badly.

"Get up!" I said again. "I'm leaving. Come with me."

"No," he moaned. "I can't move. I'm staying here."

Another mortar shell landed in the park.

I sprang up and ran all the way to the last houses, where the other men had collected and where the tanks were still sitting in the middle of the road, waiting for orders. Covered with sweat and panting from his long crawl up the ditch from the armored-car outpost, a bazookaman arrived on the scene, ready for action, but he was too late. Another bazookaman had made it earlier across the road and been killed. Marsh arrived with his face covered with blood from a bullet that had cut his forehead. He was furious at Cobb and madder still at the British tankers.

As we watched from behind the house, two shells came in almost simultaneously and knocked out the first two tanks. The lead one began to smoke. It turned right, ground forward slowly into the ditch, and stopped. Its cannon went off with a jolt, and the shell screamed into Nunen and exploded against a house. Nobody got out of the tank alive. The hatch of the second popped open, however, and three Englishmen jumped out and ran away.

"Pulling out," someone cried. "Let's go."

One by one, we crawled down the ditch under machine-gun fire to the armored car, where we stopped. Little Johnny Martin, leader of the first squad, tried to soothe Cobb, who appeared to be quite upset. "That's all right, Cobb," he said gently. "Take it easy. We're not going back in there."

With a thrumming roar, three Spitfires came out of the north at tree-top height. Their cannon blazed at us, crackcrackcrackcrack. We threw ourselves on the ground.

"Anybody got a smoke grenade?" Martin yelled. "For Chrissake, throw it!"

I pulled an orange smoke grenade for identification of friendly forces out of my pocket and threw it a few yards away. The British quickly unrolled luminescent orange cloth panels and spread them on the armored car. The Spitfires never came back.

We settled down to wait for the stragglers. Several men were still missing, including Meth, Wiseman, and Miller from our squad. Nobody knew what had happened to Wiseman and Miller. The Germans continued to mortar the west end of Nunen.

Martin went up to a British tank which had pulled back with us. "Put a shell in that church steeple," he suggested. "The Krauts are using it as an observation post."

The tank commander shook his head. "I'm sorry, we can't do it," he replied crisply. "We have orders not to destroy too much property. Friendly country, you know."

And so we mounted the tanks and pulled out without leveling Nunen, as a good American armored unit would have done, for that is how wars are won—not by fighting 50 percent or 30 percent or even 85 percent, but by fighting 100 percent with every weapon at your command.

When we got back to our old position near Eindhoven and began to clean our weapons for a rifle inspection, we learned that Sgt. William Guarnere of the second platoon, consistently the bravest man in E Company, had led a band of volunteers all the way back to the park and rescued Meth. They also found Miller—dead in a backyard. A German had seen him lying bewildered behind a log and had thrown a hand grenade on his back. Five or six other men had been killed. Two were still missing: Wiseman and Bull Randleman, a massive farm boy who was the leader of the second squad.

Considerably chastened, we spent a very quiet day in our holes, cleaning our weapons, but we were not through with Nunen yet, for at twilight we mounted the tanks again (hating the British for their slowness and their stupidity, their "waiting for orders" and "can't destroy too much property") and went back to the armored car. D Company was in the lead, with E second and Headquarters in the rear. F Company planned to come in from the left flank.

I shook and sweated every inch of the way. When we dismounted near the armored car and began to move up, I took good care to go quickly from cover to cover and lie low at the halts.

The Germans opened fire on D Company as soon as it started down the open road. From the shooting, we could tell that they had moved their outposts to the edge of town, evidently planning to make a battle of it. We hid behind trees and let them shoot.

F Company was late in arriving. The sun went down while we waited. Soon the word came to withdraw; the battalion attack had been called off on account of darkness. With cries of joy, we mounted the tanks and went back to Eindhoven.

Thus ended our rides to Nunen. The communiqués (if they mentioned it at all) probably called it "a reconnaissance in strength." As far as I was concerned, it was a mess. And for my platoon leader, I had only four-letter words.

IT WAS A BEAUTIFUL DAY for a drive in the country. The sun was warm, the sky was clear, the air was soft and balmy and yet with the smoky crispness of fall. In the mood for a drive, we piled into one of the G.I.

trucks with colored drivers that had just been assigned to the 101st Airborne Division for the Holland campaign. I took good care to settle myself near the tailgate.

Everybody was in good spirits, for we had rested a day or two after Nunen in a field near a hospitable farmhouse where there was lots of fresh fruit and milk. Wiseman and Bull Randleman had both returned to the platoon. Cut off from the rest of us, they had hid in the village overnight and listened to the Germans search for them. Bull, who had bayoneted one of the searchers, left for a rest, but Wiseman was as hale and hearty as ever. Meth had been evacuated, and Miller was dead; our squad now numbered ten.

Thinking themselves completely safe, for we had no armored escort and the British were still talking as if the war were almost over, most of the men unbuckled their harness and took off their helmets and threw their weapons on the floor.

Each truck in the 2nd Battalion convoy towed a small, open trailer that held half a squad of men. Men from F Company began to get into ours. I smiled when I saw their noncom, Gordon Mather, my first squad leader in the Army. One of the bravest men in F Company, Mather, the skinny, fiery redhead, had helped rally the Company when the S.S. counterattacked outside Carentan and his captain had cowered in his hole and refused to fight. The captain, who was always going back to Battalion "to check up" whenever his men went into the attack, was later transferred in grade to regimental special services officer and thus assured of living through the war, while Mather, who was outspoken and fiercely independent, remained a squad leader. As I watched his men get into the trailer, I looked for a familiar face, because this was my old squad, the one in which I had spent my first eighteen months in the Army. All the familiar faces were gone.

"How's it going?" I asked Mather.

"Can't complain," he said. "A goddamn ball so far."

"How's Vogel?"

"Fine."

Mather jumped into the trailer, and the convoy moved off. Our destination was said to be a village far to the north, near the Neder Rhine, where we were supposed to set up a holding position.

The convoy turned onto the main road from Eindhoven, and we settled ourselves to enjoy the scenery in comfort.

"This is a wonderful country, isn't it?" I remarked to Wiseman. "Look at those windmills! Just like the geography books, aren't they?"

"Sure are."

"The villages are just the way I thought they'd be—and so are the canals and roads and meadows. I love Holland."

"Everybody wears wooden shoes," Pace added.

"Certainly is different from Normandy," Hoobler said, joining the conversation. He hallooed to a couple of civilians who were waving at the convoy. "Those people had no use for us, did they, Web?"

"They seemed to hate us. Nobody in Normandy ever volunteered to help us or fight with us. These Dutch are different; they're fine, intelligent people. Understand a couple of Dutchmen have joined the Company as volunteers."

"That's what I hear," Rader said.

The talk died out as we passed through another village.

The villages are pure Vermeer, I thought, but the windmills are the greatest thrill of all. How fine it is to see them wherever you look!

We passed several roadside inns with ORANJE BIER signs out front and graveled play gardens for the children alongside and overtook mile after mile of British artillery units. At one place where we stopped for a short break, we met the 1st Airborne Division's rear echelon.

"Where are you headed for?" I inquired.

"Arnhem, mate."

"How's it going up there?" We had had no news since our landing.

"Sticky. The lads are having a rough go of it."

Hogwash, I said to myself. Now they're talking like Americans. Every G.I. you meet says his Company's been wiped out, it's had the heaviest casualties in the Division, there are only three old men left.

We wished the 1st Airborne luck and climbed back onto our 6 × 6. The British were brewing tea in the ditch beside their high, boxy trucks. Everything seemed so peaceful and bucolic that it was hard to believe that there was a war on and that anybody was having it rough.

Back on the highway that we had marched down almost a week before, we crossed the Wilhelmina Canal at Zon on a Bailey bridge guarded by British 40mm ackack, went through the village, which had become a headquarters of some sort, and into the pine forest to the north. A few gliders lay scattered about the jumpfield on the other side like relics of days long dead, but all the parachutes had been picked up.

Several hundred prisoners stood in long overcoats in a barbed-wire enclosure on the field. We shouted and cursed at them.

The convoy turned right at the tiny, crossroads village of St. Odenrode, bounced over a railroad track, and proceeded six or seven miles to a place called Veghel. We slowed down on a curving road in the center of town and stopped bumper to bumper. A few men got up and stretched their arms and legs.

BzzYOO . . . BAM! A high-velocity shell whipped over our heads like an angry giant bee and exploded against a house at the end of the street.

"Eighty-eights!" an officer cried. "Everybody off!"

ABANDONING WEAPONS, gear, and all self-control, the passengers leaped from the trucks in a wild panic. I knew that we were in for trouble, so I took good care to leave with my rifle in one hand and a box of machine-gun ammunition in the other. I lay down in the gutter. The truck drivers and most of the other men disappeared among the houses.

Only Mather acted like a soldier. Standing livid in his trailer and shaking his rifle at his running men, he shouted for them to come back.

"Goddamn you guys!" he bellowed. "You call yourselves *soldiers*. Get your goddamn ammo! Get your goddamn guns, you sonsofbitches!"

His men turned and came back sheepishly. Others followed them to other trucks and trailers. Mather threw gear at his squad with a steady stream of curses.

I smiled at him from the cover of the gutter, where I lay full length, between the high curb and the thick truck wheels. Mather was the finest squad leader I had ever had.

"Soldiers!" he exclaimed, clearing the last cartridge belt from the trailer and looking down at me. "Jesus Christ."

I laughed. "Looks like we're in for it now," I remarked.

"You said it."

He gathered his men and marched them back to where his platoon was forming.

An excited soldier with the white diamond of the 501 on the side of his helmet trotted down the sidewalk.

"What's going on?" I asked, standing up.

"Kraut tanks," he replied. He pointed to the head of our convoy.

"They're coming in, right on the road there. Jesus, we only got one battalion in town; our flanks are wide open. Where's your battalion commander?"

"In the rear." I jerked my head. "Name's Colonel Strayer."

He ran away.

Another shell passed overhead and burst out of sight.

Officers began to appear and organize their men. Our Company having been cut in half, with company headquarters missing somewhere north of town, we were in reserve. D Company went south toward a canal at the edge of the village, while F Company began to go north, where the tanks were. The British set up 40mm antiaircraft to fire down the side streets.

We drifted off the main road, which had become the center of enemy attention, and stopped in an alley beside a British truck parked near a wall. Squatted on the sidewalk, the driver was calmly brewing tea in a German mess cup as the shells zipped by.

"Hello, mates," he said cheerfully. "Tea time. Getting rather warm here, don't you think?" He stirred his brew.

While Pace and Wiseman distracted him with idle chatter, Hoobler and I moved to the rear of the truck, where we had noticed some loose rations lying handy. We lifted several cans of plums and stew and stuffed them into our musette bags.

"Wonder what's going on?" I said, returning to the tea party.

"Does anybody know?" Wiseman replied.

"If they do, it'll be the first time," Hoobler added.

"Boost me on top of that wall," I said. "Maybe I can see something from there."

Wiseman and Hoobler lifted me up. All I could see was alleys and backyards, with nobody in sight. I wondered where the Germans were.

"See anything up there, Webster?" a new voice inquired.

I turned and saw Lieutenant McFadden, my former platoon leader and now commander of F Company. A small, genial, sensible person, he appeared to be as baffled as we were by our truck ride's startling end.

"No, sir," I said. "I can't see a goddamn thing."

He went away, and Lieutenant Peacock came and shifted us deeper in town. After passing more 40mm, a row of dismantled 155s on trailers, and a Piat antitank gun crew hidden in a little, round, roofed bandstand in the middle of the village square, where several roads came together, we stopped in front of the village hall. Pace and I went inside for a personal tour, but since there was no food or drink, we sat down in a hallway and began to doze. I woke up with Rader shouting at me.

"Where the goddamn hell have you been?" he said. "We're moving out. Been looking all over for you."

"I've been right here all the time."

"This is no place to be. The squad's been outside."

We went back up the street and stopped behind some houses near our trucks, which were still parked bumper to bumper. Nothing happened, so Wiseman and I began to inspect the kitchens of the nearest houses. Finding them bare, we rejoined the squad, where Hoobler was needling Rice, who, as always, had begun to dig in.

"Digging to China, Rice?" Hoobler inquired, laughing.

"You go to hell, boy."

Rice turned his back, and Hoobler whistled like an incoming shell. Rice threw himself flat.

"Ha, ha, ha. Sure sucked you in on that one."

"Goddamn you, Hoobler, that's hard on a man. It's nothing to laugh at."

"Ha, ha, ha."

BzzYOO. A real 88 came in.

We dove at the ground. Hoobler stopped laughing. The 88 burst on the main street.

Going to an arched brick passageway that led from the backyard to the road to see what was going on, I found D Company halted on the sidewalks.

An Aldbourne acquaintance, Sanders, asked if I had any spare M-1 ammunition.

"I'm fresh out," he explained. "We just caught a bunch of Krauts milling around near the canal and shot the hell out of them."

"Wait a minute," I said. "I gave a bandoleer to another guy who has enough already. I'll get it off him. Be back in a jiffy."

I ran through the brick tunnel toward a large air-raid shelter in a field behind the next house where Matthews, who had my bandoleer, and the rest of the first squad had taken cover, along with thirty or forty weeping civilians. I recovered the bandoleer and started back.

An 88 shell came in so close I didn't hear it until it was right alongside. I threw myself flat.

BLANG! The shell hit a wall fifteen feet away, showering me with fragments of brick and mortar.

Choking on the smoke and dust, I got up with my ears ringing and returned to the air-raid shelter. Another shell passed by and then a barrage landed on the main road, where D Company had stopped. I did not return there with the bandoleer.

The first squad had crowded so fully into the little space left by the civilians in the shelter that I was forced to wait out the barrage half in the entrance and not fully protected.

The civilians were unnerving. Clutching their children as the shells bammed into their neat homes, they wept and wailed, shrieked and moaned, and sang dismal old Dutch hymns. Some of them knelt and prayed aloud, as if the world were coming to an end.

As far as we were concerned, they had no perspective; this was the safest place in town. Four or five feet deep and with a roof of logs and sod almost as thick, it could have withstood a direct hit from an 88— which was more than we could say for most of the houses. I found the atmosphere so depressing, however, and felt so guilty about bringing this on the little children that I left in the first lull.

Lieutenant Peacock was trying to restore order in the backyards. Nobody had been hit so far, and we were all in excellent spirits except Whytsell, who had turned apathetic. Pace thought it was a lark, and Hoobler made a joke out of every shell that went by.

Morning passed into afternoon, with the road cut at both ends of town and no relief in sight. At one or two o'clock, almost a dozen R.A.F. Typhoon fighter-bombers appeared overhead. We waved and shouted as they circled above the Germans through puffs of light flak. One by one, they peeled off and screamed down. Whoosh! they released the rockets under their wings at a target a thousand yards north of us. There was a wonderful sound of continuous booming. Several fires started to burn, and we hoped, when the Typhoons had gone away, that they had put an end to the shelling, but it soon came back as strong as ever.

We moved to an orchard by a crossroads on the northern outskirts of town and began to dig in as fast as possible. This was the frontline reserve position. The orchard was bounded by dirt roads on the west and north, the main highway on the east, and a cobblestone road on the south, where several houses were occupied by battalion headquarters and the aid station.

The soil was light and sandy, though occasionally laced with roots, and digging together, one at each end, Wiseman and I went down to water level in about ten minutes. Our slit trench—for we never dug one-man foxholes—was two feet wide, six feet long, and four and a half feet deep.

And none too soon.

BzzYOObzzYOObzzYOO . . . BAMBAMBAM!

"Jesus Christ!" I exclaimed, jumping into the hole. "They've seen us."

The shells had landed on the cobblestone road.

"Sonsofbitches," Wiseman muttered.

We looked up and grinned at each other.

"Here they come again!"

Sitting in an inch of water, I closed my eyes, gritted my teeth, held my breath, and clutched my elbows with my arms around my knees.

Three more shells came in, low and angry, and burst in the orchard.

"They're walking 'em toward us," I whispered.

I felt as if a giant with exploding iron fingers were looking for me, tearing up the ground as he came. I wanted to strike at him, to kill him, to stop him before he ripped into me, but I could do nothing. Sit and take it, sit and take it. The giant raked the orchard and tore up the roads and stumbled toward us in a terrible blind wrath as we sat in our hole with our heads between our legs and curses on our lips.

"I never felt so helpless before," I confided to Wiseman in a dry whisper an hour after the shelling started. "I'd give a foot to get out of here."

BzzYOObzzYOObzzYOO. BAMBAMBAM!

Three pounds of T.N.T. A muzzle velocity higher than a rifle bullet. Hundreds of pieces of jagged, red-hot metal. Black clouds of smoke. Eighty-eights. Death.

Three more came in. The Germans were firing in battery, probably from tanks or S.P.s. The last shell was so close that it clanged when it exploded. Three more arrived.

The ground quaked, and a rancid black thundercloud curled down into our hole, making us cough and choke. An ugly chunk of hot steel an inch square plunked into Wiseman's lap. He grinned.

"Close," I whispered. "They're traversing the orchard." I felt as if the giant were near enough to hear me, and I was afraid to raise my voice for fear it would draw him to us.

Three and then three and then three.

No wonder men went crazy in a shelling. It was the worst experience on earth. You could fight a tank and shoot back at an airplane and meet a man on equal terms, but there was nothing you could do about artillery. The Germans called it the whispering death.

A man began to moan aloud in the southeast corner of the orchard. "Medic," he called plaintively. "Somebody get a medic. Somebody help me. God, oh God, I can't stand it."

The next three shells came in so fast that their zipping sound was intermingled with the explosions. The giant grabbed our hole and shook it back and forth.

I dissolved and waited to die. Each salvo had come closer; this was the closest of all. One of the shells had hit a tin shed ten feet away. The next three would bracket us.

"They got the 3rd Bat," someone shouted, "they killed those 3rd Bat sergeants."

"Now it's us," I whispered.

"Buddy," Wiseman began. He shook his head.

The next three passed overhead and hit the crossroads fifty yards behind us.

"Whew," I said, smiling. "Thank God that's over. Now it's Strayer's turn."

"He can have it." Wiseman grinned. We stood up and looked out.

The trees around us were chopped by shell fragments and the ground littered with torn branches and frayed leaves. Black craters dotted the earth. Other men rose from their holes and greeted one another.

While we watched, amazed, two Sherman tanks waddled out of town on the main road and stopped beside the orchard. We cursed them, because we were afraid they would attract more artillery fire, but not a shell came in.

Toward the end of the afternoon, in another lull, Rader announced that our British rations, which were designed not for an individual but for a group of men, were available for supper. "Come and get 'em!" Hoobler cried, standing near Rader.

"The hell I will," I answered. "Throw mine to me here."

Lyall, Massaconi, and several others sauntered over to eat aboveground with the noncoms. Wiseman joined them. I stayed in my hole.

"It's all over, Web," Hoobler chortled. "Come on out! You're safe." The others laughed.

"Goddamn Webster's got hole-itis," Rader remarked.

Three 88s came in from the north and burst in the orchard.

Six men tumbled into Rader's hole. Wiseman landed on my feet in a high dive. I glanced over the crumbling, sandy parapet. Not a person was in sight.

"What did you say, Hoobler?" I called.

"Fuck you."

"Ha, ha, ha."

The shelling commenced as heavy as before. Wiseman shared his can of beef with me.

At twilight, our platoon sergeant, Talbert, began shouting in alarm. "Out of your holes, men!" he cried as the shells died down again. "We have to go help F Company. Krauts have broken through, outposts driven in. Bring all your ammo. Let's go!"

Well, I thought, climbing slowly out of the slit trench, the shells will catch us above-ground now. But if you have to go, you have to go. F Company's in trouble, and we have to help them. We're in reserve, so we have to go. And if we're shelled, we're shelled. There is absolutely nothing we can do about it.

I followed the other men to the north end of the orchard, where we gathered around Talbert and Lieutenant Peacock and began to wait. Lyall and some of the other replacements who had never seen a fresh dead man before drifted off to the left to inspect the shredded remains of two sergeants from G Company who had just begun to dig in when a shell landed between them. Lieutenant Peacock did not consider the sight of positive value, and so he drove them from the scene and forbade anybody else to go there. Finally we got moving.

The dusk was ominously silent. Tensed for the first shells, we edged down a dirt road to the left into a thick forest where F Company was standing in a deep, grassy ditch lined with tall poplar trees. Many of the tree trunks had been chopped by shell fragments. A 57mm antitank cannon was emplaced between two small, half-timbered houses. The men at the gun and in the ditch had a hard, sweating, detached look in their eyes and no words for anybody. All of them stared straight ahead at a narrow field of high, light-green grass and a lush forest fifty yards beyond where the enemy lay.

We passed along the whole Company and their unprotected left flank and learned that the outposts had withdrawn of their own accord and that a number of men had been killed by German tanks, including an old E Company man, bouncy little Lieutenant Smits, a breezy, popular officer from California. The second platoon's noisy Farley, however, had stopped a medium tank with a bazooka on the main road at a distance of less than one hundred feet.

Winding around to the left, we came out on the cobblestone road behind the orchard. Wiley, the big, mean cook whom Nakelski had beaten up in Aldbourne before D-Day, lay dead beside a shell hole in the road, his body sprinkled with rubble and torn leaves. The body of another man was sprawled facedown nearby. We returned to our holes as darkness set in and the evening's shells began to arrive.

I was glad that we had gone to the M.L.R., or Main Line of Resistance. The walk had relieved the tension inside me, and the sight of F Company holding firm had been immensely reassuring.

The air turned cold, and a light rain began to fall. Wiseman and I took our raincoats out of our musette bags and put them on and settled down for the night, each of us sitting in one end of the trench with his head on his knees. Our boots were wet through, and the rain and dirt kept trickling down our necks. We were so cold and miserable that we couldn't sleep, but as I remarked to Wiseman, we could thank God for one thing.

"What's that?" he inquired sleepily.

"We're in reserve."

THE GERMANS DISAPPEARED just before dawn, and so we got out of our holes a couple of hours later and began to trail them. We crossed the main road, where Farley's Mark V medium tank stood one hundred yards north of the F Company line, and went down a lesser road to the east. The ditch on our right was littered like a dirty beach, with shovels, canteens, bayonets, musette bags, and other abandoned gear.

"Hey, Whytsell," I said, "there's a shovel for you." He had been borrowing shovels for several days, and if there was one thing I hated to loan, it was a shovel.

"Uh-huh," he mumbled, not bothering to stop.

"Pick it up! You'll need it later."

He shrugged his shoulders and looked away. Rader, who had overheard us, made him get a shovel and put it on his belt.

When we reached the open farmland beyond town, the column of

British tanks that we were escorting slowed down while we spread out in skirmish lines on both sides of the road and began to move forward in search of stray Germans. Intermittent machine-gun fire encouraged us to stay close to the ditches, but our platoon found nothing to shoot at.

The second platoon's McClung, a tall, thin man with deep-sunken eyes and a rather melancholy expression, had better luck. A remarkably keen scout, who was said even to be able to smell Germans and who was therefore in great demand for patrols, flushed several enemy soldiers from hiding. He delighted the English tank crews by chasing the Germans in front of their tanks and killing them, frontier style.

Everybody got back on the road in an hour or so and proceeded in another direction at a brisker pace. A flight of C-47s towing CG4A gliders on a resupply mission passed to our right half a mile away. As they came abreast of us, some Germans on the ground threw up a mass of light flak at them.

"Rader!" Lieutenant Peacock cried. "Take four men and knock out those ackack guns!"

"Yessir."

The column continued to march.

"Pace, Wiseman, Webster, Hoobler! Let's go," Rader said.

I stopped with the others beside the road and gaped at Rader. "He's crazy," I said. "Four men to attack all those Krauts? Hell, there's at least a company over there, probably with antiaircraft half-tracks. They're half a mile away, and nobody's stopping for us. Where's the Battalion going? Does anybody know where we're going?"

A twinkle came in Rader's eye. "You and Pace go look in that house over there," he said. He pointed at a big, half-timbered farmhouse about 150 yards down a tree-lined dirt lane to our right. An old brown barn with a thatched roof stood to the left. Our own road was lined at regular intervals with leafy poplars. Pace and I stopped near one of the trees, and lying on a dirt mound, looked up and down.

"Kraut tank!" Pace exclaimed, pointing left.

I squinted. "You're full of it."

"Down in those trees about two hundred yards."

"Oh yeah, sure."

A big tank camouflaged with tree branches sat at a crossroads two hundred yards away.

"That's a Sherman," I said, studying it.

Pace shifted his worries to the farmhouse. "Kraut in the window!" he exclaimed. "Got a burp gun."

"Oh, for Chrissake."

I couldn't see anything but the reflection of the glass in a dark, second-story window. The farmhouse had an abandoned air about it. I looked to our rear and saw that the Battalion had gone down the road. Up ahead, the German antiaircraft had ceased fire.

Rader ran to us with an angry face.

"What's holding you people up?" he demanded. "Go check that farm-house!"

"Pace sees a machine gunner in the window," I replied, hoping to stall as long as possible, for I sensed that Rader was no more anxious to carry out Peacock's mission than we were.

"Well, uh, yes. Let me take a look."

Shading his eyes with his hand, he studied the building and then an-nounced that he saw nothing. "Look around that house and barn," he said, "and be snappy about it!"

"Cover me, Pace."

I ran forward about twenty yards, fell down, and covered the build-ings while Pace got up and ran past me, then fell down to cover me. We reached our goal this way, which was the recommended method of ap-proaching new areas, and went through the house without finding any sign of Germans. The barnyard was deserted even of animals, and there was nobody in the hayloft or the hired hand's bare little room, which had a crucifix on the wall and smelled very strongly of disinfectant.

"Come on back!" Rader yelled.

We trotted after the Company and caught up with them in about five minutes.

I wanted to shake Rader's hand for acting so sensibly. If we had attacked the Germans with their 20mm and 40mm cannon as ordered, we would have done it alone and unaided and would probably have disliked it thor-oughly. Lieutenant Peacock, who made no comment on our swift return, would have been miles away by the time the Germans had finished with us. I made a mental note to get out of his platoon as soon as possible.

"THIS IS GOING TO BE GOOD," Lieutenant Peacock informed us as we waited to leave the orchard again. We had returned to Veghel from the south and found it under shell fire from some Germans who had decided to cut the road there despite the violent objections of the 327th Glider Infantry, who had come up to reinforce the village. No sooner had we settled down in our holes for lunch than the word came to move out. "A British corps is sweeping up both sides of the road from Eindhoven," Lieutenant Peacock continued, "driving the Germans before them. We're going to trap the Krauts, men. We'll dig in near here and wait for them."

A column of British tanks came forth to join us. When the 2nd Battalion was finally formed, we headed east into the country, then south to the edge of an immense plain, where we stopped. Spreading out beside a winding dirt road, we dug into the banks of a deep, grassy ditch lined with gnarled willow trees and began to camouflage the fresh dirt of our parapets with branches and torn grass.

"I'm looking forward to some good shooting," I remarked to Wiseman, who, as always, had dug most of the hole. An ex-miner, he was a better digger than me, with far more strength and endurance.

He nodded and gazed out at the plain, which offered a clear field of fire for more than a mile. "I don't see any Krauts yet," he said, squinting.

"Me neither, but they'll be along, and we'll be ready for them. Hot damn! We couldn't have a better position." I imagined the Germans' surprise as they ran from the British corps and stumbled into us with no cover. It was a soldier's dream.

After an hour, we began to get restive. No Germans had appeared, and there was no sound of distant firing to herald their approach. An enemy machine gun fired several hundred yards to our right and was silent. We slipped into our holes. The afternoon began to wane.

"What happened to the big deal?" I wondered aloud.

"Snafu," Wiseman replied. "Sonsofbitches are playing this war by ear."

A jeep bounced cross-country toward us from the south. The man beside the driver kept waving an orange flag as a sign for us not to open fire.

"Limeys," Hoobler announced, handing his field glasses to Pace. "Take a look, buddy."

"Limeys, all right." Pace nodded.

The jeep came into our lines to report that the British corps was held up by stiff resistance farther south. We'd have to find the Germans ourselves.

"Christ," I muttered. "Might have known it was too good to be true. The one time we get a good position, the goddamn Krauts refuse to co-operate."

Hoobler laughed and jumped out of his hole. "If they won't come to you, you have to go to them. Come on, men, up and at 'em!"

Spread out in a meandering column of twos, we started diagonally across the field. It was late afternoon already, with an overcast sky and a wet wind from the south that promised rain.

We were in an excellent position to be ambushed, and the British tankers were not at all enthusiastic, but they were told to make the best of it and come along, because they had to go where we went whether they liked it or not. Trained in General Montgomery's leisurely tactics of massive preparation and overwhelming breakthrough power, they had no stomach for an airborne unit's hasty and impromptu maneuvers.

Another enemy machine gun fired to our right, farther down the road we had left, but none of the bullets was close. A couple of very young German deserters were flushed from the heath as we approached an oval-shaped pine forest about a quarter of a mile long with a big sand dune in front. Other deserters had abandoned their uniforms and loose items of gear in a ditch near the forest.

Captain Nixon and an S-2 patrol ran across the field to our right. When he was in the column, Nixon began to show off his helmet and tell what had happened. On advance scouting, his men had bumped into some Germans. A machine gun fired a burst that hit him in the helmet, leaving a jagged hole, but nobody had been hurt.

Cutting onto a sandy road that ran behind the little forest on the south, the lead tank went behind the dune, which was about twelve feet high and dotted with the light growth of a sand dune at the beach, and out into the open. Suddenly it stopped with a loud thump and began to smoke. Nobody got out.

"Krauts!"

A machine gun burped. The bullets crackled in the pines.

"Get some men on that sand dune!" yelled Captain Winters, our Company commander. A big, strong young man with sandy hair, he had won the Distinguished Service Cross in Normandy.

The first-squad scouts, McCreary and little Matz, a quiet boy with thick glasses, went around the west end of the dune and into a ditch beside a road there and suddenly came face-to-face with a terrified young

German in a hole. McCreary stopped, and looking beyond, saw another German covering him with an MG-42. He could have shot the first man, but he knew better, for the machine gunner would have gotten both him and Matz. He whirled around and ran behind the dune. The first German popped out of his hole and ran in the opposite direction.

The twilight thickened and rain began to fall.

F Company and E Company lined up on the crest of the sand dune and at the north edge of the pine woods and began to shoot across a meadow at a cluster of farm buildings four hundred yards north. A German machine gun returned the fire, bringing the marksmen to their bellies and moving them behind trees.

The bullets crackled overhead as we ran up to join the shooting. Lyall and Massaconi threw themselves flat.

"That's O.K., fellers," Hoobler said, trotting forward, "they can't hit you. You have the dune for cover."

McCreary came back and suggested spraying the ditch where he had been, but most of the men were more interested in shooting up the farmhouse and a small forest nearby.

"Cease fire, goddammit, cease fire!" a voice cried.

We frowned over our shoulders. Somebody was always trying to spoil our fun. Now it was Lieutenant MacFadden. "Cease fire!" he screamed, running up and down the line. "That's the 3rd Battalion over there. Pass the word along to cease fire! Boy, what a mess. Tell that goddamn tank to cease fire!"

The shooting spluttered and died out in random shots. Someone threw an orange smoke grenade into the meadow, while Sergeant Talbert mounted the crest of the dune and began to wave an orange panel back and forth.

Burrrrrp.

Talbert scrambled down to the low ground.

"3rd Battalion, hell! Shoot those sonsofbitches!"

We opened fire again. Lieutenant MacFadden unlimbered his M-1 and joined in. The second British tank commenced shooting its turret machine gun at the farmhouse.

Since nobody shot back, the men quickly lost interest and gradually ceased fire as darkness set in. An all-around defensive was organized in the manner of a wagon train halting for the night in Indian country, with E Company on the west and part of the south side of the forest and the other companies circling the rest.

Kneeling in the open beside the sandy road on the south, I tried to dig in. The roots were so thick and the ground so hard that I soon lost interest. Oh hell, I thought, putting my shovel back in its case, why bother? They're not going to shell us.

A whistle blew and there was a tremendous burst of fire near the dune for several seconds, then absolute silence.

Wondering what had happened, I glanced to the west and saw the first tank glowing dull red in the wet darkness. Its ammunition snapped and crackled and popped. A smell of burning flesh mingled with the odor of gunpowder.

"Anybody want to go on patrol?"

I looked up at Talbert, who had just come into the area, and shook my head. "Not me," I muttered. "I don't volunteer for anything."

Hoobler and all the replacements stood up. "We'll go," Hoobler said. "O.K., come on."

They followed Talbert through the dripping trees to company head- quarters. I felt small and cowardly as I watched them go. Deep inside, however, was a warmer feeling: self-preservation.

Everybody but Hoobler came back in a few minutes.

In relieved tones, Lyall explained what had happened. "We thought it was just a first-platoon patrol," he said, lying down. "Hell, it's a battalion patrol. Why should we volunteer?"

"Goddamn right," Massaconi said.

"What's it for?" I inquired.

"Well, it's an S-2 patrol," Lyall began rapidly.

"They can have it," I interrupted. "When are those bastards going to start making their own patrols?"

"Anyway, Captain Nixon wants to send a combat patrol over to the farmhouse to knock out a couple of S.P.s that he thinks are hiding there."

"Not for me," I murmured, shaking my head.

"Me neither," Pace agreed. He was squatting nearby in wet misery, looking very small and forlorn.

"So we backed out. Hoobler's going."

"He would; he's crazy."

Lyall brightened. "Remember all that shooting a while back?"

"Yes?"

"Well, the rumor is that Captain Winters wanted to send D Company across the field with all the bazookas in the Battalion, firing as they went, while F Company gave 'em overhead fire. F Company gave 'em overhead fire, all right—that's what the shooting was about—but D Company told Winters to go to hell. 'If you want to cross that open field,' Captain MacMillan says, 'use your own goddamn men.' "

I laughed. "Well, anyway it's a good story. Never spoil a good story."

Hoobler returned and began to prepare for the patrol. He put on his wool-knit cap, rubbed dirt into his face and on the backs of his hands, and borrowed a Thompson from little Mack of the mortar squad. Filling his pockets with clips of bullets, he tried to keep up a running chatter, but his voice broke, his hands trembled, and he began to stutter. It was the first time I had ever seen him show fear, and I admired him very much for forcing himself to go along.

The rain thickened, soaking through my boots and pants legs. When the water began to work down my neck, I got up and moved back among the pine trees and lay down. The tank continued to glow red-orange.

Unable to sleep, I got up and paced back and forth to keep warm. A sound of snoring filled the forest. How can they do it? I wondered, envying anybody who could sleep on the ground on a night like this.

"Hey, Web," a hoarse voice called from behind a thick pine tree.

I stopped and looked down. It was Wiseman. Cold and wet, he huddled on the ground with his knees up against his chest and his teeth chattering.

"Can't sleep, huh?"

"Never could in the field."

I sat down beside him, and since neither of us could sleep, we decided to kill the night with talk. After a couple of hours, we got up and went deeper into the woods, where we stumbled on the medics in a little draw. Begging four blankets off them, for they always carried plenty for the wounded men, we lay down and went to sleep.

Cold and cramped and stiff all over, we returned to the squad at sunrise. Hoobler reported that the patrol had gone to the farmhouse and found nothing, the Germans having pulled out in the night.

Lieutenant Welsh, the company executive officer, now bade us rise and follow him. Going beyond the burnt-out tank, which still gave off heat, we came to a highway where a convoy of British trucks had been ambushed. Scattered dead men were still at the wheel, others sprawled facedown in the road, where they had been caught trying to run away. The Germans who had killed them had dug into the roadside ditch on the east. Two or three of their rifles lay near their narrow slit trenches, and the machine gun that had covered Matz and McCreary was still in position on the lip of another. Its owner had vanished. Filthy as ever, the Germans had left behind them piles of ordure and a rank body odor that seemed appropriate to their long, oily hair and sweaty uniforms of cheap wool.

Lieutenant Welsh was particularly anxious to salvage a Volkswagen jeep that he had spotted in one of the English trucks. Close examination showed it, however, to be hopelessly out of commission, and so we contented ourselves with other souvenirs: hand-knitted Shetland sweaters, thick gray socks (which were always welcome), clean handkerchiefs, an armored corps black beret, and a late captain's jacket, complete with pips and campaign ribbons. Apparently, the Germans had taken all the food and cigarettes, because none was to be had, not even on the dead men. Never able to touch a body or go through the pockets of a corpse, I left that part of the search to less inhibited persons.

The time had come to go again. We ran back to the Company and set off in a battalion column, heading west. We crossed the road, and entering a small forest, came upon a strange and chilling tableau.

His hands raised almost in prayer, a very young American paratrooper knelt in death beneath the trees with the bodies of two giant German paratroopers facedown before him. A murmur ran through the Company as it passed by. The American, who was from the 101st, was covered with bloody spots, probably caused by a long burst from a machine pistol, and it was remarkable to everybody that he had frozen kneeling in death, instead of falling over backward.

Who was he? we wondered, and how did he come to die here alone? Who had killed the Germans? No G.I.s had fought in this area before.

The sight provided conversation for a long time afterward, as we crossed a line of sand dunes and many meadows and continued on our way. We skirted Veghel and went five or six miles north to the village of Uden without seeing any live Germans. Our great plan of entrapment was over.

———

"WHY ARE YOU DIGGING SO DEEP?" a company headquarters man inquired.

"Because I just came up from Veghel," I replied.

"Oh?"

The stranger went away and began to expand his own hole, which was about six inches deep, while Janovec and I dug down and down and down. When we were almost five feet below ground, we widened the trench so that we could lie side by side on the bottom. We got straw from a haystack on the outskirts of town and put it on the floor as a mattress, then laid logs, branches, brush, and sod on top. The company headquarters men, who had gotten through to Uden after the Germans attacked Veghel, couldn't understand why everybody else dug so deep. There had been no shelling in Uden.

When our hole was completed, we lay down for a nap. Crumbling sand dripped on us as the walls gradually dried, and a light rain came in the open end, but we were mightily pleased with our new home.

"Webster," Lieutenant Peacock called down just as I was falling asleep, "get up and come with me."

"Yessir."

I followed him through the apple orchard where D and E Companies had dug in east of Uden and along a lane from the orchard to the Eindhoven-Arnhem highway. A large farmhouse and its outbuildings stood on one side of the lane and a thick hedge on the other. In the holiday spirit of men in reserve, a squad of riflemen passed us with helmets in their hands, on their way to a pump farther down the lane which was our sole source of water. The pump squeaked and hissed and gurgled as a man from D Company worked its long, curved handle.

Lieutenant Peacock turned left and with his farmer's stride, swung down the highway past a line of British tanks and armored cars parked at the curb. He went into a three-story house on the village square, led me upstairs, and stopped in the second-floor hall.

This was sacred territory—the officers' billets—and feeling rather like a slum child in the Waldorf Astoria, I looked around in envy, for their beds, blankets, sheets, and hot and cold running water were beyond anything I could ever hope to achieve. My hole, which I had thought so splendid, paled by comparison.

Turning to me with the look of a timid, overconscientious man trying to be firm and decisive, Lieutenant Peacock pointed to a broom resting against one wall. "Sweep it out," he said.

"Yessir," I replied.

Boiling mad at my new role of scullery maid, I took the broom and flailed it against the floor to work off my anger.

Officers! I thought. How I love them.

I will be a scout and go ahead and on flank guard and run across the open fields with no cover, because these things are expected of any soldier. I will salute when I have to and stand at attention and say, "Yessir," no matter how wrong the officer may be, because that, too, is the Army and we all have to be disciplined, for without discipline, you cannot fight.

But when an officer who is sleeping indoors between sheets gets me out of a hole in the ground to sweep his house—well, that's asking too much. The officers ate on tablecloths with waiters and a wine list on the troopship when we came overseas, then came below to our tiny, sweaty, steerage mess hall and stood over us, shouting, "Hurry up, men, hurry up! There's another company waiting to get in."

I didn't like that either.

Nor did I like their seizing the Blue Board, the best pub in Aldbourne, and putting it off-limits to their own enlisted men, allowing all others to come in. That was a rotten, unfair abuse of their rank and privileges. They got away with it, because who were we? We had no rights and no way to protest. They said they were right and we were wrong, and that was that.

Yes, I will endure all the miseries of a world at war—why do they have to aggravate them by demeaning a man? Aren't they happy with their jump pay? They get $50 more a month jump pay than we do simply because they are officers and for no other reason. Their risk is no greater than ours; many of the sergeants are better jumpmasters.

How could anybody be an enlisted man in the Regular Army and put up with this crap for thirty years? Only a bum, a broken man could do it. I would sooner starve to death in civilian life than be an enlisted man in the Regular Army. And as long as I live, I will never "Sir" another man again.

These things I kept to myself, of course, for Peacock had me, and besides, I was young and cowed by rank and never sufficiently self-confident to be outspoken with officers. A real man like Wiseman or Blacky Wilson, the Oregon lumberjack in F Company, or Barnson, the wild and woolly, scar-faced Swede who had been transferred from F Company after he threw down his rifle in a company formation at Fort Bragg and told off his platoon leader, these men would have told Peacock where to put his broom. They would have been thrown out of the Company the next day, but at least they would still have their self-respect.

They were men; I was a boy still. Peacock sensed it and knew that I wouldn't have the courage to rebel against him.

Brooding on these things, I grew more and more angry. As he stood over me and picked and nagged while I banged around in throttled fury, I consoled myself by remembering what he was like in action and thinking that I was better. You could forgive almost anything of an officer who was good in action. If he wasn't good there, then he wasn't good anywhere.

I returned to the orchard in a violent sulk, washed my face in the pump's icy water, and filled my helmet for shaving. After proclaiming the great injustices that I had suffered to a grinning group of men cleaning the machine gun, I shaved and went back into Uden to be by myself for a few minutes.

Saluting all the officers that I met (and goddamning every one of them, for Peacock had soured me on the lot), I strolled through the streets until I came to a bar. I went in and found a number of British soldiers seated quietly at little round tables, drinking watery, wartime beer. The room was as neat and clean and warm as a Vermeer kitchen. It took me away from the Army to the Europe that I had always wanted to see, the Old Country of peacetime. Glad to be a whole man again, alone and on my own, I ordered a beer and sat down at an empty table.

I lingered in the bar till twilight time, then strolled back to the orchard for supper, which the cooks, who had just caught up with us, prepared from British rations, stray cows, and other gleanings of the countryside. I decided to take a shower when this was over.

The night was clear and frosty, the stars very low and winter-bright. Standing naked by the pump while another man worked the handle, I soaped myself off and rinsed the goose pimples. I had not washed all over for about ten days, and the feeling of cleanliness was like a rebirth.

Murmurs of men in their holes in the orchard and in the farmhouse reached me as I went back up the lane, breathing deeply and relaxed and smiling inside. Looking up at the stars and thinking of the men around me who made up the Regiment, I gave thanks that I was young and alive, outdoors in a fine country with an outfit that I liked. The Peacocks, actually, were few and far between. For this I was also grateful.

I WAS BELABORING PEACOCK with a broom, bam, bam, bam! He cowered in a corner and covered his head with his hands and cried for mercy. The thrill of the blows warmed my heart and made me increase the pounding.

"Get up, Webster!" someone cried.

Peacock vanished, and in the darkness I saw Janovec sitting beside me and heard Rader at the entrance to our hole.

"Oh Christ," I muttered, shaking my head. The dream had been so delightful.

"You and Janovec fall out in the lane in ten minutes for a patrol," Rader said.

"O.K., O.K."

Resenting the disturbance of my dream and feeling quite imposed upon, I took my own sweet time about putting on my boots, which I always took off at night, and stripping my cartridge belt. I did not relish the patrol, but because it had come up so suddenly and I had had no time for prolonged forebodings, I was not particularly scared. I fell out on the lane to find everybody else ready and Rader mad because I was so late.

After he had given me the usual hell for being late (a common failing of mine), he marched us out to the main road. Lyall and Wiseman had also been chosen.

We entered the battalion headquarters house, went upstairs to a bare room, and sat down with some other men from E Company and two S-2 men who were supposed to lead us. They seemed quite unconcerned. "Nothing to it," one of them said as everybody began to smoke.

Captain Nixon, a blasé young man who made quite a thing out of being a Yale man—I never let on I went to Harvard—arrived after we had waited about fifteen minutes. A dark person with a heavy beard, he looked as if he hadn't shaved for at least three days. This was his usual state. Captain Nixon was alleged to hale from a place called Nixon, New Jersey; his family was supposed to own half the town.

" 'Tenshun!" shouted one of the S-2 men, springing up.

I started to rise reluctantly from the floor, where I had been chatting with Wiseman and Lyall, but the captain raised his hand and told us to be at ease. I sagged down again.

"Come in here with me, men," the captain said, leading the way into the adjacent room, where a map was tacked to the wall.

We followed him. My fears had increased greatly in the wait. I began to sweat and swallow hard.

Captain Nixon, who slouched and never raised his voice, oriented us by pointing to the location of Uden on the map. "The Dutch Underground has told us that the Krauts have moved into the village of Volkel, near here," he said. His finger went south along the Eindhoven road, then cut east to a cluster of eight or ten houses almost three miles from Uden.

"I want you men to go down there and find out if the Krauts have really moved in. They may be planning an attack from that direction. This is a reconnaissance patrol; don't shoot and don't get in a fight if you can help it. Just look around and come back."

He introduced the two S-2 men who were to lead us, then described our route, which was essentially that traced by his finger.

The S-2 men set fire to some corks and passed them around, so that we could blacken our faces and hands. We left the house immediately afterward. Lyall was bright and cocky as ever, and Wiseman hadn't changed from his bluff heartiness, but I felt soured and scared and silent. Janovec was his own dour self.

We passed through the semi-civilian world of a village behind the lines with feelings of the greatest envy, like men who go through a great city on their way to the death chamber of a distant prison. Everybody else seemed happy and peaceful and totally careless of the fact that we were going on patrol. British tankmen were lolling about their parked vehicles, heating tea on tiny gas stoves, while dozens of paratroopers strolled up and down the sidewalks as if on leave.

The houses of Uden ended by a large Catholic building where a number of nuns lived. A British tank was on guard between the road and the nunnery, with its crew dug in around it and one man inside. They gave us the password and urged us to be silent.

"At ease!" our leader hissed.

The talking ended, and I unslung my rifle and put a bullet in the chamber. No daredevil, I had taken a position in the middle of the column, so that I could go either way if fired upon and still have contact with both the front and the rear. A man in the rear lost contact easily and never knew what was going on up front, while the point were likely to find themselves alone in an ambush. They were at an added disadvantage, for to maintain contact with the rest of the patrol, they had to be constantly looking back. As it was, it was almost impossible to maintain contact in any direction at night.

We marched down the highway at top speed and in closed ranks. Most of the men, including those from S-2, took no great pains to walk quietly. I began to wonder what kind of patrol this was. Either S-2 knew something that we didn't or else they were naturally careless. As for the others, most of them fitted the latter description—naturally careless. They always marched with slung rifles until fired upon and seldom took the precaution to be prepared for eventualities.

I erred in the other direction: I was too apprehensive. Fearful of the night, which was cold and overcast, with low, black clouds, I held my rifle ready and walked with care, looking all around as we went. I didn't trust S-2 or anybody else to look after me.

We stopped abruptly after we had gone about a thousand yards and knotted together at the edge of a bridge over a narrow creek ten feet wide. Two slit trenches were dug into the shoulder of the road on our side, with a machine-gun crew in one and a bazooka team in the other. A telephone wire ran back from the position to Uden. This was the last outpost.

The men on guard were very tense and quiet. They chided our leader for his loud and careless approach and told him to be more silent when he crossed the creek. "Four miles from here to Veghel," one of them whispered. "Christ knows how many Krauts are in between."

"Lock and load," our leader told us, "and spread out. Five yards between men. Let's go."

We crossed the bridge to no-man's-land.

A string of tracers flew into the sky parallel to us a mile or two away in the east and then an artillery barrage rumbled and flared far off to the west. The sound of our shuffling footsteps and clicking gear became unbearably loud, but on we went as fast as before.

The man ahead of me suddenly turned left. I stumbled after him into a slimy ditch, up a mound, and over a meadow of high, wet grass to a barbed-wire fence, where I ripped my pants and cursed the day that I had thrown away my wire cutters. Never having used them in Normandy, where hedges took the place of fences, I had abandoned them in Aldbourne. Now I needed them more than ever, for there were no hedges in Holland, just an endless succession of barbed-wire fences.

"Watch the wire," I whispered to the man behind me.

He groped for it and held it down while I ran to catch up with the others.

"This is a ball," Lyall remarked aloud.

"Shh! Christ."

We scrambled up the loud stones of a railway embankment and down the other side, where we stopped for a ten-minute break. From here we went across several fields to a cow path through a dense thicket. The noise of our approach was so great that I expected to be fired upon any minute.

Emerging from the tunnel, we saw a group of small houses about 150 yards away. We stopped and lay down while our leader reconnoitered the dwellings from a safe distance. He was back in a few minutes, without ever getting close to the village.

"O.K.," he whispered, "let's get out of here. No Krauts around."

We turned and hurried safely home to our holes in the orchard.

"HIT IT, HIT IT!" Rader cried. "Hubba, hubba. Put on all your gear and fall out on the double! We have to go down to Best and help the Deuce. Krauts have broken through."

Enraged at the sudden awakening, for I had only been asleep two hours, the patrol having returned at about one A.M., I decided to express my indignation with tardiness, which I knew was more irritating to Rader and Peacock than anything else I could do. I dressed slowly and climbed out of my hole to put on my boots.

Everybody else had gone. Jerking the laces tight, I slipped under my harness and ran after the platoon, which had lined up in the lane.

"Always late," Rader commented. "Goddammit, Webster, when are you going to be on time?"

"When this freaking outfit does something sensible."

"You'll never see the day," Pace said.

I laughed.

"Moving out!" Lieutenant Peacock yelled. "Let's go."

Nobody was very happy about it. Bleary and disgruntled, the whole Company muttered and shuffled through the darkness. Best was, we knew, fifteen or twenty miles to the southwest. We could expect a long hike, since someone else was using the G.I. trucks that had left us in the ambush at Veghel.

The column stopped and started, waited ten or fifteen minutes, and finally worked into position with the rest of the Battalion. A number of men were smoking and lighting cigarettes; nobody made any effort to put them out. We began to march, then stopped again near the British tank on the outskirts of town. The peculiar throbbing of German airplane motors came in low from the north. Its machine guns opened fire, pututututut, as it passed overhead, a strange black shape soon lost in the night.

"Put out those goddamn cigarettes!" an officer cried.

The smoking ceased, and the line began to move again like an unfolding accordion, as each man passed the word back to observe a five-yard interval. There were no tanks with us this time, for the British had drawn most of them north in a violent effort to break through to the paratroopers trapped in Arnhem.

A flare burst low in the east a couple of miles away, and an enemy machine gun fired a long string of tracers under it parallel to our course. A drum barrage rolled and thundered miles off in the west. The shells lit the horizon with quick white flashes; their explosions came to us faintly fifteen or twenty seconds later. A battle was in progress in the direction we were going, and we did not look forward to joining it.

The pace was so fast, however, that we had little energy for forebodings. We kept changing off on the machine gun, each man carrying it twenty minutes on his shoulder, then passing it to the man behind him, and we were so burdened with boxes of ammunition that we were very tired by the time we reached Veghel.

In the bitter, frosty cold of first light, the village looked like a Kerr Eby lithograph of First World War ruins. Many of the houses had been shelled and gutted. Mortars had blown the tiles and lathing off many roofs, and 88s had punched holes in the walls. The trees were torn, the windows smashed, telephone wires dangled from their posts. Now occupied by the 327th Glider Infantry Regiment, which had landed by air the day after we had jumped, Veghel had apparently been considered a key position, with bridges over a creek and a small canal and many roads coming together. The Germans had attacked it three or four times in an effort to keep supplies and reinforcements from reaching the 82nd Airborne Division in Nijmegen and the British 1st at Arnhem. The attacks had been partially successful; blacker and blacker news reached us of the British 1st being ground to bloody rags by German panzers.

Five or six miles south of Veghel, when we were down to ten minutes apiece on the machine gun, we passed through the village of St. Odenrode, where the Germans had also once cut the road. Several houses were smashed, and there was a dead British dispatch rider lying by the road in his leather gauntlets, knee-length boots, and round helmet.

The box of ammunition that I was carrying began to dig into my hand. Company Headquarters had a car, I noticed, but they were too busy saving their own shoe leather to make room for others' necessities.

"Why don't we get a horse and wagon for this stuff?" I said to Rader. The subject had been mentioned before, but I never wearied of discussing it.

"Peacock won't allow us to."

"God . . ."

"You know Peacock."

"Boy, do I know Peacock."

I shifted the box to the other hand.

The head of the column left the road and began to go cross-country. In spite of the chill in the air, my underclothing was soaking wet and my feet, swollen and throbbing, were burning hot. Finally the order came to take a break. We fell out on the grass.

"Want some milk, Web?" Wiseman said, nodding at a cow grazing nearby.

"I sure do."

"Let's go."

Tearing up handfuls of grass to feed her, we went to the cow and patted her and made our offering of food. As soon as she began to eat, Wiseman, who had done this many times before, squatted by her udder while I held my canteen cup below the chosen tits. An expert milkman, he filled the cup quickly. We stopped work and drank it down. The milk was warm and wonderfully rich and creamy. I had never tasted anything like it before I had come to Holland. Wiseman started to drain off another cupful.

"Let's go!" Rader cried. "Moving out."

We left the cow and continued west across slightly rolling land of poor farms, wild heath, and small pine forests. After several hours, we stopped by one of these farms and had lunch. Wiseman and I beat the others through the kitchen door and quickly found a can of milk and cheese large enough for the whole squad. The house was bare and clean, but like all the other farms we had been in, alive with biting black flies that took the edge off the neatness. A further search outdoors uncovered half a dozen eggs in the dirty hay of an empty chicken coop. Delighted with our success, we built a fire in the backyard and scrambled the eggs in an iron skillet borrowed from the kitchen. We cleaned the skillet with sand and water when we were through and put it back in the kitchen. There was no sign of the owners anywhere.

Well, I thought, as we set off again, in better spirits, if the Deuce was in trouble when they called for help this morning, they'll be wiped out by the time we get there. I did not frankly look forward to Best. Meandering around the countryside was far more pleasant than fighting.

Mounting a small rise, we came upon a British infantry outfit dug into the westward slope. A company of the Queen's Own Guards Regiment, they were the neatest soldiers I had ever seen in action. Crouching in holes as square and precise as the Germans', they were all clean-shaven and in regulation uniform, with their helmets squarely on their heads. We knew that the Guards' units were the best in the British army—every man had to be at least six feet tall and a superior soldier—but we had never realized how well disciplined they were on the field of battle. By comparison, we looked like a rabble in arms, with our beards and muddy uniforms and tattered gear. Our helmets were worn with a jaunty individuality, and most of their tops had been blackened by cooking and shaving fires, for the helmet served as an all-purpose iron pot. The Guards, who eyed us with the air of men studying a strange apparition, were, we noticed, on the alert and well down in their holes.

"What's up?" somebody asked them.

"Jerry tanks," an Englishman replied. He pointed west. "In the low ground."

The slightest elevation in a land as flat as Holland gave one command of a huge sweep of countryside. From here, at the crest of a sandy, gentle ridge, we could gaze west at least ten miles.

I squinted down the slope at the meadows and patches of woods and saw no German tanks. That did not reassure me, for I knew the English did not lie like American soldiers. Everything was so still, and the Guards, who had been in action since Normandy and who yet looked as if they had just marched out of the sentry box at St. James's Palace, were so tense and ready that I was glad when the order came to get going again.

Heading north on a sandy road that ran along the top of the ridge, we began to hear the rumble of artillery ahead. The light chatter about the Queen's Own died out. We entered a forest of the tallest pine trees we had seen so far. The slamming of many heavy doors came to us from the other side of the forest, where the 502 was fighting for Best. The artillery accentuated the stillness of the woods; we seemed to be moving through silent sleep to a nightmare.

A parachute was dangling from a tall pine fifty yards beyond the road. Two dead men from the 501 lay nearby. Farther along, brightly colored plastic communications wire led to the scattered trenches of an abandoned German position. The artillery fire increased, and a sound of small arms began to mingle with the booming.

I unslung my rifle and made sure that it was loaded.

We emerged from the forest into lush meadowland. An 88 shell passed over, making us duck low as we filed into a deep ditch lined with huge old trees. The high steeple of a very old church stared down at us a quarter of a mile away. I wondered who was using it for observation. We crowded together and began to dig in. The order came to move to another place. Only Rice dug in there. With the dry rustling of many leaves, our own artillery passed overhead, crashing to earth out of sight. The 88 fired again, lower than before, one, two, three. The shells burst in the Battalion area and killed several men in the mortar platoon of Headquarters Company, but nobody in E Company was hurt. The heavy tooming of a 50-caliber machine gun answered a crackle of German fire. A lone sniper began to shoot into the meadow.

After we had lain in fear and ignorance for at least thirty minutes, Sergeant Talbert came down the ditch from company headquarters and told us that it was a false alarm. "The Deuce has everything under control," he said. "They don't need us after all."

"Thank God," I murmured.

"On your feet, men!" he cried. "We're going back to Uden."

We stood up in full view of the steeple and filed slowly out of the ditch to a road through the forest behind us. This led in turn four or five miles to the Eindhoven-Arnhem highway.

By now it was late afternoon. We had been on our feet almost continuously for twelve hours, and our feet hurt. Men who had once gone twenty minutes on the machine gun were down to two or three; their griping warmed the air. Even Rice, who had tied his bootlaces tightly about his ankles so he wouldn't feel the pain as he carried a machine gun for F Company on the march from Toccoa to Atlanta, complained about the soreness and stiffness in his feet, ankles, and the calves of his legs.

Thoroughly irritated, I finally wearied altogether of carrying my box of ammunition about the time we passed the dead motorcyclist in St. Odenrode.

"Jesus Christ," I said to Rader, "why don't we give this goddamn ammo to company headquarters? They have a car."

"You know why."

"I jumped with this goddamn thing, and I've been stuck with it ever since."

"Tough."

"Let's get a goddamn car somewhere and use that."

"Can't. Peacock's orders."

"I'm not going to carry this thing much longer."

"Oh hell, throw it away! We have plenty more."

"Throw away ammunition?"

"Sure, we'll never miss it."

"O.K." I swung my arm back in an arc and let the box fly. It landed with a thud on the grass.

Lieutenant Peacock ran up. Afraid that he was going to make me fetch the ammunition, I tensed inside and gritted my teeth, but he passed me by, for he was interested only in a passing British truck. Part of a convoy that was also going north, it bore on its tailgate several men from the third platoon.

"Off that truck!" Peacock shouted. "Get back in line, all of you!"

The men jumped down and waited for their platoon to come up, while Peacock upbraided them. "If you men are going to fall out now, what will you do when we go to combat again?"

They shrugged their shoulders and scowled at him without bothering to reply.

Colonel Sink was waiting for us on the edge of Uden. As we limped by, he mounted his jeep with his back to the setting sun and welcomed us home.

"Do your feet hurt, men?" he called when we were even with him. "Do your feet hurt?"

Did my feet hurt! I wanted to throw my rifle at him, for the first time in two years.

YESTERDAY WAS QUITE A DAY, I mused as I hurried back from the medics: I caught diarrhea and voted for Roosevelt.

Now I was bound for the barn on the west side of Uden where we had moved from an outpost in the north several days after returning from Best. The ballot had gone on its way to the States, but I still had the diarrhea; it made me hurry faster.

The first platoon had taken over a large barn and made itself at home in the hay. Supposed to be on the M.L.R., we had posted a couple of men on 24-hour guard in the field behind us while we slept on soft hay in thin, one-man sleeping bags which had caught up with us with the last of the regiment's rear echelon. It was our most comfortable position in Holland.

But I couldn't enjoy it, because I had the worst diarrhea I had ever caught in the Army; I couldn't lie still for more than twenty minutes. Cramped and irritable, I had spent most of the day and night running back and forth to the slit-trench latrine behind the barn, with time out for a mile walk to the medics and a dose of sulfa pills.

It was all the cooks' fault, I mused as I came in sight of our quarters. Bastards always were dirty. They kill a cow and butcher it and boil it hard in pasty gravy and call it beef stew. It almost broke my teeth, but the stew wasn't to blame—it was the wash water afterward. Vile as the British seamen on the *Samaria*, who had set out cold pans of salt water for us to wash our mess kits in, they gave us a single garbage can of soapy water as a battalion rinse. By the time I got to the can, the scum was an inch thick on top. The grease clung to my pan, breeding germs, and gave me diarrhea at the next meal. I had spent last night on the run, unable to enjoy the comforts of my sleeping bag.

Well, anyway I had voted. That made me happy. I had to walk almost two miles to cast my ballot, but I would have walked ten, if necessary, because this was my first vote—I was 22 in June—and I had always wanted to cast it for Roosevelt, the greatest President we had ever had and the only one who ever gave the working man a break.

Roosevelt had faced and overcome the two great crises America had ever suffered: the worst depression in history and the world's biggest war. He was a politician, as crafty and conniving as any, for politics is a cesspool of lying lawyers, but his work was greater than the man, and the country was better for it. The rich Republicans hated Roosevelt for helping the working man, for encouraging the labor unions to wring a fair day's wage for a fair day's work out of employers who had never heard of such a thing before and for putting into effect fair-employment practices that they considered outrageously Socialistic. Roosevelt helped the unemployed when Herbert Hoover, the last Republican, an engineer who never quite understood humanity, had said, "Let every man help his brother," when he knew perfectly well that the rich weren't about to help the poor, never had and never would. I had grown up with Republicans and gone to school and college with them, and sickened by their selfishness, their cold avarice and lofty contempt for the common people, had early sworn to vote for the Democrats, who, for all their rotten political faults, were more concerned with the welfare of the country as a whole.

Delighted that I had at last fulfilled that ambition, I snapped back to the present when I saw a dozen people standing in front of our barn. A wild-eyed crone was shrieking and cackling at some soldiers while several Dutch children looked on.

"*Was ist los?*" I said to the crone.

She turned on me with a furious spate of Dutch that I could not follow. I shook my head at her. "*Ich verstebe nicht,*" I replied. Spotting an intelligent-looking boy of about 12 who was watching us with a smile, I asked him what was going on.

"She says it's her barn," he replied in excellent German.

The woman began to cry.

"*Verrucht,*" the boy commented.

"She's nuts," I told the other G.I.s. "The kid says she's nuts."

"We gathered that," Hoobler said, chuckling.

The woman wiped her face with her apron and turned on me with renewed fury, as if I were to blame. I backed away from her.

"Sick 'em, Ma!" Pace cried.

"*Es ist der Krieg,*" I said gently. Blaming everything on the war was an old excuse, but it sometimes worked.

"*Krieg! Krieg!*" she yelled, throwing up her hands.

Hoobler grinned.

"Tell her we're sorry, but we have to stay in the barn for a while," I said to the boy. "We'll take good care of it."

He translated the message and got back a hag's curse in reply.

"We won't hurt anything," I added.

But the crone was adamant. We were in her barn, she shrieked, and we had to get out of it.

"Oh, hell," I sighed, beginning to lose patience. "Tell her to go home." This only brought more tears.

I reached in my pocket, pulled out a D-ration chocolate bar, and handed it to her. "Here, for Chrissake."

The crying stopped, and her eyes brightened. "*Danke, danke,*" she murmured.

I hurried into the barn. She began to wail again, but her audience drifted away, and so she finally gave up and shuffled home, talking to herself.

The sun went down and soon the barn was filled with snores. Carl Sawosko, a quiet, pleasant man from Chicago who had joined E Company, lit a candle and put it on the floor near the door, then got his guitar, which had come up with the sleeping bags, and began to play. Hoobler and the first squad's Dukeman and Christenson, who were both good singers, gathered around. A barrage rumbled in the west as they sang.

"NOW WHERE?" I muttered as we marched toward a convoy of G.I. trucks.

I was in an irritable mood, for the diarrhea had tied my stomach in hard knots, sucked my throat dry, and galled my arms. The raw chafing made me take short steps and wince with pain. My views on life were

more jaundiced than usual, and when Peacock told us that we were going north of Nijmegen to hold a quiet defensive position, I could not
help commenting sourly that I had heard that song before.

Incredibly garbled in transit, the word had finally reached us that the
British had lost the battle for Arnhem. Montgomery's great gamble to
flank the Siegfried Line with the 1st Allied Airborne Army and turn the
armor loose in the plains of west Germany had failed—not, we were
sure, through any lack of courage or determination on the part of the
paratroopers, but through the slow ineptness of their countrymen in
tanks. A good American armored unit like the 2nd Armored Division,
which had helped us in Normandy without any tender regard for property, ammunition, or orders from the rear, would have broken through to
the 1st Airborne Division; if General Patton had been in charge of the
effort, the whole British 2nd Army would have gone through Arnhem
and far beyond.

But the gamble had failed, and so we were trying to hold what little
had been gained by the 82nd and 101st. While the British infantry took
over our old area and widened the scattered footholds into a broad corridor north to the Lower Rhine, the 82nd would remain on the defensive around Nijmegen and the 101st would dig in along the river, west of
Arnhem.

It sounded quite placid, but skeptical as ever, I took a seat near the
tailgate and kept my helmet on and my rifle in hand. The trucks moved
off.

This was our longest and loveliest drive in Holland, on the most perfect day. The air was crisp and cool, with the clean brightness of fall, and
the sky was bright blue. Autumn colors of the leaves contrasted with
the sky and the lush green grass, which had not yet turned brown.
Marveling once more at the windmills, the neat orchards, the stately
churches, the Breughel villages, and the fair and friendly people in
wooden shoes who waved to us as we went by, we agreed again and again
that there was no country as good as Holland. Cold and wet, England,
which we had all liked very much, had been too often overcast and soot-
coal dirty, while France had been a surly disappointment of indifferent
people, rotting corpses, and too much war. Both those countries had
been disappointing. Holland, on the other hand, was even better than
the geography books. None of us had imagined the depth of hate that
the Dutch felt for the Germans, whom we had always considered as

practically the same kind of people, a hate, we knew, that made us doubly welcome. The wonderful thrill of being wanted, that we had first felt in Eindhoven, was still with us.

In half an hour we passed a huge field covered with gliders for the 82nd Airborne Division and then came to the Maas River. One of three tributaries of the Rhine that wound through this part of Holland within twenty miles of each other, the Maas was spanned by a long steel bridge very similar to the one that the German paratroopers had seized at Moerdyk in the movie we had seen before D-Day. The road curved up to it on a raised approach that paralleled the river for several hundred yards. Batteries of 20mm and 40mm antiaircraft were dug in along the embankment to protect the bridge from German air raids, for the Luftwaffe was very much alive in this area.

The Maas was wide here, and the bridge was almost half a mile long, but it had been taken intact by a unit from the 504. It was a daring task for lightly equipped troops. The 504, however, was equal to it. For my money, the best regiment in the 82nd, they were old-timers who had fought in Sicily and Salerno; one battalion had won a Distinguished Unit Citation on the Anzio beachhead, where the regiment had spent several months as line infantry. Known to the press (only) as the Anzio Roughnecks, they looked down on the 506th as upstarts and referred to us as the Walky Talky Regiment. It made no difference now, when we were together in action, and after they had missed Normandy, the greatest jump of the war. The 504 preferred not to discuss Normandy.

Polish paratroopers in gray berets were on guard at the Maas-Waal Canal bridge six or seven miles farther along when we drove by. Dug in deep on both sides of the small suspension bridge, the Poles, who were great people and splendid soldiers, were protecting the crossing from a raid by German paratroopers. They waved cheerfully as we passed them with shouts of greeting. Most of their unit, we knew, had been dropped near Arnhem on the south side of the Lower Rhine in an effort to reinforce the 1st Airborne. The Poles had been severely mauled on the jumpfield by waiting Germans.

We went another mile or so and then stopped for a ten-minute break under a row of big trees with thick, spreading branches. To our left, several Typhoons and Spitfires circled and landed at an airport some two thousand yards away.

BAM! A shell burst three hundred feet from us in a field between our convoy and the airport.

I leaped off the truck and ran for a farmhouse equidistant in the opposite direction.

Another shell burst fifty yards closer.

What a country this is! I thought, hoping to find cover behind the house. British planes take off with Kraut tanks firing right under their nose. I thought the 82nd had settled everything up here. Nobody's safe anymore. The only thing to do is to get hit and sent back to the hospital in England.

I darted around the corner of the farmhouse and almost stumbled on Johnny Martin, who was relaxing in the sun, with his back to the explosions. "What the hell?" I gaped, thinking I had just broken all records for the hundred-yard dash.

"Been here for hours." He grinned.

The rest of the platoon arrived on the run. A third shell exploded near the trucks.

"All clear!" Hoobler shouted from the road. "Come on back!"

We edged across the field to the convoy and returned to our slatted wooden seats. As the trucks started off, Hoobler explained what had happened.

"Spitfire caught an ME-109," he said. "The Kraut dropped a load of butterfly bombs to try to escape, but the Spitfire got him. Skinny Sisk tried to talk him into dying." Hoobler laughed.

More at ease, we proceeded north. I continued to sit by the tailgate, however, because you just never knew what was going to happen next.

We halted again in the midst of some plowed fields a mile or two from Nijmegen to allow a long train of refugees to pass by. Several hundred in number, they streamed silently out of the city on foot and in horse-drawn carts piled high with bedding and cooking utensils. Women and children predominated. Nobody waved to us or acted as if they were glad to see us. They passed by in silence instead, with crying children and a dazed, defeated look in their eyes.

"They're evacuating the city," I commented. "Looks like we're in for trouble."

Wiseman nodded.

A movement high above the silent, pathetic stream of people (who made me feel guilty and uncomfortable) distracted me. "Look!" I said, pointing up.

The clear blue sky was laced with the cottony white vapor trails of half a dozen dogfights. So high that they appeared only as tiny black dots, the slowly twisting airplanes maneuvered for position. What caught my eye was a single Spitfire hurtling straight to earth. Closer and closer it came. I gritted my teeth and waited for the pilot to jump. A voice inside me screamed, Get out! Get out! I did not want him to die—him or anybody else, because it was too lovely a day to die. But down he came. No, no, I thought, it can't be; he still has time to jump. I loved Spitfires and had the greatest admiration for the R.A.F.

But no pilot left the plane. It screamed down the last hundred feet and hit a meadow a thousand yards west, burying its nose four feet into the ground. There was no explosion and no fire—just the sudden, quiet ending of a man's life.

The civilians had trudged beyond us, and so we began to move again. We turned sharp right at the edge of the city and drove southeast toward a high, forested ridge. More refugees passed us. We could hear very heavy artillery falling in Nijmegen. After continuing five miles, we turned up the face of the ridge, which rose at least three hundred feet above the polder. A key terrain feature originally assigned to the 82nd, this was the highest ground in all Holland.

We drove into the pine trees and stopped. The trucks took off with a rush as soon as we had dismounted, and our own shells began to whisper overhead and land far to the east.

"This is the Reichswald," Lieutenant Peacock announced. "Germany is only a few hundred yards away."

That's nice, I thought, quite content to stay where I was. The hell with Germany.

We spread out in the woods and took over a network of German trenches. An enemy strongpoint seized by the 505 or 508, all the trenches were fresh and intact. There were no bodies lying about and there was little evidence, other than some chopped trees, of a violent struggle. Wiseman, Janovec, and I staked claim on a comfortable, zigzag trench, five feet deep and eighteen inches wide, that had two zigs and a zag, one for each of us. A thick roof of logs and dirt covered most of the excavation.

"Chow call!" Hoobler cried as we began to prepare our gear for the night. We had been told that we would be in reserve here for about twenty-four hours before going north of Nijmegen to an area between the Waal and the Rhine that was known as "the island."

"Come and get it, goddammit!" Hoobler yelled.

We scrambled out of the hole and ran to him like a pack of dogs. Every meal was a competition, and we wanted to be in at the start, for they were community affairs, a little of this and a little of that, and God help the hindmost. This was due to the nature of our British rations.

We had been living on them all but the first three days, when we ate K rations and then subsisted on apples, pears, and peaches, civilian handouts, and German rations from an Eindhoven warehouse. These were mostly stone-hard biscuits, tasty canned meat, and little tubes of Limburger cheese.

The British rations were better, but that did not decrease the ill will generated at each meal. Somewhat on the heavy side, the food consisted of cans of sausage meat, beef stew, meat and vegetable stew, beefsteak and kidney stew (my favorite), and a rich fruit pudding. Biscuits and dehydrated tea rounded out the menu.

Popular with both British and Americans (who would never admit liking anything English), the tea was an ingenious mixture of dried leaves, concentrated sugar, and powdered milk. A heaping spoonful in half a canteen of boiling water made a sweet, hearty beverage unrivaled in our own larder, which had separate packets of sugar for the coffee and no milk.

Unfortunately, a squad of twelve men had to share the contents of these cans equally. It was never done. After they had been heated in the fire, there was no sitting down with one's own complete meal, as with a K or C ration, but rather a hasty sampling of transient cans, with a taste of this and a dip of that, while eleven other people watched to make sure you didn't take more than your share (which they of course expected to be less than they had taken). I hated these meals in Holland.

I sat down near Hoobler and entered the fray. The talk was combative.

"Pass the stew, Massaconi."

"Come on, Lyall, I haven't had any beef yet."

"Jesus, Pace, are you going to hold on to that can all night?"

"Let's go, Webster, give somebody else a chance."

"Keep that pudding moving, Hoobler. You've had it at least ten minutes."

"Goddammit, Janovec, you're not going to hog *all* of that, are you?"

Swiftly dipping into whatever I could grab, I kept one eye on the other cans to make sure that I wasn't missing anything. Eternal vigilance was necessary, I had learned one day, after becoming deeply involved in a can of stew, when I had looked up to see Hoobler scraping out the last of the fruit pudding.

The only fair solution, we had discovered, was to find a large can, fill it with a quart or two of water, break all our crackers into it, dump in all the cans of meat, and make a stew for the squad. We tried to do this whenever possible, because it gave each man a cupful of stew to enjoy by himself.

After supper, we rinsed our spoons in the tea, wiped our hands on our pants, and strolled twenty yards west to a clearing that afforded a beautiful view of the evening's double feature: German airplanes and Allied ackack.

The Luftwaffe flew in at dusk every day to bomb the Rhine bridges at Nijmegen, and the British and American antiaircraft guns greeted them with cascades of tracer. Viewed from a safe distance, the fireworks display was almost as good as the one I had watched from the swamp behind Utah Beach the night before D-Day.

"Beautiful, isn't it?" Hoobler sighed. He thoroughly enjoyed war.

I nodded. The spectacle surpassed any 4th of July show I had ever seen on the grounds of the Bronxville High School.

The forest behind us was filled with the murmur of men settling down for the night. My diarrhea temporarily lulled by a warm feeling of companionship and security, I sat in the clearing for almost twenty minutes, admiring the ackack and watching the 3rd Battalion, which had just arrived, move into a narrow valley directly below us to the left. Our own shells continued to whisper overhead and land deep in the Reichswald with a comforting thunder.

A lone high-velocity shell whipped out of the woods in reply just as darkness fell. Passing close to our heads, it sent us diving for the ground. The shell burst in the 3rd Battalion's bivouac.

"Time for bed," I said, jumping up and trotting to my hole.

Everybody but Hoobler ran to their trenches. He stayed awake another thirty minutes, drinking in the fireworks and chortling aloud at our sudden sleepiness.

THE 501 MOVED INTO OUR AREA in the morning, with tales of a good jump and some brisk battles afterward, but we hung around till afternoon, killing time with rifle and equipment inspections and walks in the forest, before the word came to move out again.

The ride was hurried. Under full speed, we hurtled downhill and north to Nijmegen, which was under bombardment from enemy siege guns. Extensively damaged by air raids and the 82nd's battle for possession, the city was a deserted mass of rubbly streets and battered buildings. There were no civilians anywhere. The tremendous boom of incoming shells spurred our drivers to faster speeds. In a few minutes, we mounted a rise and came to a giant, new, high-span steel bridge over the Waal River. The bridge was famous already, the story of its capture having reached us several days before.

A splendid feat of arms, the deed was done by a Battalion of the 504, which had first driven the S.S. from a little castle on the left, then gathered a patchy fleet of rowboats, canoes, and wherries and paddled several hundred yards across the swift river under heavy fire to storm the banks and take the other end of the bridge. Violent counterattacks by the Germans had been launched in conjunction with dive-bombers, but the 504 had stood its ground and the bombs had missed the bridge. The Germans had even sent frogmen swimming downstream with demolition charges, and artillery batteries had pounded the roadway—all in vain.

We raced across the span at full throttle. A sign at the north end told us that Arnhem was ten miles away.

The light faded from the sky. The air turned cold and thick, with a low, wet mist. Our trucks jogged left, followed the high riverbank for a mile or so, and descended into flat orchard country. We were on the island between the Waal and the Lower Rhine, with Germans to the north, east, and west, and the bridge we had crossed was our only link to friendly territory. The island was at war. As we passed through the rich orchards, we saw battery after battery of British field artillery camouflaged with burlap-dotted netting. The slamming of the guns made the wet dusk even more depressing. In a chastened mood, we passed a barbed-wire corral of bedraggled German prisoners without the usual curses and fist-shaking. Janovec began to complain of stomach cramps. My belly turned cold; the diarrhea stirred again. All of a sudden, the trucks jammed together and stopped.

"Everybody off!" an officer cried. "This is it."

I jumped down and stepped over to the shoulder. It was almost dark.

"Third squad over here!" Rader shouted. "Third squad over here!"

I picked up my new box of machine-gun ammunition—throwing away the old one had solved nothing—shivered convulsively with cold and apprehension, and fell in line with the rest of the men. The country was so low that it seemed to be below the level of both rivers, and the lowness increased the weight and penetration of the damp cold. I shivered again. Something told me that we were headed for trouble.

Rader spread us out five yards apart, and we started off in silence, the only noise coming from our squishing boot soles and the soft clatter of moving thighs against hanging gear. The night was very dark and oppressive. All the artillery had ceased firing.

We marched north on a narrow, black-topped road shining with moisture. A ditch filled with stagnant water stood beside the road with 105 craters in it every few yards. Looking beyond these evil black marks, I saw dimly many wet orchards bearing big, ripe apples.

Janovec, who had been muttering somewhere behind me, suddenly cried that he could not go another step. "These damn cramps," he said, falling out of the column. "Medic, medic!" He fell down in a tight, writhing bundle. Someone else yelled for the medic. The column kept moving.

Two British soldiers in fleece-lined leather jerkins met us at the next crossroads to guide us to our new position, which was at the front.

"What's it like up here?" Rader inquired.

"It's a bloody rest position, mate."

I winced. He was too cheerful.

On and on we went, thinking that we would march all night, until finally we were the only company left in the 2nd Battalion, the others having disappeared en route. D and E Companies would be on line, we were informed, while Headquarters and F were in reserve. After about five miles, we stopped in the cobblestone streets of a village of twenty or thirty small houses strung out in the lee of an immense dike that towered over their roofs.

"This is it, mates," one of the guides announced. "The village of Rand-wijk!" A column of British soldiers who had evidently been awaiting our arrival marched past us, picking up our guides as they went by.

"Spooky, isn't it?" Wiseman remarked.

I nodded, feeling the weight of the dike hanging over on us. "A ghost town. I don't like this place."

"LET'S GO, YOU GUYS. Patrol leaving in ten minutes."

"What!"

"Goddammit, there's nothing to it. Just walk along the dike and contact the Limeys. Be back."

Rader left the barn where we were billeted, and Wiseman and I rose from our bed of hay beside the stinking pigsty and put on our helmets and boots. We were quite unhappy, for it seemed as if we had marched in and fallen asleep only half an hour before.

I slid a bullet into the chamber of my .45, eased the hammer forward, and dropped the pistol into the right-hand pocket of my combat jacket. After feeling for them in the dark, I crossed a bandoleer over my chest and tightened the sling on my M-1.

"Ready?" Wiseman whispered. "Here comes Rader."

Accompanied by Pace, he led us out to the street and explained that E Company had to run a contact patrol every two hours from our village almost a mile east to a British position. "It's a snap," he commented.

"Do you mean to say," I whispered, "that almost a mile of that dike is unprotected?"

"Division's really spread out thin."

"Man, it must be."

"Antiaircraft's got an outpost in a farmhouse halfway. Between them and our patrols, we ought to know pretty quick if any Krauts come through."

"Sure. But I don't want to be the one to find out."

We passed a guard at the end of the village, left the road, and cut through an orchard to our left until we came to the dike.

Immense in the village, it seemed even larger close-up. As we hurried along its base, looking for infiltrating Germans in slit trenches that the British had dug into the slope every ten yards, I wondered if anybody was lying on top, watching us and waiting to shoot us in the back.

Rader rushed along in such careless, confident haste that I thought he would surely draw fire from a thousand yards away, so still was the night and so loud his footsteps. I kept squinting at the meadows on our right for signs of moving men and up the grassy slope of the dike, which was about thirty feet high, for a German's silhouette.

Lucky Janovec, I thought. He's out of this. I wondered where to escape if we suddenly stumbled upon the enemy. The fields offered no cover, and anybody who ran up the face of the dike was asking for death. Rader hurried on. A cluster of farm buildings loomed dark ahead.

"Halt!"

We stopped. The voice was American. It came from the shadows of the first small outbuilding and bade us advance and be recognized, after Rader had given the password.

We gathered around the guard. A small and rather fearful man who seemed very glad to be able to talk with somebody, he told us that a squad of the 81st Airborne Antiaircraft Battalion was on outpost here. Almost half a mile from the nearest friendly forces, he did not like the isolated position at all.

The reason for the outpost was obvious: It was the most logical place for the enemy to cross the dike and regroup in concealment. We did not envy the men who had to hold the place.

Then we came to another ideal entryway. Dominated by a windmill atop the dike about five hundred yards farther east, it featured a long orchard on the north that led straight to the windmill and another, even larger orchard on the south—and no friendly forces to protect them. All the enemy had to do was cross the flatland from the Lower Rhine, sneak through the trees to the dike, dart over it to the other orchard, and set up an attack at leisure. The windmill would afford observation for miles in all directions. If it was true that the German artillery pounding the island was as strong as we had heard, then he would have no trouble at all building up a strong bridgehead here.

We approached a small barn and farmhouse at the foot of the dike with our rifles ready and tiptoed among the buildings, stopping every few feet to listen for a cough or shuffle or clink of metal, but there were no Germans.

"This is a hell of a setup," I commented to Wiseman after we had left the place behind and had begun to relax. "A mile gap in our line and nobody watching a position like this. If I were the Krauts, I'd come right over here."

"This outfit's crazy," Wiseman agreed.

We strolled a few hundred yards farther to a little village, built along a raised road that sloped up to the crest of the dike, and went among the houses without being challenged. A guard finally stopped us near the top of the dike. We asked what was new, and he told us in a Cockney accent that it was bloody restful here. Leaving him, we went up for a look at the no-man's-land that lay between us and the Lower Rhine, almost a mile to the north. Nothing appeared to be stirring. Scattered outposts were supposed to warn of enemy movement from villages across the river, but these outposts had limited vision and were not always reliable.

"Let's take a look around," Wiseman suggested, leading the way to a nearby door. "Isn't this a beer joint?"

We entered a small tavern on our left. Carefully blacked out, its taps were dry, its shelves empty.

"Limeys beat us to it," Rader said. "Let's go home."

We went south along the sloping road for a mile or so, bore right on a broad highway, and turned right again after another mile. A four-engine Stirling bomber lay on its belly in a pasture near the last intersection.

"Let's take a look at it," I suggested. "Maybe we can find some souvenirs." What I had in mind was warm gloves or a fleece-lined flying jacket.

We walked over to the plane and looked inside, but there was nothing portable.

"Goddamn Limeys beat us to it again," Wiseman muttered. "They sure picked this country clean."

We left the bomber in disgust and went down a side road to our pigsty.

WISEMAN AND I woke up hungry; in fact, we were always hungry, for neither British nor American combat rations were enough to fill a man. You could subsist on them, to be sure, but you were never full. That is why we were always on the lookout for food. We picked ripe fruit from the trees, milked the cows, and filched whatever victuals the civilians had abandoned in their houses. And now came our greatest opportunity to feast on livestock: The village of Randwijk was fluttering and squealing with homeless ducks, chickens, and suckling pigs, all begging to be roasted, fried, baked, or broiled. We planned a royal feast.

But alas, Rader told us that we couldn't even light a fire, for fear of attracting heavy artillery. Dug in along a chain of wooded hills over a mile away, on the other side of the Rhine, the Germans had the whole island under observation, and although our village was hidden by the dike, the least sign of smoke would have brought a barrage down upon us. We preferred to leave the animals alive.

Our only alternative was to search the houses. Accordingly, Wiseman and I set off after breakfast with an empty pillowcase, and going from door to door, carefully examined the kitchens, attics, and cellars of those places not occupied by soldiers. Nobody interfered with our hunt, for the British, who were administering the area, had moved all the civilians several thousand yards to the rear. A lone young man met us at an intersection, chatted with us briefly in a German that sounded more German than Dutch, and strolled off toward the Lower Rhine, leaving us to wonder whether or not we had been talking to a spy. We didn't let this distraction interfere with our main pursuit, however.

By the time the morning was over, we had filled the pillowcase with a couple of pounds of sugar, some ersatz coffee, and a dozen Mason jars of jam, meat, and preserved fruit. At one house we found a bottle labeled "Brand Spirits" that smelled like pure alcohol to me. I tried a drink and couldn't talk for five minutes; the liquid burned—and tasted—like smoke from a tar fire. Wiseman, who was more durable in many ways, claimed that it was merely a Dutch version of white lightning and offered to split the jug with me, so that we could both get drunk, but I declined. I wanted to get drunk, but not that badly.

We returned to the squad when we had run out of kitchens, and moved from the barn to a clean little house nearby, where we spread our sleeping bags on the tile floor of a half basement and ate lunch. Keeping the liquor to himself, Wiseman provided milk for us from a passing cow.

The owner of the house made an appearance. A pale, fragile, coughing man in his middle 30s, he had gotten permission to return for some medicine that he kept in a cabinet in his bedroom. One of our varlets had already broken into the cabinet and scattered its contents about the floor, like some destructive child in malicious mischief, but the civilian shrugged it off with a quiet smile, got what he wanted, and left with our promise to take better care of his property.

Just when we were lying down for a nap, Rader announced that his squad had been detailed to bury a horse and calf whose rotting carcasses were stinking up the neighborhood. Killed by shell fire, the bloated animals lay on the grass behind one of the houses. While we worked all afternoon on this melancholy task, the first squad, which was ahead of us even on details, hurriedly buried two or three goats and a pig and then reclined indoors. Since our orders did not cover people, nobody bothered with the dead civilian lying facedown in his black suit in a puddle beside the road.

Both the village and its surrounding meadows had been the scene of rather brisk fighting. Dead animals littered the streets and yards; several of the houses, hit by mortars and artillery, had burned to the ground; and there were shell holes and empty ammo boxes and machine-gun belts everywhere. Having found scattered German gear in the houses we had visited, we surmised that the Germans had first held the village and then been driven out by British infantry with tanks, whose tracks twisted through the yards like sunken roads.

The sun faded into thick mist by the time our burial detail was over. Offered the choice of guard or another contact patrol, Wiseman and I chose the latter, since neither of us could stand the rigid monotony of guard duty. Rader told us he'd wake us at four A.M.

The Germans started to bombard a position several miles east of us at sundown. Dusk and dawn were their favorite times of attack, and the steady detonations, which came in at about ten-second intervals, set us on edge and made sleep difficult.

Rader woke us at midnight. "Changed the orders," he said, explaining that the first squad would go out at four. We cursed and grumbled, then left the village. The cannonading had increased in both volume and intensity while we had slept; now a shell came in every five seconds or so. I remarked to Wiseman that trouble was brewing.

"Those Kraut sonsofbitches are up to no good," he agreed.

We hurried through the patrol and found that the 501 had relieved the British in the little village that sloped up to the crest of the dike. They, too, were nervous about the bombardment.

Cold with fear and diarrhea, I returned to our house and fell asleep on the hard tile floor.

The German artillery was coming in very fast now: a 105 or 155 shell every second. Evil was afoot.

"THE KRAUTS HAVE broken through! Get up, everybody up!"

I blinked and sat bolt upright.

"Quick! Get ready for a dawn attack!"

I unzipped my sleeping bag, ripped out of it, yanked on my boots, and grabbing my helmet, rifle, and harness, ran outside with my bootlaces clicking behind me. This was no time for delay.

Men were pouring from all the other houses. A thick fog lay over the land, and the air was very damp and cold. The enemy artillery had ceased firing; an ominous silence filled the void.

We assembled behind the house that held the first-platoon C.P. and began to wait. The initial excitement wore off quickly, and after fifteen minutes, I began to feel that this was just another of Peacock's false alarms. Always cautious, he loved to prepare us for dawn attacks that never materialized.

The only thing we ever had in common, I thought, watching him move about with a tense, worried look on his face, was diarrhea, and we both have that now. I went into the garden, scraped out a catlike little hole, and squatted over it in pain and aggravation.

The platoon took advantage of Peacock's diarrhea by drifting silently back into the houses while he was absent on missions of relief. I watched them disappear one by one and then scurried back to my own cellar when he went into the garden again. I had just lain down with some other men when we heard a great commotion in the yard. Peacock appeared at the head of our basement stairs.

"Get out!" he shrieked. "Goddamn you people, the Krauts have broken through. Everybody outside on the double!"

"Oh shit," I muttered as I passed by him.

"Leave your musette bags here," he said. "We're only going to be gone a couple of hours."

We formed quickly on the road, where we learned that the Germans had come over the dike in the dark and that we were going to cross over to their side and cut them off in the rear while F Company attacked from the south and the second and third platoons held our village. Captain Winters ran up with a group that included Carson, a radioman, Hale, and two volunteers, the second platoon's calm and fearless Sergeant Guarnere, decorated with the Silver Star in Normandy, and the third platoon's fine medic, Roe, who had a warm, brave heart.

"Let's go!" the captain shouted.

We trotted down the road and into an orchard on our left. The fog was so thick that we could only see fifty yards.

When will it come? I wondered. We're going to run right into it in the fog. My fingers, clenching my M-1, were stiff with cold, but I was sweating freely. My heart pounded like a machine gun.

Strung out Indian file, we ran along the base of the dike to the first group of buildings, where half a dozen antiaircraft men joined us with a stretcher and a 30-caliber light machine-gun.

Still running, we suddenly came on McCreary, Matthews, Sawosko, and another man from the first squad moving slowly back toward the village. On the four A.M. patrol originally scheduled for us, they had run into a company of Germans digging into the orchard behind the windmill. McCreary was shot in the neck, Sawosko shot through the leg, but nobody had been killed. Matthews appeared to be badly frightened, and Sawosko, who was limping and whose pants leg was covered with blood, had a glazed look in his eyes. Our platoon medic, Longo, dropped out to take care of them.

"Go left!" Captain Winters shouted. "Over the dike, over the dike!"

One by one, we ran up the slope, across a two-lane road on top, and down the other side to a wide drainage ditch about a yard deep. We were in no-man's-land. A flat stretch in full view of the enemy hills across the Rhine, it ran about a thousand yards from this point to the river, and though cut by ditches, offered no cover or concealment. There were no houses nearby, no woods, no walls. I dreaded the time when the fog would lift, as lift it would.

We lay in the ditch and waited for the rest of the platoon to come over. Rice began to dig in, while the rest of us, figuring that we had enough protection and not much time, lay flat and hoped for the best.

The fog began to lift, revealing the windmill only a few hundred yards away. Its great arms silent, it seemed to be staring right down at us. I wanted to burn it to the ground.

"Let's go!" Rader said. "Third squad follow me."

Ducking low, we ran up the ditch toward the windmill, then cut left and stopped in another ditch. Rice began a second hole.

A shell whistled above us and burst, kuRACK! Right above the men we had left behind.

"Dukeman's dead," someone cried. "They got Duke."

While we watched, Christenson crawled up and took his cigarettes and Carson threw an overcoat over him.

"Poor Duke," Hoobler murmured, shaking his head.

The fog continued to thin. I wanted to return to my own side of the dike very badly. Higher and higher the mist rose as the sun warmed its top. Soon we could see patches of blue sky. The houses, high brick factory chimneys, and round kilns of the enemy villages of Renkum and Wageningen looked down at us from across the Rhine. The hills behind them seemed very high. We could distinctly see the pine trees that covered their slopes.

Captain Winters brought up the rest of the platoon and then shifted us forward to a ditch that paralleled the raised road leading to the windmill. There was a large factory building by the river at the opposite end of the road.

"Krauts!" someone yelled. "Kill 'em! Kill the sonsofbitches!"

Their chests and heads in sharp silhouette, almost a dozen Germans ran along a ditch on the other side of the road like clinking targets in a shooting gallery. We threw down on them with cries of joy and began firing. The range was only one hundred yards.

Farther down our ditch, Muck and Penkala, who had spotted an enemy machine-gun crew setting up to fire at us from the corner where the road joined the dike, put their 60mm mortar into action. With a loud pop, the first projectile soared into the air, arched high, and then tumbled to earth. The explosion blew both gunners off the ground, killing them instantly. Muck and Penkala walked the next shells down the ditch toward Wageningen.

"Beautiful, isn't it, Web." Hoobler smiled.

I laughed. The shooting had relieved my tension and tightened my bowels. My shoulder hurt from the slamming rifle, but I was glad to be fighting at last.

Captain Winters stood up. "Fix bayonets and prepare to charge!" he yelled.

Nobody cheered the order. Apprehensive about crossing a hundred yards of open ground without cover and in full view of the windmill, we rammed the bayonets on our rifles and rose to a crouching position.

Captain Winters jumped out of the ditch. "Let's go! Let's hear a little noise! Kill 'em! Kill 'em all!"

Screaming like Comanches, we ran out into the field, firing from the hip.

I began to sidle toward a ditch on the left when I was halfway across. Christenson, who was just ahead of me, wheeled about and goddamned me for shooting so close to him.

"Relax," I said. "I was nowhere near you."

I jumped into the ditch and ran down that. Three or four other men followed suit. Our charge ended at the raised road.

It was an anticlimax. Expecting to rush the Germans, we had stopped short with an obstacle still between us.

"That's O.K.," somebody said who had climbed a hedge and peeked across the road. "All the Krauts are dead. Mortar got most of 'em."

We sat down and began to wait. The mist was almost gone.

"I don't like this," I commented to Christenson, who was sitting beside me. "We're too exposed. Look!"

A barrage of airbursts crumped over a field three hundred yards behind us.

"They're feeling for us, those sonsofbitches," Christenson said in a low voice. "And when they get the range, God help us."

"This is a hell of a place to take a break," I added. "Why don't they do something?"

"Anybody up here speak German?" a voice inquired.

"Yeah, I do!" I answered.

"Come here quick! Bunch of Krauts in a garden."

Glad to be on the move again, I got up and ran north beside the road a hundred yards or so to a four-foot embankment that paralleled the dike. Several riflemen and Riley, a big, quiet Headquarters Company machine gunner attached to E Company, were lying on the mound, covering a patch of high green vegetables about seventy-five feet square. "Krauts," Riley said. "A couple have already surrendered."

Pointing my rifle down at the greenery, I stood on the mound and began to shout. *"Heraus, heraus!"* I yelled. *"Schnell! Hande hoch. Mach' schnell!"* I told them to surrender or be killed. They were surrounded, and they had just one minute to lay down their weapons and come in with their hands high. "You'll go to America," I promised. "Good food, no more war. *Heraus!"*

One by one, half a dozen burly Germans in spotted ponchos rose like sprouting flowers with their hands in the air. We frisked them as they came over the mound and sent them to the rear. Hard-eyed and almost middle-aged, they bore the double lightning insignia of the S.S. on their collar tabs. *"Polski,"* they cried, *"wir sind Polski,"* but their German sounded remarkably good to me. We waved them on.

I shouted once more at the garden and then told Riley to spray it with his machine gun to make sure we eliminated any stragglers. He grinned and swung his gun back and forth with a steady tooming.

A shell came in from the south with a loud swishing and burst among the vegetables fifteen yards away.

"Our own artillery," I yelled. "Let's get out of here!"

Another shell burst about thirty yards behind us. Joe Liebgott, the platoon interpreter, screamed with pain and clutched his elbow.

"One short and one long," I said. "Now they'll fire for effect." I began to run away from the mound. The others ran with me.

"Tell the artillery to cease fire!" we screamed. "They're hitting our own men. Tell 'em to cease fire! Cease fire, cease fire, cease fire!" We could see Captain Winters talking on the radio a couple of hundred yards south.

Peacock, who was much closer, ignored the cry and ran at us with a boiling face.

"Get back up there!" he screamed. "Goddammit, you can't run back to the rear!"

I gaped at him. "They'll kill us," I said. "Those shells will kill us all. Tell the artillery to cease fire."

"Go back, go back, goddammit, go back all you men!"

"Jesus," I said. "Oh God." I did not want to be killed by our own barrage.

One of the German prisoners, standing nearby, began to laugh at Liebgott, who had been interrogating him when hit by a shell fragment. Liebgott, who was Jewish and who hated the S.S., pulled out his trench knife and slashed and stabbed at the German.

Calling us deserters and waving his carbine at us, Peacock continued to shout for us to go back. Never having once come to the mound to help or direct us, he now drove us back there with frantic curses, then stopped well in the rear without bothering to send a runner back to Captain Winters.

Furious with helpless anger, we lay down on the embankment and waited for the barrage to fall on us. It was all we could do; we were obeying orders. The words that we had for Peacock were unprintable. For the first and only time, I felt like killing an officer. Talk of shooting this lieutenant or that captain was so much talk, I knew, for you were glad to have anybody along in action regardless of how rotten he was in garrison, but for once I truly understood the sentiment and sympathized with it. I would have shot him if I had had the chance. I had more against Peacock than I ever had against the Germans, who, after all, were just soldiers doing what they had to do.

"Smoke?" Riley said, offering a pack of Chelseas.

I shook my head. Goddamn the Army and every officer in it. And double damn Peacock. What a time he picked to exercise his authority! Where has he been the last eighteen days? He's so timid he'll get his own men killed before he'll go to a higher officer and ask a favor of him—especially a favor like telling the artillery to cease fire.

We are disciplined, so we lie here and take it, because, in the end, we are more afraid of defying the authority of an officer, backed up by the whole Army and a court-martial composed of officers like him, than we are of death by shell fire. Discipline is fear, not leadership, and we are afraid—not of Peacock but of the irresistible force that he represents. Afraid for our lives, we are more afraid of the system that holds us in thrall, and so we lie here and wait to be killed, because an officer tells us to lie here.

Several minutes passed. We began to relax. Soon the fear passed and with it most of the hate. I no longer wanted to kill Peacock, just to pound his face with a rifle butt.

Rader came up and told me to move back a few yards to a gap in the hedge across the road, and keep watch on the fields to our east. I took a stand by a wooden gate and began to stare toward Arnhem, which was about eight miles distant. A salvo of enemy airbursts cracked in the air three fields away, leaving a cluster of black smoke puffs behind them. They were getting closer; it was only a matter of time before they found our range. Pace and Hoobler came up to chat.

A German soldier sprang from a ditch two hundred yards to our direct front and ran across an open meadow toward the river. Amazed that a lone man would have the nerve to expose himself on a day like this, I jerked my rifle to my shoulder and began to trail him. When the muzzle was pointed at the leading edge of his chest, I squeezed the trigger. The German dropped as if he had been flattened by a pile driver.

"Yippee!" Pace cried. "You got him." He fired a tracer at the body.

Hoobler chuckled with delight and opened fire with his M-1. The shots made the German's body twitch and jump. I fired twice more to make sure, for I had a feeling that this was a runner, streaking back for reinforcements, and I wanted to make sure he stayed put.

With a kettledrum booming, a cluster of mortar shells walked toward us from the direction of the dike. I wondered why nobody bothered to shoot up the windmill. It was the only logical point of observation. If we lingered too long in one place, sooner or later the observer would be able to adjust fire right on top of us. He was coming closer and closer as it was. I wanted desperately to leave this open tableland for the comfort of Randwijk's cellars.

"We're going to attack the factory," Hoobler remarked, staring toward the Rhine. "Captain Winters thinks that's where the Krauts are coming from."

"Oh?" I said, feeling sick at the prospect of going a thousand yards deeper into enemy territory to storm a huge building with a handful of twenty or thirty men. "I don't want to do that. We'll be wiped out in the process."

Hoobler shrugged his shoulders.

Captain Winters brought the rest of the men across the road and moved us through the gate into a ditch that paralleled the dike. We lay down and began to wait.

We were beyond the windmill now. There was no front and no rear. From the windmill and the hills beyond the Rhine, the Germans had the observation on us. They laid down strings of mortar and artillery shells in the fields and ditches around us, coming closer and closer and closer. I wanted to get up and run all the way back to our village.

A squad of Germans rose from the ground about three hundred yards east and ran toward the dike. They had only gone a few feet when the British artillery caught them with a remarkably accurate barrage that knocked them flat in two seconds.

We cheered. The British were master artillerymen, and as long as Captain Winters' radio worked and we had contact with them, we would be assured of some measure of protection.

A cluster of mortar shells landed in the meadow beyond our ditch.

We threw ourselves flat and lay still until the order came to get going again, then rose to our hands and knees and began to crawl forward. Captain Winters was still talking about attacking the factory.

Thirty men attack a factory? I wondered, trembling with fear as another barrage landed nearby. God, isn't there an honorable way out of this?

We crawled over a big, freshly killed German whose face and chest were dotted with little red bullet holes and then lay down again. The cracking, banging, crumping death seemed to be all around us. I wanted to dig my way into the earth a thousand feet and pull all the dirt in after me.

Our ditch ended at a hedge some thirty feet ahead that cut off our forward vision. Curious about what lay beyond, Hoobler mounted a yard-high mound to our right and looked over.

"Krauts!" he yelled. "Jesus Christ, Krauts!"

He fired a shot at a point just beyond the hedge.

"I got one, I got one! Yahoo!"

Martin, another man, and I ran toward the hedge to open fire. We had only gone a few feet when a German machine gun fired a short burst at us.

A 200-pound man swung a baseball bat and drove a spike clean through my leg. The force of the blow spun me around and knocked me down.

"They got me!" I cried.

WHAT A CLICHÉ! I thought as I lay on the ground. "They got me!" I've been seeing too many movies.

Ashamed at my lack of originality, I watched the other men run back a few yards and turn around. Hoobler remained where he was. I got to my hands and knees, stood up, and limped to Roe, who was crouching in the ditch some thirty feet away. Shot through the right calf, I could feel blood flowing down my leg into my boot. There was no pain, however—only a stiff, pulling sensation every time I took a step.

I had gotten my wish—a million-dollar wound. My sole concern now was to withdraw to Randwijk. Over the dike, I said to myself, I have to get over that goddamn dike. I stopped beside Roe.

"Lie down," he said. "I'll fix it."

He rolled up my pants leg and inspected the damage. It was a very clean wound, enough to get me out of combat for a couple of weeks but not permanently disabling. The bullet, fired upward, had gone in one side and come out three inches higher on the other without mushing or tearing the muscle.

"Not bad," Roe commented.

He sprinkled both punctures with sulfalanamide and wrapped a shell dressing around my calf, then told me to go to the rear.

I grinned. Free at last—from Peacock, from the Army, and above all, from attacking the factory. "Thanks," I said. "This is what I've been hoping for."

"Good luck, buddy. Think you can make it?"

"Hell yes! I'll run all the way."

Seeing Guarnere close at hand and lightly armed without elaborate webbing or extra ammunition, I offered him my bandoleers. "I won't need them anymore," I explained.

Completely at ease on his elbow in the ditch, he held out his hand and took the bandoleers. I gave my hand grenades to a couple of other men and began to limp west as fast as I could go. Everybody wished me luck.

The antiaircraft medics were the last men in line. Some shells came in close as I approached them, so I lay flat until the firing had ceased, then got up again. My leg was growing stiffer, but there was still no pain, only a pulling. The medics tried to stop me as I went by.

"Stay here, buddy," one of them urged. "We'll take you out on the stretcher as soon as things quiet down."

"No thanks," I replied. "I'm not going to hang around this goddamn place one more minute."

"Can you make it?"

"Damn right I can. I'm not going to stop till I reach the regimental aid station." They smiled, and I laughed and told them that I did not intend to lie here and let the artillery zero in on me. They couldn't understand why I refused their help.

Taking a deep breath, I jumped out of the ditch, crossed a field, and went as fast as I could limp to the raised road where we had killed the Germans. I was on my own now, several hundred yards from the platoon and even farther from Randwijk, and I kept my eyes wide open, constantly searching, and my rifle ready, because I had no idea where the Germans were or whether we still held this area. At last I was across the road, with the windmill behind me.

I had two choices: to wriggle through two ditches in a long L to the dike or to cut across a couple of meadows at a 45-degree angle from here and hope that nobody would knock me down in the process. Impatient to reach safety, I decided to run for it.

I forced my way through the hedge, dropped into a ditch, picked myself up, and ran into the field where we had made the bayonet charge. A loud whishing came in after several seconds, and an artillery shell blew up behind me. My speed increased.

Another shell came in, much closer.

They're shooting at me, I thought, feeling the iron fingers of the giant clutch at my heels. The dirty bastards are firing artillery at a lone man, and a wounded one at that. Don't they know I'm through with all this crap?

WhishwhishwhishWHISH . . . BLANG!

I did not think it possible to move faster, but the last shell showed how wrong I was; it gave me wings.

A German poncho caught my fancy as I approached a grassy embankment two feet high. Make a good souvenir for my sister's boy, I thought. I scooped it up and ran on.

A barbed-wire fence prevented me from sailing over the mound to safety. I threw one leg over in such a hurry that my pants got caught on the wire. Four or five artillery shells of about 75mm caliber exploded in the field beyond the mound.

Christ, I thought, they'll kill me yet.

I ripped free of the wire and flopped down behind the low embankment, which barely concealed me. Panting and utterly exhausted, I contemplated another decision: whether to get up and run across the field to the dike or crawl beside the mound a hundred yards west, then follow another ditch south to the foot of the dike. The choice was obvious: I crawled.

Flat on the ground, digging the sides of my boots into the turf and dragging my rifle beside me, I moved with painful slowness through sticky old mud and fresh piles of cow dung. This was a heavily traveled cow path, but I was no longer particular; in fact, I would have crawled up the longest sewer in the world under the same circumstances. It was a terrible feeling to know that somebody was watching for me and would drop another barrage around me the moment I came up again.

Pausing for a rest after twenty or thirty yards, I glanced up at the dike and saw two 506th machine-gun crews setting up their guns on the crest.

They're insane, I thought. Don't they know what a perfect target they make?

The knowledge gave me selfish comfort, however, for I knew that no artilleryman would waste shells on a lone man when he could drop them on two machine guns. I got out my identification scarf and began waving it and shouting at the men on the dike to make sure they didn't shoot me.

"Don't shoot!" I yelled, standing up and running at the dike. "Don't shoot! Don't shoot!"

The gunners ignored me as they lay down and began to adjust their elevating and traversing mechanisms.

Stopping for breath at the first ditch we had entered when we had come over the dike, I knelt beside Dukeman's body and patted his shoulder and said goodbye. He was a long way from Colorado, the high, clean mountains that had never known the filth of war.

The machine gunners began to fire rapidly at a target near the raised road to the windmill.

I charged up the face of the dike, across the road between the gunners and the village, and down the south slope. Safety lay in the rear, I knew, and not in Randwijk, which was about 150 yards to my right, for the Germans might be there now. This was no time to find out.

I went into a ditch on the border of the first pasture beyond the dike and stopped for another break.

Three shells landed with a great roar on top of the dike where the machine gunners had been. I winced.

Artillery began to fall on Randwijk like heavy rain. Roofs shot into the air with tremendous booms and clouds of smoke and shards from the red tile. It was the end of our rest position.

There's nothing for me here, I thought. I have to go back, far back, back where the civilians are.

More determined than ever to stay alive, I crouched low and waded through a stinking, stagnant watery ditch to a line of poplars. They won't get me now, I kept telling myself, they won't get me now. Nobody's going to keep me from that hospital.

My leg was knotting badly, and movement had at last become painful, but I knew that I had to keep going. No medics would pick me up here, and there were no ambulances. Actually, I was quite happy to be on my own. Looking out for myself was something I always liked to do. It was the one thing I could do better than anybody else.

When I had trudged a weary two miles from the dike and was beyond the sound of firing, I came across a large farmhouse standing by a dirt road and a narrow drainage canal that ran from east to west. The hike through plowed fields, over fences in and out of mucky ditches, and through hedges had exhausted me so much that I decided to stop here until some G.I.s found me.

A middle-aged Dutchman saw me come into the barnyard, leaning on my rifle, and ran out to help me. He took my arm and led me gently indoors to a wonderful big kitchen where a number of other civilians, evacuated from the villages along the front, had gathered together. The center of attention, I went to a chair and sat down while a dozen people stared at me and murmured with pity in a language so thickly Dutch that I could barely understand one word in ten.

It was not surprising to be stared at, for, dung- and mud-smeared as I was, I would hardly be presentable even in a pigsty. I hadn't shaved for almost a week, my boots were filthy, and one leg of my pants was covered with dry blood. I told them that I was a wounded American paratrooper and asked them to send somebody for help. A boy was dispatched while the farmer's wife went to the stove and prepared some refreshment. I swallowed eight sulfathiasole pills to prevent infection and sat back and enjoyed the warmth and the attention. German pancakes almost a foot in diameter were set before me with strawberry jam and cups of hot coffee and warm milk. Several children clopped into the room on wooden shoes to stand at a safe distance and stare and whisper.

"*Danke, danke,*" I said, finishing a second pancake. "*Wunderbar.*"

The civilians nodded and smiled and murmured together.

I didn't care if I ever got to England. This was a better show by far.

Two men from F Company came in the door as I downed my third pancake. One, Haney, was familiar to me, but the other was a replacement who had joined the Company after I had been thrown out.

Haney sighed in disgust. "Oh Christ, Webster, it's you," he said. "The civilian told us a Limey soldier was dying up here."

I laughed. "All for nothing, isn't it? Well, give me a hand. I suppose I have to get out of here." Hating to leave the farmhouse, I stood up and thanked the civilians for their hospitality.

Haney and the other man helped me outside to a bicycle that they had brought with them and put me on it. My leg was so stiff that I could hardly walk. With one man on each side, we started down the dirt road beside the small canal.

"I thought F Company was attacking the windmill," I remarked to Haney. "How come you're still back here?"

"Only one platoon went out. The others are still in reserve. How is it up there?"

"It's a mess, just a goddamn mess."

"Isn't it always?"

They left me at a little road junction with an earnest young civilian with some sort of armband on and a bazooka team that had dug in beside the canal and told me to lie down and wait for the battalion medical jeep, which was making periodic trips through here from the front.

Free at last to relax, I gave my rifle and webbing to one of the bazookamen and took off my helmet and rubbed my scalp, which always itched under long confinement. I rolled up my .45 in my identification scarf and hid it in a jacket pocket, to keep it from being stolen by the rear-echelon medics. The jeep arrived a few minutes later.

Driven by an old sick-call acquaintance, it bore on a rear stretcher Sergeant Boyle of E Company, who had been hit in the shelling of our village. A fragment had laid open the back of his thigh from knee to buttock.

"Hold tight," the medics said, putting me on a stretcher over the hood, "we're in a hurry. Have to get Boyle back as fast as possible."

After driving about a mile and a half at top speed, we pulled into the village of Zetten-Andelot and stopped at the schoolhouse, a low building of dark red brick that served as the regimental aid station. I got off the stretcher, went indoors, and sat in the dusty sunlight of a back window. Covered with G.I. blankets, the bodies of four dead paratroopers lay beyond the window in a narrow alley.

God, I thought, looking out at them, how long does this have to go on?

A dead-white civilian in a black suit lay moaning on a large table in the center of the room while Major Kent, the regimental surgeon, and Doc Feiler, our wrenching little dentist from Greenwich Village, worked over him. Several enlisted men from Regimental Headquarters Company moved about in the background.

This was the first place in the evacuation chain where a wounded man could get really adequate first-aid treatment, and there was a saying that if a man could live till he got here, then he would probably live all the way to the general hospital. Morphine injections and plasma transfusions could be given by almost any aid man at the front, but the really vital attention started here. Whenever possible, the regimental aid station was set up indoors in the sturdiest building available, whether a story, factory, office, church, or railroad station.

Other men, more seriously wounded than I, were brought in moaning, cared for briefly, and taken away in ambulances, while I and the other walking wounded sat in silence against the wall with our backs to the dead men and waited for our turn. It was a strange waiting room, with its little desks and chairs and schoolroom pictures on the walls, the dying civilian on the table—they were giving him plasma now—and the dead men on stretchers outside. Everybody talked low. The only sound was the moaning of the civilian.

Worn out by my day over the dike and so many sleepless nights before, I felt an overwhelming urge to cry, a hate and disgust that I could not stifle.

Enough, enough of this! I thought, seeing Dukeman dead, the shells falling on the dike, our little village blown to pieces, Sergeant Boyle in agony on the rear stretcher. Oh God, get me out of this now and forever more.

Our Home Was Secure

I CAME BACK TO THE OUTFIT WHEN THE SNOW WAS MELTING ON the 7th Army front in Alsace. It was February, 1945, eight months after D-Day, and it seemed to me as if the war would never end.

Europe, I thought, spitting over the tailgate of the truck that was taking me from the last replacement depot to E Company, God, how I hate Europe. I glared at the cold, wet countryside. Gray snow still lay in the north hollows, but the rest of the low, bare hills were slimy brown with rain.

We were moving up to the front. The rumble of artillery fire got louder, hushing the chatter of the other men in the truck, and I looked away from a Europe that I hated and watched my companions to see if they were as depressed as I was. We had all been wounded in Holland or Bastogne and had been weeks or months away from the outfit.

Only four men are left now, I noticed with a start. An hour ago we had a truckload, and it was noisy and cheerful. But that was before the artillery got so loud; now the men are quiet, lonely, preoccupied. They're probably thinking the same thoughts that I am—thoughts of home.

Home! I laughed to myself.

Home is a hole in the mud, a bedroll in a haystack, a night in a wet ditch lined with dead men. Home is the 88s, sucking wind, that burst with a blinding clang. Home is the mortars that walk around you in the lifeless meadows. Home is the airbursts cracking one field over and the bullets that snap and pop in the leaves above.

It's some home, I thought, gripping my rifle hard and trying to shut out the steady bamming of the artillery as it came closer and closer, but where else can I go? This is the only place in the Army for me. I know most of the officers and men by name or reputation. We've shared all the jumps from Georgia to Holland; been on the same dull field problems; slept with the same whores in London. I could never be a clerk or truck driver after that; I have no bond with the rest of the Army, who are playing it safe without fear or courage or camaraderie. They go to town sloppy and whine like sick dogs. I don't want any part of them; they're too soft, too smart, too slick. If I can't be in the paratroops, I don't want to be in the Army. I'll never go back to rear echelon.

I turned my head and glanced out to see where we were. The truck hit a dip, splattering my face with mud. I cursed and felt like crying. The cannons were very close now.

It's a lousy world, I thought, staring at the rainy farmland. All those sullen, silent half-timbered houses; the rutted roads dug deeper by an army of trucks and tanks; the shelled fields and chopped trees and piles of manure in the front yards. This is Europe, poor damned, drained, and beaten Europe. Why can't we fight at home? Think of all the liquor you'd get in a place like Greenwich.

A G.I. who had stopped on the shoulder to let our truck pass caught my eye as he stood and watched us. His green jumpsuit with its big canvas side pockets was black with smoke and rain and dirt and mud, and he was so dead and passive that he didn't even curse our driver as he splashed him, but his helmet bore a white spade with a short white bar below—the markings of the 2nd Battalion, 506th—and the sight of him made my heart leap. My outfit, I thought, looking forward to seeing my friends again, that's my outfit.

The truck passed a straggling column of men with mess kits in their hands, slowed down, and stopped at a large, white, stucco farmhouse. "2nd Battalion!" the driver yelled back at us. "Anybody for the 2nd Battalion?"

"Ho, ho!" I replied, very excited. I wondered who would be left and what kind of stories they would tell and where we would go next. I stood up, shifting my .45 to my right side, slung my rifle over my right shoulder, and jumped off the tailgate. One of the other men, who was from the 3rd Battalion, handed me my duffel bag. "All clear!" he shouted to the driver. "Let's get the hell outa here!" The truck lurched forward, leaving me alone in the road.

I sighed and stared at my surroundings. It was a muddy little village of old houses with steep, German roofs. Everything looked tired and cold and wet and shut down. Where do I go now? I wondered, and who will be left when I get there? I started toward the house.

Bill Morganti, the tattooed man with the pirate mustache, the great wit, and the warm heart, came around the corner with a dark green bottle in his hand with a white-enamel snap-on cork. "Webster," he said, "where the hell have you been?"

I was so glad to see him still alive that I could hardly talk.

Noticing my eyes drop to the bottle, he smiled and said, "Schnapps." I nodded. "The local Krauts make it out of potato peels. Good schnapps is made from cherries; this stuff is made out of potato peels."

He weaved a little, and I asked where E Company was located.

"C.P.'s in the next house," he replied. "We just came off the line. We're moving out tonight, but the bastards made F Company pull a patrol anyway. No sense at all, but they had to keep the men busy. Killed a couple of good men. This freaking outfit."

Morganti walked off, and I began to wonder whether I should have come back after all.

I TURNED RIGHT and walked across a cobblestone courtyard thick with slippery mud and manure to the C.P. building, where I knocked on the door.

"Come in!" a voice cried.

I entered a narrow hallway piled with Army radios and musette bags and bazooka ammunition. The air was warm and close and rich with the homey fragrance of coffee and cigarettes and sweaty clothes.

This is a good deal, I thought, looking around, but it can't be too good or too permanent, because they're not taking care of it, they don't even bother to wipe their feet or scrape the mud off the floor. I guess they're just passing through; if they were settling down, they'd clean it up and keep it neat. I went through an open door on the left to a room where I heard conversation.

It was a large, whitewashed parlor with a low, beamed ceiling. A tall, square, blue-and-white porcelain German stove stood in one corner, filling the room with a fierce, wonderful heat. I looked from the stove, which fascinated me because it was the kind I had read about in fairy tales but had never seen before, and saw two men watching me from behind a bare wooden table. I was surprised to see them, because they had not been in E Company when I had left.

One was a thin young man with a rather plump, almost babylike face and large brown eyes. His hands were white and clean, his face smooth, his jumpsuit looked as if it had just been laundered. He was the 1st sergeant, age 22.

I glanced from him to the Company commander and frowned. What had happened to our old Company commander? I knew what had happened to the old 1st sergeant—his thigh had been ripped open from knee to buttock by a shell fragment in Holland, and we had ridden from the front in the same jeep—but our old Captain Winters, the medal winner, who was big and hard and aggressive, seemed like the kind of man who would live forever. Now he was gone.

Still frowning and puzzled, I took off my helmet and stood before the two men, scratching my head and reluctant to salute. "Is this E Company's C.P.?" I inquired.

"Sure is," the 1st sergeant replied with a warm enthusiasm that made me think he might not be so bad after all.

"Hello, Mann," I said. "When did you transfer from F Company?" I smiled at the captain. "I thought you were in D Company, sir." I had heard of his reputation as a reckless, savage man, and I was glad to have him for a Company commander.

"We came in at Bastogne," the captain said. His name was Speirs. He came from Boston. His voice was hard and harsh, his eyes cold and narrow, his teeth stained with tobacco, but his smile was honest and sincere. "Captain Winters is a major now, up at Battalion. Glad to have you back, Webster." He smiled again, and I knew that we would get along well. "We need men like you. Better get some chow. We're moving out in a few minutes. Going south to Haguenau."

"Yeah," Sergeant Mann butted in. "Half the town is ours, and half is Kraut. The rumor is that we're going to take the other half. Guy in S-2 says they're using railroad guns and the Maginot Line on the doggies. Shells are coming in at the rate of eight hundred a day. It looks rough as a cob."

"I hope it isn't *too* rough," I said. "I want to break in easy." I nodded to them and left the house in search of the chow line.

A soldier with an empty mess kit in his hand came out of the second house away and started toward me. Something in his gait and bearing caught my eye. The posture was familiar—straight as a ruler, shoulders back, head high and challenging—and I recognized the helmet cocked flat against the left side of his head, the long, hard, finely chiseled face, the German black leather belt with its Gott mit Uns buckle and the Luger slung on the right hip.

"Marsh!" I yelled. "For Chrissake."

His eyes lit up, and he hurried over. "Webster! Keed, it's been a long time."

We shook hands. I was so happy to find him alive and strong that I felt warm all over. I had never been sure that he had liked me before.

Suddenly a battery of parachute artillery dug in behind the village fired a barrage: BOPBOPBOP! BOPBOPBOP! BOPBOPBOP! I ducked for the ground. Marsh smiled and pulled me up.

"That's hokay, keed," he said. "It's our own artillery. You'll get used to it again. Better hit the chow line. There ain't much left." He went down the street to a barn, and I started for the mess hall.

Two men from the 2nd Battalion walked out the front door as I went in. They glared at me with the assurance of old soldiers mentally spitting on a green replacement. Irritated by their air, I glared back. Who the hell are you? I wondered, you sonsofbitches. Old men! Probably came in after Holland. I started with this outfit at Toccoa. Who the hell are you?

Then I shrugged my shoulders fatalistically, knowing that it wasn't important anymore, remembering that it was always like this when men returned to the outfit: strangers everywhere, the old-timers thinning out. The Toccoa men are the strangers now, I thought. The replacements have taken over. We're outdated; we don't belong here anymore.

I went through the door into air that held suspended a rich promise of hot coffee and burnt stew and walked back to a large, medieval kitchen, where two 7th Army cooks were wrestling a thirty-gallon aluminum pot to a dumping position at the back door. They paused when they saw me.

"Just in time, buddy," one of them said, wiping the sweat from his face. "You almost missed the boat; we thought you guys were through. Here!" He plopped two pieces of toast on my mess kit and ladled a dipper of brown goo over them that looked like Grape Nuts in gravy. "Shit on a shingle."

I laughed, and he piled apricots and hard biscuits and jam on my other pan. I filled my cup with coffee and left.

The living room, which had been filled with soldiers when I had entered the house, was now empty. I sat down on an officer's bedroll, put my meal on the floor, and began to eat slowly and with great relish. It was the first chance in two months in the replacement depots that I had had to sit down and eat comfortably in a warm, well-lighted place. This is the rich, full life, I mused as I ate. Home cooking.

When I was halfway through the stew, I heard shouting outside. My stomach tightened and grew cold, and I began to eat as fast as I could. The shouting was followed by a rattling of weapons, the cursing of non-coms, the subdued griping of soldiers moving out. Someone opened the front door. "Hit it, hit it!" he yelled. "On the road! We're moving out."

The door slammed, and I shook my head sadly. The Army never changed. You could never get anything worthwhile accomplished. Go to the latrine, drop your pants, and bam! another formation. Start to read a magazine on your bunk and "Everybody outside!" Write a letter, and after the first paragraph, "Let's go! Chow call." Fall asleep in the field, and it was always, "On your feet, soldier! Break's over." Goddamn Army.

I dumped my leftovers into the stove in the center of the room, put the biscuits in my pocket, slung my rifle, and went outdoors.

The Regiment was moving out, and the artillery was giving them a covering barrage in farewell. BOPBOPBOP! BOPBOPBOP! BOPBOP-BOP! went the muzzle blasts. Whishwhishwhish. Whishwhishwhish. Whishwhishwhish, the shells whispered overhead. The salvo crashed a few seconds later in the enemy lines on the snowy side of the bare hills: bambambambambambambambambam.

I trembled. The sound was ominous. No good would come of it.

The guns rested a minute or two, then fired again. And again. And again. The guns reared back and belched black smoke, and the shells whispered high above and slammed down like heavy doors, and soon a dull, thick rain started to fall, as if in answer. The 506th was going to Haguenau.

Already, the 2nd Battalion was assembling for the move on the shoulder of the road. The men dribbled reluctantly out of the warm houses and stood wet and cold in the gray twilight, waiting, waiting, always waiting.

What are we waiting for now? their eyes said. For more of this? What's next? Who gets killed there and who gets wounded and who is captured or loses a leg or an arm and goes home to the States? No matter; we will find out soon enough. Whatever we are waiting for and wherever it is, it will keep. Why rush it? Why hurry?

They had been in a hurry once, before D-Day—they had marched

115 miles in three days and run a seven-mile mountain in forty-five minutes—but that was long ago, in the days of innocence, when they were
easily impressed and could be made to hurry. They were in a hurry no
longer. Normandy, Holland, Bastogne, Alsace—what are we waiting for
now?

"Easy Company, over here!" Sergeant Mann shouted. He moved about
briskly, clean and young and still quite eager, and lined the men up
three abreast, but it took some time, for the men could no longer be
hurried.

About forty of them finally straggled from the barn where Marsh had
gone. They wore a motley array of raincoats and field jackets and German shelter halves. Some of them wore woolen G.I. overcoats, others
truck drivers' mackinaws or tankers' jackets that they had found in the
Bulge. Some men had piled little rolled sleeping bags on top of their
musette bags and lashed them down with bootlaces, while many more
made hobo bedrolls and looped them in a horseshoe over one shoulder
with the ends tied, Russian style. There were many German pistols on
their belts and no gas masks, and the griping was both universal and
profane and yet strangely cheerful, for every move made them talkative.
The next place, they hopefully rationalized, couldn't *possibly* be this bad.

I passed the column on the run, my mess kit clattering, got my gear,
and came back. "Goldbricks up front!" someone yelled as I went by the
third platoon. I grinned. It was good to be back where you were known.

I stopped at the first platoon, which was at the head of the column,
behind company headquarters, and stared at them dumbfounded.
There are only eleven men; a platoon should have forty. I counted them
again to make sure, but there were still eleven. I felt like crying.

McCreary threw back his head and laughed. "Well, well, howdoyoudo," he said. "Where the hell have you been?" He and I had wound
up in the same hospital ward in England after evacuation from Holland,
but he had rushed back to the outfit when he learned that they had returned to base camp, because he wanted to set up a pressing shop with
Matthews.

"Where have I been?" I said. "Replacement depots. And rough it was,
too." I grinned. "How's the tailoring racket, McCreary? Press a lot of
pants in the Bulge?"

"Bite me, buddy, bite me. You're in the first squad now, Webster, the
better half of the first platoon: six men. We're loaded, we've got eleven

men in the platoon now." He shook the water off his Thompson and patted its barrel. I fell in beside him, because he was always good company and cool in action.

A sound of heavy tramping came up behind us on the road. I turned and saw the 3rd Battalion, which had left base camp at Mourmelon December 18th with more than five hundred men. There were about 150 left. They came on in four company groups ten yards apart, and they were out of step and wet and dirty and quiet with the silence that always set in near the front.

A man in the second platoon raised his voice in greeting. "Hey, hey," he shouted, "look at the glider-riders! Whattayasay, rear echelon?"

"Strayer's strays," one of them replied with a laugh. "It's the Walky Talky battalion." He waved to me as he passed, for we had both gone through the replacement depots together. "Hello, Webster. Seems like old times, don't it?"

I grinned. "Hi, Widdess. Let's go back to the 10th Replacement."

Widdess waved goodbye, and the 3rd Battalion filed out of sight downhill in the rain. It was followed a minute later by D Company, 35 men strong, leading the 2nd Battalion as it often led the Regiment. After they had passed, Captain Speirs turned and faced us and, marking time in place, shouted, "Let's go, E! Don't forget your ammo." He did an about-face and led us onto the road ten yards behind D Company.

The parachute artillery's pack howitzers were thundering in the background. Cold, heavy, winter rain fell on our helmets and bedrolls and ran down our rifle barrels and dripped off the bottoms of our raincoats onto shins that were already soaking wet. The cannon blasted, the shells whispered and landed with far-off, door-slamming crashes, and I bit my lip and thought of how old and familiar it all was and how depressing. And yet it was bearable, because I was back with friends.

MCCREARY BROKE OFF his favorite song and looked at me with a sly twinkle in his eyes. We had left the village behind with relief, as if something unpleasant had been buried there, and the farther we marched from it, the higher our spirits rose. One or two men even ventured to whistle. McCreary was the only singer.

"What's the story, Webster?" he inquired. "Where are we going?"

Marsh, who was marching on his other side, asked about the rumors at company headquarters.

"Mann says we're going to a place called Haguenau," I said. "Krauts got half, we got half. We're supposed to take the other half. Mann claims they're using railroad guns and the Maginot Line—shells coming in at the rate of eight hundred a day."

"Sounds like another rest position to me," Marsh commented with a wink.

"Rest position!" McCreary exploded. "My ass. Every goddamned rest position we've been in we've gotten the hell beat out of us. I don't like 'em."

"Aw, what's the matter, Mick?" Marsh asked. "You getting chicken? You want to be back in rear echelon with Matthews, drinking cognac and looting the B bags?"

"You're goddamn right, buddy, who doesn't? Well, here's the convoy."

In the light of the artillery flashes and what was left of the day, the trucks seemed as tired and dirty and battered as the men now gathering around them. Their windshields were cracked and punctured by bullets; bullet holes and the rusty gashes of shell fragments marked their bodies and fenders. Some of the doors and tailgates were sprung, and shrapnel had slashed long, thin slits in a few of the canvas tops.

This outfit's taken a beating, I thought; our trucks never looked so bad before. More than two months they've been going now—from the middle of December to the middle of February—and there appears to be no end.

Sergeant Mann, who had been conferring with Captain Speirs at the head of the column, turned around and yelled for the first platoon and company headquarters to get in the first truck and the second and third platoons in the next one. "Load 'em up!" he cried.

I boosted McCreary over the tailgate and handed him our weapons, then climbed in with the others and tried to settle myself comfortably in the tiny space left. After unbuckling my cartridge belt and setting my rifle butt down on the steel floor between my knees, I inhaled and pushed my shoulders back to force the people apart who were crowding me in on both sides. When I was finally at ease, I pushed my helmet on the back of my head and studied the men across from me, searching for a familiar face.

Well, I thought, smiling, if it isn't Sholty, "Moldy" Sholty, as Matthews
called him, the Jet. Sholty was a green replacement just before Holland.
Now he's an old man. I wonder what happened to the others; all that's
left are Sholty, Wiseman, Marsh, McCreary Cobb, Lyall, Martin, Rader,
Liebgott, and an ex–second platoon man, V.D.

"Hi, Sholty," I said. "Where'd you get the B.A.R.?"

"Hi, Web, long time no see. They gave me this up in the Bulge. All the
platoons have 'em now. Supposed to be one in every squad. An 88 got
our machine gun."

"Won any crap games lately?" For an amateur with an air of slow ami-
ability, Sholty was one of the luckiest crapshooters in the Regiment. He
was buying a farm in Indiana with his winnings.

"Haven't hit a game since Mourmelon," he replied. "We haven't been
paid for two months."

The driver raced his motor, and I turned to Marsh and asked what
had happened to the other men. "Where's Sawosko?"

"Got it at Foy."

"Oh? And what about Muck and Penkala?"

"They got it at Noville. Shell came right in their hole."

"God . . . Where's Julian?"

"He's dead, too, Web. Got it on patrol."

I wondered about the third squad. Where was everybody?

"Pace and Janovec got trench foot; they'll be back. Rice—you remember Rice, always digging in?—lost a leg in a barrage that hurt nobody else. Whytsell's been transferred to a diesel-repair outfit, and
Massaconi is back in rear echelon."

"And Hoobler. Where's Hoobler?"

"Dead."

Marsh looked away, and McCreary told me how he had died while the
medic was off looting the dead. They wanted to shoot the medic when
they caught him, but it was all talk, and so he was never punished.

"It isn't fair," I murmured. "It just doesn't seem right. They were the
old boys who had never been hit before." I had learned in the replacement depots that Mather had also died. My first and finest squad leader,
the noisy, reckless redhead, unwounded in two campaigns, he had been
killed at a crossroads by a distant machine gun while moving up to the
front. His best friend, Vogel, couldn't eat for two days afterward.

"A lot of guys who were never hit before died in that goddamned

Bulge," McCreary said. "I'm telling you, buddy, it was a rough sonofa-bitch."

I nodded. But there was one person missing who would not be missed. "Say," I said, smiling, "where's Lieutenant Peacock?"

"Home on rotation."

"No kidding? I'll be goddamned."

"Yeah." Marsh grinned. "Mick was so glad to hear he was leaving that he got out of his hole and ran over and shook his hand. Peacock thought he liked him." Marsh laughed. "Mick told him it couldn't have happened to a better guy."

The Army, I thought: All the good men killed, and Peacock sent home on rotation.

Our driver, who had let his motor idle, shifted into first, and the truck lunged forward. I closed my eyes and thought of Muck and Penkala, who were small, clean-cut men, close as brothers, and of little Julian, who was that great rarity, a gentle Southerner. Hoobler was dead too. It did not seem possible. He was the only person I ever met who thoroughly en-joyed war, and now he was gone.

The cold iron truck bounced stiffly up and down, slamming us from side to side, and the rain fell on the canvas with a drumming patter. Karl Sawosko was dead. Where was his guitar? He and Hoobler had stayed up half the night in the barn at Uden, just singing songs. Now they were both gone. But Peacock was alive and home on leave.

A gust of anger blew through me. Then I sighed and closed my eyes, because I knew that anger was useless. I could not change war or the Army.

"Send me a letter," Sawosko used to sing, "send it by mail. Send it in care of the 506th jail."

I fell asleep and began to dream of the Camp Mackall guardhouse and of its carefree AWOLs, who used to sing the same song. How warm and cozy it was, and what a good time the AWOLs had there!

The rain fell, the guns went off, other soldiers passed in the night, and I smiled in my sleep. There was no camp like Camp Mackall.

THE TRUCK JOLTED to a halt, as if it had hit a wall, and I woke up in vi-olent fear, terrified by the night and the airless silence that had sud-denly replaced the noise and motion of travel. I hope it's only a dream, I thought, seeing nothing. I hope I wake up in the English Speaking Union. Or maybe I'll be in the hospital—that would be even better.

Then my eyes adjusted to the darkness, and seeing the men around me, I knew, with a sudden feeling of despair and depression, that it was no dream. There was Marsh, McCreary, Wiseman, Sholty, Rader, Liebgott, Lyall, Martin, and Cobb. The rain was still falling, the night was even blacker, the front was close. I should have known better than to dream, for whatever dreams I might have had all ended when I was sixteen and had run away to Gloucester to ship out on a fishing schooner. The schooners were diesel hulks, so I went back to school. That was the way my dreams always ended. The Army was no different.

Men were talking low outside and banging their weapons on the ground as they unloaded from the trucks ahead. Everything was unseen and unknown and mysterious. I gulped with the fear that always came over me when we moved into a new position at night.

Sergeant Mann raised the back flap and told us to get out. I stood up and watched the scene that was unveiled as Marsh and McCreary rolled up the flap.

We had stopped in the middle of a wide street that had been heavily shelled. Gutted white houses, grinning with black shell holes, stood like skulls squeezed flat behind the sidewalks. The rubble that had fallen into the street in the shelling had been bulldozed back against them in a mound five feet high. Concrete telephone poles with black wires that dangled like broken gut leaders ran up into the sky at regular intervals from the rubble. The cobblestone road was pocked with shining, water-filled shell craters. Several men were whispering together on the opposite sidewalk as if they were afraid to break the spell of death and desolation that lay over everything.

After we got out, we crowded together until Sergeant Mann came back and told us to spread out. We shuffled apart a little until he left, then drew together again, for the air of the city made each man long for company. Sergeant Mann returned a few minutes later. "Lock and load," he said. "We're going on outpost."

Outpost! I said to myself, visualizing two men in a slit trench three hundred yards ahead of the Main Line of Resistance. I certainly picked a fine time to come back.

The night was a collie that barked and whirled around us, and we were the sheep, pushing together for warmth and courage. We stumbled

after the 1st sergeant for several blocks and then bumped to a halt beside a high wall topped with concertina barbed wire.

Always the cautious soldier, I looked carefully for cover from shell fire
and saw none. My stomach felt cold and tight, and I breathed as lightly
as possible, afraid that the least noise would call down a barrage. The
only sounds were a few whispers and the far-off rumble of the idling
trucks' motors. The rain felt very cold. I waited stiffly for the first
rustling of the shells that had been promised in such large quantities.

The trucks left with the dry grating peculiar to their kind and slam-
banged out of sight. A single cannon fired in the distance.

I held my breath as the shell whispered overhead and landed with a
faraway bam in the other end of town. The explosion echoed up and
down the empty streets. I exhaled in relief. The other platoons moved
out.

Now Marsh, who was our acting squad leader, conferred with Mann.
The latter went off with the rest of the Company, leaving us alone on the
sidewalk. Marsh told us to wait till a guide came who would lead us to
our positions.

"Let's get off this sidewalk and find a little cover," I suggested.

McCreary, who was nearby, feigned surprise. "What's the matter with
you?" he asked sarcastically. "Nervous?" He shook his head and clucked
his tongue. "You were always too careful."

"Hmmm." I stared at the empty street, looking for cover. The house
across the street had possibilities; it had only been hit once. Well, I can
always run for it and hope a door or window is open. I heard a man's
footsteps approach and glanced away in fright.

It was an infantryman with the Cross of Lorraine patch of the 79th
Division on his shoulder. Perfectly unconcerned, he kicked and scuffed
his way toward us with his rifle slung. "You guys going to relieve us?" he
inquired aloud.

"O.P. 2?" Marsh replied.

"Yes."

"That's us, buddy. We always get the shaft." He raised his voice at the
men huddled around him in the rain and said, "Let's go. Moving out.
Five-yard interval."

I took my M-1 off my shoulder, tightened the sling, and checked the
chamber to make sure the gun was loaded, then ran to catch up with the
others. The infantryman had already moved off at a fast, careless pace,

with Marsh and McCreary beside him, and I did not want to lose them any more than a dog likes to lose its master in a thick crowd. We went through the silent city, stumbling over rubble, falling off high curbs, tripping on chunks of brick, and wading in flooded shell holes, until McCreary broke the silence by asking about the position.

"Watch the wire!" the guide said, holding down a strand of barbed wire that curled across our path. "Here's the deal: outpost in houses."

"Houses!" McCreary exclaimed. "I'll be goddamned. Who ever heard of outpost in houses?"

"Sure, it's a snap. The Krauts sit in their houses, and we sit in ours, and the reserve Battalion makes the patrols. We get a little artillery and a few mortars. Haven't had a direct hit yet."

"Sounds like the peacetime Army." Marsh grinned. The guide nodded.

Two smiling infantrymen passed us on their way to the rear. Their hands were filled with bandoleers that clacked together and swung back and forth like pendulums. I hurried after them and asked if they could give me some ammunition.

"Sure, buddy. Here, take a couple. We don't need 'em anymore; we're pulling out. Going back to rest camp. Hot damn!"

I crossed the bandoleers over my chest and ran to catch up with the others. I felt much better now. If you had too much ammunition, you could always leave it by the wayside. But if you had too little . . .

After winding in and out of streets and alleys and across backyards and vacant lots until we seemed to be hopelessly lost, we came to a big, open parade ground, about two hundred yards square, that was surfaced with stone paving blocks shining in the rain. Long, dark, Victorian brick barracks three stories high, with very steep slate roofs, bordered three sides of the parade ground. The fourth, or south side, ended at a low stable. All the buildings had been heavily shelled, and there were craters scattered irregularly about the open space.

The guide raised his hand and halted us. "Spread out," he whispered. "They got this place zeroed in." He unslung his rifle, and holding it ready, trotted onto the drillfield.

He went along the front of the west barracks, darted across a narrow road, and hurried close to the north building. A safety catch snapped off a rifle in the darkness of a big doorway with a pointed arch in the center of the barracks. "Halt!" someone hissed. The guide gave the password, and we moved into the doorway.

We walked up a flight of stone steps ten feet wide and six feet high and halted in a level entryway, where a guard stood watch in the shadows. This was the platoon C.P., he told Marsh. Martin, who was the acting platoon sergeant, took Wilson, Lyall, Liebgott, V.D., Rader, and a new man, Crist, in with him.

"I guess you guys are on outpost," the guide said to us. "Let's go."

We walked close to the C.P. building, dashed across an open gap, and went into the stable. Picking our way over fallen beams and piles of rotten hay and old manure, we came to a hole in the back wall about a yard wide and four feet high. One by one, we crouched, and passing through the hole, dropped down four feet to a bare, cratered field fifty yards square.

Diagonally across from us on the left, on the other side of a narrow road, was a ghostly white house as tall and square as a Gordon's Gin bottle. Its roof was a patchy mass of loose shingles and uneven mortar holes. Shells of a large caliber had punched other holes in its front and blown out all the windows. From the lines of bullet holes that crossed and recrossed the walls, it appeared to have once been a strongpoint that had been taken by direct assault.

The house was probably the neat and placid home of a middle-class family before the war, but it was an outpost now, our guide told us. He had no idea what had happened to its owners. The mother and little children had probably been taken off to slave labor camps by the Germans and the father gassed or shot or worked to death in a lager.

We crossed the cratered field on a slippery mud path and scurried over the road to an eight-foot iron fence that enclosed the front yard. The road ran north on our left a hundred yards to the bank of a creek, where it curved and went between it and the east barracks. A small house stood alone on the other side of the creek, 150 yards away. To our right, the road went straight for 50 yards to a wooden Army bridge over a slough that emptied into the stream. Beyond the bridge was a triangular grove of beech trees so stripped and withered by shell bursts that they were more like bare poles than living trees. The grove was about a hundred yards wide at its base. A line of houses, dark and dim in the falling rain, lay beyond the trees.

When everybody was across the road, we followed the iron fence south to a sloping driveway converted by the artillery into a rock garden of jagged masonry. We went down the driveway to a two-car garage in a half basement. There were three inches of water underfoot, and the air smelled strongly of urine ammonia and the chocolate of ordure.

Almost a dozen infantrymen were crowded together at the far end of the garage, impatiently awaiting our arrival. They were loaded with gear and moving about like restless horses. One of them shined a pencil flashlight on McCreary. "101st Airborne, huh?" he said. "The Battered Bastards. We read about you guys at Bastogne. You done a hell of a job."

McCreary smiled complacently and was about to agree with him and tell him all about it, when the guide, who was apparently a noncom, told the men to leave. They trotted out without another word.

I watched them with gritted teeth. "Rest position, my ass," I said to McCreary. "I never saw guys so anxious to pull out of a rest position. No good's going to come of this place, no good at all."

WE HESITATED BRIEFLY in the garage, as if unwilling to face the fact that we were once again on line, and then Marsh snapped us forward with a "Well, goddammit, let's get out of this swamp!" and led us through a door in the right wall.

We crossed a concrete hallway that evidently served as the community garbage dump. It had everything—ashes, ordure, urine, empty ration cans, wet cardboard boxes, old bandoleers, broken china, a torn blanket, and a mound of potato peels—but most of all it had a smell, the smell of a French railroad station where troop trains stopped and thousands of men had relieved themselves.

From here we entered another, more promising room. About fifteen feet by twenty, it was lit by an open kerosene lamp that gurgled and flickered and flared sideways with the drafts. A steel double bunk with dirty, stained mattresses stood against one wall. At the north end, beside the lamp, stood a sandbagged 50-caliber air-cooled machine gun on a sturdy wooden table, its muzzle pointed at a piece of fiberboard, covered with rags, that served as a blackout for the only window. A field phone lay next to the gun. To one side of the table was a square, flat-topped tile stove. It threw off a terribly dry heat. The stove had an oven and was evidently stoked with a pile of coal briquettes at its foot. A rough board bed stood opposite the double bunk. Its mattress was spotted and stained and smelled very moldy. Two other mattresses, covered with dirty civilian blankets, lay on the floor in one corner. Near them were three boxes of C rations and a box of D-ration chocolate bars.

The occupants, who had been hastily donning their gear, paused and surveyed us with interest. We clustered around the stove, holding our hands out to its heat, and one of the infantrymen frowned at us and asked where the rest of our men were.

"We're all here," McCreary said. "Six men and a B.A.R."

The infantryman shook his head. "We have eighteen men and two machine guns, and we'd still have a hell of a time holding this place if the Krauts ever came over."

McCreary snorted. He had little use for the infantry, who did everything with tanks and heavy artillery and were not inclined to be wild or reckless or high-spirited. "We can handle it, buddy," he said complacently. "We've been in worse places than this."

"You can have it." Our guide smiled. "Are you the squad leader?"

"No, Marsh here is."

"Then you both come with me while I show you the setup. It's a pushover. All you have to do is stand guard at night and scrounge all day. Officers never bother you, and the artillery isn't much." He paused and looked down at McCreary, who seemed awfully small. "You guys did a good job up in the Bulge. We read about you in the *Stars and Stripes.*"

"Oh yeah? Well, that was a lot of crap, saying we weren't trapped and we weren't rescued. Don't you believe it, friend. We were surrounded, and the 4th Armored saved our ass. Don't believe that goddamn *Stars and Stripes;* it's full of shit anyway. We had a rough time at Bastogne. No parkas, no shoepaks, no ammo, no nothing. When we pulled into Bastogne after riding all night in those open semitrailers, all we saw was a line of stragglers drifting out of town without helmets or weapons, mumbling to themselves. I asked an M.P. directing traffic what's going on, and he says, 'All these other outfits are pulling out, and the 101st is coming in.' . . . But the worst part of the Bulge came after the 4th Armored broke through and saved our ass. Hell, when we were surrounded, we were dug in good and the Krauts had to get out of their holes and come at us with no cover. But when we went into the attack with the tankers, then we had no cover and lost a lot more men than we had when we were surrounded. . . . Where's the nearest Krauts, buddy?"

"Did you notice that little house across the stream about 150 yards north of here?" McCreary nodded, and I listened closely. "We think it's a Kraut listening post, but we're not sure, because we've never seen them. That creek is the front. It's called the Moder River."

The sergeant led him and Marsh through the hall to another basement room, which was less comfortably furnished than the first one. I followed them, because I wanted to learn all I could about the position. We went through a squeaky wooden door in the east wall and climbed a wooden staircase powdered with rubble. Now we were on the first floor, about six feet above ground on the road side and ten feet above the river, which was some fifteen yards wide. We turned left and scuffed through a narrow hall that was ankle-deep in plaster and bits of brick and lath and halted at two French doors at the south end. The doors framed a small, outside balcony with a waist-high iron railing. Through them we had a commanding view of the woods and the stream below.

A rifleman stood watch at one of the doors. He turned when he heard us and looked at the sergeant, who told him to go below and prepare to move out. The sergeant beckoned McCreary and Marsh alongside with a jerk of his head. "Watch those woods!" he whispered. "If the Krauts ever come over, they'll probably land at the edge of the woods and sneak through 'em to take you in the rear. Another company's got a machine gun dug in near the road at the other side of the woods, but you'd better keep your eye on them all the time anyway. And stay away from the water! The engineers have mined all the bushes on the banks."

"What about the big field out there?" I inquired. I could barely make out a wide plain stretching away from the opposite riverbank.

"Nothing there for a mile but a big farmhouse five hundred yards southeast of here. There must be Krauts in it, because the artillery is always shelling the place, but we've never seen any. A mile away, on some low hills, is the Haguenau Forest. It's lousy with Krauts. You can see 'em moving around like ants in the daytime, but they won't bother you." He led us back into the hall and through a door on the left into a small room, saying over his shoulder that this was where they kept their heavy 30.

Two men lounging by a 30-caliber water-cooled machine gun sandbagged on a marble-topped table with thick, claw legs twisted their heads at our approach. The sergeant nodded to them and patted the gun barrel, which was aimed at the woods below. "This is a good place for your B.A.R.," he said. He told the others to bring their gun down to the cellar and get ready to leave. The gunners smiled and started fling-ing sandbags to the floor.

"Our living room," the sergeant said as we entered a high, white room that faced west and south. In worse condition than any other room, it had apparently been the center of resistance when the house had been taken. We went through it and across the hall to another balcony, which faced east and directly overlooked the creek. "A good guard post," the sergeant commented. "Who knows? The Krauts may get the notion to come straight over some night."

Before we returned to the basement, he paused in the hall and jerked his head up at the ceiling. "There's nothing much above here," he said. "Just two empty floors and an attic. We burned all the woodwork, the banisters, shutters, and doors, before we found coal for our stove. There's a toilet in the attic, but no running water. We use it when there's no artillery coming in."

The two machine gunners crowded past us and hurried downstairs, kicking the debris ahead of them. We followed after.

By now, all the infantrymen but our guide and the gun crew had gone away. We watched these last men gather their gear and ammunition. When they were ready to leave, McCreary, who was very friendly and well mannered, escorted them to the garage door and bade them farewell. They wished us luck and disappeared into the night.

Overwhelmed by the sybaritic luxury of good beds, a warm room, a hot stove, and lots of food and rations, McCreary smiled at us when he came back. "Boys," he said, picking out a can of Meat and Beans and set-ting it on the stove, "we got it made."

"LOOKS GOOD TO ME," Cobb said, sitting up on the top bunk and swinging his legs back and forth. "Where's the nearest Krauts?"

"Hundred and fifty yards north." McCreary pointed at the blackout board with his left hand while he turned the ration can with his right.

"That's nice, but isn't it just a little close?"

"Aw, hell, it's only a listening post."

"Who are they listening to—us?"

"The hell with the Krauts," said Winn, a new man. "I've had enough of 'em. Where's the booze?"

"Any gals in the neighborhood?" Cobb inquired.

"When do we eat?" Sholty asked. "I haven't eaten since supper."

"You fellows shut up and let me sleep," Marsh grumbled. He lay on a floor mattress, with his face to the wall.

"Let's not be antisocial, Marsh," McCreary snapped. "Just for that, you'll be the first man here to stand guard. We still have a war to fight. Sholty, get your B.A.R. and come with Marsh and me." He blew the ash off his cigarette and continued, "We'll stand guard an hour apiece at the French doors upstairs and then put in another hour on the phone down here. The phone man will wake up the next guy to go upstairs. O.K.? Now, Marsh, for Chrissake, wake up!" He yanked off Marsh's covers and rolled him away from the wall.

"Jesus Christ, Mick, why pick on me?" Marsh muttered. "You're the goddamnedest would-be squad leader I ever saw." He got up, stretched sleepily, put on his helmet, slung his rifle, and trudged after McCreary.

A mortar coughed while they were gone. We stopped talking and held our breath, but there was no explosion. "Must have been a flare," Cobb said. "Maybe they heard us." We started to talk again, more quietly than before. A high-velocity shell whipped past the garage door, sucking wind, and crashed near the stable with a report that was muffled by the rain.

"Eighty-eight," Winn said.

"Awful close," I added, shivering. "Well, hell." I started to unlace my boots.

McCreary and Sholty came back, and a flickering, smoky peace descended on the phone room. I loaded my .45 and put it beside my head on the mattress and closed my eyes. Cobb was already snoring on the top bunk, and Winn began to doze in a chair beside the telephone table. Soon the only sound was Cobb's snoring. We were on outpost.

A COPPER-COLORED C-ration can sailed through the air and landed with a bang in a wooden box in one corner of the living room, where we kept the phone.

"God," I hissed, "Meat and Vegetable Stew!"

"Corned Beef Hash," McCreary muttered, spitting out the words as if cleansing his mouth of something distasteful. He threw the can after mine.

"Meat and Vegetable Stew."

"Corned Beef Hash."

"Meat and Vegetable Stew."

"That goddamned 79th Division! Why didn't they leave us some decent chow?"

It was the next morning. The rain had cleared, and the sun had come up strong and bright, making the fears and forebodings of the night before seem asinine. Everybody was in a gay mood. McCreary and I were squatting like fakirs over three cartons of C rations bequeathed us by the former tenants and were passing judgment on the contents as we sorted them out. The undesirable brands were goddamned and flung angrily into an empty box, where they would be held in reserve, for use only in an emergency.

"Think we'll ever get any of those new C rations?" I inquired. I knew perfectly well what the answer would be, but I wanted to stir McCreary up a little.

"When the war is over," he replied, sucking on a cigarette stub, "they'll hand 'em to us as a bonus when we come down the gangplank in New York. The Quartermaster and the Air Corps are getting 'em now—like the good cigarettes. We have to settle for Chelseas and Raleighs and Corned Beef Hash."

"And Lemon Juice Powder, Synthetic," I said. I threw the glassine envelope at the box with all the force I could muster.

"What are we having for breakfast?" Marsh said, poking at the fire in the stove.

"Meat and Beans, buddy," McCreary replied. "Any water left for coffee?"

"Just a little."

"I seen a well in them woods," Cobb said. "Any volunteers?"

"I'll go," I said, putting on my helmet. I fetched a white enamel pail near the stove and went out to the well. An 88 zipped close overhead when I was crossing the bridge on the way back, and I told the others to move fast outdoors, adding that I thought the 88 was watching this place. McCreary put a frying pan on top of the stove and started heating a mess of Meat and Beans. "If only I had some garlic," he murmured, "even this might taste good." Cobb began to heat the coffee water.

The smell and the excitement of breakfast stirred us into action. We pulled out our G.I. spoons or folding German spoon-and-fork combinations and wiped them on our pants and prepared our mess kits. All converged on McCreary at the same time, but he held us off and bade us wait till our food was properly cooked, and so we talked of other things.

"Let's go scrounging today," Marsh suggested. He peeked over the chef's shoulder and noticed that the meat was sticking to the frying pan. "Better stir it some more, Mick."

"Bite me."

"We need skid," Cobb said.

"And lush."

"And spuds."

"And coal."

"And garlic."

"And women. Jesus, I could screw a sheep."

McCreary laughed and, opening two breakfast cans of dry C rations (which contained the biscuits, candy, sugar, and powdered beverage that complemented the meat cans), removed their packets of powdered coffee and set them on the table. "Couldn't be a better layout," he said, passing around the biscuits. "I could stay here forever; this is the way to fight a war."

Wheet, wheet, someone whistled for attention on the phone. I picked it up. "O.P. 2. Webster speaking." I listened with a scowl, then slammed the phone down. "Dirty bastards are planning a patrol for E Company. Everybody stand by. Shh!"

Cobb's hand paused en route to the frying pan. McCreary stopped in front of Marsh with a biscuit-can extended. Sholty, who was brushing his teeth, stared dully ahead, seeing nothing, his toothbrush firm on his upper gums. Marsh's hands stiffened on the bootlaces he was tightening.

The noise, which we had all heard, grew louder: a freight train puffing and chuffing in the sky. It came in from the east, choochoochooCHOO-CHOO. As it passed overhead, everybody involuntarily ducked toward the floor.

The train went on. A couple of seconds later there was a tremendous explosion a quarter of a mile to our rear. The house rocked back and forth.

"Hit him again!" McCreary shouted, shaking his fist at the sound. "He's Irish."

Everybody relaxed and started talking fast.

"Heavy stuff," I said excitedly. "A railroad gun on the Maginot Line."

We discussed the railroad gun for a while and how we hoped that it was true that large-caliber artillery was usually saved for rear echelon, and then started eating. When we were through, Sholty poured water into the frying pan to clean it.

McCreary was outraged. "Sholty!" he screamed. "Where's your manners? Don't ever clean a frying pan with water! It ruins the flavor of the food." He was livid.

Sholty belched at him and replied with a condescension that filled the room that the best cooks always washed their frying pans.

"Buddy," McCreary replied hotly, "where I come from, they clean 'em with a rag. A good chef would no more think of washing a frying pan than of drinking wine a day old. You have to learn those things, Sholty."

The phone tweeted again. With an air of I'll-straighten-you-out-later, McCreary answered the call. He listened for a while and then set it down with a sigh. "Portugee's giving us a new phone," he said. "The 79th Division wants this one back. Rader says Captain Speirs and Major Winters are coming down here to study the situation and terrain for the patrol, so nobody leaves till they're gone. Better clean your weapons; they just might hold an inspection."

"I wouldn't doubt it," I snapped. I wrenched my rifle toward me, as if it were to blame, and overcome with a propensity to gripe that had resulted in my being thrown out of F Company, cursed the Regiment for infinite chickenshit. I recalled the time in Normandy when we were dug in beside a swamp near St. Come du Mont and they rousted us from our holes to police the area for German and American equipment. "And no sooner do we get back to England than they start basic training all over again, seven days and two nights a week." The memory made me boil. " 'Have to work the replacements in,' the colonel says. My ass. Then we go to Holland and Peacock makes me sweep out his goddamned house—and me living in a wet slit trench!" I yanked a patch through my rifle bore and held the gun up to the light.

There was a scuffling in the rubble outside, followed by splashing footsteps as someone came in the garage. A thin, dark boy with a long, animated face and pop eyes darted in. "Hiya, fellows."

"Whattayasay, Portugee?" McCreary replied.

"Can't say it here, ha, ha, ha. How are the Krauts treating you?"

"We've been welcomed," Sholty said. "An 88, a 270, and a mortar."

"I still say it's the best goddamned setup we ever had," McCreary said. He looked around challengingly. "Tell us about company headquarters, Luz."

"Say, if you think you got it made, you ought to see those bastards! Freaking blue-star commandos." Luz was in company headquarters as a radioman, but his loyalty remained with the first platoon, where he had started. He bent over the table and detached the old phone from its cord and put a German one in its place. He had unrolled the German wire on the way from the platoon C.P. in the north barracks, and now he would roll up the 79th Division's American Signal Corps' wire on his return.

But company headquarters, a political scene not admired by riflemen, was still on his mind. "Them rear-echelon bastards are sleeping on *sheets*!" We couldn't have been more astounded if he had said they were walking on water. "They have running water, electric lights, and two cooks. *Two* cooks! One ain't enough for twelve men. Better start cleaning your gats, men. Some of you are going on patrol."

"Is that official?" Marsh inquired.

"From the company headquarters' latrine. Know any better source, Marsh?"

Luz rose from the table and, snapping his fingers as he went, jitterbugged to him and asked him to dance. He grabbed his wrists and started off. "Hotcha man, doing the Lambeth Walk." He yipped and yahooed. A former exchange student with the British 6th Airborne Division, Luz, who was a great mimic and consistently entertaining in both garrison and combat, turned on his English accent. "Blimey, I'm a Limey. Covent Garden, 'ere we come."

Marsh blushed and wrenched free. Luz trucked and pranced, while the rest of us laughed and clapped our hands. Everybody liked Luz.

"Whassamatter, kid, no sense of rhythm?" he said to Marsh. "I'm going C.E., I hear voices." He stopped and cupped a hand to his ear. Two men were talking in the yard outside.

"Must be the captain," Luz said. "Him and Winters left the C.P. right after yours truly. Let's go watch 'em draw fire." He led the way out to the garage.

The officers stood in the middle of the yard, below the French doors, on a slight mound like Napoleonic marshals at Austerlitz, and swept the scene with their arms, now pointing at the woods, now at the Moden River, now at the farmhouse strongpoint and the distant forest, where enemy soldiers were crawling about like upright ants among the pine trees. It was a clear blue day, with unlimited visibility, but they showed no concern.

We watched them awhile, muttering low about their attracting the attention of the 88s to our home, and then went indoors. Luz fetched the G.I. phone and started back, rolling up its wire on a hand reel as he went.

McCreary alone remained outside. When the officers saw him, they joined him on the threshold of the garage. "Hello, Major," he said pleasantly, as one equal to another. "Hello, Captain. Patrol going out soon?" He leaned against the wall with a cigarette dangling limply from a corner of his mouth.

"Yes, McCreary," Captain Speirs replied. "In just a few days. Platoon leaders will pick the men. S-2 wants some prisoners."

"They always do. Why don't they get 'em themselves, sir?"

The officers laughed and said goodbye, and McCreary returned to the basement in a thoughtful mood. "O.K., men," he said quietly, "the coast is clear for scrounging. Sholty, do you want to stay by the phone while we look around?"

"May as well. I have to clean the B.A.R. anyway. Hurry back."

"Remember," McCreary said to the men getting ready to leave, "everybody home before dark." He turned to me. "Let's go together. There ought to be a lot of stuff in these houses."

WE WENT OUT THE DOOR and through the musty, foul-smelling hall to the open end of the garage, where we paused to reconnoiter.

The flat, bare, brown land beyond the river was silent and peaceful, as if catching its breath after the rain, and there seemed to be a touch of spring in the air. Three P-47 fighter planes were circling lazily amid tiny black puffs of flak far to our right rear (for we were actually on the very tip of a long, thin finger thrust deep into enemy territory by the 7th Army on the Rhine plain of Alsace), but there was no sound of war on the ground. The sky was a clear blue that seemed even clearer after days of storm and overcast, and the air smelled fresh and wet and countrylike, with the fragrance of moist earth and decayed leaves. The snow had disappeared from the north hollows; hard little green buds were already pushing out on the tree branches.

I smiled. It's going to be an early spring, I thought, feeling a great relief. Maybe things will be better now; they are always better in the spring. I breathed deeply, grateful to be alive to enjoy the simple pleasures of earth and sky, and listened for shells. There were none. "Great day, isn't it?" I murmured.

"It sure is. Spring, goddamn!" McCreary inhaled. Everything was running in our favor, even the weather. "They say it was the worst winter in fifty years," he remarked, blinking at the sky and smiling. "Thank God it's over. Let's go."

He scurried up the driveway to the road, turned left, and ran across the bridge over the slough and past the base of the woods to the first house. "Dammit," he muttered. "We're too late." He pointed through the open door.

Two soldiers were leisurely pulling out wardrobe drawers and flinging their contents behind them with both hands to the floor of what appeared to be the parlor. One of the men, a square, squat person with wide shoulders, a long trunk, and very short legs, held up a tablecloth, examined it critically, and remarked in a wonderfully rich Brooklyn accent, "This'd make a choice scarf."

"Yeah," his assistant replied sarcastically, without looking up, for he thought he felt a camera hidden in the corner of the drawer, "if you got a neck like Gargantua, it'd make a hell of a scarf, a hell of a scarf, Eddie. It's O.K. for you, but it ain't for me, it just ain't my style. Goddamn! No camera."

I nudged McCreary, and we both walked in. When he heard us come, Eddie quickly shoved the tablecloth into a big pants pocket and stared at us belligerently until he recognized us. Then a huge grin spread across his lined, brown face, and he said, "A couple of boys from E Company. What are you guys doing here? This is protected territory; D Company got the franchise."

"We're just looking around, Weeks," I said. "Any houses left for us?"

"Sure, sure—across the bridge. Help yourself. Where are you guys located?"

We told him and invited him to pay a visit, adding that we were always home.

"Thanks. We got a 50-caliber in a dugout in the woods. Swiped it off the 10th Armored at Bastogne." Having noticed that his buddy had just slipped a crucifix and a pile of handkerchiefs into his pockets while he was playing host, Eddie Weeks, the former boxer and general character of D Company, dashed back to the wardrobe to get his share.

"Come on, McCreary," I suggested. "These guys won't leave us anything." I raised my voice and said goodbye to Weeks, but he didn't hear me, for he had had a sudden inspiration: He was on his hands and knees, rolling up the rug in search of a floor safe.

We ran back across the bridge and over the cratered field to the shelter of the stable wall, where McCreary stopped and lit a cigarette. Even outside, the stable gave off a disturbing odor of burnt powder, moldy hay, old manure, and horse piss. After lingering here a minute or two, we decided to follow the course of the slough back to a group of houses several hundred yards west, instead of going through the hole in the wall to the barracks area, where we knew some machine gunners and the men from the platoon C.P. were at large.

"This is a beautiful deal, isn't it?" I said. "We're warm and clean. No holes to sleep in, no officers riding herd on us. Eat all day and watch the war all night. We've got a ringside seat—with room service."

"Best deal we ever had, buddy, best deal we ever had." McCreary started off.

I walked beside him, sniffing the air as we went. It was a wonderful day to be alive—so much to see and do, so many roads and houses to explore. I had come back at the right time after all.

We turned onto a narrow street and walked along a sidewalk marked with white tape.

"Isn't that a minefield marker?" I inquired.

"No, it's just a night guide. Probably once led to a C.P."

Unconvinced, I walked as close to the tape as possible, knowing that it must be safe or the person who had laid it would have been blown up. The deserted houses all around us suddenly turned ominous. I loosened my .45 and put a bullet in the chamber.

We followed the tape for a block and then picked a house at random and went in, wrinkling our noses at the musty smell and stale air. We could tell immediately what had happened here, for everything was more or less intact, though somewhat rearranged.

Apparently soldiers had come to the door one day and told the civilians to leave immediately, without taking anything with them. The soldiers had then taken over. One of them had ripped off a heavy lace curtain, while another had broken some of the dark, Victorian furniture. A German or American bravo (but more likely the latter, for the Germans usually took better care of their billets) had flung a large Mason jar of preserved peaches at a four-foot wall mirror, breaking them both. The broken glass and the garbage lay where they had fallen. Smashed cut-glass decanters were strewn about the floor. The bureau drawers had all been pulled open, for this was the first act of any invader, drawers often being hiding places for jewelry, watches, cameras, sweaters, and wool socks. Some of the men also liked to fondle women's underwear.

It always embarrassed me and made me feel ashamed. I wanted to apologize to the owners for the mess that we made, to tell them that we were only looking for little comforts to make our life more bearable, but I would have been lying, for deep in all our hearts we hoped to find more rewarding treasures than socks or sweaters.

"That freaking infantry," McCreary grumbled, surveying the scene with disgust. "They beat us to it, just like in the Bulge. I'm telling you, buddy, we have to jump in combat to get first crack at the houses."

"Oh hell, if it isn't the infantry, it's the Krauts. You can't win in a place that's been fought over as much as this. Let's check all the rooms, to make double sure. They might have missed a lump of coal or something."

We drifted slowly through the house. I loved to explore abandoned homes, to see how other people lived, and although I majored in food and liquor and never took clocks or ashtrays or any other kind of Atlantic City–type souvenir (later lost or thrown away) that appealed to so many men, I joined every scrounging expedition just for a chance to go sightseeing. I liked to try to visualize the owners of these strange, deserted places. How many in the family? This looks like a little girl's room. And that picture on the mantel of the kid in the German uniform must be the son. What's the father's occupation? Lots of history books in the parlor. Maybe he is a teacher. The war's been on for five years—or is it six? How well have they been eating? This ersatz coffee is worse than Sanka. How can they chew bread so hard and heavy? Well, at least they're still canning pears and peaches. I love fruit.

There was nothing left for us in the kitchen: no food, no drink, no pot, pan, or bucket. McCreary muttered low and absentmindedly cranked a hand pump at the sink, bringing up a gush of old-smelling water that splashed into the dusty basin. He let the handle fall and then went up the back stairs. I washed my face at the pump and followed him.

The second story was in worse shape than the first, for the house had been hit by mortars. Chunks of lath and plaster lay white and chalky on the floor, and the bedclothes in one room had been ripped by shrapnel. From the bloodstains on the sheets it was apparent that someone had died here when the shelling had started. I stared at it and wondered who he had been, whether a soldier or civilian. How would you like to come home to this? I asked myself. A wrecked house and a bloody bed, smashed mirrors and torn furniture. I hope I never have a family that has to go through a war.

We returned to the kitchen and tried all the doors until we found one that led to the cellar. McCreary blinked at the semidarkness and felt his way down sideways, lighting a match at the foot.

The basement was flooded with black water that appeared to be rather deep. "Spuds!" McCreary exclaimed, pausing on the last step. "Looks like coal too." He eased his foot into the water. It was only four inches deep.

Lighting matches as he went, he swished to an empty gunnysack near the stairs, lifted it, and carried it to a pile of potatoes in the far corner. "Wonder how the infantry missed these?" he speculated. He began to throw them into the bag as if he feared that someone would catch him in the act and make him give them up.

I went to a mound of coal in another corner, picked up a gunnysack, and slipped the briquettes into it one by one. About six inches long by two thick and three wide, they were an excellent fuel.

When our bags were so full that we could barely lift them, we felt our way in the dark back to the kitchen. McCreary set his load down in the front hall, straightened up, and suggested that we take a break.

We stood erect, inhaling and throwing back our shoulders and working them around and around, and stared dully out the front door, which we had left open. A bird twittered far away, but there was no other sound.

With a great, ringing roar, a shell landed on the sidewalk five yards to our left. We threw ourselves flat and cursed. The day had seemed so perfect.

"Mortar," I hissed. Where had it come from? Who had been watching us? We were at least three hundred yards behind the front, hidden from enemy view by many buildings, and yet somebody had seen us and called down fire. "They've seen us, they've seen us," I said in a panic.

McCreary made no reply. Instead, he lifted his head quickly, like a dog that hears someone approach, and squinted outside. He appeared to be concentrating on something far away.

A few seconds later, another shell exploded, only a yard or two from the front door. The bitter black smoke puffed into the room. McCreary snapped to his feet, grabbed his sack of potatoes, and darted off.

Coughing and gasping and almost paralyzed with fright, I lay flat and shook my head to stop the ringing caused by the detonation. I felt lonely, abandoned, hopeless. We're hidden from the Germans, I thought, and yet somebody has seen us and told them to shell us. And it's not area fire, because it's too accurate. I couldn't understand it.

I waited several minutes for another mortar, then stood up and shouldered my sack. I listened very carefully for the faint whisper, almost never audible in the field, that was a mortar shell's only warning, and heard nothing, not even the tweeting bird.

They'll get me if I stay here, I thought, and if I go out, I'm likely to run smack into one of those damned things. Mick would laugh me to death; I'd sooner meet the mortar. He's probably laughing at me now. Oh well, the hell with it.

I jumped out the door, ran down the steps, and took off on the taped path. "McCreary!" I yelled. "McCreary, where are you?"

Shouting his name, I ran a short block that seemed very long, turned sharply with the tape, and bumped into McCreary, who was leaning against a brick wall, smoking a cigarette and waiting for me.

"What's the matter?" he inquired innocently, his eyes twinkling. "Scared?" He blew the ash off his cigarette and gazed up into the sky.

Still trembling and so excited I could barely talk, I wiped the sweat off my face and took a deep breath and told him I was afraid I'd lost him.

"You have to listen for those shells, buddy," he said in a rather professorial tone, "you have to time 'em. Walk slow and listen for 'em, and when you hear 'em coming, hit the dirt." He blew a smoke ring. "You ought to know that by now, Webster."

I looked down at him, so calm and cocky, and smiled, for he did not fit the popular conception of a paratrooper as a big, lean man; no artist would have asked him to pose for a recruiting poster. Short and fairly plump, his general appearance was genial and comfort-loving. He never exercised if it could be avoided, religiously dodged all details, and concentrated his energy on the pursuit of food, liquor, cigarettes, and women. Nevertheless, he was always calm and cool and forward in action. His humor and confidence was more stable and reassuring than Hoobler's had been, for Hoobler was a very rare person who actually liked war and continued to like it till the day he died. McCreary, who did not like war, was more like the rest of us and was therefore more intelligible. In some ways, he was an even better soldier than Marsh, who was lean and rough, fought in bars, and looked like the ideal paratrooper.

But still I disagree with his artillery thesis. "I don't listen for shells when I'm out in the open," I said. "Not me. I run like hell from cover to cover. The slower you move, the more time they have to hit you. You can't hear a mortar most of the time anyway."

"I can hear 'em, buddy, and that's good enough for me. Let's go." He blew the ash off his cigarette, swung his potato sack on his back, and started off.

We entered our house so quietly that we surprised Sholty in the act of taking inventory of the ration boxes. McCreary, who was by no means unsuspicious, stopped and watched him pick up a packet of coffee. "Well, well," he commented, startling Sholty, "howdoyoudo! Conning us on the chow, Moldy?"

A sheepish grin spread across Sholty's wide, Dutch face. "I wouldn't do a thing like that," he drawled. "I was just planning to fix you boys a little java. Anyway, it doesn't matter how much of this stuff we take now, because we's getting 10-in-1 rations tonight."

We nodded and dropped our sacks on the floor and began to empty them.

Sholty grinned. "Boy," he said, "spuds and coal! That's swell. You guys really did all right."

SUPPER THAT NIGHT was a gala affair. Each of us had returned with food or fuel or household knickknacks, and Cobb regaled us with tales of his explorations of the battalion front with his buddy Morganti, who had wind of a liquor cache lying close to a German position. Morganti, he said, was in O.P. 3, the first barracks near us, where two squads of Headquarters Company machine gunners were stationed.

Now Marsh was standing at the stove, stirring a pan of diced potatoes. For the time being, he had been appointed head of the household by our platoon leader, but he still deferred to McCreary in matters concerning the finer things of life. "Think they're done yet, Mick?" he said.

Sholty, who had been dozing on the top bunk, woke up and blinked down at them. "Aw, you guys don't know how to fix spuds," he said with disdain. "You have to slice 'em real thin and leave 'em in water awhile. Them's not thin enough."

"Nobody's asking you to eat 'em," Marsh said quietly. "There's plenty of C rations left—help yourself." He looked at McCreary, who was poking around in the potatoes with a trench knife, and sought his approval before lifting the meal from the stove. McCreary went on poking, so he speared a slice that looked especially appetizing and handed it to him on a fork. "Try this one," he urged.

His buddy took the fork daintily, popped the offering into his mouth, chewed it lightly, rolled his eyes toward the ceiling, and nodded approvingly. Marsh removed the pan from the fire. "Come and get it, men!" he yelled.

We hit the pan with a wild, scraping clatter. Sholty played a very active role in the assault.

"Well, well, howdoyoudo, Sholty," McCreary exclaimed. "I thought they weren't good enough for you. Come on, now, leave a little for the rest of us."

When the potatoes were finished, we relaxed on the beds to wait for darkness and guard duty upstairs. Still hungry, I decided to make a pudding. While the other men, who somehow never acquired a taste for them, watched in horrified fascination, I took four fruit bars that I had been hoarding from my pocket and laid them beside me. Duty-bound to be generous, I inquired dully whether anybody else would like one.

"I'd sooner eat Chopped Pork and Egg Yolk," Winn responded.

"You can say that again," Sholty added.

Cobb held his nose, Marsh frowned, and McCreary shook his head in benign tolerance.

"In that event," I said, brightening, "I think I'll make a fruit pudding."

"God."

I laughed and fetched my canteen cup. After unwrapping the fruit bars, which were composed of mixed dried fruit and were quite dark and heavy and sweet, I crumbled two dry crackers into the cup, added chunks of fruit, stirred in a little water for pliability and a little grease from the frying pan to give it a plum-pudding richness, and carefully tamped the dark mass into the cup with my fingertips, then set it on top of the stove.

The others watched in silence. Finally, Winn stood up and stared down into the cup. "Have I eaten it?" he asked, "or will I?"

"Wiseman's sending up three dozen more bars from the C.P.," I told him. "Want some?"

He shook his head. Eating fruit bars was something that was just not done in the Army.

McCreary, who was a gourmet at heart, was more understanding. He had been watching closely, with a smile of approval that he would never have expressed aloud, and as the rich pudding smells rose from the cup, he decided to try a novelty of his own. "Think I'll make a cheeseburger."

He got a can of K-ration cheese, opened it, and removed the contents, which resembled an inch-thick slice of orange log almost three inches in diameter, and sliced it in half. Next he took a similar can of Chopped Pork and Egg Yolk and dropped its contents in the frying pan. When this was brown on one side, he turned it over and laid the cheese beside it. Then he set the meat on one piece of cheese, put the other on top of it, and flipped the burger over and over until the cheese was singed and melted onto the pork. He ate it with a gusto heightened by the others' disapproval.

"Mick!" Winn exclaimed. "How could you?"

"The trouble with you guys," McCreary said loftily, "is you ain't sophisticated, you got no taste. Webster and me, we're connoisseurs."

I nodded. "Tell us about that tailor shop you were going to start in base camp. How'd you make out?" I addressed the others, for it was a good story.

"McCreary was so hot to press pants, he left the hospital before Thanksgiving. 'Stick around,' I kept saying. 'This is a good deal. If you go back to the outfit and they're in base camp, you'll be swimming in chickenshit. And if it's still on the line in Holland—well, why rush back to that? At least stay here for Thanksgiving; this is the best chow we've ever had. You know what those 506th cooks will do to the turkey—the same thing they do to chicken: chop it up with cleavers and boil it in flour paste, pinfeathers and all.' "

McCreary snorted.

"But he wouldn't listen to the voice of experience," I continued. " 'I got a racket, buddy,' he insisted. 'Matthews and I are going to set up a battalion tailor shop. I used to be a spotter in civilian life.' So he left before Thanksgiving.

"Me, I had no racket; all I could look forward to was details, field problems, and chickenshit. So I waited till Thanksgiving and payday and then started back. It took me two months, because they lost my records in the replacement depots. McCreary, though, had a racket. Tell me, did you press a lot of pants in the Bulge?"

"Yeah." Marsh grinned. "He sure did. Pressed himself into the ground every time he heard a burp gun."

McCreary bolted a mouthful of cheese and spluttered at Marsh for kidding his courage. "Now, now, you know that ain't true," he said hotly. "Tell the kid how rough it was. Tell him about Bastogne and Foy and Noville. Tell him about the buzz bombs and screaming meemies and 88s."

"Listen," I said, deadpan, "if you think it was rough in the Bulge, you should have been in the 10th Replacement. We had to stand retreat every night. Every goddamned night! Did you stand retreat at Bastogne, McCreary?"

"Oh, blow it."

The phone whistled. McCreary hmmphed at me and lifted it up. "O.P. 2," he said. He listened thoughtfully and nodded his head from time to time. "They won't like it and neither will I. . . . O.K., buddy, I'll tell 'em."

He hung up the phone and sighed. "That goddamn patrol. The lieutenant's picked the men."

Everybody stopped eating and looked at him. Who would it be?

"He picked 'em, not me, so don't cry in my beer. We're so damn short-handed down here that we can't spare anybody, but they're taking half of us anyway. It's the same in all the other platoons. That's right, Cobb, you're one of 'em. I'm another. And Winn, you'll carry the B.A.R. Sholty's just got a pass to Paris."

"MY GOD!" McCreary exclaimed, after the initial burst of complaint from the patrolmen had died down into muttered curses. "Dark, and we have no guard." He glanced at me.

"I'll go," I said, wanting to make up for a guilty feeling that had come

Public haircuts were given to girls who collaborated with the Germans in Eidhoven after the city was liberated on September 18, 1944. (Photo by Hans Wesenhajen).

Celebrating the liberation of Eidhoven. The soldier on the right, Webster wrote on the back of the photo, is Wiseman, "who dug most of my foxholes for me...He was a brave, rough and tough miner." (Photo by Hans Wesenhajen).

David Kenyon Webster in Eidhoven, September 1944. (Photo by Hans Wesenhajen).

The Berghof, Hitler's house for guests in Berchtesgaden, at the end of the war. The author and his friends joined in raiding the wine cellar.

*Captain
Ronald Speirs*

*Private
Ralph Trapazano*

Colonel Robert F. Sink.
(Courtesy U. S. Signal
Corps).

*Corporal
Donald Hoobler*

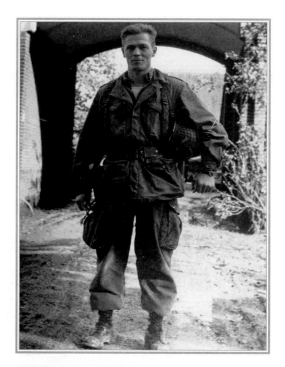

*Captain
Richard D. Winters
in Holland,
October 1944.*

*Private
Robert Marsh*

Illustration by David Webster.

*David Kenyon Webster—what the well-dressed rifleman will wear.
(the pistol is not issued).*

David Kenyon Webster is 4th row from the top, 5th from left. E Co. 506th in Austria, June 1945.

over me when others with more time on line had been chosen for the patrol. Winn, I knew, had not missed a day's action since the Bulge started, while Cobb and McCreary had both seen the main part of Holland and all of the Ardennes. For a moment, I had thought of volunteering to take Winn's place, for he was relatively new to the outfit and claimed that he had not missed a single E Company patrol so far, but the moment had passed. Though my guilt remained, I tried to comfort myself with the reflection that the new lieutenant, a mild young man not very sure of himself, probably would have sent me along, if he had known me as well as Peacock did. Not knowing me, he had chosen Winn instead. McCreary and Cobb, I knew, could take care of themselves, so I didn't feel as badly about them as about Winn. I was frankly relieved not to have been chosen, for a patrol in a city as settled and heavily mined as Haguenau was bound to be a rather unquiet venture.

I borrowed Sholty's wristwatch, put on my helmet, dropped my .45 and two hand grenades in the pockets of the truck driver's mackinaw that I had acquired in the replacement depots, slung a bandoleer across my chest, and with my M-1 in hand, went slowly upstairs.

The cold night air, coming so soon after the hot, stuffy cellar, made me shiver and cough, but I soon adjusted to it. Leaning against the wall by the left-hand French door, I stared past the balcony at the scene below.

The weather had turned damp again; it was a close, drizzly night that made me think of London. I longed for it very much, as I recalled the steaming, wild, wild bars and the girls waiting outside, one pound quick time, three pounds all night. It's been a long time since I got drunk, I mused, wishing that I were back in Piccadilly.

I shook myself out of the reverie, and blinking at the woods, began to think that this was not the night to be on outpost. The Germans liked bad weather, and I could only see about a hundred yards.

Usually the 7th Army searchlights, dug in by antiaircraft batteries in the hills several miles behind us, lit the front by throwing their beams straight up into the sky. The reflected glare was almost as good as a full moon, but the lights weren't very good in fog or rain or thick overcast. We were on our own tonight.

I frowned at the Moder River. Swollen with spring rains and the melting snow, it looked like boiling lead mixed with tar. The bare trees on its near bank seemed to be wet ghosts walking toward me.

A German rifle popped far off and was answered by an American machine gun, toomtoomtoom. How simple it would be for a combat patrol to slip across the river and surround our house.

And when the Germans send a patrol, they make it big, they send everybody. They creep through the dark, thirty or forty at a time, ready to fight a platoon and break through to the rear, which they know is always careless. What should I do if they come and I see them first? Should I play it safe, like the man in Uden the day we went to Best who watched them march in at noon? They stole a car and marched out again, and he never fired a single shot at them. The officers said he was wrong, but who were they to talk—it wasn't their life. I would have shot at them, thrown my hand grenades, and run, but that was long ago, when I was still somewhat eager. Now I know better. I'm not looking for trouble anymore.

But if they come tonight and I don't attack them, they will surround the house and wipe us out. I could hide upstairs, but they would kill my friends. I'm not heel enough to let them do that. The others are trapped in the cellar; one bazooka round would get them all. I have a fighting chance up here, they have none. A cellar's a grave.

Or is it? Look what happened in the 3rd Battalion.

It was a story that was going the rounds then. A large group of 3rd Battalion men—some said ten or fifteen, others twenty or thirty—were in reserve, sleeping peacefully in a basement behind the lines in Holland. Thinking themselves secure (a popular fallacy when in reserve), they hadn't bothered to post a guard at the door. Shortly after midnight, a giant German opened the door and stopped on the threshold with a Schmeisser machine pistol in one hand and a squeegee flashlight in the other. He swept the sleepers with the light. "Get your clothes on and come with me!" he shouted in perfect English. "The house is surrounded."

The men looked up in amazement. "For Chrissake," one of them said disgustedly, "somebody shoot the sonofabitch."

And somebody did. Another man calmly pulled out a .45, cocked it, and holding it with both hands, aimed carefully at the huge German framed in the doorway. He fired, and the German fell over dead. The rest of the men grabbed their weapons, rushed outside, and drove off the surrounding Germans.

Those things happen occasionally, I thought. They make the war interesting—if you live through them. But it's all luck. It was the German's night to die, and no matter how good a patrol he pulled, he died. The 3rd Bat's number wasn't up, that's all.

I stiffened with fright.

Swish . . . Swish . . . Swish.

I shivered and threw my rifle up to my shoulder.

Swish . . . Swish . . . Swish.

My scalp tightened till my hair stood stiff and wiry. Somebody was wading in the river out of sight to my left. I held my breath and listened carefully, to make sure it wasn't my imagination.

Swish . . . Swish . . . Swish.

Here they come, oh God, here they come! I pushed the safety catch forward in the trigger guard and eased out on the balcony for a better look.

Swish . . . Swish . . . Swish.

I stepped back inside, with my heart pounding in my head. Wide-eyed with fright, I turned and ran downstairs. "McCreary! McCreary!" I cried. "They're crossing the creek!"

Mick jumped out of the chair, where he had been dozing. "Krauts!" he yelled into the phone. "They're coming over." He slammed down the receiver, grabbed his Thompson and two loose clips, and woke up the others. "Shoot a flare, Marsh! Krauts! Winn, Cobb, out by the garage! I'm going upstairs with Webster."

"There must be a platoon of them," I said as we ran back to the balcony. "They've been wading across for ten minutes."

We listened to the swishing, and then went to the front porch, which directly overlooked the sound. The shadows and the stream and the drizzle all combined to render invisible the exact location of the crossing.

Meanwhile, Marsh had run out to the gatepost by the road. He fumbled with the tape that sealed the flare container, which was about a foot long and an inch and a half in diameter. He removed the top and slid the aluminum canister into his hand. A quick wrench and the cork plug was out of its firing end. He took the bell ammunition from his rifle, inserted a blank cartridge into the chamber, and dropped the flare on the grenade launcher attached to the muzzle of his M-1. Now he was ready to fire. He tilted the barrel at about an eighty-degree angle, put the butt on the ground, and squeezed the trigger.

The canister shot a hundred yards into the air and burst over the northeast corner of the house, illuminating the area with a blinding white light.

McCreary and I studied the creek intensely. "I don't see anything," he whispered skeptically. The swishing continued, at regular intervals. "Let's go outside and take a look."

We went down the stairs and out the garage door, where Winn and Cobb stood ready. "Tell Marsh to shoot another flare in a couple of minutes," McCreary said.

Turning left, we walked slowly around the house to three slit trenches that had been dug in the lawn, facing the river, but they were empty and half-filled with water. Nobody was hiding in or near them; we made sure of that. From here, the lawn sloped gently to a line of yard-high bushes on the river's edge. They had been mined by the 79th Division, and nobody was hiding in them either.

Greatly emboldened, we went on carelessly through long, wet grass and chunks of debris to the place where the swishing was coming from.

A German mortar coughed in the distance among the enemy houses to our left. We froze and looked down, so that our faces wouldn't shine if a flare went off. The shell landed far behind us. Marsh shot his second flare.

It burst right over the house. In its light, McCreary pointed to the river and exclaimed, "There's your goddamn Krauts! Platoon, my ass. For Chrissake, you ought to be ashamed of yourself, Webster."

I followed his finger and grinned.

As the river swept down, its current dragged the branches of a half-submerged bush with it. When the branches had stretched their limit, they snapped back with a loud swish that sounded exactly like a man wading.

"It certainly sounded like Krauts," I said, laughing and slinging my rifle.

McCreary sighed and told me to go back on guard.

ANOTHER DAY PASSED, with further expeditions to the nearby houses, some close shells, and a 105 that bracketed the house, driving Cobb down from the upstairs toilet with his pants around his ankles. We swept the refuse in the hall into a far corner, cleaned off the stairs, and hauled water from the well in the woods. Now it was night again. McCreary and I were getting ready to go to company headquarters and fetch the rations. McCreary wanted to borrow Marsh's Luger.

Marsh hated to loan it. "Gee, Mick, goddamn it," he said, shaking his head. "That's the only souvenir I've got. Been saving it for my bub."

McCreary's jaw dropped in mock astonishment. "Why, Marsh!" he exclaimed, looking him up and down. "You talk like a little kiiiiiiid. Imagine a great, big, grown man like you talking like that."

Marsh snorted and blushed and tried to think of a wisecrack, but he was not as quick-tongued as McCreary, so he just muttered a few goddamns, unbuckled the Gott mit Uns belt that held the Luger holster, and handed it to him.

I dropped my .45 into the pocket of my mackinaw and stood up impatiently, anxious to be off.

But McCreary was in no hurry. His eyes gleamed as he examined the Luger very carefully. It was indeed a beautiful pistol. "Give you a hundred francs for it," he said.

Marsh roared with the laughter. The going price was closer to five thousand francs, or $100. He watched his buddy slide the Luger back into its stiff leather holster and then looked away, as if he couldn't bear to see it leave his possession. McCreary put on his helmet and joined me in the hall.

We went across the road and through the stable to the platoon C.P., where Rader and V.D., a bulky, grinning young man with a wide mouth and bright black eyes, were waiting to join us. The C.P. building, we learned, had once been a German military hospital. Its staircase walls were lined with amusing murals of enemy goldbricks at sick call, and the building itself was very solidly built. Down in the cellar, where the men lived, the walls were two feet thick. Martin, Rader, and the new officer slept in one part of the basement, near the phone, while Liebgott, Lyall, V.D., Wiseman, and the new replacement, Crist, occupied another adjacent room. Though the nearest German house was less than fifty yards away, the cellar was so cool and dark and the walls so thick that I felt more secure there than in my own house. The stoves were not as good, however, nor were the men as congenial, for they were split into two distinct cliques—the headquarters, which stayed by the phone, and the riflemen, who kept watch by a window on the fourth floor.

"It's about time you guys got here," Rader remarked to McCreary as

we came in the basement. "Heard you boys are getting nervous in the
service."

Any reflection on his courage was sure to bring McCreary's temper to
the surface to leap and splash for all to see, and he hit the line and sent
the reel spinning. "Trade jobs with you anytime, buddy," he snapped. His
eyes lit up. "Well, well, howdoyoudo, if it isn't old V.D. Getting plenty up
here, V.D.?" He offered his hand for a shake. "Congratulations. Let me be
the first. Heard you got the Combat Infantry Badge for leaving the cellar yesterday."

Everybody laughed.

V.D. dropped his hand. "Kiss my ass." He grinned. His long, thin-lipped
mouth snapped shut on a piece of gum, and he commenced chewing it
like a catfish mouthing flour balls. "Let's go and get it over with," he said
to Rader. "I don't hanker to stay outside any more'n I can help."

"We know, buddy," McCreary murmured, "we know."

V.D. snapped his mouth shut with a curse and waited for Rader to
rise. When he was ready, we left the house and wound through the rubbly streets to company headquarters.

This was located five or six blocks west of the barracks square in an
undamaged three-story house on a wide intersection and was by far the
best of the Company's billets. Directly across the street in a small vacant
lot, the company's three 60mm mortars were set up for battery fire in
separate holes five feet square by four deep. They were laying down a
barrage as we approached.

The muzzle blasts lit the scene with quick flashes, and the noise was
deafening. They would fire three or six or nine, and then there would be
a lull that in its way was as deafening as the coughing thunder that had
gone before. A noncom shouted, and the men rose out of the earth like
black geysers and slid shells down the tubes and ducked back into the
earth as the shells went off. It was like some hideous, noisy nightmare.

Rader led us through the front door of the C.P. and held it open for
us. When we were all in, he closed it, so that no light would show outdoors, and opened a door to the left. We entered single file.

"My God!" McCreary exclaimed, overcome by the contrast with the
violent scene outdoors. "Civilians."

We had entered the living room. Clean rugs, overstuffed furniture,
framed pictures on the wall, electric lights burning—everything was in
order. There was even a player piano.

Sergeant Mann was playing gin rummy on a blanket-covered table in the center with one of the louder, more objectionable cooks, while Luz, who was sprawled comfortably on a fringed couch, cleaned a P-38 pistol. A couple of runners and radiomen were chatting in the far corner.

Luz brightened when he saw us. "You guys hungry again?" he inquired, throwing a D ration at McCreary. "Think fast!"

"We're always hungry," I said, inspecting the room with obvious envy. "We're hungry because you guys get the rations first."

McCreary, who had caught the D ration, dropped it on the floor with loathing. "Boy, have you got it made," he remarked. "How do you get a deal like this?"

"We're 4F, buddy," Luz replied. "Company headquarters. Kraut generator runs the lights. We swiped it in the Bulge." He commenced cleaning his P-38 again. Nobody else greeted us.

The mortars stopped coughing, and just when the silence was growing unbearable, a group of men came in from each of the other platoons. They nodded to us and stood against the wall, muttering at the luxury. Absorbed in his card game, Sergeant Mann ignored them just as he had ignored us. When he had finished his hand, he looked up and asked if everybody was here. "Tonight we get P.X. rations and 10-in-1s," he announced.

"It's about time," someone remarked.

"At ease! I'll do the talking here."

The men glared at him.

"We've broken them down as fairly as possible, so don't feel gypped if you get Chelseas and razor blades instead of Camels and Hershey bars. . . . O.K., Luz, pass 'em out. Each platoon take one of these empty boxes for its P.X. rations."

McCreary, who was constantly improving himself and who suspected everybody else of doing the same, had no faith in these ration breakdowns. He had a nose for fraud and did not intend to have his men shorted by liars, politicians, dog-robbers, cooks, and company clerks. He watched with narrowed eyes and a projecting lower lip as the rations were distributed. Two cartons of Luckies went to the third platoon, two Chesterfields to the second, and Raleighs to the first. McCreary exploded.

"Wait a minute, Portugee!" he hissed, low enough so that Mann wouldn't hear him. "Give me those Camels down in the box! Yeah, them. You're not gypping the first platoon, buddy." He frowned.

Luz jerked his head at the 1st sergeant, who was absorbed in other trivia, muttered something about "goddamn orders," and quickly switched brands. He liked the first platoon; there was nothing, he claimed, that he wouldn't do for it—"after I've done it for myself." He left McCreary and dropped equal shares of gum, toothpaste, soap, razor blades, V-mail, and Tropical Chocolate in the three platoon boxes.

McCreary's eyes had been dancing all over the room, seeking other treasures, especially those short-stopped by company headquarters. He nudged Rader and pointed to a carton of Hershey bars on the table at Mann's elbow. "What's the deal, buddy?" he hissed. "Ask him, ask him who gets the Hershey bars!"

Rader was reluctant. Not inclined to argue with those above him, he usually took all rations and details without question or complaint. He cleared his throat, coughed, and asked, "Uh, Sergeant Mann, who are them Hershey bars for?"

"Company headquarters," Mann snapped, plainly showing that he regretted not having hidden them. He sighed, for the ration breakdown was always contentious. The platoons came in like hungry wolves and circled and snapped and howled whenever they saw a decent cigarette or a good piece of candy go to someone else. He sighed again and repeated that they were for company headquarters. "We didn't have enough for everybody," he explained, "so I thought it'd save a lot of bitching if we held on to 'em and equalized it next time."

"Next time, my ass," McCreary grunted. "You guys . . . Time you get through with the rations, we're lucky to eat Chopped Pork and Egg Yolk." He disliked Mann and knew that he could get away with open griping, now that the latter was on the defensive, so he raised his voice for the benefit of the other dissidents.

"We ought to be glad," he said, "that rear echelon even lets us eat. Look what happens to the stuff on the way to the front! When it comes off the boat in the E.T.O., the port battalion stevedores break open a case or two and help themselves. Then the railroad battalions lose a couple of dozen cartons—look at that nest of thieves they just caught in France: colonel and all in the black market! After that, the quartermaster truck companies undercount a couple of more boxes. And holy God, by the time Division and Regiment and Battalion supply take *their* cut, we're lucky we even get a bar of soap. So I tell you what: Be grateful, men, goddammit!"

He shouldered a case of 10-in-1s (a day's ration for ten men in one box) and headed for the door. "Nothing's too good for the American soldier—if his buddies don't gyp him out of it." He slammed the door behind him.

Mann grinned. A small man mad was a sight to see.

Rader shrugged his shoulders, as if to disassociate himself from McCreary in Mann's eyes, and lifted the box of P.X. rations. I took a five-gallon German jerrican for water, and V.D. picked up two round, red tin containers filled with kerosene for our lamps.

"What's the matter with Mick?" Luz inquired as we started to go. "He sounds bitter. He never used to bitch like that before."

"Well, uh, all the boys are pissed off," Rader said. "They want to go back to Mourmelon."

"Don't we all, don't we all."

"TIME TO TAKE DOWN the blackout," Marsh said, for morning had come again.

I removed the stick that propped shut our window covering at night and gently lowered the board, with its padded edges of ripped blanket that kept the light from shining out through the cracks.

The little German house across the river caught my eye and made me frown. Something was wrong over there, something had changed. "Jesus," I whispered, "Krauts."

"Where?" McCreary asked. He almost fell over the stove in his haste to reach the window. The others looked around for their weapons.

I set the board to one side and pointed at the house a hundred yards north of us.

"Uh-oh," Cobb murmured.

"We have company," McCreary said.

"I noticed the shutters were closed last night," I said. "Now they're all open. If we don't get them, they'll get us." I ran for my rifle.

"Nah, hold it up!" McCreary snapped. "I have a better idea. That place is too close for mortars or artillery, and shooting an M-1 will only let 'em know for sure that we are here. I have it. We'll bazooka the joint." Keeping his eyes on the house, he picked up the phone and whistled for the C.P.

"O.P. 2, McCreary speaking. We spotted a houseful of Krauts. Think you can get us a bazooka, quick? It's the first place north of here, right across from O.P. 3. Step on it, buddy! They've probably seen us too."

He set the phone down, and Marsh began to organize protection for the bazookaman. I was to cover him outside, while the rest of the men watched from upstairs windows and McCreary remained by the phone.

Someone whistled in the mouthpiece a few minutes later and told him that Luz had just passed the platoon C.P. on the run. He was carrying a bazooka. Marsh suggested that the C.P. tell the machine gunners in O.P. 3, who had been getting rather close fire from the 88 around their top-floor lookout, to cover the house, in case any Germans tried to escape from its rear. "This is going to be good," Marsh remarked.

Someone pounded and clattered across the road and into the garage and then burst into the phone room. It was Luz, with a bazooka in one hand and a bag of ammunition in the other.

"Hiya, fellows," he gasped, panting hard. "Ran all the way." His face was covered with sweat. "Where are the Krauts? Oh man, let me at 'em, let me blast 'em, let me blast 'em!" He mimicked Jimmy Durante. "Show 'em to me, just show 'em to me!"

"Hi, keed," Marsh said. "What's new in rear echelon? Come here and we'll show you some Krauts."

Luz stepped to the window and slapped McCreary on the shoulder. "Hiya, Mick, what's new? Look at Sholty, all dressed up like a soldier."

Sholty grinned. "How's it feel to be up front, Luz? Different?"

"It's a change. A man gets tired of easy living."

Marsh nodded at the house while Sholty, who was due to leave today on his pass to Paris, took the B.A.R. and went upstairs to cover the house from a window there. "We saw 'em airing it out a little while ago," Marsh said. "Better put a couple of rounds in the basement. We'll cover you. Webster'll go out with you."

Luz turned to me. "Hiya, Dan'l. How's the dictionary?" He trotted outside. "Let's go up the road to the last fence post," he suggested. "You lie down and cover me, and I'll shoot from behind the post. Got three rounds; may as well use 'em up. Hell, we're not paying for 'em, are we, kid?"

I smiled.

We strolled up the sidewalk beside the iron fence that enclosed our front yard, which we considered our backyard, since the river was our front, tactically speaking, and studied the situation and the terrain. The

road on our left ran straight north to the bank of the creek, and then between the machine gunners' building and the Moder River. Concertina
barbed wire was strung along its edge there, opposite the German
house, which stood by itself in the open. Almost equidistant from our
place and O.P. 3, the house was at least two hundred yards away from the
congested dwellings in the enemy part of Haguenau.

We stopped at the last fence post, which was of fieldstone and about
two feet square, and Luz's eyes narrowed as he gauged the distance to
the target. He leaned the bazooka against the post, removed three shells
from their fiberboard cases, and laid them neatly in a row on the sidewalk.

"Are you ready?" I asked nervously, keeping my eyes on the house.
There was no sign of life in the dwelling.

"I'll give 'em a reveille they'll never forget." Luz laughed hoarsely. He
slid a round into the bazooka's rear, knelt, and tilted the muzzle up,
ready to fire. "Lie out in the road there, will you, buddy?" he said to me.
"Cover me, kid, cover me."

I walked out into the street ten feet and lay down in full view of the
house, with my M-1 pointed at the nearest window. The cobblestones
near my nose smelled wet and flinty, reminding me of some rocks that I
had found in the Yosemite River when I was 10 years old. I felt very
homesick and tired of the war and suddenly wondered if I would ever
see the States again. Luz hissed, and I nodded. "Give it to 'em."

BLOW! The rocket shot out of the bazooka and streaking fire and
smoke, burst with a terrific concussion against a basement window,
blowing off the shutters. Luz reloaded quickly and fired another round
at a second window, with the same result. The third round went upstairs
and blew up indoors.

"How's that for shooting?" Luz inquired. He laughed, and I smiled.

We both stood up and stared at the house. It appeared to be totally
lifeless. There was no sound, no movement. A few wisps of smoke clung
to the walls, drifting up toward the sky, and then a bird twittered briefly
in a bush near the river.

"Let's go inside," I said, tense and somehow unsatisfied. "I guess
they've had it."

"Like shooting fish in a rain barrel," Luz remarked. "I haven't had so
much fun since I shot my mother-in-law."

He slung the bazooka over his shoulder, and we turned and started back. There was still no noise or movement in the house.

"God!" I exclaimed, ducking low.

A high-velocity shell whipped past us with a terrible, angry buzz and burst against O.P. 3. We looked up. The shell had hit only a few feet away from the machine gunners' lookout post on the top floor. We began to run for the basement.

"Some shooting," I panted. "They're sniping again. That 88'll be the death of us yet."

Marsh met us at the garage door. "Nice going, Portugee," he said, slapping his back. "You sure put 'em in there."

"I gave 'em a reveille they'll never forget," Luz replied, laughing. "Anytime you want anybody blasted up here, just give me a ring. Ask the operator for Luz. Demolition's our specialty. Found any safes yet, Marsh?"

"Nope, but we're looking."

McCreary came out and invited Luz in for a cup of coffee, but he said he had to leave right away. "No safes, no Luz," he explained. He said goodbye and walked off.

Marsh watched him go, with admiration in his eyes. "That crazy Portugee's got more guts than anybody else in E Company," he remarked. "He's one of the few guys who doesn't change from combat to garrison, he's always the same—crazy."

After we returned to the phone room, we studied the German house. It appeared to be completely dead.

"Well," Sholty said, "I guess those guys will keep their blackouts up from now on."

"And so will we, buddy, so will we," McCreary replied, lifting our board and jamming it tight against the window. "From now on, this thing stays up day and night."

FOUR DAYS AND FIVE NIGHTS.

We've only been here four days and five nights, and yet everything seems to be coming to a head.

The patrol, the 88, the 105, the railroad gun, and the mortars: They're going to come together. But there's nothing we can do about it.

We're five miles offshore in a flat calm, with the sheet loose and the boom swinging back and forth in the ground swell. We see the squall ruffling the water, but we can't do anything about it. Nothing. Just sit and wait.

Every time I go outside, I feel self-conscious. All those silent houses across the river, so close together. I'll bet there's a squad of Germans in every one.

That strongpoint, riding the open field like a brig on a tidal wave.

The way they bracket this house with heavy artillery.

And that 88. They level it on anybody who moves too slow. The direct hit on O.P. 3. Lucky nobody was hurt, but there will be other times. Maybe we're next. One shell can punch a hole in the wall and kill us all.

Somebody is watching us. We don't see them, but we can feel them.

The people are too German. The houses are German. The stoves. The furnishings. All the street signs end in "strasse."

They've left their mark on this town, as if they intended to reclaim it someday, and somebody is watching us.

Maybe it's the civilians. They drift by us during the day. How do we know they're not Krauts? They walk slowly and study us carefully, mentally counting, calculating, adjusting fire. I don't like it a bit.

And now we've got this goddamned raft to haul from company headquarters to O.P. 2. It'll be stored in the garage until the patrol leaves tomorrow night.

I stumbled, with a whispered curse. The raft was terribly heavy and sticky. It had been rolled into a bulging, uneven bundle, about four feet long and two feet thick, that was too awkward for even four men to carry without staggering and stumbling and losing their grip.

It was eight o'clock, black and unpleasant as burnt toast, and the four of us—Marsh, Cobb, Winn, and I—were feeling our way angrily along the empty streets. We carried the raft until we could hold it no longer and then let it fall and sat down on it to rest. Each leg of the trip was shorter than the one before.

"I wish I was back in the cellar," Winn said, wiping the sweat from his face. "I'll bet McCreary is really raising hell with all those rations."

We got up again with a sigh and started out into the barracks square, which was under sporadic mortar fire. Winn and I had almost been hit by two shells there earlier in the day, and so we wanted to hurry through the open space as fast as possible.

But we couldn't hurry any more, for the raft, which had been captured from the Germans, had grown heavier as we grew weaker. We stopped for a break and moved on, stopped for a break and moved on. At last we reached the stable. In a sweating state of hateful exhaustion, we manhandled the bundle through the hole in the wall and let it fall without caring how much noise it made.

"About time for another break, isn't it?" Winn said, panting.

Marsh wiped off his face with a sleeve, gasped for air, and sat down on the raft. "Hokay, keed," he said, panting, "we'll take a long one right here."

A German machine gun fired a long burst to our left, in second-platoon territory, and a flare burst over the barracks square, then everything was dark and still again.

"Let's go," Marsh said.

We lifted the raft and bore it to the garage, where McCreary met us.

"I hate to see that thing," he remarked, kicking the rubber bundle. "That makes the patrol final."

"We'll set her down at the far end," Marsh said, "and blow her up to-morrow."

After we had rid ourselves of the raft, we gathered in the phone room and worked up the guard roster, which had been forgotten in the sudden call for a detail to go to company headquarters. Winn was the first man upstairs.

He stood shivering at the French doors and studied the scene outside. Bushes and trees and rocks and houses that were innocent and harmless in the daytime had a way of becoming quite ominous at night, and the closer the patrol came and the more he thought about it, the more the shadows looked like men, the more the noises sounded like Germans creeping over the rubble. The searchlights were on tonight; probably a patrol going out. Patrol—he hated the word. Suddenly his mind snapped alert, and he leaned forward and stared southeast, at the Haguenau Forest.

Little blue lights had begun to move about in the trees, a mile away, blinking on and off as they passed behind the trunks.

He ran downstairs to Marsh, who was gossiping on the party line with the C.P. and a kibitzer from O.P. 3, and said breathlessly, "I saw lights out in those woods full of Krauts, little blue lights. Maybe they're bringing in tanks. Jesus, Marsh, we couldn't stop 'em. They can cross the big field before the artillery could zero in on 'em."

"Hold it, fellers," Marsh called over the phone. "Winn thinks the Krauts are bringing tanks into those woods on our right front." He told Cobb to stay below, and went upstairs with the rest of us, each with a weapon in his hand, for we were all anxious to see this great phenomenon—lights at night.

As we crowded around the balcony, we saw the lights wink on and off. They were scattered through the woods like fireflies.

They have a lot of nerve, I thought, showing lights on the front. Either they're crazy or careless or very strong, or else it's some kind of trick. A sane man wouldn't even light a match at night.

"Looks bad," Marsh murmured. "Might be tanks, might be supply trucks or troop carriers. I don't like it, keed, I don't like it a bit." He scowled.

"What'll we do?" Winn asked. "They're too far away for 60 mortars."

"Let's get the artillery; they can blast 'em right out of there." He pulled a compass from his pocket, raised its lid, and sighting through its aperture, took an azimuth reading. "How far do you think it is?"

"About a mile," I volunteered.

"Nearer a thousand yards," McCreary said.

"I'd say a mile," Winn said. "Looks that far in the daytime."

Marsh shrugged his shoulders. No two men ever agreed on distance, especially at night. He thought it was a thousand yards. "Keep an eye on 'em, Winn," he said, snapping the compass shut, "and let me know if they start moving across the field. Come on, fellers, let's go down and call the artillery."

We trooped below, where he blew in the mouthpiece until he got a response from the C.P. "Say, Martin," he exclaimed, "we saw half a dozen blue lights moving around in those woods way off to our right. The boys think that maybe the Krauts are bringing tanks up for an attack. It sure is a good artillery target."

A call for artillery had to go through channels, from outpost to platoon to Company to Battalion to Regiment to Division to Artillery Battalion to gun battery, and the thought of it apparently so exhausted Martin that he heaved a sigh that was audible to everybody in our cellar. "O.K.," he said apathetically, "I'll ask Company about it. What's the range and azimuth?"

"A thousand yards at eighty degrees, Johnny."

"Sit tight. We'll let you know when the shells are on the way."

Marsh smiled and set the phone down and lit a cigarette. He took a long drag while the rest of us chatted about the artillery and the joy that it could bring and then lay back on a bunk and blew a smoke ring at the ceiling. Suddenly, as if struck by an afterthought, he jumped up and went to the lookout post. "See anything more?" he inquired.

Winn shook his head. "They're still moving around. Looks like eight or ten of 'em now."

"Hokay, keed, you stay put and watch the artillery. See how far off it lands and tell me, so we can adjust it smack on the woods. Martin says he'll warn us when they're on the way."

"Good."

Marsh sat by the phone, smoking nervously, for it was the first time he had ever dealt with the artillery. He hoped that everything would go off well. Men had been killed by amateurs (usually officers) who played with artillery without the knowledge or experience that it required. When the phone hissed, he jumped up and snatched at it greedily. "Another five minutes, huh? Hokay, keed, I'll tell Winn."

We smiled, and he went back upstairs. Winn was very glad to see him, confiding that the cold and the darkness and blue lights and the coming patrol were beginning to get on his nerves. Marsh patted him on the back and returned to the phone.

Martin was calling. The shells were on the way, he said.

"On the way," Marsh repeated to us. He leaned back and stretched out his feet. "This is going to be good: Let the artillery do it."

Three howitzers fired a salvo in the hills behind Haguenau.

We heard the shells' quick whispers come right at the house, whish-whishWHISH.

"Hit it!" Marsh cried.

We dove for the floor.

Three shells exploded almost simultaneously in the front yard, between our house and the road. The ground rocked and heaved and a rain of rocks hit the wall.

"My God," McCreary gasped, "they're shelling the house!"

Marsh rose from the floor in a fit of violent anger and grabbed the phone just as Winn rushed in.

"Marsh, Marsh," Winn yelled, "they're shelling us! Stop 'em, stop 'em, tell 'em to cease fire!"

"Hello," a cool voice replied from the depths of the big brick C.P. building, "Martin speaking."

"Jesus Christ, tell the artillery to cease fire!" Marsh shouted at him. "They're landing on our doorstep."

"Ha, ha, ha. You're getting chickenshit. They're nowhere near you."

"Goddamn you, come here and listen to 'em! They shook the house."

"You're nervous in the service."

"Goddamn you, you'll get us all killed! Call that goddamned artillery right now or I'll come up there with an M-1 and *make* you call 'em! You hear me, you hear me?"

He slammed the phone down with tears of anger in his eyes and exploded into a rage against Martin. " 'They're nowheres near you,' he says. By God, someday I'll whomp the stuffing out of him. I'll whomp him and stomp him and beat the living bejesus out of him, and watch out, buddy, watch out. Old Marsh hasn't been whipped yet."

We waited a long time, and finally, when no further shells came in, went up and watched the lights again. All of us were angry at Martin and even madder about the artillery, which had apparently taken the thousand yards from our house to the woods as the total range, instead of adding it to the distance from the cannon to the house.

"Well, hell," I sighed. "Maybe it's just trucks on resupply."

An 88 zipped past us and burst several hundred yards away.

"I saw it!" I exclaimed. "I saw the muzzle flash. Give me your compass, Marsh. I'll take a reading on the next one."

There was another flash a few seconds later. I pinpointed it and counted till I heard the thump of the cannon's report. "A thousand yards at fifty degrees," I said, repeating it over and over to fix it in my memory. "We've finally spotted that 88. Must be dug in out there. Let's put the artillery on it."

Marsh looked at me incredulously. "No thanks, keed," he drawled. "We've had enough artillery for tonight."

"But if we don't knock it out, it's going to get all of us one of these days!"

"Nope. No artillery. Not tonight."

"Marsh is right," McCreary said, ending the discussion. "Those guys at the C.P. will only louse up again if we start messing with the artillery. If they loused up once, they'll do it again. I got no faith in 'em. Just remember one thing, buddy: If the Krauts ever come over here, we'll have to beat 'em off with M-1s and hand grenades. There's nothing else to count on and nobody else to help you."

MY TURN HAD COME for guard. The excitement over the artillery and the blue lights had died down, and everybody else had gone to sleep except Marsh, who was by the phone, keeping the watch below. The blue lights still flickered and twinkled in the forest. They mocked us with calm assurance, and staring at them savagely, I wanted to knock them all out, to level all the trees with every cannon in the 7th Army. The patrol was going out tomorrow; it did not seem right that the Germans should suddenly be so active.

A wagon creaked slowly, with the ungreased grating of dry wood on dry wood, and began to move about among the German houses to my left. My hair stiffened. The wagon stopped and then rolled a few more feet and stopped again. It appeared to be moving slowly across the front, near the platoon C.P.

I clenched my rifle and leaned back against the door sill, wondering what had come over the Germans and why they had come to life. A flare popped over a D Company outpost in a small factory five hundred yards down the creek. Deep in town, a German machine gun clashed with an American 50-caliber. A 105 shell whispered overhead and landed far behind the barracks square. The wagon began to move again, jolting and creaking and clattering among the cobblestone streets.

It must be the ghost that's followed us through Europe, I thought with a shiver, for the sound did not seem wholly real—who would have the nerve to walk a horse-drawn wagon along the front in a city under such heavy artillery fire?

The rumors and stories came back to me full force. I had heard Captain Nixon of Battalion S-2 discuss this wagon once. He claimed that it had first appeared outside Carentan, when the 2nd Battalion had one hedgerow and the S.S. the next. Every night they heard a wooden wagon moving about behind the German lines. They even heard the horse's neighing and clopping and the country jingle of his harness. "We put mortars and artillery on it," the captain had said, "but that damned thing just kept going."

Some of the men used to speculate about it. They thought that it was the ghost of a supply cart that had gotten a direct hit and that the driver was homesick for his old outfit. So every night he'd come back and visit his buddies on the line.

The 3rd Battalion reported hearing the same wagon in Holland, near Opheusden, where they had a terrible battle and many men were killed. British tankers who were with them heard it too. They said it was a curse on the Regiment, brought on by some of the things that were done to prisoners in Normandy, where viciousness reached its peak.

And when I was in the 7th Army's forward battalion replacement depot, an S-2 man from Regiment told me that the wagon had followed them to Bastogne. They heard it crunching in the snow, he claimed, but they never saw it or hit it.

Well, hell, there's nothing I can do about it. Thank God I won't make the patrol.

Other sounds began to rise in the still, cold night. A lone dog that I had heard before (and wanted to shoot) barked and howled in the German streets. I shivered again.

If there was a firefight or if a few shells were coming and going, I would have felt better, because then I would have known that the Germans were occupied. Now, when the front was so quiet—for there had been no shooting for about fifteen minutes—and I could hear all the weird little noises, I became quite alarmed. No good ever came of a silent front.

Something clanked and rattled at the farmhouse strongpoint, and a cow mooed plaintively for attention. It was not a new sound, for I had heard it the first night, but now it seemed eerie, a sure sign that the Germans were in the house. They must have kept the cow in an underground shelter during the day and turned it out at night. I could not blame them for wanting fresh milk. It was a great luxury in wartime.

The cow clanked and mooed, the dog barked, the wagon creaked, and the little blue lights twisted and turned. Finally, when I thought that I would scream, Cobb stumbled upstairs and relieved me.

After my hour on the phone was over, I took off my helmet and lay down on a floor mattress and went to sleep. I dreamt of a cow that mooed and dragged a clanking chain after the patrol. When the patrol was deep in town and had surrounded a house that was their objective, a dog started to bark at them. Suddenly the whole street was lit by blue lights, and Germans came running out of all the houses, firing from the hip. I woke up sweating all over.

McCREARY, COBB, AND WINN left for the patrol at twilight, but we were not as understrength as we had been the day before, when they had gone back to the Rhine-Marne Canal for the rehearsal, for we had just received four replacements to help us hold the house tonight. Fresh from basic training and four weeks' jump school, they had arrived in Europe only a week or two before. It was the first time we had ever received replacements on line, and none of us liked it, because we thought it meant that we would stay in combat much longer than usual. We immediately cleared out the southeast room, which was most in line with the 88 and closest to the woods, and put the replacements in it, keeping the warmer, safer phone room for ourselves.

Products of the 18-year-old draft, our newcomers seemed terribly young and green and we all felt sorry for them, coming so suddenly to an outfit on line. Previously it had been the custom to receive replacements in base camp and work them into the Regiment there, so that they could get to know the other men before they went into action. Now they just threw them in and let them take their chances. I did not envy them.

Of the four, Lamb appeared to be the most competent, probably because he was a Southerner, and I never met a Southerner who wouldn't fight. An Alabama boy, Lamby was stocky and calm and self-assured. Kohler was more talkative. A preacher's son from Baltimore, he appeared to be quite good-natured and friendly, with a great deal of common sense. His swearing was the kind expected from a preacher's son—virulent. The third man, Hickman, was a sturdy, smiling, talkative Indiana farm boy who wanted very much to kill a German. Hudson, the fourth replacement, was so quiet and shy that he seemed to require the most looking after of anybody.

While they were chatting together in their new quarters, I went to the garage entrance to check the weather. I wore my usual daytime indoor ensemble—a wool undershirt, jump pants with suspenders, and unlaced jump boots—and found the weather quite cool.

Another twilight, I thought, with the feeling of sadness that often came with that time of day. There certainly isn't much daylight anymore. When we jumped in Normandy, it was light from five A.M. to eleven P.M. Now it's light only from eight to four.

I don't feel right in Europe, I mused, listening to the rain on the leaves and the murmuring of the replacements indoors. There's something tentative and embarrassing about the dead land and the drab, defeated people in black that reminds me of a trip to the slums. I want to get away from it, not to know about it. Hit me again, and send me back to England. If only I could go back to our box stall with a lardy cake and a couple of milk stouts under my belt.

I sighed and unrolled the rubber raft, fetched a bicycle pump, and began to inflate the raft, which the patrol would use to cross the Moder River tonight.

Things are changing now, I thought as I heaved up and down on the wooden pump handle. The replacements have added a new dimension, robbing us of our exclusiveness. And trouble has started already; it was bound to start as soon as Cobb and Morganti had found some liquor.

The house where it was hidden was under direct observation of the Germans, but they had darted into it and found several cases of schnapps. Accompanied by Wiseman, they had stacked the cases in a courtyard. Alas, the Germans heard them and put mortars on the area. The cases were smashed, but they managed to salvage two bottles apiece. The Germans shot at them with rifles as they ran off, and Wiseman was nicked in the knee. They got drunk that night. Cobb went upstairs to run a belt through the machine gun that we had been given recently to supplement our B.A.R., but Marsh, who had never loved or admired him, went after him and beat him off in a free-for-all that left Cobb with a black eye and a bloody nose. Wiseman told off our little lieutenant in the platoon C.P. and then drifted back to the company C.P. and got in a violent argument with Captain Speirs.

Things are always changing, I mused. Just when you have a nice place, something comes along to mess it up. The essence of life is change, not stability, but I can't get used to it; I want everything to stay the way it is.

"Next, next!" I shouted, straightening my back and panting, for the pumping had been hard work. "Who's next on the pump?"

Marsh came out, with the replacements, and they all took turns while we stood around and talked. Since two other rafts had been brought to the house, we were still at it when night fell. The talk centered about the patrol.

For two days the artillery had been zeroing in on key crossroads, known enemy houses and strongpoints, and all the streets leading to the patrol's objectives. The company and battalion mortars had registered on closer targets. Every man in the patrol had been thoroughly briefed, both in the rear and at the windows of O.P. 1, which looked out on the houses they were to surround.

Lieutenant Jones, a tall, likable young man, just out of West Point, who had recently taken command of the second platoon, had volunteered to act as patrol leader. Sergeant Mann was supposed to assist him. The third platoon's McClung, the one who could smell Kraut, would be the lead scout. A tall, thin, quiet man with deep-set black eyes and remarkably keen senses, he was more like a hunter than a soldier and could flush Germans from the thickest cover. He had astounded and delighted British tankers in Holland by chasing Germans among their tanks and shooting them.

These men would have lots of company. Noisy McGuire from Company Headquarters would carry an S.C.R. 300 for radio communication with the rear, while the third platoon's Mercier would shoot the rifle grenades. Big and hard, with a pitted face and cold eyes, Mercier was ambitious and extremely frustrated, for Regiment, for reasons of its own, had made lesser men into officers and passed him by. One of the best combat men in E Company, he was a platoon sergeant now. The harsh, New England bitterness that he felt seemed to make him particularly good in action. In addition to him and McGuire, an officer from Battalion S-2 and several enlisted men from Regiment would go along as observers and German linguists, for the whole object of the patrol was not to fight but to capture prisoners and from them learn the latest rumors on the other side of the river. Just in case of trouble, more than a squad of riflemen and B.A.R. men would also make the trip.

Already they had begun to rendezvous at a D Company house, where they planned to eat a hearty supper and drink coffee till ten o'clock, when the patrol would begin. At ten they would come into our garage for the rubber boats, carry them through the woods, and cross the stream near the point formed by a bend in the river. A rope was to be fastened to a concrete telephone pole on the enemy side and a tree on ours for the men to pull the raft across. Once ashore, they would split in half, one section going away from us into town, while the other surrounded one of the houses opposite O.P. 3. Rifle grenades would be shot into the cellar windows, prisoners would be taken, and any Germans who tried to get away would be shot. The leader of the first group to get a prisoner was to blow a whistle and start back as fast as possible. Upon hearing the whistle, the other section was to follow immediately, regardless.

There would be plenty of support. An artillery observer was already waiting in O.P. 1 to call down fire on all points on which the guns had registered. The whistle was his signal; as soon as he heard it, he would tell the mortars and 75s and 105s to commence firing. A splendid barrage was promised. There was even a 57mm antitank gun ready. Smuggled up to the front, it would soon be emplaced in the darkness at a street between O.P. 1 and the machine gunners' building and would fire into the basement of a house which, because of its proximity to the platoon O.P., could not be safely hit by indirect mortar or artillery fire. Eddie Weeks and the D Company 50-caliber machine gun were to provide overhead fire upstream toward town, along the river line, while our own machine gun, now sited on the marble-topped table upstairs, would be shifted to the balcony that overlooked the river on the east and would cover the bazookaed house. After the patrol had passed by, it would be shifted to the stream crossing to cover the return.

It sounded like a fine patrol, with all eventualities covered and plenty of time for preparations, but I was still glad that I was not going along. F Company had tried a patrol only recently and had been stopped at the river's edge. There was little reason to be optimistic about this one.

Now the rafts were ready. Marsh and I lingered briefly and then went to the road to investigate a noise that we had heard there.

Its front sandbagged against Panzerfausts, a heavy tank squeaked and clanked toward us on the pavement. It stopped between our house and the little wooden bridge and, holding one tread stationary, ground around until its 76mm cannon covered the big field. We went up to it.

"Hi," I said to a man lounging in the turret. "Sure is good to see you guys."

He nodded, dimly visible in the thickening darkness. "Say, buddy," he said, leaning over, "where's this big farmhouse we're supposed to cover?"

Marsh told him. The tanker nodded again, and Marsh added that if the Germans sent up a flare, they would see the farmhouse all right. "You can't miss it," he said. "It's the only living thing in that whole goddamned field."

"Watch yourself," I suggested. "There's an 88 zeroed in on this area. If you have to shoot, you'd better get behind our house right afterward or it'll be your ass."

Marsh gave him the azimuth of the farmhouse, and he swung the cannon till it pointed at it. "O.K., buddy," the tanker said. "We're ready."

MARSH LIT THE LAMP. "Lucky Sholty," he said, "on a pass to Paris. And Mick—I sure hope nothing happens to Mick."

"He'll be back," I said, but I wasn't too sure, for the night was too quiet and ominous.

"Poor Mick. I'd hate to think of losing that little guy. Winn can't swim, you know."

"I know." My sense of guilt was greater than ever before. After two months in the hospital and two months in replacement depots, I had come back and let a man who had not had any rest for almost seventy days go on a patrol that I should have volunteered for. The patrol had to cross a swift stream, and that man couldn't swim. If he died, I would be guilty. Nobody else felt this, but I knew it would be on my conscience. Winn, you have to make it, I thought, you have to make it.

In the next room, Kohler and Hickman were talking about the time they had gone on pass together in Baltimore. I could hear subdued laughter. Hudson and Lamby were upstairs, on guard together.

"Well, keed, it's nine o'clock." Marsh sighed. "Let's go." He told Kohler to watch the phone and led the way up to the machine gun, which we moved to the porch that overlooked the river and faced due east. Working as quietly as possible, we set the gun up on the wide stone railing with the muzzle pointing at the basement of the bazookaed house.

"Damn dark," Marsh whispered. "No searchlights tonight." He pulled the bolt handle back and eased it forward.

The gun was half-cocked. One more yank on the bolt handle, and it would be loaded and ready to fire. We kept it half-cocked as a safety measure.

A flare burst. We froze.

Facing the enemy, in the most exposed position in the house, we knew that we were asking for trouble if we ever shot from here, for the muzzle blast would be visible to all and especially the 88, which we dreaded above everything else. But this was the only place where we could give the patrol adequate covering fire. If it was ambushed from the nearest house, we would run three belts through the gun if necessary, because the lives of the patrol would depend on us. I was not brave,

but I knew enough about war and fighting to see the value of our position and the necessity of our using it to help the patrol, even if it meant
almost certain death for us.

"I'm going down and tell Kohler to let us know when the patrol has
left," Marsh said after the flare had died out. Before I could reply, he was
gone.

I did not like it there alone. The front was remarkably quiet, as if lying in wait. The 88 seemed to have fallen asleep. Enemy mortars shot
one or two flares off to the left, over town, and no high-explosive. Our
own artillery, warned of the patrol, rested on its guns and waited for the
whistle signal for their great barrage. The searchlights were out. We did
not want to illuminate our own men. Our side shot no flares. There was
no small-arms firing. There was no moon, there were no stars. Silent and
tense, the outposts on both sides of the Moder River watched and
waited for the first burst of fire.

I heard a scraping sound behind me and turned to see Marsh coming
back. The patrol had left the house, he said, adding that we would carry
the machine gun down through the woods to the bank of the creek as
soon as we heard the men pass below us on the opposite shore.

"Eeeyah!" somebody screamed at the crossing point. There was a
thrashing in the water and then silence.

"God," I murmured. "Winn." I pictured him dragged underwater to his
death by the weight of his B.A.R. belt.

We waited and waited. Marsh sighted along the barrel to make sure
the gun was aimed properly and adjusted the elevating and traversing
mechanism. "Poor Winn," he said. "Wonder what happened to those
other guys? I don't hear anything."

"Maybe they lost the rafts."

Marsh shrugged his shoulders.

I held my breath and listened for footsteps, but there was only the
soft hiss of the light rain on the bushes below. A shingle slid off the roof
with a terrifying clatter. "Jesus Christ!" I exclaimed, jumping.

"Spooky, isn't it?"

"Man, I'll say. Where is that damned patrol?"

This balcony gives me the creeps, I said to myself. It's too exposed.
That 88'll pick us off as soon as it sees our tracers.

Putut . . . Pututut . . . Putututututut.

"A Thompson! They've surrounded the house already."

The patrol had passed by us so quietly that we hadn't even heard them. Now they were assaulting the first objective, the house far in town. Rifle grenades crashed, fragmentation grenades thumped low, and M-1s joined the Thompson with their heavy bamming.

"Come on, let's go!" Marsh cried. He pulled the bolt back, yanked out the belt of ammunition and pushed it into its box, swung the gun to his shoulder, tripod and all, and hurried for the stairs. I picked up two boxes of ammunition and told Kohler and Hudson, who had come up to us, to take the other two.

We ran recklessly down the stairs, through the cellar, and out the garage. Marsh led the way along a slippery mud path through the woods and threw the machine gun down by the rope across the stream. Wiggling on his belly, he twisted and turned until the gun covered the farmhouse strongpoint. I flopped beside him and fed the belt into the gun. Kohler and Hudson dropped the other boxes beside us and lay down five yards to the rear, ready to move up in case we were hit. The small-arms firing continued.

Bleep, bleep! We heard the piercing whistle.

"Get ready, boys," Marsh said. "Here comes the artillery."

THE 60s COUGHED AND BELCHED sheets of flame. The 81s lit the night with volcanic flashes. Lightning of the 75s and 105s flared up behind the western ridges. Salvo after salvo of shells whispered through the sky above us and fell like thunderous rain on the silent city. The barrage had begun.

As the exploding shells flashed red and orange and the night came alive with the coughing and bopping of the mortar and artillery batteries and the door-slamming detonations of the patrol's covering fire, we smiled and shook our heads in wonderous admiration.

"Beautiful," I murmured. "Isn't it beautiful?"

"Them poor Krauts." Marsh smiled.

It was the best barrage we had ever seen, and we lay still and rejoiced in it. As we stared up at town, we heard a harsh, crashing report near the platoon C.P. and saw a sheet of flame and a red ball dart across the river into the basement of a German house. The 57 had commenced firing.

"Look!" Marsh exclaimed, pointing straight ahead.

A house had started to burn half a mile away.

"I hope they burn the whole town down," I said, feeling very relaxed and safe and strong.

Toomtoomtoom . . . toomtoomtoom . . . toomtoomtoom, the D Company machine gun fired up the river.

Burrp . . . burrrrrrrrrrp, an enemy machine gun replied. It aimed straight at Eddie Weeks' position in the woods behind us. We flattened ourselves and watched the two guns duel, their bright-red tracers crossing and recrossing above us with vicious crackles.

There was a frantic shouting on our left, a rattling of weapons, a screaming of orders. The patrol was returning.

"Let's get out of here," I said.

"Hokay, keed," Marsh replied. "We've done what we were supposed to."

He jumped up and started back toward the house with the gun. We followed him indoors, for our job was done. We had covered the closest house while the patrol had gone out and had covered the farmhouse for their return. Now we wanted to get back to the cellar before the enemy reacted with mortars and artillery.

An 88 buzzed over us like a huge, angry bee and smashed into the D Company dugout. The 50-caliber ceased firing. German mortars began to cough in town, while enemy rifle and machine-gun fire welled up among the houses.

"Just in time," I muttered, darting into the phone room. "My God," I exclaimed, rearing back.

McCreary, Cobb, and Winn were sitting calmly around the table, having a cup of coffee. They were very happy. They had started to cross the creek, they said, when their boat had capsized. All of them had lost their weapons. Winn, who had given the shriek we had heard, had drifted downstream a hundred yards, but had wiggled through the mined bushes on the bank and saved himself. The boat drifted away. They had hurried back to the house, borrowed more clothes from the replacements, and tried again, but had not been able to cross the swift-moving stream. So much time had already been lost that Lieutenant Jones had ordered them to stay inside while the patrol went on. They were overjoyed. The S-2 officer, who had also been repulsed by the river, had stayed with them.

An 88 shell burst with a ringing crash in the trees thirty yards away, and soon another crashed on the road.

Down at the crossing, exposed by an enemy flare, the patrol scrambled across the creek on the rope or pulled themselves over in the sole remaining boat. We could hear them shouting and arguing. Vest, the company mail clerk, drew his pistol to kill a prisoner wounded so badly he wasn't worth ferrying across, but Mann ordered him not to shoot, so they left the dying German on the other bank.

We heard them running through the woods toward us. They burst into the garage just as the 88 ranged in around the house. I watched the men run in, all black-faced and furious, and saw two shells burst in the yard just beyond the driveway.

Everybody crowded into the phone room as the shells darted around the house in search of stragglers. Their drawn, blackened faces lit by the flickering, black-edged flame of our little lamp, the twenty-odd men of the patrol filled every foot of floor space, crammed together on the bunks and mattresses, making the small room seem even smaller and more close.

They were wild with hate and the fierce release of men who have just made a successful attack, and having risked being killed, have instead done the killing. They surged viciously around two small, sallow, very calm prisoners in long-visored cloth caps, so eager to kill them that the least wrong word or movement on their part would have meant their death.

But the Germans were older men, without the cruelty and hot blood of the young, and they knew how to act under the circumstances. They stood calmly and stared without expression at their captors. Mortars coughed in the background, shells rang closer and closer to the walls, the machine gun burped over the river, the house rocked with near-misses, and through it all the prisoners stood coldly unconcerned and even slightly amused, as if they thought that we were taking the war too seriously. When someone who was particularly exercised elbowed them or shouted at them or yanked them about, they merely shrugged their shoulders and rolled with the punches.

A salvo of shells burst near the road, and a small man from company headquarters who had been wounded in the head by a fragment from a German hand grenade screamed in pain and fright, "Kill me, kill me, somebody kill me! Oh Christ, I can't stand it." He began to cry.

The room went quiet, and the Germans stiffened as everybody's eyes shifted from the wounded man to them, for as Germans, they were held responsible. The man was eased to a bunk, and the eyes spoke a single thought: I'll kill you for this. If he dies, you go with him.

Marsh turned to McCreary for a bandage. The little man opened his eyes and saw the Germans in their long-visored caps. He cried out and began to thrash with pain.

"Lemme kill 'em, lemme kill 'em!" Vest yelled. He pulled out a pistol and rushed at the Germans.

"Get outa here, Vest!" Mercier said, holding him back. "They want those bastards back at Battalion."

Vest put the pistol back in his holster with muttered goddamns.

His face red with blood, the little man kicked and squirmed and sobbed aloud. It was almost more than I could stand to watch him. "Morphine," I said. "Give him some morphine."

Somebody else opened a first-aid packet and pushed a morphine syrette into the wounded man's arm.

McCreary snatched up the phone. "For Chrissake," he hissed to Rader, "call Company and get a stretcher down here quick!" He chewed on a dead cigarette with tears in his eyes.

"Kill me! Somebody kill me! Oh, oh, oh. Mercier. I want Mercier. Where's Mercier?" the wounded man cried like a frightened child calling for its mother.

Mercier stepped over to him and held his hand. "That's O.K., buddy," he murmured, "that's O.K. You'll be all right." The man subsided, and Mercier patted his hand and wiped his own eyes with his sleeve.

Three shells came in so fast and close together that the detonations and sound of their flight intermingled. The house quaked.

The wounded man started up with a piercing shriek.

"Take it easy, buddy," Mercier said, easing him back. "Everything's going to be all right."

I watched them with wet eyes. Mercier was so big and hard and strong, and the wounded man seemed small and pitiful enough to be his hurt little boy. I knew he was going to die—I could tell by looking at him—and I didn't want to see it. I had had enough. I left the room.

One more scene like this, I thought as I went out to the garage, and I am through for good.

"Oh, kill me!"

I gritted my teeth and stared at the night, not caring how close the shells came. The night smelled cold and old and wet. Burnt gunpowder of the 88s gave it a special flavor.

In a lull, I heard footsteps pound across the vacant lot and into the garage. Roe and another medic stopped when they saw me. "Where is he?" Roe panted.

"In the back room," I replied. "I'll show you."

Our own artillery was still falling in town. The enemy house burned brighter than ever. Flares popped and glowed all along the river line. German mortar barrages kuRUMPed around the house, in the woods, along the banks of the creek. The wounded man was numb to it all. Relaxed at last by the morphine, he lay limp and moaned softly.

Roe quickly unrolled the stretcher and then he and Mercier and the other medic slid their arms under the wounded man and lowered him to it. The movement made him shriek with pain.

McCreary sucked hard on his dead cigarette, and my eyes clouded over again.

The Germans watched the wounded man without sympathy and relaxed when he was ready to go. Their crisis had passed, they knew; no longer were they in danger of being killed.

The patrol filed out of the room. When the way was clear, Roe took the front of the stretcher and the other medic the rear. They lifted it gently and started off. Mercier walked beside them, holding his friend's hand and telling him over and over again that everything was going to be all right.

Some more shells came into the yard, so they set the stretcher down in the garage and waited for a lull. When the firing stopped and they judged that it was time, they started off again. I watched them till they disappeared and then went back indoors.

OUR ROOM SEEMED AS EMPTY as a nightclub after a large, noisy party has left. We could even hear the flickering of the lamp's flame, or imagined that we could: It was that quiet.

The quiet indoors was a remarkable contrast to the night outside. Once so still and ominous, it was now a heaving volcano of fire and flashes and flares, as the enemy reacted to the patrol and the artillery barrage. German mortars walked up and down both banks of the river, across the open field, through the woods, along the road, and around the barracks square. The machine gun died out, but the 88 continued to make us twitch with its angry buzzes and ringing explosions. Alien and strident in a situation where neither side dared to show the tiniest match flame, the burning house stood out in the dark city like an angel in hell.

While we busied ourselves preparing for a restless night that we feared might even bring a counterattack, the upstairs guard became aware of a strange noise down by the crossing. The noise was a gargling, choking, wheezing sound that could have been made only by a man shot through the lungs; the abandoned prisoner was still alive.

"Let him die," McCreary said when he heard the news. "He doesn't have long to go."

"No," I replied. "If we leave him alone, the Krauts are likely to hear him and come back for him. He'll tell 'em about our house, and they'll put the 88 on it."

"Oh hell."

"I mean it. Look at the way the 88 followed the patrol into the house. Look what it did to D Company's 50-caliber."

Marsh nodded his head. "Pretty risky out there with all those mortars," he said.

"I'll go," I replied. "It's him or us."

"You're crazy."

"No, I'm cautious. I'm going to swim the creek and finish him off with a trench knife. That way they won't hear anything. I don't like that 88."

I changed into a pair of wet fatigues that I had washed in the afternoon, put my trench knife in my pocket, and went outside.

Alone in the darkness, I found my courage less strong than it had been in the company of other men in the phone room. The fear of the 88 kept me going, however, until I was well into the woods.

With a tremendous roar, half a dozen mortar shells landed together on the other side of the creek.

I went back to the house.

McCreary welcomed me. "We were really sweating you out," he said. "Thought maybe the Krauts would be using that guy as bait for an ambush."

"We'll get him with hand grenades," Marsh suggested. "O.K., Web?"

I nodded.

We tiptoed back down the forest path through the bare, black, dripping trees, and stopped behind a two-foot mound that ran along the river's edge. The rope that the patrol had used was still in position. The wounded German lay out of sight on his back near the other end, which was tied to a concrete telephone pole about fifteen yards from us.

He must have heard us coming. For a few moments he held his breath and stopped groaning and gasping and wheezing, evidently hoping that we would not notice him. But he couldn't stay quiet long, and soon the ghastly, sucking wheezes commenced again, loud as ever.

Poor bastard, I thought, listening to him. He's trying to hide from us. He's dying, and he knows we want to kill him. What a fate: to gasp your life out all alone in the mud of a dirty little creek, helpless to hold off the slow death that is inside you and the quicker death that is walking up on you on the other side of the water. A death without love, a death without hope. God, who invented war?

But if he gets back alive, I may be dead.

"O.K.," Marsh whispered, "let's throw 'em."

We pulled the pins on our hand grenades and arched them across the river at the sound of the wheezing. One of the grenades exploded, the other was a dud. There was no change in the breathing noises. We went into the house, got two more grenades, and tried again, without success. The German continued to moan and wheeze.

"The hell with it," Marsh said. "Let him die. They won't come after him."

We gave up and went to bed.

Just before sunrise, Cobb, who had also considered swimming—until he had heard the mortars—strolled down to the creek, threw one grenade, and killed the helpless, dying German.

Our home was secure for another day.

Hitler's
Champagne

IT WAS SPRING AGAIN, THE EARLY SPRING OF 1945, AND WE WERE
deep in the enemy's country, on the plains of Bavaria. By this time, many
of the mourners who had bowed their heads at Littlecote were in turn
themselves mourned, and a squad of twelve counted itself lucky if it had
two men left who had jumped in Normandy.

We had been searching for the front for several weeks and hadn't
found it yet. From the Rhine River, where we had lived in apartment
houses on the west bank and listened to the infantry mop up the Ruhr
Pocket on the opposite shore, we had ridden in a huge semicircle
through Germany, Holland, Belgium, Luxembourg, and France, and
back into Germany again.

Our journey was delightfully noncombatant. The air was warm and
sweet, the countryside newly green. Bedded down in hay provided by
Colonel Sink, who knew what we wanted, we hung our feet over the side
of our little boxcars, munched K rations, shot at passing trees, and admired landscapes that were not crowned with airbursts. We passed as
tourists through cities like Aachen, Sarrbrucken, Kaiserslautern, Luxembourg City, and Sarreguimines, and finally stopped at Ludwigshaven,
where we switched to D.U.K.W.s and set off with the 7th Army in search
of the front.

All the rumors were encouraging. A G.I. in the Transportation Corps
said that the front had broken up completely. The Germans were surrendering by the thousands, an M.P. told us. A Red Cross girl claimed
that organized resistance had ceased altogether.

We drove through Ludwigshaven and crossed the Rhine on the long,
swaying, Ernie Pyle pontoon bridge. From the ruins of Mannheim (dead
rotting in the rubble, no civilians on the streets), we turned east, and
going uphill, entered beautiful country very like the Catskill Mountains.
Heidelberg stood undamaged by the lovely Neckar River, but we continued through it and eventually crossed the Danube at Ulm on another

pontoon bridge. On we went, still looking for the front, through the Pfalz, Baden, Wurttemburg, the prettiest part of southern Germany, gathering a battle star for a campaign that involved no shooting.

The once mighty German army was in a state of utter dissolution. Everywhere we went, enemy soldiers flowed to the roads like rivulets running downhill after a rain. We relieved them of their watches, pistols, and binoculars and sent them on their way to rear echelon, for we couldn't be bothered with them now; there were just too many of them. They had been a novelty at first—live Germans by the hundreds—but the novelty wore off quickly and we grew bored with them, so merciless in victory, so fawning in defeat.

We sunbathed on the breaks and spent each night in a village, where we commandeered the dwellings and bade the civilians be on their way till morning. We ate fried eggs and canned beef and drank the liquors of a continent, ranging from French cognac and German schnapps to Russian vodka and Hungarian kirsch. We slept between sheets and took hot baths, and nobody traveled without a corkscrew, a frying pan, and a radio. Though it was forbidden by the clean-minded young men at S.H.A.E.F. (farther in the rear than ever before), some of us even fraternized with the local *Mädchen. Kommen Sie* here, baby!

WE HAD PULLED OFF the Munich-Salzburg Autobahn at twilight, after the 3rd Battalion, which was in the lead, had been ambushed at a blown bridge. It was the Regiment's first action in southern Germany. A pocket of Germans who had apparently not heard the news of their nation's collapse had opened fire on the 3rd Battalion as it halted at the gap in the great, six-lane superhighway. Several men were killed who had been with the Regiment since its start. The rest dismounted and spent the night climbing a mountain and flanking the ambush.

We enjoyed a more civilian evening. After backing up and turning around, we went to a Hansel-and-Gretel village, filled with wounded S.S. men, a couple of miles north of the Autobahn and spent the night frying eggs and drinking new milk and old brandy. We switched on the electric stove in our chalet and fried a few dozen Grade A. We slept between sheets on soft double beds, and we did not envy the 3rd Battalion.

Now another day had come. "Hit it, hit it!" the C.Q. had cried. "Moving out in half an hour."

I wriggled out of my mummy-type, one-man sleeping bag and sat up on the living room floor, where I had gone to sleep. The C.Q. had left the door open behind him, and the icy blast of air that came in made me shiver and cringe. It was still dark outside.

Muttering obscenities, I looked at my watch. It was only 4:30, an hour before the normal reveille. I shuddered. We only rose this early for a dawn attack. I did not look forward to fighting again. It was too late in the war to risk being killed. I was an acting noncom, a squad leader, but I still did not want to get killed.

My assistant, V.D., and I were the only men who had been in Normandy. The other ten had come in as replacements afterward. Not one of us had been in this same squad a year ago. In fact, half the men were young boys from the 18-year-old draft who had been in the Army long enough to take 13 weeks' basic and 4 weeks' jump training before going overseas as replacements. It was a good squad, though, and I was glad to have it while my regular squad leader, Marsh, was on furlough in the Riviera.

After I had gotten the men up, we gathered in the warm kitchen and ate breakfast. The dawn attack was the main topic of conversation. With the Alps running like jagged sharks' teeth on the southern horizon only ten or fifteen miles away, we were all concerned about the so-called National Redoubt, the mountainous stronghold where Hitler had allegedly ordered the S.S. to make their last stand. It was one of those fight-to-the-last-man stands he was always ordering (and how seldom they were executed!), but its basic idiocy did not make it any less menacing to us. We did not look forward to cleaning out the Alps in a tedious mountain campaign, now that the war was almost over.

We lingered so long in the kitchen that our platoon sergeant had to come in and roust us with an obscene blast for holding up the Company. He left, and I went to the living room and put on my musette bag and harness. Still the cautious soldier, I checked my cartridge belt to make sure I had everything. I would never move out unless I had everything.

Yes, it was all there: bayonet, canteen, shovel, compass, wire cutters, first-aid packet, and the .45 I had bought to keep from getting my throat cut on the jumpfield in Holland. I took two hand grenades from my pockets and hung them on my suspenders. My rifle was loaded, my stomach full, a fifth of kirsch was in my pocket. I was ready to go into action. I picked up a box of machine-gun ammunition, told V.D. to check the house for misplaced or deliberately forgotten grenades and ammunition, and led the squad outside.

I was bitter cold. The puddles in the roadside ditches had frozen over in the night, and a heavy frost shone like the moonlight of D-Day on the roads and fields. The ground was frozen hard.

We ran down to where the rest of E Company was stamping its feet and milling about in a cloud of frozen curses, fell in place in front of the second squad, which was our rival in all scrounging and the avoidance of details, and came to attention under the glare of Captain Speirs. After a count had been taken, he gave us at ease and explained our mission.

"We're going into the Alps," he said, "as soon as the goddamn D.U.K.W.s get here. The war's almost over—just a couple of more days now—and I don't want to lose any of you men in an ambush, so keep your weapons handy and be ready to fight the minute you hear the first shot."

A runner pounded up the road and saluted. They talked briefly and then he left and the captain informed us that we had to meet the D.U.K.W.s on the other side of town. He faced us in the direction and gave us route step. D Company was already moving out ahead of us.

The village was asleep; there were no civilians or wounded Germans on the streets. The only sound was the distant crowing of a rooster and the heavy tramp and muffled clatter of the Battalion as it marched along.

I breathed deeply and threw my shoulders back, for it was good to be outdoors again in the cold country air that was so fresh and clean at dawn. I had always loved the outdoors, but growing up in a New York suburb, I had never experienced it so fully or satisfactorily as in the Army.

The marching column was a part of that love, for the two seemed to go together, the wonderful sweep of the open country and the long, bobbing line of broad shoulders, olive-green helmets, dark-brown rifles, and swinging arms. It was something I had searched for all my life, without consciously knowing it, something strong and open and manly. There was no sound as inspiring or reassuring as the heavy tramp of jump boots and the soft clatter of shovels and bayonets on moving legs.

This was where I belonged. I had come back to it twice, after minor wounds in Normandy and Holland, and I wanted to stay with it to the end. I did not like the Army and I would never "Sir" anybody again as long as I lived, but as long as I had to be in the Army, I wanted to be in the 506th.

I looked at the sky and then at my watch. Five-thirty and already getting light. But it was a dull light, with no clear sky and a mass of very dark clouds lowering on the earth as for a thunderstorm.

We passed a grocery store that had just been abandoned by company headquarters. A wild mass of slave laborers and ex–prisoners of war was rushing in and out of the doors and windows, scrambling for boxes and cans and shouting and shoving and tearing at each other like hungry tigers. Some were short Mongolians, others big Nordic men, but all were Russians, with homemade red stars in their buttonholes.

"Rooski, Rooski!" we shouted, waving to them.

They grinned at us and commenced scrambling again. A few of the stronger—huge, rough-looking men in padded coats and fur caps with earflaps—who had managed to wrench some groceries from their compatriots started to trot past us. They yelled and waved and gave the V sign. How wonderful it is! their faces said, the war is almost over. *Deutschland kaput!*

The gray light spread out from the east, lighting from below the mass of black clouds overhead. Suddenly, as always at dawn, the air seemed much colder than it had at night. I pushed the box of machine-gun ammunition that I was carrying under a suspender and thrust my hands into my pants pockets to keep them warm.

"So this is May?" I said to McCreary, the second-squad leader, who was marching alongside.

"They can have it, buddy," he replied. "I'd hate to be here in December."

We continued a quarter of a mile beyond the village before we saw a convoy of D.U.K.W.s moving slowly toward us. Colonel Strayer stopped the first one and asked where the hell they had been. A red-eyed, irritated 1st lieutenant told him.

He said the D.U.K.W.s had been assigned to the 1st Battalion, then shifted to the 3rd and at three o'clock this morning to the 2nd. His men hadn't had regular rations or a good night's sleep for two weeks. They had made the invasion of southern France in August with the 7th Army and had been with them ever since, from the Riviera to the Vosges Mountains and the Danube crossing, but they had never worked with such an erratic, improvised outfit as this airborne division. "We're used to solid, well-organized outfits like the 3rd and the 36th Divisions," he said defensively. Colonel Strayer told him what he thought of truck drivers and bade him turn his barges around in the nearest field and take his men aboard.

We halted on the road while the D.U.K.W.s smashed down a fence, made a half circle on a frozen meadow to our left, came back on the road, and lined up bumper to bumper, facing south. The maneuver, which took twenty minutes, was accompanied by stamping feet and impatient cursing as the men got colder and colder. The last D.U.K.W. made its turn, the lowering sky broke up, and it started to snow. We climbed in.

I took a stand near the front, to see what was going on, while the others, who were less curious, huddled together on the cold metal floor. Finally the convoy moved off with the waddling motion peculiar to these vehicles, which resembled a pontoon on wheels and rode like a sailboat in a gentle swell. The cursing subsided to snores, shivers, and lewd mutters of complaint.

It was snowing so hard that we could only see about fifty yards ahead. The D.U.K.W.s went up and down some low hillocks, turned left on the Autobahn, moved tentatively ahead a mile, and halted.

I shook the snow off my helmet and checked my watch—6:20. It was going to be an awfully late dawn attack—perhaps it would never come? I could be home frying eggs.

The memory of the kitchen reminded me of other warm things, and suddenly I recalled the kirsch. I snaked the bottle out of my pocket and glanced casually around the D.U.K.W. The coast was clear; most of the men were sleeping with their arms folded on top of their knees and their heads buried in their arms. Nobody was watching me but V.D., a big replacement named Smith, our lieutenant and platoon sergeant, and Joe Liebgott, now the first platoon's interpreter-radioman. I unscrewed the cap and took a drink. The warm, sweet liquor made my body glow. I took another drink.

"Dibs," said Liebgott.

I nodded and handed the bottle to Smith, who had priority because he was in my squad. He called it "cough syrup, worse than rum" and drank more than I had. Liebgott was next.

"That stuff'll kill you," McCreary said, blinking up at us. He extended his arm. "Give me a drink."

Liebgott passed the bottle to V.D., who tilted his head back and gargled. The bizarre noise woke the rest of the men, and they studied him with thirsty eyes. I cursed him for drawing attention to the kirsch. "We could have kept it up at this end," I said. "Now we have to pass it around."

The snow stopped and a cold wind came off the Alps to clear the sky and chill us further. In the light of a sun that glared without warmth, we saw a blown bridge half a mile downhill from us. There were three small houses just this side of the bridge. Men were dismounting from the D.U.K.W.s ahead and running up and down on the pavement, shadow-boxing and waving their arms and clapping their hands together to warm up. Others started to heat their rations over little cardboard fires lit in cleared spaces on the highway.

Captain Speirs came alongside and told us that we could dismount if we wanted to. "We're in for a long wait," he explained. Three or four men jumped out and started to run up and down, whooping and hollering.

An old man left one of the houses on a bicycle and pedaled slowly toward us. He got off as the road grew steeper and walked beside his bicycle. While the rest of us watched in jeering disgust, two braves held him up.

He was a very old man, pale and frail and hollow-looking, with a goatee and a black serge suit, and he was panting deeply from his uphill climb. He looked as if he were dressed for church. For all we knew, it might even have been Sunday; days of the week meant nothing to us in the field.

"*Hande hoch!*" one of the heroes yelled, covering him with a Luger.

We snickered. "Look at the brave soldiers!" someone shouted. "*Combat men.*"

The old man dropped his bike so fast, its lamp broke. His hands shot in the air. He trembled violently.

One of the bravos frisked him and yanked out a heavy silver pocket watch. He waved it triumphantly in the air. The whole Company hissed him. His buddy fished through the civilian's wallet and displayed a handful of paper money. He, too, was hissed. The old man pleaded with them tearfully, but they sent him on his way.

I looked at them both and shook my head. Tough guys. The biggest looters were seldom the bravest soldiers. In fact, as Captain Speirs, who had been decorated three times for bravery, more than once remarked, there was an inverse ratio between courage and looting. Ashamed of the deed and yet powerless to undo it, since one of the men was in company headquarters and the other was a noncom (politically appointed, through court intrigue in our former captain's quarters), I glanced away from the old man's pleading eyes as he shuffled timidly by, and began to study the snow on a tree across the road. This was indeed some dawn attack.

The men ahead swarmed back into their D.U.K.W.s, and the 1st sergeant shouted for us to load up and pass the word along. "We're moving out," he said.

The snow fell off the branch that I was watching, the conquered foe wheeled his bicycle out of sight, and we jolted toward the Alps.

WE TURNED RIGHT almost at the blown bridge and squeaked and swayed and slipped down a narrow dirt road into a cold, dark valley. The D.U.K.W.s that had gone before us had churned the snow to a black slime that offered no footing; our driver wrestled and cursed to keep from sliding off the crown into a rutted ditch alongside. Tall, overhanging pine trees, brushed in passing, softly dumped their loads of snow on us, and soon the column slowed down to less than a walk as more and more of the ponderous vehicles floundered from their course and struggled to regain it. The temperature in the valley was below freezing, and the air very still and ominous.

We left the road, nosed up onto a railway roadbed, and jolted along the cavities where the ties had been. In their retreat, the Germans had ripped up both ties and rails with one of those wasteful machines that are only good for war. The tracks lay off to one side in strange, twisted shapes. Gradually the roadbed curved to the left. As we crossed a little wooden trestle spanning a rocky brook, we saw, half a mile away, the gap in the Autobahn that we were bypassing. The bridge foundations jutted out into the air fifteen or twenty feet on both sides, and the crumpled black mass of the span lay in a rocky gorge a hundred yards below.

Most of the men were sound asleep by now, for it was not a very exciting journey. Only V.D. and I stood erect. We had finished the kirsch between us, and thus fortified, were ready to face whatever perils or adventures lay ahead.

"I don't like it," I said thickly, swaying with the D.U.K.W. "It's too quiet."

We passed a snowy clearing with a cluster of little gingerbread houses right out of Grimm's Fairy Tales. V.D. frowned at them.

"Look at that," he said. "All closed up and not a civilian in sight."

"And no white flags. They always put up white flags before."

I shook my head. You could count on trouble when the civilians took off.

"Maybe this is the start of the Redoubt," V.D. said. "We're in the foothills of the Alps now."

We lapsed into silence and studied the land around us. Nothing moved, nothing made a sound. There were no birds or cows, no cheerful farm noises or children calling to each other.

"We're due for a fight," I muttered, gripping my M-1 very hard. "We've had it too easy: no patrols, no attacks, no combat, no artillery. All we've done in Germany is sleep in houses and eat fresh eggs. It can't last forever."

"I don't like it either. It's just too goddamn quiet."

We swung around a corner, left the roadbed for a country lane, and stopped. Somebody banged a rifle butt against the hollow side and told us to unload. We got out.

The convoy was halted at a steep hill on which a D.U.K.W. had skidded halfway up. The D.U.K.W. was lying across the road with its rear wheels stuck in a ditch. A group of men stood around it like sidewalk superintendents, offering lewd advice to the driver. We marched past them. An officer came up and made the superintendents pile brush under the rear wheels, for the stern had sunk so low that the propeller, which was centered between the wheels, was buried in the ground. The driver sighed and lit a cigarette. "This goddamn outfit," he began as we passed by.

"Don't bitch"—Liebgott grinned—"transfer." He laughed and went on.

"This goddamn outfit," the driver continued. "I never seen anything like it. Talk about efficiency!"

One of the detail who was gathering faggots chuckled and told him that he hadn't seen anything yet.

"Nothing's left." The driver sighed. "Nothing's left."

We went up the hill and came out on the Autobahn again, where the head of the convoy was waiting for us. Our detour was apparently over. Perhaps the National Redoubt was never to come.

Men had already set to work frisking the German soldiers drifting along the Autobahn. Two heroes stripped a pair of soft-leather, fleece-lined flying pants off a Luftwaffe sergeant and turned him loose in a sweater and his long underpants to surrender elsewhere. Another man found a Wehrmacht captain with Zeiss binoculars and a canteen full of brandy.

The wind had died down, the sun grown warm, the snow was melting fast. For the first time today, we could see the Alps. They looked much closer in the bright, clear morning air than they had at twilight, when they had appeared to be ten or fifteen miles away.

The ditched D.U.K.W. struggled free at last and ground slowly up to the Autobahn, with the tail of the convoy dragging behind. We mounted and got under way again, rolling down the great, six-lane highway at top speed.

The surrendering Germans swelled from rivulets into tidal waves. In one meadow we saw several thousand squatting in a docile encampment guarded by three bored American M.P.s. When others came to us on breaks and with a strange and almost touching but still typically German mixture of pride, arrogance, and humility begged to be allowed to surrender to a high-class airborne unit, we waved them off and airily told them we couldn't be bothered. They would have to swallow their pride and surrender to rear echelon.

It was a time of great gaiety. Victory was in the air, and the Wehrmacht was melting away before our eyes into a shabby mass of bewildered men wandering sullenly along the same road on which they had marched in triumph five years before, when their chosen leader had launched them on history's darkest wave of barbarism and extermination. Trucks and tanks from other American units came onto the Autobahn at every intersection and passed us with waves and shouts. The drivers all wore bright scarves and old civilian hats; even the tank commanders, who normally never shifted their eyes from the terrain ahead, called and waved and gave the V sign.

Wherever a P.W. enclosure or slave-labor lager had been liberated, the ragged, hungry inmates poured onto the highway that a maniac had built to enslave them and their children and their children's children. *"Deutschland kaput!"* they cried to us. No matter how tattered their clothes, the freed men had all taken pains to fashion tiny ornaments of their national colors for their buttonholes. They wore them as proudly as a medal for bravery: the red star of Russia; the tricolor of France; red and green for Italy; blue, white, and gold for Yugoslavia. There were Poles, Czechs, Greeks, Belgians, Dutch, Magyars, Slovenes, Lithuanians, and many others, all former slave laborers or prisoners of war.

I was glad, when I saw them, that I had come back to the outfit and gone into Germany, for the trip, with its views of the lagers and prison camps, had finally convinced me of the need to drive the Germans from the face of Europe. How could a civilized nation run concentration camps and murder millions—and still fight for that way of life? How could a man fight for a nation that broke up millions of families, that put old women and little children to work in slave-labor lagers? The Third Reich was a cancer on the face of Western man. I was glad now that I had played a part, however small, in helping to remove that cancer. Herbert Hoover, with his methodical, engineer's mind, could admire the Germans as an efficient and industrious race, but I was only sorry that I had not shot more of them.

Soon we started to pass the remnants of Germany's lowest triumph, the concentration camps. The sight, after so many years of propaganda, of those striped uniforms, so like pajamas, that signified endless death on the widest and most coldly methodical scale was very chilling.

A lone man from Dachau wandered out of a field when we were halted by the road and talked in a dazed way of the death that the Germans had planned for the world. He spoke of his years in Dachau and the thousands that he had seen die there. Others came up shortly afterward, and soon we passed them by the score. It made us feel good to think that our Army had set them free.

The D.U.K.W.s rolled on, past der Chiemsee, a lovely blue lake with a yacht basin, now a resort hotel that had been converted into a Wehrmacht hospital, and then pulled off onto a grassy shoulder for a ten-minute break. We dismounted to relieve ourselves and stretch our legs and frisk the passing Germans.

While we were lolling on the grass, someone motioned for silence. "Do you hear that?" he inquired, jerking his head toward the Alps. "Sounds like thunder."

I listened carefully. There were no clouds to make a thunderstorm, but there was thunder.

"Man, Web," V.D. said with a worried look on his face, "it doesn't sound good, does it?"

"No," I replied, biting my lip, for I recognized the sound, "it doesn't." It was a rolling barrage.

WE LEFT THE AUTOBAHN at the next side road and plunged down toward the artillery fire. Our mood changed from holiday excitement to silent foreboding as we descended and came upon more evidence of war than we had seen since Ulm.

Knocked out by aircraft, two yellow-brown Wehrmacht half-tracks stood at the edge of the first forest trail. There were three fresh graves in the woods nearby, with German helmets on the top of rough, pine-bough crosses. A P-47 fighter plane lay tilted like a great, stiffened, silver fish among the tall, dark pine trees farther on. We passed foxholes and slit trenches and a burnt-out antiaircraft half-track at a crossroads. Its dead cannon still pointed at the sky.

The sound of firing got louder and louder, the Alps came nearer and nearer. This was the National Redoubt, and we were going into it.

Nobody slept in the D.U.K.W.s anymore. Instead, the men stood ready with their weapons in their hands and stared anxiously at the cold, gloomy woods all around us. The road circled a low, bare hill where the enemy had abandoned four 105mm cannon in the snow on the reverse slope and went through a pass pocked with shell holes and strewn with smashed trees and abandoned G.I. gear and helmets. We started down to the valley where the shells were falling with the slam of heavy doors.

My stomach turned to water. "Jesus," I murmured, "I don't like this." My enthusiasm for war, limited even at the start, had vanished completely in the slit trench in Veghl.

The valley ahead of us was about three miles wide and four or five long. Its floor, patches of green meadow and golden grainland, was composed of low, gently rolling hills. Bigger, steeper, pine-covered hills bounded the valley on three sides. The Alps rose on the fourth, or south, side.

They were dark and ominous, gigantic, immense, towering, towering over all wars and all humanity. Everything about them was cold and hostile: the gray rocks, the thick grass and heavy moss that ran from tree level to the rocks, and the blue-green pine forests that cloaked their massive bases. A bitter wind blew down at us from the blinding white snow on the fangs that were their summits.

"Get ready for an ambush," I said, trying to appear calm and not quite succeeding.

The other men nodded and said nothing. They had been ready ever since we had left the Autobahn.

Our convoy rolled onto the valley floor and turned right. A jeep from another unit overtook us with a steady honking. "Off the road, off the road!" yelled a major standing beside the driver. He waved us aside with a violent gesture.

We went to the shoulder with a quick swing and stopped. The artillery fire was very close now. I felt like vomiting.

Their fronts sandbagged against Panzerfausts, a column of heavy tanks clattered past us in the wake of the jeep. Crouching, clinging infantrymen with fixed bayonets covered their tops and knelt behind the turrets. They passed us without a word or wave of greeting and were gone as swiftly as they had come. The artillery fell like summer thunder.

Our D.U.K.W.s returned to the road and commenced their journey in a silence of their own. They turned left, away from the bombardment, and then right, and came out on a muddy lane running straight toward the Alps. A convoy of trucks and half-tracks several hundred yards long was parked on the left shoulder. They bore the cross of Lorraine insignia of the French 2nd Armored Division, a unit manned by former sailors, now in green combat suits, who still wore black berets with bright-red pompons. The D.U.K.W.s slowed down by them and stopped suddenly, jamming up together.

Pep! A sound like the report of a German rifle went off to the right of our D.U.K.W.

"S.S.! S.S.!" a Frenchman cried from a half-track opposite us. He pointed excitedly in the direction of the sound.

"Ambush!" I yelled, clicking the safety catch off my rifle. I started over the side, then looked out and froze in position. "Jesus," I whispered.

A French tankman stood ankle-deep in the snow in a young pine forest beside the D.U.K.W. with a smoking Belgian automatic in his hand

and a cigarette in the corner of his mouth. A young German boy in his early teens lay dead at his feet in a long Wehrmacht overcoat. Hatless and unarmed, his body bore no gear whatsoever.

Two other boys, similarly clad, knelt behind the body, their mouths and eyes wide open, their faces paralyzed with fright. As they stared helplessly at the Frenchman, he blew the ash off his cigarette, put the pistol against the second boy's forehead, and splattered his brains red and yellow and purple on the snow behind him.

One of our replacements turned fish-belly white and vomited over the side. "God, oh God, oh God," he moaned.

The Frenchman stepped up to his last prisoner.

This boy was the youngest of the three. He had never shaved. He had soft brown eyes and a fresh, cheerful, pink adolescent face that had never been creased by worry or the awareness of death. All the thoughts that old men have but that he had never had before crowded in an instant into his mind and came out in his eyes and on his forehead. Framed by the dark pines, he put his hands together and prayed and cried softly and waited to die.

The D.U.K.W. moved forward, and we heard the shot from the distance.

I turned to a cocky, bubbling, young replacement who had been eager to see action. "There's your goddamned war!" I said. "Did you like it, did you like it?"

He gulped and shook his head.

OUR CONVOY PASSED an armored reconnaissance car at the head of the French column at the moment the artillery ceased firing. There was a great burst of crackling, popping small-arms fire behind us as the infantry attacked the shelled positions. We turned east and left it all behind.

A narrow pass through a dripping, rocky gorge took us out of the valley and through the foothills into the Alps themselves. The men relaxed and lay down and began to doze off. We wound round and round, up and down, till it seemed to those of us who were still awake that we must be hopelessly lost.

At last our side road joined a better one near a dark brook, where a lone enemy soldier stood beside a signpost in a black tanker's uniform, the same kind worn by S.S. armored troops. Liebgott, who was Jewish and had no love for the S.S., studied him with narrowed eyes.

"*Sind Sie S.S.?*" he inquired, leaning toward him with his rifle at his hip.

"*Nein. Ioh bin Panzergrenadier.*"

Unconvinced, Liebgott clicked the safety off his M-1.

"Hold your fire!" we shouted, not wishing to witness another murder. "He's harmless."

Liebgott ignored us. He was from the Far West, and he had something else in mind.

"*Sie sind S.S.!*" he yelled. "Dance, you sonofabitch!" He began to shoot around the German's feet.

The German pranced and cavorted. I didn't know whether to laugh or cry.

Captain Speirs yelled back for Liebgott to cease fire. He lifted his rifle with a grin, and we drove off, leaving a bewildered German behind.

Roused by the shots, the rest of the men came to life. They stood up and yawned and stretched their arms and legs and studied the mountains and admired the speed with which we were traveling, for we were going downhill in a great rush, as if the drivers had finally found out where we were going and were in a hurry to get there. Rounding a bend, we popped out of the dark gorge and raced toward a little Alpine village that sloped up very prettily from a rocky river ten yards wide.

There was a sign at a bridge we had to cross to get into town. When we read what the sign said, we screamed with joy.

It was Berchtesgaden.

WHITE FLAGS HUNG from the carved wooden balconies of the hotels and inns that lined the steep, narrow streets, and a few of the older civilians came outdoors to watch us drive in. The D.U.K.W.s crept slowly into the center of town and stopped.

"This calls for a drink," one of our replacements said.

V.D. and I gaped as he pulled a fifth of Gordon's Gin out of a big pants pocket. "Found it in the last billet," he explained, passing it around. Four fingers were left when it reached me.

"Bet I can drink it in one minute," I said, hoisting the bottle. "A thousand francs. Any takers?"

"I'll bet you can't," the replacement, Neumann, said. "Another fifth says you can't."

"You have another one too? Man, you guys learn fast. Here goes."

I upended the bottle and started to drink. Neumann timed me and the rest of the squad looked on. The gin was gone in forty seconds. I put the new fifth in my musette bag and began to enjoy Berchtesgaden.

A bright, clean resort village of about eight thousand inhabitants, Berchtesgaden rested for the most part on the south slope of a hill surrounded by glittering mountains of breathtaking beauty. The houses were built in the traditional Alpine style, with rocks on the roof, carved wooden balconies at each end, and fresco paintings of pastoral or religious scenes on the stucco walls. The village had been a modest German mountain resort long before Hitler had made it famous.

Even after six years of war, the shops still catered to tourists. There were camera stores (with no cameras), chocolate shops (without chocolate), and restaurants (without food). The places that had sold resort wear had no clothing—it had all gone for the war—and the ski shops had no skis. Innkeeping was the major occupation, and almost every building bore the sign of a hotel, inn, or Gasthof.

None of the natives could say, as they had in other towns, that they had not liked Hitler, for their absolute loyalty to the Nazi cause had been assured years before by the S.S. and the S.D., who allowed only certified, bonded, 100-proof Nazis to live so close to their leader's chalet. It was said that the British had dropped spies into the surrounding mountains on three different occasions with orders to take up residence in Berchtesgaden—and had never heard from any of them again. All the civilians were so well-known and thoroughly registered and suspicious of strangers that a newcomer was reported to the police the instant he strolled into town.

The gentleman who had so popularized this once obscure village that its name was known throughout the world had not lived in Berchtesgaden proper. He had taken to himself, instead, a private mountain, der Kehlstein, which rose abruptly from the river we had just crossed, on the town's southern fringe. Der Kehlstein was fenced off, guarded, and maintained as an S.S. preserve, with its own heavily patroled roads and massive, camouflaged barracks. Halfway up to an elevator that ran through solid rock to the Eagle's Nest stood a chalet, der Berghof, which served as a guesthouse.

It was a neat arrangement, worthy of a knave who gloried in murder and lived in fear, and so the British, in one of the light, personal gestures that they used so well to brighten the war, had bombed the mountainside with blockbusters. The S.S. had vanished among the craters thirty feet deep, and the tidy estate had been converted in an instant to a landscape resembling the face of the moon. The former owner died far north in Berlin in the crumbling, rotten ruins of his Thousand-Year Reich, and a new day came for Berchtesgaden.

So great had been the rivalry among American units racing for its capture that when Colonel Sink had radioed corps' headquarters for permission to use a bypass that would have enabled the 506th to be first in, corps had replied that everybody and his brother were trying to get into that town. A brigadier general from the 3rd Division had pulled rank on the colonel and held the Regiment up at another bypass, thus enabling the 3rd Division to reach Berchtesgaden first. It was a Pyrrhic victory, however, for our own Major General Taylor, who outranked the brigadier, promptly ordered him to lead his men back into the wilderness. This left us in possession—at 9:30 in the morning, just three hours after we had left our last billet, fully expecting to have to shoot our way into the National Redoubt.

We lingered in town awhile, then moved off to a large house beyond, where I fell asleep under a pine tree. The D.U.K.W.s left us without regret, having found us too casual for their taste, and at 2:30 a convoy of G.I. trucks took us to a settlement of long, white, two-story chalets on a highway about a mile and a half north of Berchtesgaden. The new billets were laid out as precisely as an Army camp and were separated from the road by a smooth lawn a hundred feet wide.

After a long wait while the civilians decamped and the billeting officer apportioned our quarters, Captain Speirs made a little speech. "We're going to live in these houses," he said. "They were built as apartments for the families of the Gestapo police that used to guard Hitler, so we don't care what you do to them or take from them as long as you keep them neat. Not a single civilian will be allowed in the area. The whole town is S.S., and if you don't want to lose your jump pay for six months for fraternizing, you won't be talking to any Krauts around here."

He paused, and I blinked at him, barely able to stand up. The gin had done its work. All I wanted to do was go to sleep.

"We'll stand guard on the road and around the apartments to keep the civilians out and be ready in case the S.S. comes back down the mountain to raid us; a lot of 'em haven't been accounted for yet. The Krauts will be turning themselves in at a big P.W. enclosure a mile down the road from here. The second platoon will guard this enclosure. Rest of the Company stays here."

The 1st sergeant came up and saluted. "It's O.K. to move in now, Captain," he said. "Trucks are waiting to take the second platoon away."

The Company split up at the captain's order. McCreary's squad and mine wound up in the last chalet to the north. V.D. and I staked a claim on the best bedroom by throwing our gear on the floor and then set out to reconnoiter the billet.

It was the best we had had in Germany. There were three big bedrooms in the upstairs apartment that we occupied, with a full-sized living room, a separate dining room, a tiled lavatory with a modern tub and toilet, and best of all, a large kitchen at the south end with three exposures.

The kitchen was painted a warm yellow, with red flowers on the drawers and cupboards. It featured a massive icebox, a six-burner electric stove, and a table long enough to seat half the squad at a time. Pots, pans, chinaware, and condiments were all in place; nothing had been removed or disturbed. We began to brew a pot of ersatz coffee.

The other men fell asleep or busied themselves putting away their belongings. The only noise came from a pair who were tuning in the squad radio, which we had acquired in a place called Buchloe. "There's a rumor the Krauts have all surrendered!" one of them shouted excitedly. "Looks like the war's over."

"*Yahoo!*" I yelled, pounding V.D. on the back.

While the rest of the men hurried to the kitchen to discuss the rumor, V.D. and I slipped downstairs to the basement, where we hoped to find some valuable S.S. loot hidden away.

The door was already open. We looked in and saw that the room was piled high with trunks, suitcases, and fiberboard boxes. We smiled, then frowned when we noticed that McCreary's men had beaten us to it. They were already busily at work, smashing the locks with bayonets and rifle butts.

"Man has to get up early in the morning to beat that goddamn second squad," V.D. muttered.

"Hell, they've only begun," I said. "Come on."

I ran to the coal pile, which was in a far corner and was the most logical hiding place, picked up a long iron bar lying beside the furnace, and rammed it deep into the coal.

It struck something solid. Picturing a pirate's chest of rubies, diamonds, and gold coins, I dropped the bar and tore at the coal with my bare hands until I reached the box.

It was a case of tinned beef.

"Sonofabitch!" I exclaimed.

"We can cook it upstairs."

"Who the goddamn hell wants to cook?"

Someone from the second squad took the iron bar and began smashing at the locked trunks with all the fury of a Goth in Rome. In half an hour, the floor was covered with a wild array of clothes and home furnishings.

One of the former tenants, a middle-aged woman who had been permitted to return for some forgotten article, stopped in the doorway and gasped at the destruction. Her face quivered, and she burst into tears and went back outside.

Losing my taste for the sport, which was not at all remunerative, I lifted the case of beef and carried it up to the squad.

Our coffee was brewed. We sprawled around in the bright, warm kitchen and listened to the radio, which had been brought in. The sky had clouded over outside, and a thin, cold drizzle began to fall as the sun went down. The kitchen seemed very warm and cozy.

Christenson, who was now our platoon guide, came in with an air of whiskey and a wide grin on his face. He waved a piece of paper in the air. "At ease, goddammit!" he shouted. "Get a load of this."

We nodded.

"It's from corps. Just came in on the 300. Here's what it says: 'Effective immediately, all troops will stand fast on present positions. German Army Group G in this section has surrendered. No firing on Germans unless fired upon. Notify French units in vicinity. Full details, to be broadcast, will be issued by S.H.A.E.F.' "

We let out a great cry of joy.

"Yessir," Christenson said, "looks like the war is over. We couldn't end it in a better place."

"Whattayagot there?"

I stood shivering in the drizzle near the front door and frowned at Luz, the company comedian, as raucous and funny in combat as in garrison, and O'Keefe, who was one of our younger and more gentlemanly replacements. They had just pulled up in a boatlike vehicle that resembled a miniature D.U.K.W. A mortarman, Garcia, sat in back.

"A Schwimmwagen," Luz replied. "Took it off a Kraut down the road." He got out, and O'Keefe and Garcia stood up in back and heaved the front end of a large wooden packing case over the side for him to grasp.

I looked in the box. My eyes widened, for it was filled with bottles. "What the hell?"

"Champagne," O'Keefe said. He had gotten down to take the rear of the box. "O.K.," he grunted, "I got it." Staggering under the load, he, Garcia, and Luz started indoors. I followed them like a hungry dog.

"Where the hell?"

"Hitler's cellar."

"What!"

"Sure. From his hideout, der Berghof, the halfway house."

"Well, here, let me give you a hand. My God, we have to get this upstairs before McCreary sees it. I'll be goddamned."

We strained, stiff-armed and panting, to carry the champagne quickly beyond the reach of the second squad and unloaded it in my room, where V.D. promised to keep an eye on it. "T.O. equipment," Luz said. "Every man gets a jug."

While the rest of the squad crowded around, whistling in astonishment, I dropped my voice and asked Luz and his helpers what they were waiting for. "Let's get some more," I suggested, snatching up my helmet and buckling on my pistol belt. We ran down to the Schwimmwagen.

McCreary was in the driver's seat, tinkering with the starter. He smiled, blinked at us brightly, and said, "Well, well, howdoyoudo. Look at the abandoned vehicle."

"On the road, Mick," Luz said. "Get your own kiddy car. There's a million of 'em at the P.W. enclosure."

McCreary laughed and climbed out. We swarmed aboard like pirates boarding a galleon and drove off before he could discover our destination. "Well, well," he murmured. "I'll be goddamned." He stared after us and chewed on his cigarette. Something was up; somebody had found a good deal somewhere. That goddamn first squad, always screwing some-body, I know it, I just know it.

But he didn't know it was Hitler.

Luz was at the wheel, and he was in his element—noisy recklessness. "I should have been a midget-auto racer," he remarked, zooming into the first curve. He slammed on the brakes. The Schwimmwagen skidded around the corner, and he spun the wheel and straightened her out. My heart beat in my throat. O'Keefe and Garcia clutched the side and said nothing.

"Out of the way, you sonsabitches!" Luz roared at the night. He gunned the motor, pressed on the horn, and blared his way through Berchtesgaden at fifty miles an hour. "Goddamn Nazis."

I nodded and looked ahead, grating my teeth together and blinking at the darkness. "Oh my God," I gasped as he headed straight for a stone wall. I braced my feet against the floorboards, stiffened my legs, and closed my eyes. We skidded again, and I opened my eyes and saw the wall go by six inches away. *"Sieg oder Sibierien"* was painted on the wall in huge white letters.

Victory or Siberia, I thought. If Goebbels could only see us now.

Luz hurtled recklessly through the wet streets to the south end of town and across the narrow bridge there. We passed a concrete block-house and the high, barbed-wire fence that bounded Hitler's private mountain and then started uphill.

A G.I. with the 3rd Division patch on his sleeve reeled and retched his way down the middle of the road. Luz honked and told him to get out of the way, but he was too happy to care. He had a bottle of champagne in one hand and a P-38 in the other. "Whoopee!" he shouted, firing the pistol in the air, bambam.

"We have to hurry," Luz said. "The dogfaces are drinking it dry." He pushed the accelerator to the floor and swung wide to pass a slow-moving G.I. truck filled with shouting Frenchmen. A command car hur-tled out of the darkness at him, and he jerked the Schwimmwagen back on the right with such force that it skidded sideways until it stopped two feet from the edge of an immense bomb crater.

The craters were all around us now, but fortunately none of them blocked the road. There were shattered trees and the grotesque ruins of barracks and other buildings on both sides. The torn, volcanic land-scape looked like the surface of the moon.

Luz cursed and jammed on the brakes and barely missed knocking down two drunken paratroopers stumbling along the right side of the road with their arms over each other's shoulders. They were singing, "When the war is over, we will all enlist again," and they soon wandered from the pavement to sit in a muddy field and hold their heads awhile.

Luz accelerated. It seemed as if the whole world were racing for der Berghof, and he didn't want to come in last. The higher he went, the thicker grew the stream of vehicles, until it became an almost solid mass, bumper to bumper. Recon cars, command cars, jeeps, D.U.K.W.s, half-tracks, Volkswagens, Schwimmwagens—all were headed for the wine cellar. Luz drove on the left and passed as many of them as he could, but finally the traffic was so thick that he had to fall in line.

The road leveled off at last. We rounded a curve, and I gasped at the sight ahead.

It was an unforgettable sight: the nightmare looting of der Berghof, Hitler's secondary chalet. None of the blockbusters that the British had dropped in the vicinity had hit the house, but several smaller bombs had caved in the roof, shattered the windows, and rearranged the lawn. Spoilsport S.S. men had finished the job by setting the place afire. The front yard was a hideous mass of bomb craters, blackened timbers, broken glass, and jagged chunks of brick and mortar. Scores of paratroopers, Frenchmen, and 3rd Division soldiers lurched around noisily, stumbling in and out of the house.

Der Berghof was built on the side of a hill adjoining the mountain that bore the more famous Adlerhorst, or Eagle's Nest, which stood three thousand feet above us. The road to the elevator to der Adlerhorst was blocked by bomb damage, so for tonight we had to be content with der Berghof.

Luz drove into a parking place opposite the concrete chalet and stopped. A couple of French tankers in G.I. overcoats and dark-blue berets with bright-red pompons came up and greeted us. Was it true, they asked, that the war was over?

We nodded. O'Keefe, who had studied French, told them of the latest news on the radio. *"La guerre est finie,"* he said. It was May 5th and peace was still a rumor, but the rumor was strong enough to convert to fact.

The Frenchmen grinned and shook our hands. *"La guerre est finie!"* they shouted, yanking their pistols from their holsters. *"La guerre est finie! La guerre est finie!"* They fired wildly into the air.

The shooting stopped all motion. The souvenir hunters froze in their tracks and looked around at the night. There was a scramble for weapons in all the vehicles.

"S.S.!" someone shouted. "It's an ambush! They've come back."

"*La guerre est finie!*" the Frenchmen yelled, louder than before.

"The war's over!" we chorused. "The war's over!"

"The war's over!" everybody shouted. "*La guerre est finie!*"

Those who had pistols fired them at the night. Riflemen shot rifles, officers their carbines. Someone splattered a mudbank, pututut, with a Thompson. A truck driver seized the 50-caliber antiaircraft machine gun on the top of his cab and poured a belt of tracer at the opposing Kehlstein.

The shots and shouts echoed happily through the Alps. Men danced and shook hands and slapped backs and drank toasts to peace amid the monster's ruins. It was a wonderful scene, so far removed from that night before D-Day, when we had first entered Europe, as to seem another world.

"Come on," I said impatiently. "Let's get going." I looked at Luz. "Somebody had better stay here and watch the car. I don't trust anybody on this mountain." Luz shrugged his shoulders and said he'd stay; he had already seen the cellar. O'Keefe and I grabbed the empty packing case and headed for the house. Garcia brought up the rear.

We stumbled blindly across the muddy rubble to some wide stone stairs at the east end of the building and felt our way down to the first level. It was totally dark here but not quite deserted, for a swirling, livid mob of soldiers banged and cursed and tripped and fell all around us.

We groped forward to the first room, lit a match, and saw several dozen fine radios sitting on the floor and tables. Ordinarily these would have absorbed our energy and attention, but we had not come to Hitler's home to take his radios. What were radios beside the thrill of drinking Hitler's liquor? We returned to the stairs and felt our way down one more level to the wine cellar. A sound of drinking and carousing, of cursing and bottle breaking rose from there. We hurried to the bacchanalia as filings to a magnet.

The wine cellar was on the lowest level of the hillside house. A huge room chiseled out of bedrock, it was about fifty feet long, thirty wide, and ten high. It was filled to the ceiling with metal bottle racks on which a few thousand fifths, liters, and magnums still remained. Wild-eyed warriors lit matches, held candles, worked squeegee German flashlights, while their buddies snatched the bottles off the racks and put them in pockets, bags, boxes, and other containers. Everybody appeared to be both drinking and drunk. In their haste, they had broken so many bottles that the floor was flooded with wine. The room smelled like the inside of an old sauterne bottle.

"You hold the matches," I said to O'Keefe, "we'll get the jugs." I was vastly excited by the tumult. "We have to work fast." The mob was pouring downstairs like commuters to the Times Square shuttle. Garcia and I reached up, snatched trophy after trophy, and laid them carefully in the wooden box. Soon my arms began to tire. Working more slowly, I had the leisure to read the labels.

"That dirty cheapskate," I said in a disappointed tone of voice. "Nothing but wine: Rhine wine, red wine, white wine, liebfraumilch, Chilean Riesling. Where's the hard liquor?"

"He didn't have any. At least, if he did, we couldn't find it."

"I'll be darned. Imagine a man that powerful drinking such cheap booze? If it was me, I'd have filled this place with calvados, cognac, and Johnny Walker's black label." I clucked my tongue, very disappointed in Hitler.

Four men from F Company lined up beside us and began to strip the bottles methodically from the racks. One of them reached in front of me for a bottle of Mumm's.

"Take it easy, buddy," I said, snatching a Piper-Heidsieck from a rack below his knees. "There's enough for everybody."

"Better hurry, Web," O'Keefe said. "We're almost out of matches. Stick to champagne. That other stuff doesn't taste as good."

I nodded and moved off to a dark spot where a row of Piper-Heidsieck lay undisturbed. Four layers of bottles now rested in our box. Another would fill it. The box was quite large—over a yard long by two feet wide and deep—and it would be very heavy to carry up two flights of slippery stairs.

"That's it," O'Keefe sighed as the match burned down. "Goddamn!" He threw the stub away and shook his hand up and down.

The box was heavy indeed. When we bent to lift it, we found that we could only carry it about a foot off the floor, with frequent breaks. Weakened by the liquor and constantly thrown off balance by the uncertain footing and the newcomers who almost knocked us down as they plunged toward the cellar, we had to stop and rest every few feet. Our trip out took a good twenty minutes.

We stopped at the head of the stairs to straighten our backs, and breathing deeply, watched the spectacle outside. Hitler's last garden party, an insane confusion of lights, drunks, rubble, and rain, was twice confounded by the shouting, pushing horde of soldiers who had come up the mountain while we had been below. It would only be a matter of thirty or forty minutes, we knew, before the cellar would be drained dry.

As we stood and stared, we noticed something very unusual: The Frenchmen weren't putting any liquor in *their* trucks. A practical people, more grasping and materialistic than any American, they were making off with more durable souvenirs, gathered by an antlike procession of men going in and out of a tunnel in a hillside across the road. The tunnel contained Berghof furnishings stored underground for protection against air raids, and the Frenchmen came out of it with Hitler's soupspoons, Hitler's tablecloths, and Hitler's towels and chairs.

Too tired to follow them, we carried our swag over to the Schwimmwagen and wrestled it aboard.

"This calls for a drink," I said as we started back to town. I reached behind the seat and pulled a bottle of Mumm's from the packing case. I tore off the seal and the wire fastener, fired the cork at a passing weapons carrier, and gave the bottle to Luz. The four of us killed it quickly, then started on another, which we finished at the foot of the mountain.

The drizzle turned to heavy mountain rain so cold that it froze our bare hands and the tops of our knees, but we were numb to it all. We drank a third bottle of Hitler's champagne and smashed its carcass against a German's house. Careening through the empty streets of Berchtesgaden, we broke into the chorus of "Roll Me Over" ("in the clover, roll me over, lay me down, do it again").

We came to der Barchtesgadener Hof, the best hotel in town and now the residence of Colonel Sink. I stood up and shouted at the guard at the door, "Where'sh Hiller?"

The guard laughed.

"Where'sh Hiller? We gotta fine Hiller; he set 'em up. We gotta thank Hiller."

We passed the hotel. Turning and cupping my hands, I called back to the guard, "If you ever shee Hiller, give the shunofabish our regardsh."

WHAT A PARTY we had that night! Take a squad of twelve young men who had set out for war and found Berchtesgaden instead, add thirty bottles of Hitler's champagne, mix with the strongest rumors of peace, shake well in the Alps in spring, and you've poured our party.

Popping corks, spilling champagne, breaking bottles. Raucous laughter, ringing shouts, loud choruses of lewd ditties. Have another glash. Here, goddammit, lemme pop that cork! Ish'n thish wunnerful? Shugalug. Fill 'er up, O'Keefe. It'sh all on Hiller.

V.E. Day came three days later, but we didn't wait to celebrate. We celebrated the night of the fifth.

And the sixth.

And the seventh, which was V.E. Day proper, a glorious blue day that Captain Speirs spent throwing his empty champagne bottles off the balcony of his chalet and shooting at them blearily with a .45.

Somebody found a cognac factory down the road and wheeled in a hogshead for the first platoon. When this had been drained—it was rather green but speedy—we simply fetched another from the same source.

Wine, beer, and all blends and ages of hard liquor were available for the asking in almost every house and Bierstube within short driving range. If a sudden thirst overwhelmed you en route, you stopped the first stray German soldier and took his canteen. None of them ever carried water.

Other things were also free. The Regiment, always so short of vehicles that it had to use farm carts and captured trucks the first few days in action and borrow transportation like D.U.K.W.s thereafter, suddenly found itself completely motorized, with every man who could drive the proud owner of his own near-new vehicle. Some rode motorcycles, others preferred Volkswagens or Schwimmwagens. The cowboys rode S.S. horses and soon formed the 506th Parachute Cavalry, a marching, racing, and polo society that lasted till the horses were finally worn out. Each squad had two or three Opel Blitz trucks, standard in the German army, for military duties and at least one informal vehicle for scrounging and Fraulein expeditions. Our platoon sergeant went helling down the highways, siren shrieking and bell clanging, in a civilian fire engine. He was the terror of Bavaria.

Colonel Sink, of course, got the grand prize: Goering's (or was it Hitler's or Himmler's?) Mercedes Benz. This magnificent black cabriolet was a hoodlum's dream. It had bulletproof glass and a bulletproof body, one of the smoothest, most powerful engines on earth, and a glittering, silver front as imposing as any Rolls Royce's. Colonel Sink knew quality and how to treat it. He put a P.F.C. behind the wheel in a Class A uniform and drove through the Alps in oriental splendor, smoking cigars back in the rear seat, king of the world.

Captain Speirs also had a Mercedes, but his was a sadder tale, more Army than idyllic. The car was a duplicate of the colonel's, and he cherished it dearly. But alas, it caught the eye of the battalion commander, Colonel Strayer. He asked for it, but Captain Speirs was adamant. Possession, he claimed, is nine points of the law, and I've got possession. Colonel Strayer argued and then ended the discussion with a direct order. Gimme that car! Tomorrow, Captain Speirs replied. And aside to his dog-robber, Now we'll see if this car is *really* bulletproof.

He returned to the company area and loaded his M-1 with armor-piercing bullets. While we looked on aghast, for we all admired that great car, he opened fire on the Mercedes at five yards, shattering its windows.

And now, Captain Speirs, who could be ferociously vindictive when he was crossed, said to his audience, We'll see just how goddamn indestructible these cars are. He started the motor, drove up the road to a cliff, and slid out of the driver's seat just before the car plunged into the abyss.

And that was the end of Colonel Strayer's Mercedes.

FROM A DISTANCE the caravan looked pink in the setting sun, but those who passed it on the road saw that it was mostly green and yellow-brown. The green was the uniform of the passengers, the brown the standard color of their vehicles.

It was an enemy battle group composed of scattered units that had retreated so far into the mountains that they could retreat no farther, and now it had come down from a distant Alpine valley to surrender. There were division headquarters units, Volkssturm companies, antiaircraft platoons, quartermaster supply battalions—left with no supplies and no one to give them to if they had had them, for almost the whole army had disintegrated in the broken terrain and the wild scattering of the last few days of war.

Strung out along the highway north of Berchtesgaden, they looked more like a tribal movement than a military convoy of the nation that had been the scourge of all decent civilization only a few months before. The cars and trucks and wagons were piled high with tents and bedding and cooking utensils, and they moved without precision or uniformity. Since many of the vehicles were drawn by horses (for the Wehrmacht had relied heavily on animals for its transport), the convoy's speed was geared to the pace of its slowest dray. A rifleman walked twice as fast.

Stretched out on their belongings, the soldiers, who had lost their purpose on V.E. Day, rode languidly on this last trickle of a once mighty flood. None of them carried weapons or wore helmets; the only reminder of an age that had passed was an occasional clanking half-track or self-propelled gun.

The convoy was more than a mile long, and our men, who stood and watched it pass the compound for almost an hour, all commented on the profusion of women. The American Army, which liked women just as well, we noted, had nothing like it. There were German Wacs, Luftwaffe *Mädchen*, young refugees from bombed cities who had attached themselves to the soldiers for bed and board. The German men studied the Americans with a professional interest that was returned in full, but the women, who had no such fraternal curiosity, saw us only as the enemy and looked away when we whistled and shouted, "*Kommen Sie* here, baby!"

The sun went down behind the jagged wall of western mountains just as the first vehicle in the convoy turned into the auto park beside the P.W. enclosure a mile north of us on the main road from Berchtesgaden to Munich. This was the concentration point for all surrendering Germans in the region. A guard told the lead vehicle where to park, and the passengers got out and marched with their gear through the main gate to a group of camouflaged green huts in a pine forest just inside the enclosure.

The camp had served an opposite purpose ten days before, when the Germans had run it and held captive several thousand Allied prisoners. Now under the management of our second platoon, it stood in a thin pine forest on the sloping base of a mountain. It was almost half a mile square and was surrounded by double barbed-wire fences. Guards stood watch in rough wooden huts on stilts at each corner, while others patrolled the wire on foot. The buildings, which were spotted around the entrance, were one-story barracks so adroitly camouflaged with dappled-green paint that they were almost invisible from two hundred yards away.

The auto park beyond the wire, at the south end of the enclosure, was rapidly filling up with every conceivable type of civil and military vehicle. All were available for the taking. News of the giveaway spread with the speed of light, and the throng of paratroopers who came to help themselves gave the place the Sunday air of a giant used-car lot where everything was free and nothing was guaranteed. Men argued over choice staff cars, while others raced motors, tested brakes, or siphoned gas to refuel previously selected autos. Amateur mechanics had a field day.

The camp was also filling up, but nobody came to claim the Germans except for K.P. and other details. The barracks had long since been occupied and the overflow sent forth beyond to pitch their tents by units in the open. As night came on and the sky turned pale green in the east and a deep blue overhead and the stars came out very bright and close—for the stars were always close in the Alps—the German soldiers lit hundreds of small campfires on the slope and gathered around them, as soldiers had for thousands of years, to cook and chat and laugh and sing. For them the war was over.

Now they would be given discharges and sent home afoot or by whatever vehicles could be spared. The second platoon, assisted by S-2 and counterintelligence officers, had examined their *Soldbucher,* or Pay Books, which gave their unit and service record, had taken away their weapons and ammunition, and were holding them while their names were checked against a master list of war criminals. Every country in Europe had supplied names for this list, mostly from S.S. units that had murdered villages and wiped out provinces of people behind the lines in Poland and Russia. Nothing would bring back the murdered civilians, but it was hoped that at least a few of the murderers would be punished. The bulk of the captives, of course, were innocent. They would be turned loose in a few days to find their way home to what was left of their homes, while the war criminals would be transferred to maximum-security prisons for trial and punishment.

The second platoon thoroughly enjoyed their work in the camp, for it was not without its rewards—both day and night. They stripped the incoming prisoners of watches, cameras, field glasses, pistols, and liquor, and when darkness came, invited the choicer camp followers to come into their barracks and bundle. Only one thing spoiled the soldiers' heaven: guard duty. They had to walk the fence twenty-four hours a day. How, they wondered, can we make things easier?

Christenson was the first man to see the solution, although he didn't know it at the time. Off exploring the Alps by himself one day, he suddenly heard the sound of marching feet and singing men. Stopping by the road, he was amazed to see a regiment of S.S. mountain troops round a bend and head straight for him. The Germans were dressed in beautiful, moss-green uniforms with hobnailed ski boots and carried full battle gear and loaded weapons.

Christenson was spellbound and not a little afraid. Armed only with his father's old Frontier six-shooter, he stood alone against a regiment of the most vicious men in the German army. The S.S. did not like to take prisoners.

But for once they did nothing. In fact, they ignored him completely. Proudly erect, with their eyes forward and their legs and arms swinging in time, they passed in review, singing the *"Horst Wessel Lied."* Chris said it was the most stirring parade he had ever seen.

He later discovered that they were on their way to Berchtesgaden to surrender to the 506th. They had set up a defensive position in a far valley to prevent the French tankers who had accompanied us from massacring them in revenge for S.S. butcheries in Occupied France, where they were best remembered for the murder of over 150 women and children in the church of Oradur sur Glade, a village completely wiped out by the Das Reich S.S. Division in retaliation for an alleged attack on two Germans forty miles away. Now that the French had gone off to their own occupation zone, the S.S. had come in to surrender. They knew that the Americans, who had never been occupied by Germany, would treat them more gently than any Europeans would.

They hardly reckoned on pulling guard on their fellow countrymen, but that, of all things, is exactly what happened.

A selected number of S.S. men were organized as a guard and told to shoot anybody who went over the fence. Each drew a machine pistol with ammunition and went forth at rigid attention to guard the other

Germans, who disliked the S.S. for their cruelty and the special treatment that they had received as favored wards of Hitler. The second platoon then mounted machine guns on the corner towers to guard the
guards.

It was a wonderful sight to see: thousands of German soldiers from
every branch of the service camped out in little pup tents in the pine
forest; the prickly barbed wire, ten feet high, that surrounded them; the
crisp, erect S.S. men in field caps walking the fence with loaded
Schmeissers; and the second platoon sunbathing behind their rooftop
machine guns.

IMPATIENT TO EXPLORE the mountains for the vast loot that was pop-
ularly believed to have been hidden around Berchtesgaden, three of us
decided to set off in search of easy money. Strong rumors said that there
were art treasures hidden nearby in secret cellars, that dripping caves
were stacked high with gold bars. We mounted V.D.'s vehicle and left
the company area one morning. A German army ambulance, the con-
veyance had already carried V.D. on a series of rather disappointing
searches for loose women.

"Gotta get some fratranizing," V.D. said as he tooted at the gate guard
and turned right on the road to town. He jerked his head at the back
compartment, where a mattress lay covered with blankets and com-
forters. "Man's gotta be ready all the time! Can't tell when some little old
gal is going to jump in and throw it at you."

McCreary, who was also with us, laughed. "That goddamn V.D."

Colonel Sink flashed by in his massive black Mercedes, with Blacky
Wilson, a former mortarman in F Company, at the wheel. We grinned;
everybody liked to see the colonel having a good time.

With a great shrieking and clanging, a boxy gray vehicle overtook us,
siren on and bell tolling. V.D., who had been absorbed in a discussion of
the colonel's pleasures in Germany, jumped and pulled over to the side.

The other car passed. "Off the road!" its driver shouted.

We looked and saw our platoon sergeant, Hale, shaking his fist at us
and grinning as Pace rang the bell.

His ambulance hopelessly outclassed, V.D. lapsed into a surly silence
and drove through Berchtesgaden to its eastern outskirts. He checked
the gas gauge, muttered, "Low again, goddammit," and pulled into a

service station. Nobody came out to help us. "Self-service," he said, jumping down and going to one of the pumps. "You hold the nozzle, Web, and I'll crank her till she's full."

He heaved the handle round and round, but still nobody came out of the station, which was built of rustic wood and adjoined a small Alpine house. When the tank was full, he hung the hose back on its hook and drove off.

"Isn't this the life?" he commented. "Everything on the house. Want a car? Take your pick. Need gas? Help yourself. *Deutschland kaput.*" He honked at a German cavalryman and tried to make his horse shy.

"Let's keep on the side roads," I suggested. "The G.I.s have probably checked these ones pretty thoroughly by now."

V.D. turned off on the first dirt track and followed it to the foot of a big mountain.

"Hold it up!" I exclaimed. "I saw a door in the mountain."

"Oh hell, doors in mountains . . ."

"There it is. See?"

V.D. hit the brakes, and the ambulance coasted to a halt in twenty yards. The brakes were rather weak.

We backed up until we were alongside a wooden door set into a wall of rock. The door, which was partially hidden by undergrowth, appeared to be very sturdy. We leaped out and ran up to it.

"This is the kind of place," I said excitedly. "I'll bet they hid the loot right here." Visions of gold bars and chests of jewels danced through my head.

We smashed the lock with our rifle butts and surged in.

A mine shaft, higher than a man, it ran straight back into the mountain and was completely empty except for a couple of picks and shovels near the door. McCreary lit a match and started in, then lit another and another. The shaft ended before the third match went out. We turned back cursing and hurried into the warm daylight.

"Well, hell." I sighed. "The only thing to do is keep looking. I'll bet there's a pile of dough around here somewhere. It's a logical hiding place. All we have to do is find the right tunnel."

Continuing our search, we inspected two more along the same road, but neither contained the national treasury.

V.D. WAS GETTING RESTLESS. He found women more alluring than any hole in the ground.

"Speak to 'em, Web, speak to 'em!" he panted. "Goddamn, will you look at that?"

We had come to a little meadow near a stream, where a group of twenty or thirty German soldiers and their girls had tied their horses and wagons to trees and pitched tents on the grass. Four of the girls were washing breakfast dishes in the creek, while others sunned themselves on its banks or busied themselves with various domestic tasks. The dishwashers raised their eyes when we stopped across from them but quickly looked away when they saw that we were Americans. Lounging on the grass in the usual manner of German males, who let women do all the work, the soldiers watched us uneasily, obviously fearing that we had come to shatter their pastoral paradise.

"Speak to 'em, Web!" V.D. urged again. He had his eye on a long-legged golden blonde.

"Why bother?" I sighed. "They don't want to have anything to do with us; too many of their countrymen watching them."

"Come on, come on."

"O.K. Christ." I raised my voice. *"Guten Tag."*

The girls scrubbed harder.

"Wie gehts?"

No answer.

"Let's go. Goddammit. There's plenty more women up here. These girls are taken. You have to get 'em away from their men. Take it easy, V.D., you'll get laid. You'll get laid, but not by these ones."

V.D. cursed and drove off. "Goddamn Krauts."

We followed the sandy, rutted little road around the base of one mountain after another, trying this mine shaft and that and becoming progressively less enthusiastic. Finally we spotted a heavy wooden door on a footpath more than a hundred yards above the valley floor and decided that this would be our last. It appeared to be the most promising, because it was the most inaccessible and because someone had taken pains to camouflage it with pine boughs. We dismounted and climbed up.

The padlock was four inches long, an inch thick, and so rusted that it failed to yield to several butt strokes. I decided to shoot it off, then thought better and gave it the hardest blow I could. The cover broke and the lock's guts fell out. I was glad that I had not shot when I looked inside, for the cave was filled with boxes of blasting powder.

"Enough of this crap," McCreary said, starting back for the ambulance.

"You can have your goddamn treasure hunt," V.D. echoed. "I'll take women any day. Let's round up a couple of those Luftwaffe *Mädchens* and have ourselves a ball."

We drove out to the nearest highway and continued west till we came to a signpost at an intersection. I studied the place-names and, since none of them was familiar, suggested that we go straight ahead. "There's a lake four kilometers from here," I explained. "It's called der Konigsee, the King's Lake. Let's take a look at it."

V.D. banged a tune on the horn and sang, "Shave and a haircut, two bits. All the girls have two tits." Off we went.

We were not the first arrivals at the lake. Scores of G.I.s were running in and out of little resort buildings on the shore, while others made off with rowboats and canoes or sunned themselves on a sandy beach that curved around the north end of the lake, which ran about three miles from north to south and varied in width from a quarter to half a mile. Nobody was in swimming.

V.D. sized up the situation and took immediate action. The main body of soldiers was concentrated along the beach, while practically nobody was exploring a group of two-story boathouses to our left. This was the place to go. He stepped on the gas and darted up to the third boathouse just as two men from the second platoon came outside with a big red and black Nazi flag in their hands.

"Where'd you get it?" I asked. Like everybody else, I had always wanted an enemy flag for a souvenir.

"Up in the loft."

We jumped down and ran indoors. The loft was a high-ceilinged attic filled with all kinds of awnings, tarpaulins, oars, and other boat gear. Standing against one wall were three ships' flagpoles. We grabbed them, unrolled the flags and cut them free, and stuffed them into our big pants pockets.

"Let's go," V.D. suggested. "Maybe there's a boat downstairs."

A door in the loft led down a flight of creaking, musty wooden stairs to a covered slip below, where two electric sightseeing launches were tied to narrow wooden docks. About thirty feet long, the boats had rows of padded seats on deck astern, a striped awning overhead with fringed sides, and a wheelhouse close to the bow. V.D. went there and started to tinker with the controls.

"Anybody in there?" someone shouted.

"We're all here," I replied. "Come on! We're going for a ride."

Half a dozen men from the second and third platoons came out on the dock and jumped aboard. Four of them were carrying cases of Lowenbrau beer.

The motor started to purr softly, and V.D. shouted, "All aboard! Let's go, goddammit, moving out."

McCreary and I cast off the hawsers while V.D., who claimed to have manned a craft like this at home, backed her into the stream.

"Port the helm!" he cried. "Avast the rudder! Starboard the bilges! All ashore that are going ashore! You don't 'ave to go 'ome, but you cahn't sty 'ere."

We slid out into the sunlit lake, and V.D. leaned out and goddamned a couple of G.I.s who cut across our bow, then swung us around till we were headed for the far end. The others started opening the beer. The label was good—in fact, one of the best in Europe—but the taste was bad, for the beer was weak, watery, wartime stuff, not worthy of its name. Nevertheless, it was beer, and we pretended to enjoy it.

As we finished each bottle, we cast it into our wake and opened fire on it with our pistols and rifles. The shots echoed and reechoed among the stone mountain walls that surrounded the Konigsee on all but the north side, and G.I.s in lesser craft ducked and cursed our zinging ricochets.

"Did you hear what they found down the road a couple of hundred yards from the bathhouses?" a second-platoon man inquired. "Goering's art collection! The fat sonofabitch hid it in a special cellar, then poured cement over the door. Worth millions of dollars. And do you know what the 1st Bat found? Four million dollars in gold!"

"No kidding?"

"Hell yes. They're opening safes with bazookas at regimental headquarters."

"I feel so good I can't stand it," I announced. I had just finished my fourth bottle of beer. "I'm going for a swim." I took off my pants, combat jacket, and wool undershirt and went to the bow in my cotton underwear. Taking a breath, I dove into the lake. The water was paralyzingly cold; the shock made me gasp and thrash hard to keep from knotting up. I lunged for a ladder amidships and scrambled back aboard, shivering convulsively. "Jesus, is that cold!" I exclaimed. "I'll bet it's one degree above freezing. No wonder nobody's in swimming."

V.D. drew alongside two paratroopers traveling north and asked what was at the south end of the lake.

"S.S.," they said, frowning, "S.S." They rowed on.

"I don't believe it," V.D. said, narrowing his eyes. "There's something fishy going on here. Those bastards found a good deal down there and are trying to keep it secret." He turned to the men aft under the awning. "Want to go down to the other end of the lake?"

"Hell yes."

"G.I.s say there's S.S. men down there."

"We'll whip 'em."

They fired a salvo at Hitler's mountain to prove it.

"O.K., we're off."

The boat purred down the lake until we were more than halfway to the far end. No shots were fired at us from S.S. men in ambuscade, and so we relaxed and finished the beer. V.D. began to head for what appeared to be a white church to starboard. It stood on a flat peninsula of about 250 acres of meadowland at the foot of a big split between two mountains. Three or four farmhouses dotted the meadow behind the church, which was close to a stone pier that ran out into the lake. The pier was lined almost solid with canoes and rowboats. Dozens of G.I.s were sauntering on the quay, going in and out of the church, or sitting by little round tables in a beer garden opposite the front door. V.D. worked the launch into an empty space and we leapt out and headed for the beer garden.

We shouted at several other E Company men sitting under a tree with steins of beer in hand and then went into the church, which appeared to be a medieval monastery converted to a fine, Old World inn. The dining room was cool, whitewashed, and with a high, beamed ceiling that made it seem like some castle hall. It was still serving beer and lunch, we noted, but the tourists were all in brown and very few of them were paying.

We sat down on rough wooden benches at a big table and greeted the waitress who came to serve us. She rattled off the menu. *"Gut, gut,"* I said, understanding only half of what she had said, *"und viel Bier. Wir haben Bier sahr gern."*

It was a splendid meal—soup, roast veal, boiled potatoes, cabbage, Swiss cheese, and pumpernickel bread—and the price was incredible—about forty cents apiece, including two beers.

"You going to pay her?" one of the other men inquired indignantly. "Goddamn Krauts."

"Why not? The money isn't worth anything. Anyway, V.D.'s loaded. Give her some of that money you got in Buchloe, V.D. Military government says it's no good, but she won't know the difference."

He peeled off half a dozen bills from a dirty wad that he always carried in his pocket and threw them on the table. I counted them mentally. They came to ten times the price of the meal. I slipped a couple of cigarettes under my plate as a tip and told the waitress how much we had enjoyed the food. She grinned and said, *"Danke, danke."*

We walked out slowly into the warm summer day and gazed about us at the blue lake and the great, steep mountains.

"Isn't this great?" I commented as we strolled back to the launch. "I'd like to come back here someday as a civilian and spend a weekend."

"We got to Berchtesgaden at the right time," V.D. agreed. "You can't beat it."

BUT IT WAS TOO GOOD to be true. Just when we were comfortably settled and had P.W.s doing our K.P. and other household chores and were unofficially organizing the area into regimental territories, the division staff got wind of our homestead and decided to oust us.

A few days later, an advance detail from the 327th Glider Infantry Regiment stalked into our chalet suburb and, without so much as a by-your-leave, began to chalk "Major So and So and Captain Such and Such" and "10 officers" and "20 enlisted men" on our doors. When we asked what was going on, they informed us with obvious relish that the 327th was going to take over Berchtesgaden. The 506th, they leered, was being exiled to an obscure valley farther south in Austria.

We moved out at night and after several hours' drive wound up in the attic of a chalet smack against a mountainside. Now it was noon of the first day in Austria.

After the
Fighting

"Hey, Web, Christenson wants you at the C.P. Shake a leg!"

I jumped off my bed, where I had been looking at back copies of the *Berline Illustrierte Zeitung,* a picture weekly in which the whole war had the dreamy quality of a vast lie and the German soldiers were always on the attack *("Deutsche Soldaten greifen an!"),* even when the Russians were in Prussia, and ran downstairs and up the street to the next house, where Christenson, Hale, and Liebgott lived with our platoon leader and half a dozen men from company headquarters. I knocked on Christenson's door.

"Come in."

"You wanted me?"

"Got a deal for you."

"Oh?" A deal was usually a euphemism for something undesirable.

"You've been after me for the next advance detail. Now's your chance."

I smiled. Advance detail meant first crack at the new billets, perhaps two days in advance of the Company.

"Liebgott and Neumann have had plenty; today it's your turn."

"Thanks."

"Pack your gear and report to the C.P. at nine o'clock."

I lingered a moment to inquire why we were moving out so suddenly. We had been in Kaprun only two nights and a day.

"You know the Army, so don't ask me why." Christenson sighed. "Goddamn if I know why we're leaving or where we're going. Do you want to go or don't you?"

"Sure, sure."

"Better get going. It's 8:35 now. And don't tell Liebgott I sent you. Krauts can't understand his Yiddish, but he's jealous as hell of these deals, so just keep your mouth shut."

"O.K."

I ran back to my billet and began to pack. One souvenir I particularly wanted to keep was the issue of the *Illustrierte Zeitung* that was almost wholly devoted to a German account of the defeat of the British 1st Airborne Division at Arnhem. The magazine was filled with pictures of dazed, badly wounded paratroopers with a scared look in their eyes and grinning Germans all around them. Poor guys, I thought, as I rolled up my sleeping bag. If it had been Patton's 4th Armored Division, they would have made it. A paratrooper could only hold out a couple of days till the tanks broke through, and the British tanks did not break through, not because they were not brave but because they were inefficient and inept. They simply did not know how to use armor. So the 1st Airborne waited for them in vain and fought a terrible, grinding battle against two panzer divisions. When it was over, the Germans, who were so cold and cruel, marched the wounded men back from the front on foot to Germany for several hundred miles. It could have happened to paratroopers anywhere. How could men whose heaviest weapons were bazookas and 81mm mortars stand off two panzer divisions?

I slipped into my harness, hunched my musette bag into a comfortable position on my back, buckled my cartridge belt, slung my rifle, and went to the C.P., where a jeep was waiting with a driver and an interpreter from each of the other platoons.

"Going along?" one of them inquired jovially.

I nodded.

"Maybe this time we'll find all the gold that Himmler dug out of the Jew boys' teeth."

The Camera Killer came out the front door and jumped into the front seat. We started off.

God, I thought, staring at the back of his head, why does this guy have to come along? Of all the officers that could have been in charge . . . I had first met the lieutenant when, as an S-2 officer, he slept through the patrol in Haguenau. Switching to E Company for the trip through Germany, he had distinguished himself by seizing a camera from a German woman in a Bavarian village, throwing it to the ground, and shooting it with his pistol. For this exploit he had been dubbed the Camera Killer.

"Anybody know where we're going?" I asked.

"Nope," the man next to me replied. "Someplace far away, I hope. I want to line up a shack job before the Company pulls in. Nice day, isn't it?"

"Wonderful. This is the prettiest country in the world. I've been all over the States, but I never saw anything as pretty as these Alps. They're even better than the Tetons."

We dipped into the valley's floor and crossed a stream that ran down its center. Now we were passing a clean little white church on a grassy knoll that overlooked the village of Kaprun. Surrounded by rich green meadows, Kaprun was a small settlement of about four hundred people in very old chalets and Gasthof. It had once been a minor resort, catering to bicycle tourists too poor for the more famous places in the Tyrol. Two inns with carved wooden balconies lined with gay flower boxes faced a dusty little village square, and there was a scattering of small shops on the tree-lined streets. In all, Kaprun was a lovely country town. Even the G.I. shorts drying on the balconies, the soldiers shouting from the windows and galloping along the street on S.S. horses failed to disturb the summer tranquillity. If anything, they brought Kaprun to life, just as they had revived Aldbourne in days past. KREIS SALZBURG, a sign said on the outskirts: Salzburg Province.

We left the village on an uphill road and wound round to the right, passing two children in shirts made from parachute silk evidently sent home by their father from some drop zone overrun by the Germans. I wondered what had become of the parachute's owner. The square, gray ruins of a medieval castle next appeared on our left, commanding the approach to the Kaprun Valley. The walls of the castle still stood, but the roof had tumbled in years before. Through the open gate, we could see a wild mass of trees and shrubs growing in the courtyard where other soldiers once had drilled.

From here we had a splendid view of the land ahead in all its rich summer colors. Pink, white, red, and gold flowers dotted the green meadows. Above them on all sides, blue-green pine trees flowed up to gray rocks and clean white snow on the mountaintops. The Kaprun Valley joined a larger one here at right angles that was two or three miles wide and that ran east to west between a snowcapped mountain range on the south and a lesser range on the north. The mountains ran as far as the eye could see. Straight ahead to the north at a distance of about five miles, a bright blue lake sparkled between two wooded mountain ranges. A village dominated by a church with a high, Norman spire ran out into the lake on a promontory at midpoint.

"That's Zell am See," the Camera Killer remarked. "Regimental headquarters and the 3rd Battalion. Beautiful, isn't it?"

"Yessir."

"They got it made down there. Colonel's living in a hotel on the lake with a trailer of Hennessy right outside the door. See that mountain behind town?"

"Yessir."

"Got a ski lodge on top. Place used to be a big resort. Good skiing in the winter. Cable cars run up to the lodge. Colonel wanted to put his headquarters up there." He laughed. "Colonel likes to live high, ha, ha, ha. But soon as the general heard about it, he nixed the deal. Said he'd be goddamned if he'd ride a cable car to see anybody, ha, ha, ha."

"Ha, ha, ha."

"Jesus, isn't this the country, though?"

"Yessir."

"Makes you wonder how the Krauts can come from a country like this and be so goddamn mean. You'd think a man growing up here or in Bavaria would be so happy with the world that he'd like everybody, but it didn't work out like that, did it?"

"No sir."

"The trouble with Germany is that it's wasted on the Germans."

"Ha, ha, ha."

We had come down from the castle while the lieutenant was talking and were now in the big valley, near a grassy airfield with a small, camouflaged hangar where several G.I. trucks were parked. Paratroopers were climbing in and out of three or four light planes and a big, three-motored JU-87 transport nearby.

"They claim a Kraut general on the lam landed up here," the Camera Killer noted. "That's his plane, the old Ford trimotor. Haven't caught the sonofabitch yet. Boys ought to stay away from those planes; I wouldn't trust any of 'em. Might be booby-trapped."

The road curved left and then right along the end of the lake, and he pointed at a farmhouse high on the mountain to the west and said, "Third Bat found a big rocket scientist hiding out up there. Going to ship him back to the States. Isn't that a pistol? We win the war, and they ship the Krauts back to the States."

To our right, a path and the tracks of an electric railway ran side by side along the lake into town. Paratroopers on horseback and afoot moved about with noisy gaiety under trees along the path, while civilians by the dozen fished in the lake and other G.I.s rowed or canoed on the water.

"Summer in the park," our lieutenant noted. "Isn't it great? There's the colonel's hotel. Best in town; you know the colonel." He laughed and pointed down a side street to a lovely old gabled building on a point. Officers sat at little iron tables on a veranda nearby.

"This town used to be a big Kraut resort," the lieutenant continued. "Nothing but hotels and inns. Beats Columbus, Georgia, doesn't it?"

"Yessir."

"Lake's three miles long and a mile wide. You men ever get the time and the transportation, you ought to go for a swim. Colonel's going to give the best beach club in town to the Regiment. Nothing but the best for the colonel."

"Yessir."

"I heard rumors the Krauts sunk a lot of gold bars in the lake to hide 'em for the next war. Colonel's got a detail on it now."

We continued through Zell am See and down the valley in which it lay for another six or seven miles, past some very small villages and a burnt-out enemy half-track at a crossroads, and entered another, smaller valley that ran at 90-degree angles to this one. A large village rose before us on a low hill in the center of the new valley.

"This is it," the Camera Killer announced, "this is Saalfelden. Last big intersection on the road to Germany. That rocky pass straight ahead in those mountains leads to Berchtesgaden."

We stopped at a house marked with a Headquarters Company guidon, where he chatted briefly with a 2nd lieutenant who appeared to be an old acquaintance, then drove farther into town and stopped again.

"Everybody off," the Camera Killer said brusquely. "E Company's got this street for its billets. You men take the first four houses. Run the Krauts out and get enough space for your platoons."

He turned to me. "You—what's your name?—come with me. We'll get the billets for company headquarters and the first platoon."

THE OTHER INTERPRETERS went into the first house without knocking and began to shout, *"Raus, raus, schnell!"* The Camera Killer and I hurried to a clean, whitewashed three-story home and beat on the door.

A pale, thin young man with thick glasses and timid, watery blue eyes opened the door and blinked at us in fright.

"Guten Tag," I said.

"I speak English," he replied. "What do you want?"

"Your house," the Camera Killer said. "You have thirty minutes to move. Get going!"

"Better leave the radios and cameras," I added. "Cameras are *strengstens verboten."*

The young man swallowed hard. His face wrinkled as if for tears, and he shook his head and frowned and whined that he had a very sick father. "He's a dentist," he explained. "He can't move because he's sick and because he has very valuable equipment here. Take that house next door; it has lots of rooms. There are many kitchens. Your soldiers will like it very much. See, it is an apartment house, with three flats. It is much better for you than this."

"You have half an hour," the Camera Killer said with an edge in his voice.

"But my father is sick. He is old. He is a dentist. This is a very uncomfortable house; you will like that one much better. There is not enough room here. We do not have enough beds. My father . . ."

"Shut up!"

The Camera Killer took a piece of chalk from his pocket and wrote, "Co. Hq., E Co.," on the door.

"Get your goddamn father out of here in thirty minutes or we'll throw him out."

We moved on to the next place. The young man, obviously 4F and therefore doubly contemptible in our eyes, for he was quite unlikable without any physical defects, stood in the doorway and wept softly and made no move to obey the order.

"Some companies let the Krauts live in the basement," the Camera Killer noted as we entered the next house and started up the stairs. "They keep 'em around to cook and wash the dishes and sweep the floors and do the laundry, but Captain Speirs doesn't believe in that and neither do I. Krauts only get in your hair if you let 'em stay in their own houses. I say, move 'em the hell out! The bastards moved everybody else out of Europe, made 'em slave laborers, put 'em in concentration camps. You have to be hard on these people."

His voice carried into all the apartments, which the weak young man had so strongly recommended, and soon every door was open and the whole building, which was three stories high, was filled with whispers of fear as the residents peeked out and saw us climb the stairs.

We reached the third floor and knocked at the apartment there. A German officer about 35 years old answered the knock. I greeted him and looked beyond at the living room, which was bright and sunny and gay with pretty yellow wallpaper and Van Gogh prints on the walls.

A smell of milk and diapers and powder and soap filled the air. Four small children who had been playing on the carpet scrambled to their feet and ran to their mothers in tears. The crying set off a chain reaction in two wicker bassinettes and in a baby at a mother's breast, for the room was like a veritable maternity ward of babies and mothers. They gathered their children around them and talked softly and patted their backs and stared at us with frightened eyes. There were four women altogether.

I couldn't do it. Turning to the lieutenant, I said, "Let's try another place, sir. We can't run little children out in the street."

"The hell we can't! They're Krauts, aren't they? Tell 'em to get out in half an hour."

"But sir?"

"Goddammit, tell 'em to get out!"

The infant wailing reached a crescendo.

"God," I muttered. Raising my voice, I explained to the German officer that we were requisitioning the house for our billets. He and the women and children had thirty minutes to pack up and go.

"But where will we go?" the German inquired. "Every place in Saalfelden is filled with refugees from Salzburg and Vienna. The inns are all military hospitals. There is no place for us to go. My wife and I are doctors; we are taking care of these women; there is no one else to look after them; they have come with us from Vienna; their husbands were all killed on the Russian front."

"I'll see what I can do."

"What's eating that sonofabitch?"

"He says there's no place to go."

"Tough."

"He says the town's filled with wounded Krauts and refugees from Vienna and Salzburg. We can find another billet, sir. Hell, we don't have to run these little kids out."

"Bah. *Raus, raus, raus!*"

The women joined their children in tears. This only aggravated the Camera Killer.

"They didn't give the Jews a chance to stay home, did they?" he shouted in a voice that shook the building. "They're Krauts, and they have to go."

"But innocent women, sir? Little children?"

"Goddammit, soldier, quit stalling! They're Krauts. They have to go."

"They're Austrians, sir."

"Same thing."

"But little children?"

"Goddammit, soldier, I'm sick and tired of your back talk. Move these sonsabitches out! The Company's due in twenty minutes. They have to have a place to stay. They're staying here. They can't wait on a roomful of sniveling little Kraut bastards."

"But sir . . ."

"We don't have time to be nice to these sonsabitches. Goddamn 'em anyway. They started the war. Now see how they like it. We're bringing the war home to them like they brought it to everybody else the last five years, only we're not going to murder them or put 'em in a concentration camp."

He paused for breath, and the women looked helplessly to the German officer to protect them from this violent, flushed-face man who had come to the door. The officer stepped up to the lieutenant. *"Bitte,"* he began.

" *'Bitte,'* hell, you sonofabitch! You didn't give the Jews a chance. Get going!" He pulled out a pistol and waved it under the German's nose. The women gasped. The officer shrugged his shoulders and bade the women start packing.

"And make it snappy! You have only fifteen minutes. Clear this house in fifteen minutes or I'll blow your goddamn brains out!"

The Camera Killer left the apartment and started downstairs, shouting, *"Raus, raus!* Everybody *raus!* Get out, you Kraut sonsabitches!"

I stared at the little children. It was not right. I had never believed in the war until I had gone into Germany and seen what the Germans had in mind for the world: the slave-labor lagers, the broken families, the men from Dachau; old women and little children worked to death in Ruhr factories. To me the Germans were a nation of barbarous psychopaths responsible for the first-degree murder of ten to fifteen million Poles, Russians, and Jews, innocent civilians whose only crime was to have been born—Poles, Russians, or Jews. They had filled hundreds and hundreds of tank ditches with the bodies of men, women, and children, had denied God and Christ to follow a satanic Messiah who promised them only murder on the vilest and vastest scale in history. A nation of animal lovers who had never understood people, the Germans had set out deliberately to exterminate the Slav, to annihilate the Jew, to murder all whom they disliked or who would not love them as animals loved them that had been taught to obey and beg for food. I wanted the Germans to be thoroughly punished, to help seek out those responsible for the mass murders—if I could ever catch Himmler or Hitler or Goering, I would take the greatest delight in making them die slowly— but I did not blame all the Germans, I did not think it right to return barbarism with injustice, to take out on little children the crimes of sadistic countrymen.

"I'm sorry," I said to the officer. "I didn't want to do it. But the lieutenant is an officer and I am a private, so I had no choice. I wish I could help the children. It isn't right."

The German sighed. "What can you do?" he said softly. "It is the war."

"How come the mortar squad gets stuck in the attic?"

"Third squad was on the ground floor in the last billet; they get all the good deals."

"First squad's sleeping two men to a bed. Second's got a bed apiece."

"Who picked these goddamn billets? Second platoon's got the best houses in town."

"Company headquarters has a place big enough for forty men. We should have had that instead."

Christenson sighed. He had heard it all before: the weeping and wailing and gnashing of teeth every time we moved into new billets. Nobody was happy; everybody else's place was better than theirs. If he put the mortar squad in a barn and the rest of the men in a schoolhouse, Henderson screamed about the hay and the horseflies. If he gave Henderson a break and put McCreary in the barn, then the whole second squad filed a protest. If the second squad got the ground floor (an important location, since it offered first crack at the meals as they were distributed in Marmite cans), then V.D., Marsh, and I stormed in to complain of persecution and discrimination. Everybody protested Hale and Liebgott's taking ways on the advance detail, and nobody ever saw company headquarters in a bad location.

No sooner did these initial rumblings settle into the disturbed earth from which they had come in fuming geysers of hate and invective (all meaningless, all part of the old Army game: to claim discrimination and hold what you have) than men came by from the second and third platoons to check on the accommodations in a casual way that fooled nobody.

"Pretty good deal you got here."

"We've had better. No hot water. Goddamn Krauts took all the blankets with 'em."

"Blankets! We don't even have beds."

The platoon leaders went to the captain and complained of favoritism, while he in turn visited them all with an eye to shifting his own people to better quarters.

"Jesus, this is better than we have."

"It looks good from the outside, Captain, but it's a mess indoors. No running water, no toilets, no electric lights."

"Looks good to me."

"The place you have now is much more centrally located, sir. It's near everything. We're sort of out of the way here, Captain."

Each man running down his own billet to noncoms and outsiders, each defending it from rival squads and platoons: It was always the same, all the way through Germany. A strain for the first half hour, the conflict died out as soon as another diversion came up. Billeting was a balancing of opposing forces. All a man could do was try to be fair in his assignments and then nod and talk quietly until the storm blew over. That time had come at last.

The women and children had moved out, the first platoon had moved in, company headquarters had evicted the dentist's son at gunpoint. Lunch had come and gone. Now it was three o'clock. Christenson was sitting on a chair enjoying the lazy peace of a summer afternoon, while I, as usual, poured out complaints.

"Don't ever put me on the advance detail again," I said. I was cleaning the Luger I had taken from the S.S. man at the Kesselfalls Hotel. "I can't take it."

"What happened?" Chris asked languidly. He tilted back with a cigar in his mouth and his feet on the windowsill and stared at the Alps, while I described the billeting.

"You've been after Liebgott's job ever since Mourmelon," he remarked when I was through. "When you get it, you don't like it. How come?"

"I can't talk German good enough. And besides, I don't have the guts to throw a year-old baby out in the street. I'd rather sleep on the ground than do that."

"O.K., you had your chance and you muffed it. On top of that, you let Hale swipe our radio and the civilians walk out with all the food. Man on advance detail has to stake his claim; can't let anybody else beat us out of anything."

The door flew open, and V.D. and McCreary ran in with a whooping thunder. "Look out the window!" they shouted. "Look out the window!"

Christenson banged forward and swung from his chair to a standing position while the rest of us gathered around.

Our window overlooked the backs of a U of houses built around an open space of small vegetable gardens. Wehrmacht trucks and tents filled the gardens and the backyards, where a hundred-odd German soldiers had made a bivouac. V.D. pointed at a house directly opposite ours.

A German girl of about 20 was undressing at a window in full view of the bivouac. She had already taken off her blouse. Now, with a born stripper's air of unconcern, she pulled her slip over her head and un-buckled her bra and let it fall. She had big breasts with large nipples.

"Yippee!" V.D. bellowed. He pawed the floor like a bull in heat.

McCreary waved to her. "Hiya, honey."

"*Kommen Sie* here, baby!" Chris called.

"How'd you like to chew on them tits?" V.D. inquired. "God*damn!*"

The girl started to undo the side of her army skirt.

A movement behind Christenson caught his eye, and he turned and saw our platoon leader standing in the door. " 'Ten*shun!*" he cried.

We scrambled back from the window to positions of attention.

"At ease, rest," the lieutenant said. "What's going on here?"

"Kraut broad." V.D. grinned. "Biggest tits you ever saw. Get a load of that." He pointed.

"I'd like to get a lot of that. Goddamn Krauts know how to fight a war, don't they? Bring the women along with 'em. This is a hell of a time to say it, but we're moving out in fifteen minutes."

"Oh Christ," I groaned. "When are we going to settle down?"

The girl dropped her skirt and lowered the window shade. We heaved a collective sigh and concentrated on our platoon leader and the task at hand.

"Where now, sir?" McCreary inquired. "Italy?"

"Other end of town. Start packing."

"Good!" V.D. exclaimed with his eyes still on the girl's window. "Did you get her phone number, Mick?"

McCreary grinned.

The lieutenant left, and we started to pack. By the time we marched out to the trucks, word of our departure had spread throughout the neighborhood, bringing the dentist's boy, the doctor, and several other evictees to the curb opposite our front door. None of the mothers was in sight.

The ride to the next billet, an old hotel by a railroad station a mile west of the main part of Saalfelden, was brief and the first impression disappointing, for the hotel was plain and poor.

We filed up the stone front steps into a dark lobby paneled with dark oak. The cooks were preparing supper in the kitchen straight ahead. On our right was a small dining room, obviously the officers' mess, for it had linen on the tables. A larger dining room stood on our left. While we milled about in the old-smelling lobby with its worn carpets, V.D. went to the registration desk, tapped its bell, and proclaimed in the ensuing silence that this was a clean hotel. "We're going to live Y.M.C.A. style," he said. "No women or liquor." He was loudly booed. "Before ten in the morning." He reached over the counter, pulled out a picture postcard, and asked me what it said.

I translated it literally: "Anton Dick's Gasthof. Thirty rooms from 1.20 kroner up, tourists' quarters from .60 kroner up. Shady garden with veranda, billiard room. Famous for its good cooking. Advantageous junction for sightseeing trips."

"At ease, men," our platoon leader called from the stairs behind the counter. "This is going to be our home for the next few weeks, as far as we know. We have the two top floors. The first and second squads will have the third floor, the rest of the platoon the second. Cooks will sleep down here, since the hotel will also be the company mess hall. I don't want any of you men swiping food from the kitchen or the storerooms. This is also the officers' mess, so keep your fun down to a dull roar.

"We're here for a purpose. Saalfelden is now Field Marshal Kesselring's headquarters. It has four or five military hospitals and a couple of hospital trains parked outside. There are two big Kraut ammunition dumps in the woods nearby, and this station is the junction for trains to Munich. That crossroads we went through on the way over is the last big one on level ground before Germany. Our job here is to help funnel all the Krauts out of Austria. Kesselring is in charge of this movement. Krauts with armbands are on his staff and can keep their pistols. They'll be coming and going all the time, so don't bother 'em. Captain Speirs will help Kesselring coordinate his troop movements with the American Army. Mortar squad'll guard the hotel and the station, while the others take turns at the crossroads. Squad leaders billet your men now. Chow in fifteen minutes. Get going!"

"We have to beat McCreary," I whispered to Marsh and V.D. "Let's run."

We broke from the crowd and bounded upstairs, reaching the top floor well in advance of the second squad, but McCreary caught up with us when we hesitated whether to turn right or left.

"Thought you'd beat me to it, huh?" he panted. "Like hell, buddy, like hell. Nobody's beating McCreary. Not by a long shot." He inhaled. "Let's be reasonable about this. Our men get along good together, so let's organize the floor without any goddamn connivery. Come on."

We went on a quick tour. The rooms were very much alike in both their arrangement and accommodations. Each had two or three big beds, simple and sturdy, high closets with drawers below, and plain white dressers. The walls were whitewashed and generously cracked, the reed rugs torn and frayed. Bits of wooden flooring peeked through underfoot in the hall, which was covered by an old red carpet. There was a china pitcher and a washbowl in each room; the only running water was in a lavatory beside the stairs, and the hotel's sole bathtub, we discovered, was one floor below.

We agreed to give the first squad, which was Marsh's and mine, the southern half of the floor and the second squad the north. Since the hotel ran from north to south, this gave each of us a view of the two main sights: the mountains on the east and the railroad station on the west.

The men quickly dispersed and started to unpack. After supper, which we ate in the tourists' dining room, we lay around until it got dark and cold and then went to bed. Our day, however, was not quite over.

McCreary, who had gone for a walk, returned to my room a few minutes after we had switched off the light and woke up Marsh and me. "Come on, come on!" he said excitedly, shouting us awake. "Warehouse full of liquor."

WE RAN INTO THE HALL without bothering to tie our boots or put jackets over our undershirts.

"Shh," McCreary cautioned. "We don't want to spread this around." He beckoned to Sholty and Matthews, who were waiting near the stairs. Matthews had come up to us in Berchtesgaden after remaining in France with the Regiment's rear echelon from Holland on. A lively, witty person, he was always welcome on a foray or a party.

We padded downstairs, nodded to the guard at the front doors, and followed McCreary at a dead run around the south end of the station, across the railroad tracks, and two hundred yards down a gravel lane to a corrugated-iron warehouse on the western outskirts of town. A guard challenged us at the entrance, but McCreary, who had apparently spoken to him before, reassured him, and he stood aside and let us go in.

"Second platoon," McCreary whispered. "The rookie doesn't know what he's got in here. Cases of gin, buddy, cases of gin. Wait'll those guys find out we've been cutting into their territory." He chuckled softly.

Sholty stumbled on a soft bundle in the hay underfoot as we groped toward the far end of the building, which was about seventy-five feet long. Someone cursed him in German. "Krauts," Sholty said. "Step on their faces."

We shuffled slowly through thick darkness past oddly shaped machinery and over grunting, moaning, tossing sleepers until we came to a row of wooden packing boxes along the west wall. Each box was about a yard high and wide by four feet long.

"Come on, Matt!" McCreary hissed as he bent over and shoved his fingers under the bottom of one. "Get on the front of this sonofabitch."

Matthews grabbed it and started backing out of the warehouse. We followed with another. Tripping and shuffling and grunting and straining muscles that hadn't been used for months, we moved from one end of the building to the other, leaving in our wake a trail of crushed hands and German curses. There were many enemy soldiers asleep on the floor.

The guard frowned and peered in McCreary's face as we went out the door. His suspicions aroused by our haste, he asked what company we were from.

"C Company," McCreary replied briskly. "1st Battalion. We're on detached service." He hurried on.

The guard's eyes narrowed and he shook his head, as if to say, I'll have to tell somebody about this. It don't seem right.

We staggered back down the gravel road under a full moon and stopped for a break after fifty yards.

"I sure hope it's a case of lush," Matthews remarked, panting. "I'd hate to work this hard for monkey wrenches."

"Hardest I ever worked in the Army," Sholty agreed.

I grinned. It was the first time I had ever seen Matthews or McCreary do physical labor. We bent to the task once more and by easy stages moved the two cases into the hotel, where we paused again in the lobby. So far, our only witness, who didn't count because he was in another platoon and new to the Company, was the guard at the hotel's steps. But now another man hurried toward us from the back of the hotel. It was Miller, one of the least objectionable of the cooks.

"Booze, huh?" He grinned. "Here, let me give you a hand."

"No thanks, we'll manage."

"Why don't you store it in our rooms? The officers never come around there."

"Ha, ha, ha."

We hurried up to the room that Marsh and I shared and, with one man posted as lookout by the door, quickly broke open McCreary's case. He and Matthews filled their arms and pockets with tall, clear liter bottles of Wacholder Verschnitt, or German gin. The labels were crude, almost homemade, and stated that the gin was *"nur für* Wehrmacht," for Wehrmacht use only.

"You guys hide the rest," McCreary suggested. "Better to keep it in one place than have it spread all over the hotel."

"O.K."

"I'll pass the word around the squad for the boys to drop in any time they want a snort."

He and Matthews left, and Marsh, Sholty, and I set to work hiding the remainder of the broken case, which contained forty-eight bottles. We put them in drawers, jump boots, pillows, musette bags, on top of the dresser and under the mattresses. Each of us sipped on a liter as we worked, and though it was raw and green and smelled sickeningly sweet, we delighted in it. When all the bottles were out of the rough excelsior that had cushioned them, we carried the broken box outdoors and left it behind the hotel to fuel the washpots. The other box was covered with a tablecloth and set under our window.

Hale and our platoon leader came by on inspection the next day. Everything was fine until they reached the box. Since we had not told the second floor of our find, having little rapport with platoon headquarters or the squads there, we dreaded Hale's discovering our treasure. He ignored the box, however. Our platoon leader was not quite so oblivious.

"What's in that box?" he inquired.

My heart dropped to my knees.

"Squad equipment, sir," Marsh replied.

The inspection team grunted and left the room. When the door was shut, we yelled with joy.

"Buddy," Marsh said with a smile, "nobody's going to cut into our liquor."

"HAVE ANOTHER DRINK."

"Don't mind if I do."

The little man lifted a white china pitcher from the washbowl on top of the wardrobe and filled the big man's glass. Everybody else was asleep or on guard.

"Iced tea and gin."

"I know. I'm getting used to it."

"Webster had to slip the cooks a couple of jugs to get the iced tea, but it's worth it. Not a bad drink at all. A man can't drink gin straight."

"No sir, he can't."

"Some party last night, huh?"

"Yessir, I can see it now: Webster out cold; Matthews lisping and stuttering; Marsh bragging about how the squad obeys him; Winn laughing and shouting about Bastogne; and Gilmore—that goddamn Gilmore—pressing clothes like crazy. Why does Gilmore always press clothes when he gets drunk?"

"Goddamn if I know. Boys in the platoon C.P. are having a pretty good time, too, only they're drinking cognac."

"Yeah, I sat in on one of those things. Enough to make you sick. Hale slobbering over Pace; Rader out cold in an armchair; Chris watching 'em all in disgust; and that Texas loudmouth wrestling with that slob platoon leader of ours. Him and his familiarity and sunglasses and pasty, pimply goddamn face. I can't stand the guy."

"Me neither. Well, it's been fun the last week anyway."

"Sure has."

They stopped talking and stared out the window, which overlooked a big stone barn, half as long as the hotel and parallel to it ten yards away, that served as home for several dozen displaced persons and refugees from the bombed cities of Austria and Germany. Poles and Czechs who had once worked in the hotel still occupied dark, damp little rooms in the barn's half cellar.

A line of three sooty washpots had been set up below the window near a ramp that led to the barn's huge front door. The last late eaters were still dipping their utensils in the gray water, which had been discolored by the company wash an hour before. There was no G.I. can for garbage, as in the States, for nothing was wasted in Europe, where all the people were hungry. At every meal, a pathetic band of timid, bony children and quivering old women begged for our leftovers before they could be thrown away. They took everything: the coffee grounds, the orange peels, the pork-chop bones.

A Wehrmacht trailer containing sleeping quarters and a fully equipped dental office was parked about twenty yards to the right of the washpots. The only other military activity was a platoon encampment of German soldiers a hundred yards farther on.

To the left, a gray brook with a charming, shaded gravel path curved toward the barn, then swung away from it and continued through small truck gardens toward the main part of Saalfelden, almost a mile distant.

The ground beyond the brook was level meadowland for two miles to a row of gray, snowcapped mountains that formed the northern boundary of the valley. A picturesque, 13th-century castle stood in the meadow halfway to the mountains.

"Been out to the castle yet?" the little man inquired, blinking at its fairy-tale silhouette, now fading in the dusk. The castle was occupied by a colony of Polish farmworkers brought here as slave labor by the Germans.

"Heck yes."

"How'd you make out?"

"Think I got something lined up. She's a honey: brown hair, blue eyes, big tits."

"Got an armband?"

"I'm getting one."

"That makes it legal, huh?"

"Sure. Boys at Regiment are putting 'em on all their Krauts, and man, they got some honeys. Real high-class—countesses and that kind of stuff. Know that little Polak in the barn? One that used to be a chambermaid? Does our laundry?"

"Uh-huh." She was a frightened young girl of 15, barely formed, whom the Germans had taken from her parents' farm three years before and shipped to Austria to work as a chambermaid. Her parents had been marched off to oblivion to dig emplacements on the Russian front, and because the innkeeper had pitied her and treated her more as an adopted child than as a servant, the hotel had become her home. When we had taken over, she had remained undisturbed, for she had no home anymore, and we preferred to give our work and rations to Displaced Persons like her than to the Germans.

"Nice little girl," the small man commented. He preferred women over 30.

"Ducatelli's in love with her."

"Stop it, will you? Nobody's in love."

"So help me. I can tell by the way he's been mooning around, holding her hand, and bringing her chow and flowers and every other goddamn thing."

"Well, whattayaknow? Love. Hmmm."

"Have another drink."

"Thanks, I'll force one."

"Stuff creeps up on you, doesn't it? Goes down like iced tea, comes up like gin."

The big man laughed and set the pitcher back in the bowl. He stood near the window for a couple of minutes, inhaling deeply, then tensed and frowned at something that had caught his eye below.

It was a cook, an object of universal contempt, and he was clad in the cooks' uniform: a greasy, sweaty, long-sleeved wool undershirt and a pair of sooty, grease-splattered fatigue pants. Drunker by far than either of these observers, he had lurched out the back door of the kitchen and was zigzagging to the trailer.

"Slopshits are drunk again," the big man commented. "Sonsofbitches haven't been sober overseas."

The cook pounded on the trailer's door, then stumbled inside.

"Couple of slick Krauts down there."

"Who's that?"

"Them dentists. They're cleaning everybody's teeth for cigarettes and Hershey bars."

"That's smart."

"They got women too."

"Oh?"

The little man stood up and looked out the window. The twilight was over; it was so dark and misty now that they could barely see the trailer.

"Cooks been screwing 'em in their rooms. They're swapping chow for ass. They're living filthy."

"They always did."

"Look, look!"

Another cook staggered out of the kitchen and knocked at the trailer door. The first one came out in reply with a rather heavy, well-built woman. Watched by one of the dentists, who held the door open, a similar female followed. The dentist shut the door and turned out the light as soon as she was outside. This was the signal for the assault: The cooks whirled on the women, threw their arms around their waists, kissed them passionately, and clutched their bottoms. The women were by no means unattractive.

While the two men at the window clenched their fists and pushed their stomachs tight against their belts, the cooks swayed back and forth in ardent embracement until the women, who appeared to be sober, wrenched free of them and led them into the barn.

The little man downed the last of his drink and set his canteen cup on the dresser. His eyes were sparkling. "Let's move in on 'em," he said softly.

The big man grinned.

"They're so goddamn drunk they're going to pass out as soon as they lie down. Those broads know what they're doing. We have to catch 'em before they roll 'em off and run back to the trailer. Come on."

Later they told us what happened. They padded downstairs to the lobby. A redheaded British major from S.H.A.E.F., who spoke German with a Scotch accent and who had come with the outfit from Berchtesgaden to seek war criminals hiding in the Austrian Alps, was sitting in the officers' mess, talking with Captain Speirs and another officer. None of them looked up as the two men slipped around the newel post and darted into the kitchen.

As they passed some open crates of oranges and eggs, the big man nudged his companion and winked.

"We'll get 'em later, buddy," the little man said, "on the way back." He nodded at a cook who had come at them from the shadows of a storeroom behind the crates. "Whattayasay, Miller?"

"What are you men doing in the kitchen?"

"Just passing through. Going to get a little fresh air."

"Keep your hands in your pockets and keep moving. Too many of you guys swiping rations already."

"Not us, Miller, not us. We wouldn't take anything off a cook. Chrissake, all you guys done for us!"

Laughing to themselves, they went through the kitchen to a narrow corridor that led to the back door. A short walk took them into the barn.

They stopped in the door, which was always open, until their eyes had grown accustomed to the darkness. The snoring and grunting and tossing of the refugees in the hay sounded like a barracks after lights out. A panting came to them from the far left, a panting and thrashing, then a woman's "Oh, hoh, oh, ohhhhhhhh."

"Watch it," the little man said as he started for the sound. "Floor's covered with people."

He bent over and felt ahead of him so that he wouldn't step on anybody. He had seen these people in the daytime—the bewildered old men, the crying children, the widows who had lost men, family, and household in the war—and he did not want to hurt them any more. They had been hurt enough already, he had once said. It did not matter whether they were Germans, Russians, Poles, Czechs, or Yugoslavs; they had all suffered. Torn from their homes and pushed on by the flood of war, as a wall of water uproots even the oldest trees with the deepest roots and carries them along a huge, muddy river, most of them had never wanted war. They were the average people of the world, he had claimed, and, helpless in the hands of governments that controlled the tanks and airplanes, they had suffered the most.

He paused, and pulling his companion to him, pointed to the left, where a woman had just rolled a man off her with a German curse and was whispering to another woman near her. The man mumbled drunkenly and shook himself, then lay still. Another man was asleep near the other woman.

"Cooks passed out," the little man whispered. "Now it's our turn."

He crawled to the first woman and panted, "Fooken, fooken."

The cook stirred drunkenly and went back to sleep. The big man was already kissing and caressing his date.

The little man unbuckled his belt and let fall his trousers and underpants, while his girl sighed bitterly and pulled up her skirt and settled into position. Her friend followed suit, for both had been trained to oblige soldiers. Soon the hay was alive with a double creaking.

The steady rhythms slowly penetrated the cooks' addled brains, making them toss and moan and gradually come to. When the little man in his passion accidentally kicked the cook beside him, the man sat up and shook his head.

"What the hell?" he said thickly, blinking at the heaving figures beside him. He reached over and felt the little man's bare bottom.

The little man chuckled to himself at the cook's discovery. It was too late; he had already had his fun.

The cook started yelling in the foulest language and grabbed for him, but the little man was too quick for him. He gave him a shove and stood up and hoisted his pants. The other cook came to and contemplated the big man, who was still in the act of love. Before he could act, his rival's body relaxed and the little man hissed at the big man to get going.

The cook lunged at him again. He hit him in the stomach and ran for the door. The big man followed, clutching his pants.

"Rape! Rape!" the cooks shouted. "Stop 'em!"

The refugees moaned and tossed and rolled over in the hay. War and soldiers and the nights were always the same. Would it ever end?

OUR ONLY DUTY WAS GUARD. The mortar squad guarded the hotel and depot, while the three rifle squads alternated on the crossroads where the main street between Saalfelden and the railroad station crossed the highway to Germany. The second and third platoons watched the ammunition dumps in the forest nearby. Elevated to the post of city manager and contact man with Field Marshal Kesselring, Captain Speirs took up residence in the latter's private train, which we raided one night for a case of Hennessy cognac, and company headquarters set up an information and dispatch office to handle offers of surrender, issue passes for German convoys, and arrange for deportation into the Reich of the remaining enemy soldiers. While their job was interesting, ours, on the crossroad, was even more so, for it had the most movement of any post in the Company.

Noncoms stood guard here once every three days, privates every other day. We wore woolen uniforms and helmet liners and stood in the middle of each road and stopped every German driver to find out where he was going and why. All vehicles' passes were checked, and what with the constant procession of men and cars, the time passed very quickly. For the first time in my life, I actually found myself looking forward to guard.

German M.P.s helped to make it interesting. One for each of us, they were big, tired men who had seen service as infantry in the First World War and as combat M.P.s in this one. They wore as their badge of office a heavy neck chain bearing a brassard with the word "Feldgendarmerie" inscribed on it in raised letters, and it was a pleasure to work with them, because they were such good soldiers. They saluted with a great heel-clicking; they handled German vehicles and information-seekers with cold efficiency; and they obeyed orders like robots. I am sure that if we had told them to shoot every other pedestrian, they would have done so without the least qualm, because that was the order. Real soldiers. For all their discipline and snap, these men were, however, rather pathetic figures, in the army so long that they almost dreaded a return to the disorder of civilian life.

One of them was in the highway now, with his hand raised as a signal to halt. A Wehrmacht Opel Blitz truck stopped in front of him. First in a convoy of about a dozen vehicles, it was loaded like the rest with rations, bedding, haversacks, blank-faced men in German uniforms, and subdued, overworked women. The Feldgendarm clicked his heels and saluted the person sitting beside the driver. *"Passkarte, bitte,"* he said as I strolled over with Trapuzzano, a slender, eager young replacement who had come in just before the Bulge.

The Wehrmacht officer on the front seat returned the M.P.'s salute, reached in his pocket, and handed out a folded sheet of white paper. The M.P. nodded and passed it on to me.

"Hauptmann Ernst Meutzig has the permission of the military government at Zell am See," it said, "to transport his unit with ten trucks to Berchtesgaden."

"Soldbuch, bitte," I said to Captain Meutzig. He gave it to me, and I checked his identification against the pass. They were always correct, but it was part of our job to make sure, so I went through the routine, primarily because I did not like the captain's looks. I returned the pass and the Soldbuch with a *"Gut, gut."*

"Darf Ich?" the captain started to say.

"Ja, ja. Mach' schnell!" the M.P. barked. He saluted again. Trapuzzano also saluted.

The captain returned the salutes, and the convoy passed through us slowly and without friendliness or greeting. None of the Germans was happy about being removed from Austria, which they had apparently come to regard as their own.

"This is the kind of guard I like," I commented as the trucks crossed the plain toward the dark, rocky pass a mile or so north that led to Germany.

"Nothing to it, is there?" Trapuzzano agreed. "Too bad we missed the shooting. I'd like to have seen that."

I nodded. A Wehrmacht staff car had tried to run the roadblock a few days before. It was shot off the road by a rifleman in the third squad who killed the driver and his passenger in the process. The German M.P.s, strong authoritarians, had approved of the action, for the driver had also disobeyed their shouts and orders to halt. They had a generally low regard for our discipline, muttering among themselves that they were trying to preserve law, order, and respect for authority in spite of us and not because of us, and they were pleased to see an American exhibit strength on the proper occasion.

"You don't have to salute these Krauts," I said to Trapuzzano. "I'd never salute anybody in another army, especially the German army. Bad enough to salute the pricks in ours."

"Oh, hell, I get a kick out of it."

"Suit yourself. Ah, the doctor."

A sporty little tan convertible slowed down and stopped beside us. It was manned by a crew of two with whom we had already become quite familiar: a racy, fast-talking, middle-aged German who claimed to be a doctor and who talked a garbled American slang, and a quiet, decorative blonde of about 25 who looked expensive and said nothing.

"Good morning," I said, smiling at the blonde. "How are you?"

"O.K., G.I., O.K.," the doctor replied. The blonde was silent. "What say?"

"Can't say it here."

"Ha, ha, very good, ha, ha. O.K."

"Going to Berchtesgaden?"

"You betcha. Some fun, huh?"

I laughed, and the blonde smiled at me, warming my skin from head to toe. "Let me see your pass," I said. The doctor handed it to me, and I studied it and frowned. "No good. I can't let you go."

The doctor's face stiffened. "It's good," he said coldly. "I know it's good; your Major Winters gave it to me."

The blonde stared straight ahead and bit her lip.

I laughed and handed back the pass. The doctor returned to joviality. "O.K., G.I.?"

The car spurted toward the rocky pass.

"Slick sonofabitch," I murmured. "I don't trust anybody that friendly. He's always going to Berchtesgaden, always with the same excuse. Probably organizing an underground or running messages for S.S. men in the mountains. He's too smooth, too sure of himself."

"How about that gal?" Trapuzzano said. "Isn't she a honey?"

"Krauts and their women—I've never seen anything like it. Wonder how she got lashed up with a phony like that."

An elderly couple in peasant costume passed us timidly, nodding and afraid. We smiled and said good day. I left Trapuzzano and walked over to

Janovec, who was standing at the corner where the traffic halted coming out of Saalfelden.

He was holding up a Luftwaffe convoy of four trucks while he checked the leader's credentials. "Sonsofbitches are all going home." He grinned. "How about us, Web? When do we go home?" He returned the driver's pass and yelled for him to take off. The bulging, wheezing trucks went into the intersection and turned right, toward Germany.

We stood side by side and watched the convoy till it disappeared between the sheer gray sides of the pass. "They're moving all the Krauts out of Austria," Janovec commented softly, "even the civilians. Pretty soon we'll have the place to ourselves. Jesus, what would you do if you were a Kraut returning to a place like Cologne with nothing but a uniform too tight in the chest and six sizes too big in the ass and no job or place to live and your country just lost the war? Poor sonsofbitches. I'd take a pistol home with me and make a living that way."

"I don't envy them. Well, maybe we'll go home too. There's talk of a point system coming up that'll let some of us out."

"Hope so."

Another familiar couple approached us. Daily visitors to the roadblock, they were a pale, quiet Frenchman and a young blonde woman. Although most of their fellow countrymen had already gone home, they apparently preferred to linger, for reasons of their own. Perhaps a rope was waiting for them in France; we never found out.

"Hello," the man said. "What is new today?"

I told him what I could of the *Stars and Stripes'* latest stories about De Gaulle, while he listened intently, pathetically eager for news from home. When I was finished, he tipped his hat and thanked me, she nodded curtly, then both strolled away, a sad, lonely couple in the land of their nation's enemies. I went on to Smith's post.

A big, sensible young man who had come to us in Haguenau, Smith had the easiest post of all, stopping the German traffic coming into the area from Berchtesgaden. Since almost none came in, he had very little to do for two hours.

We chatted awhile, then he left for a few minutes' relief, and I began to talk with his German M.P. Of all the Feldgendarmerie, he was the oldest, the friendliest, and the most talkative. In five years of war, he had once said, his outfit had been in almost every country in Europe. France was the best by far *("prima, prima")*, with Italy a close second. With the exception of the Ukraine, Russia was not a desirable assignment, even for an M.P. The German army's feelings about Russia were best expressed, he had told me, by a sign posted on a road to the front: HIER BEGINNT DIE AUSSERWELT. "The Outer World starts here."

I asked what was new, and he said that his unit was finally going to be discharged; they would leave for Berchtesgaden as soon as their captain got the transportation. "This is the end of my second war," he said. "I hope it is the last."

"What will you do now?"

"I don't know."

"Where do you live?"

"Mannheim."

Mannheim, I thought, remembering a city almost totally destroyed.

"My home was burned in an air raid, the factory where I worked was bombed; I have no home and no job. My wife and daughter are living in a public air-raid shelter, and both my sons are missing in Russia. I am 55." He sighed. "It is time to go home."

A camouflaged Buick staff car that had stopped for Trapuzzano passed by, and the German snapped to attention, clicked his heels, and saluted. Two enemy officers in tailor-made uniforms with many ribbons and medals returned the salute from the rear seat. They had red collar tabs and red bands around their stiff-visored garrison caps.

"Oberkommando der Wehrmacht," the M.P. said in the hushed tones of one who has seen God or Eisenhower. "General Luttwitz."

Smith, who had come back, grunted and asked what he had said.

"German general staff," I replied. "I'd like to shoot 'em both."

Smith grinned. Every soldier wanted to shoot a general.

"Buddy at regimental headquarters says the outfit won't go C.B.I."

"That's O.K. by me. I have no urge to fight the Japs. All I want to do now is go home."

"Outfit's going to be occupational—strategic reserve. Point system's going to start soon. Buddy tells me one of the short-time airborne divisions, the 18th or the 17th, is going to be made a high-point outfit to take the old men home."

"I hope it's true."

A horse-drawn wagon with firewood pulled up while we were talking. The driver, who was leading a team of two beautiful Percherons on foot, looked at us questioningly. Smith waved him by. I moved on to Kohler, the preacher's son who had come in at the same time as Smith and who was a bright, chatty person, selected, like the others on my relief, for his congeniality.

"Here comes that goddamn Nazi," Kohler said after we had exchanged greetings. "Sonofabitching Hitler Youth."

A boy of about 14 walked out of Saalfelden and through the intersection toward us. A very handsome blond, he was the most poised, arrogant adolescent I had ever seen. Unlike the peasants and townsfolk and wounded Germans who passed us on convalescent walks, the boy, who wore high woolen socks, a short-sleeved white shirt, and very small Lederhosen, never spoke to us, never smiled at us, never even looked at us. He moved in a cloud of hate that was more irritating than the most offensive civilian driver.

"They'll make the next war," I commented as he went by. "Snotty little bastard. Hitler filled 'em with his hogwash, and they never had it beaten out of them in action the way the soldiers did. You wait and see. They remind me of the teenage kids I saw in Japan in 1935, when the Japs were getting ready for war. The older people were nice to us, but the kids hated us like this kid does. They're the ones who fought the war."

A one-legged German soldier with a pack on his back bounced out of Saalfelden and stopped by Janovec. I went over to see what he wanted. He had a thin, bright face and a jaunty air that was somehow enhanced by his primitive crutches, which were olive-green saplings with the bark still on them.

"*Guten Tag,*" he said, smiling and leaning on his crutches. "*Ich bin entlassen.*"

"Good!"

Janovec frowned, and I explained that he had been discharged. "Want a cigarette?"

I lit it for him, and the German thanked me, inhaled deeply, and said that it was the best smoke he'd had in six years. Nodding at his right leg, which was off at the knee, he coughed, ahff! and grinned. "*Granatwerfer.*"

"Ah." I smiled. "A mortar."

He nodded pleasantly and continued to grin. A 1st lieutenant, he told us that the Americans were letting him go home. "For me the war is over."

A civilian car stopped by Trapuzzano. "Where's he going?" I yelled.

"Munich."

"Want to go to Munich?"

The cripple smiled. *"Ja, ja."*

The car came up to us as we moved into the middle of the crossroads and stopped again. Its driver, a fat civilian, appeared to be quite surly.

"This soldier needs a ride to Munich," I said, opening the back door. The driver grunted. "Get in," I said to the lieutenant.

He banged up to the door, stopped on his one leg, handed me his crutches, swung inside, and sat down. I passed in the crutches.

"Danke," he said, smiling, *"danke scher."*

The car drove off.

"A good man," I remarked to Trapuzzano, who had come up. "With a sense of humor like that, he must have been a very good officer."

"Makes you sorry for those sonsofbitches, doesn't it?"

"It sure does. They have no V.A., no pensions, no fancy hospitals, no jobs, nobody to look after 'em. Hell, they don't even have a country of their own anymore."

We stood and watched a convoy of about a dozen G.I. trucks go by. The canvas tops were off, and the backs were packed tight with a picnic crowd of singing, shouting civilians wearing tricolors in their button-holes and waving homemade French flags. Someone threw a bouquet of violets at our feet, and they were gone.

"Slave laborers," I commented. "Going home and glad to go. But I wouldn't want to return to a country as dead and beaten as France. Germany has more vitality; France just seems drained dry. They haven't even picked up the rubble from D-Day. I have no love for the Germans, but at least they work together. In France, it's every man for himself; they never get together and never get anything done."

"Goddamn Frogs," Trapuzzano muttered.

Continuing the circle of posts, I returned to Janovec just as a pretty girl pedaled up and got off her bicycle.

"Hello, honey," Janovec said.

"Please?"

He laughed, and I asked what she wanted.

"I must go to see my aunt. She is sick. May I go by the railroad sta-tion?"

"Certainly. We stop only vehicles."

A boxy white panel truck marked with small red crosses pulled up with a German enlisted man at the wheel and a heavy, severe nurse beside him. Janovec winked at her, and she pursed her lips and gave him the pass.

I went around to the rear, opened the doors, and looked inside. Four gray-faced German soldiers lay on stretchers inside, staring dully at the ceiling as if they saw death hanging over them. I shut the doors softly. It could have happened to anybody. "O.K., let 'em go," I said.

"Hey, Web!" Trapuzzano shouted. "Guy wants to trade for a 7.65."

"I'm coming."

It was a private from the 502, touring the area on a captured motorcycle. He said he'd swap a G.I. wristwatch for a 7.65, a small automatic pistol that would be more convenient in civilian life than a Luger or a P-38.

"You're talking to the man with the 7.65s," I said. "Let's go to my billet." I climbed on the rear seat, roared down to the hotel, made the exchange, and came back, all within five minutes.

There was a great commotion at the roadblock when I returned. Two German M.P.s were screaming at an excited civilian in a small black car, while Janovec stood by with a wide grin on his face.

"Get a load of this," he said. "They're fighting the war all over again."

The Germans turned on me with such a flood of gutturals that I could not follow them. Finally I gathered that they wanted to take the civilian prisoner.

"Why?" I asked, staring at him. A thin young man in his late 20s, he had curly red hair, wild blue eyes, and a tricolor in his lapel.

"He is bad. He has been robbing the civilians. We have orders to arrest him."

The Frenchman made a remark that turned both Germans on him, shouting and waving their fists. Their eyes were narrowed in hate, but he only smirked at them. Janovec grinned.

"We have no such orders," I said. I told the Frenchman to drive on.

"*Deutschland kaput!*" he yelled, racing away.

"*Schweinhund,*" one of the Germans muttered. A corporal, he was as big and old as the other M.P.s but considerably harder and less sociable. Where the others were benign and fatherly, he was critical, harsh, and precise.

"You should have arrested him," he said. "He is a bad Frenchman. He stole that car. He has a pistol. With it, he has been robbing the people for miles around. Your military government has issued a warrant for his arrest."

I nodded, "Uh-huh," and looked at the car. I could still shoot it off the road. If it had been an S.S. man or some other renegade German, I would have done it, but a Frenchman? No. I would never shoot a Frenchman, especially to please a German.

"You must keep order, you must preserve respect for law."

"*Ja, ja, ja.*"

I walked away, leaving the Germans to mutter at our casual airs and the lawlessness of the French. A fetching brunette in a tight blue skirt and a shapely sweater approached on foot, with two second-platoon men behind her, whistling. She tried to ignore them but finally broke down in a smile as she went by. The two G.I.s who had been trailing her like stiff-legged dogs stopped to chat.

"How's the fratanizing here?"

"No dice on the roadblock."

We exchanged rumors and they went on. The news was good: Pistols would be issued through company headquarters; the point system was about to start; and the Camera Killer had been detached from active command of any of us and placed in charge of the area's Displaced Persons.

My stomach shriveled as a familiar figure pedaled toward us from Saalfelden. I checked my new watch and glanced toward the railroad station in hopes that the relief was on its way, for my buddy was approaching and I did not want to chat with him.

My buddy was an artist without talent, a pest, and a bore who wore plus fours and considered himself a gentleman. He bummed cigarettes. We started talking the first time I was on guard, and I had been unable to avoid him since.

Fastening himself on me, he pedals down from a cabin in the hills where he is living with his beautiful, talented wife, also an artist but far better, while she waits in bed to have a baby, and tries to wheedle me into recommending him for the post of company interpreter. Desired by every civilian who can speak two words of English, this post is firmly held by Liebgott, who does not want any competition or interference. Nevertheless, he pesters him too. Liebgott hates him.

My buddy is a Viennese without Vienna, for the Russians are there now, and he does not like them. "What were the Russians like?" I asked him one day.

"Subhuman," he replied.

Wounded in the Caucasus, he told me that the Russians were excellent artillerymen but that their infantry attacks were old-fashioned, "masses of men." He described one attack in which his battalion beat off two regiments of Cossacks mounted on horses.

"They come on screaming, hundreds of them in a great cloud of dust. The ground quakes. My battalion commander, a brave Prussian, walks from hole to hole. 'Do not fire till I signal,' he says. 'Be calm, be steady, let them come close.' It is fantastic: a cavalry charge like the Napoleonic wars. When the Russians are a hundred meters distant, our commander shouts for us to fire.

"The slaughter is terrible. Horses scream and writhe on the ground, the field is covered with dead and wounded Cossacks, the first wave dies out in running men and riderless horses. Still they attack, wave after wave.

"Our machine guns are so hot that we cannot touch them. Ammunition runs out, but brave men bring up more. A counterattack is ordered, and we break up the next wave. From prisoners we learn that these Cossack regiments are being punished; they have been ordered to attack until their units are annihilated.

"The battle continues: attack, counterattack, attack. Artillery falls heavily on our positions, but we hold. By late afternoon, only a company of our men are left alive. They beat off a final attack, and the Russians withdraw in defeat, leaving two regiments dead on the field."

It was a good story that I never tired of. I could see it clearly: the brave Prussian striding from hole to hole; the Germans dug in fine and fighting with spirit and efficiency; the screaming Cossacks from another century riding to their death.

But when the artist tells me that we are all soldiers together and should let bygones be bygones, I grew less friendly. Certainly, most Germans were drafted, just as most of us were drafted, for no big war was ever fought by volunteers, and they had to fight, just as we had to fight who originally believed that most of the news about slave labor and concentration camps was propaganda. But this war was Germany's war, and they had to answer for it, for the millions of innocent people murdered in Russia and Poland and the other millions who died in Dachau, Auschwitz, Buchenwald, and all the other German factories of death. I could talk with the artist and all the others and be sociable to a certain extent, but I could not let bygones be bygones.

Besides, he had nothing I wanted, for he was no artist but only a pathetic dabbler in stiff, amateurish parlor landscapes. His wife was the artist. Christenson and I visited their cabin one day, and she did an excellent portrait of me in charcoal that I immediately sent home. It was the best souvenir of the war, better than any pistol or watch or shelter half. I gave her a large can of Wehrmacht meat and a bottle of Italian liqueur as payment and brought them some more food later, because I felt sorry for her, cut off from Vienna and married to a proud bore without talent. Ever since then, he had become increasingly tiresome.

"Hello," he said, stopping his bicycle. "How are you today?"

"O.K. How's the wife?"

"Very good, thank you. Do you perhaps have a cigarette?"

McCreary marched up with the relief. I gave my buddy a cigarette and told him I had to go. He continued to hang around.

Ignoring him, I greeted McCreary.

"Any special orders?" he inquired.

"No."

McCreary sent his men to the four corners while mine formed in a column of twos and I fell in beside them. "It's all yours," I said. "We'll be back in four hours."

"See you, buddy. Anything new?"

"Nope. Just the same old routine."

DEAD DRUNK ON iced tea and gin, I had fallen into bed at about nine P.M. and gone to sleep in my fatigues. Now somebody was shaking me awake.

"Get up, Web!" he yelled. "For Chrissake, get up!"

"Uh-uh," I groaned, turning away from the bright light.

"Grant's been shot. Go out on the roadblock!"

I sat up and rubbed my eyes. "What?"

"A G.I. shot Grant. The bastard's loose in town. Captain wants a noncom on the roadblock right away."

Still drunk, I got out of bed, wrenched into my jump boots, shoved the laces into the tops, and stumbled out the door with my M-1 in hand.

Grant, the sunny, quiet, golden-haired boy from California, had been shot. I never knew him personally, but suddenly I felt as if I had and wanted to avenge him. An old Toccoa man, he was a noncom with a fine combat record who had knocked out an 88 in Eindhoven and been wounded in Nunen. He had made all of the Bulge and had become platoon sergeant after Guarnere lost a leg at Bastogne.

The person who had woken me up told me. Grant was forming his relief for guard in the main part of Saalfalden when a S.H.A.E.F. major standing nearby saw a German vehicle rushing upon the relief. He stepped into the road and halted it. The driver, a G.I., jumped out with a pistol in his hand and shot the major to death. Grant ran up, shouting for him to surrender his pistol. The G.I. shot him in the head and ran away. Grant was now in a German hospital, undergoing a very delicate operation on his brain, and the G.I. was loose in Saalfelden. The whole Company had been alerted to find him.

"Everybody up!" Liebgott shouted as I started downstairs. "Grant's been shot. Outside on the double!"

So drunk that I saw the stairwell as a crazy, whirling, tilting tube, I reached for the handrail, missed it, and ran down full speed. I hit the landing, thinking it was another step, and pitched forward on my face. "Sonofabitch," I muttered, shaking my head and rising to all fours. "I'll make it yet." I picked up my rifle and went down more carefully to the second floor.

All the lights were on; men ran from room to room and floor to floor; the hotel was seething.

I smiled at the hubbub. The outfit moved fast, once it was stirred up.

Stopping on the front steps, I rubbed my face and loaded my M-1 with a clip from the bandoleer that I had slung over my shoulder on awakening. Things were steadying somewhat now; I could make out individual men forming by squads at the foot of the stairs. I ran past them to the left and down the road to the highway crossing. Since there was little traffic at night, no noncom stood here after dark. He posted his men and slept until time to wake up the relief. I usually left that job to someone reliable like Janovec, for with a gin party every night, I was seldom in condition to wake anybody else up.

Captain Speirs passed me in his jeep when I was a few yards beyond the company headquarters' house, which was about two-thirds of the way to the roadblock. I was zigzagging from one side of the road to the other, trying to run fast with my rifle at high port and inhaling sobering breaths of cold night air. The captain leaned out of the jeep. "Kill him, Webster!" he cried.

"I will, sir," I panted, glancing sideways at the jeep. It was loaded with half a dozen angry armed men. "I'll kill him."

The captain grinned and drove on toward Saalfelden.

I staggered into the intersection with my jacket unbuttoned, my bootlaces clicking behind me, and my rifle ready. The guards were all standing together in the center like cows in a thunderstorm, fingering their weapons and whispering and watching the night for the death that might come at them any moment. I told them to break it up and scatter out, one man at each road. "Lie down in the shadows at the edge, so you can see him coming. That way he'll be silhouetted, but he won't see you. Tell him to halt, and if he keeps coming, shoot him."

The guards scattered, and I ran in place and did arm exercises with my M-1 to keep warm and sober up. Gradually the gin and the excitement died down and were replaced by cold and a sense of anticlimax. Half an hour passed and then an hour. The other men had all risen and were moving about restlessly. "When's the relief coming?" one of them asked. "They're thirty minutes overdue."

"I don't know," I replied. I was thinking of Grant and the G.I. who shot him, wondering who he was and why he had murdered the S.H.A.E.F. major and shot Chuck. It was a terrible thing to happen to a man who had lived through the war and would soon go home. Liquor and pistols: That was the trouble. Too much liquor, too many pistols, everybody running wild in his own vehicle. It had to end soon.

The jeep came back a few minutes later.

"Seen him yet?" the captain asked.

"No sir."

"We'll find that sonofabitch if we have to go through every house in town. Keep your eyes open, Webster, he's likely to steal a car and make a run for it to the mountains."

"Yessir."

The jeep whirred away. Another carload of riflemen came through and brought us up-to-date. Men were watching all the roads out of

Saalfelden, they said. Mounted patrols were circling the town in German jeeps and command cars. The Camera Killer was taking a squad through the houses near the scene of the shooting. The man couldn't possibly escape. A loud, unpopular replacement from the 3rd Battalion who had seen no action, the murderer had already been identified by regimental headquarters, which had reported that he had shot and killed two German soldiers and stolen their car. It was rumored that the colonel did not want this man taken prisoner—his body would be enough.

The relief marched up the road a few minutes later and informed us that he had been captured. Grant's platoon leader had found a babbling G.I. wandering aimlessly along a back street with a dull, unseeing look in his eye. Instead of shooting him on the spot, as we agreed would have been fitting and proper, the lieutenant brought him into company headquarters. He was thrown into a chair and beaten senseless. "I've killed better men than you," Captain Speirs had cried, smashing his face with a rifle butt. One of Grant's buddies had burst into the C.P. with a pistol in hand to finish him off, but four men grabbed him and held him back. Beaten unconscious, the murderer was now on his way to the regimental guardhouse in Zell am See for further treatment.

We marched back to the hotel, wondering aloud why Grant's platoon leader hadn't killed his captive. I took another large tumbler of iced tea and gin, went to bed, and slept restlessly for a few more hours.

Achtung! Achtung!
You are now entering
the city of

ZELL AM SEE

home of the

506th PARACHUTE INFANTRY RGT.
(Fallschirmjager)

Welcome!

Christenson and I smiled at the huge billboard that Colonel Sink had erected at the city limits of Zell. "I guess the world knows who's running this town." I chuckled. Chris nodded. Dodging duty in Saalfelden, which had become more than guard after Grant's shooting, we had hitched a ride to Zell am See for a day's outing. Our driver let us off farther in town, and we cut left and went downhill toward the lake.

It was 9:30, and the wet coolness of the night was still rising in faint steam from grassy lawns and vacant lots, where the dew sparkled like tiny drops of ice. The lake, which got choppy when the wind came up at noon, was so calm and flat that it resembled a sheet of pale-green glass. The cool, sweet, summer-morning freshness of the air made us happy and alert.

We passed a sign that said, ANY G.I. CAUGHT WITH AN UNREGISTERED D.P. FEMALE WILL BE TAKEN OFF JUMP PAY PERMANENTLY, turned right at a chalet that bore the legend, "This place for American officers only," and went to a low, windowless wooden shed labeled NUR FÜR BESITZTRUPPEN.

"What's it mean?" Christenson inquired.

"Occupation troops only," I replied. "This was a private beach club when we first got here. You should have seen the blondes! French bathing suits. Rich refugees from Vienna. The rich never suffer."

We went to the entrance and stopped at a turnstile by a counter where a Mexican G.I. was lounging. "Two of us," I said. "Do you have two pairs of trunks?"

"Sure, buddy. Here's your key."

We passed through the turnstile into a quadrangle bordered on three sides by the U-shaped bathhouse and the lake on the fourth. Rough brown sand filled the open space, with raised sun platforms of wooden slats laid across 2×4s scattered about. The beach was clear except for some rowboats and canoes partially ashore. More boats were moored to a narrow, L-shaped pier that ran into the lake on thin piles. A twenty-foot sightseeing launch was tied up at its end.

A Victrola started to play a very old recording of "Singin' in the Rain." I nodded to a German soldier sweeping out the bathhouses and went into ours.

"That Kraut used to be a captain in the 6th Parachute Regiment. A nice guy. He remembers the 101st; fought us in Normandy, Holland, and Bastogne."

"No kidding?" Christenson studied the ex-captain, a stocky, handsome blond with an open, friendly face, and shook his head. "It certainly is a small world." He shut the door, and we changed into our trunks. The little room had the damp, musty smell of all bathhouses.

"A captain policing butts for a living," I mused. "Well, at least he has a job, and that's more than most Krauts can say."

We went out, locking the door behind us, and ran across the wet sand to a couple of sun platforms and sat down on them. The sun was very warm and comfortable.

"They certainly have this place posted," I remarked, jerking my head at a notice tacked to one end of the building. "East side of lake off-limits," it said.

"Times are changing." Chris sighed. "The chickenshit is setting in."

"As always. Who the hell is Lopez?" I read off another sign, "Motor-boat operated by Private Lopez only."

"Oh, that guy. I thought his face was familiar. Me and him went round and round one night in Rheims. He came in the outfit after the Bulge, and now he's running the beach clubs."

"It should have gone to an old man."

"Politics, Web, it's all politics." Chris, who had wanted to be platoon sergeant, having risen from private to squad leader and platoon guide, had been passed over in favor of a radioman who had spent his time in company headquarters. "The Army's all politics," he continued. "How else did a major like Eisenhower get to be a four-star general in five years? Politics."

"Oh, well, what the hell."

After a few more minutes' sunbathing, Chris suggested that we go for a swim. We walked out to the end of the pier and dove in.

The water was wonderfully cool and clear—not too cold and as clear as glass. Loving the exhilaration and the beauty of the mountains on all sides, we swam out until Chris complained that smoking had ruined his wind, then lay on our backs and rested.

"This is heaven," I remarked. "What a shame all those guys who were killed couldn't have lived for this—this and Berchtesgaden. They would have liked it." I looked up at the blue sky, the snowcapped mountains north and south, the wooded mountains that sloped into the lake to the east and west, and thanked God that I was alive.

"Someday, when we get time, let's take a long hike along the ridges," Chris suggested. "I'd like to explore this country. We can bring our M-1s and shoot deer for food."

"O.K. I want to go to Salzburg, too, and Bad Gastein. They're not very far from here."

We swam back to the beach, rested in the sun, went for a row, swam once more, and got dressed for lunch, which we hoped to bum with the athletes at the Hotel Austria or at some other mess hall in town. On previous visits, I had managed to slip into alien chow lines without detection. There were lots of transients and a quick pitch usually sufficed to get by a suspicious cook or mess officer.

A car honked at us as we walked up the narrow, cobblestone lane that led from the main road to the Hotel Austria, which was almost at the base of the Schmittenhohe Mountain behind town. We stepped to the curb and waited for the car to pass. A black, 1938 Chevrolet panel truck with rough white stars painted on its hood and sides, it stopped by us. "Off the road, dogfaces!" the driver yelled.

It was V.D. Sometime radioman, assistant squad leader, and general goldbrick, he was now the athletic noncom. We greeted him, and he opened the door and offered us a lift. "Us athletes have to look out for the working men." He grinned.

"Where's your sweatsuit?" I inquired. "Everybody else in town is wearing S.S. sweatsuits. How come you're in O.D.s?"

"Athletic noncom has to dress up. Isn't this the life? See that stuff in back?" He jerked his thumb at a net and two volleyballs lying on the floor. "Those are for Major Winters. He's the regimental athletic officer now. All I have to do is see that he has his volleyball game set up every afternoon."

"What a deal! Man, I tried to be an athlete—even volunteered for track, because I once ran the mile—but Hale wouldn't let me go. He said it was either me or Chris, so I backed out. Chris went, didn't you, but now we're both stuck in Saalfelden."

Christenson nodded. "How do you do it, V.D.?" he asked.

"Get close to the right people."

"Politics."

"You know it."

"What else do you do?"

"Make out a list of the daily softball games in the Regiment. Keep score. Major Winters gave me this Shivvy to run around in; T.O. equipment for the athletic noncom."

"Any girls up here? There's none left in Saalfelden, now that the Krauts have pulled out."

"Got a dishwasher's wife—one of them heavy blondes. What a lay! Makes me tired to think of it. Well, here's the hotel. See you in room 405. Have to park the car."

Christenson and I got out and went up the front steps. A crowd of loungers watched us languidly in a fly-buzzing summer drowsiness. New arrivals from the far-off, distasteful world of close-order drill and military courtesy and discipline, we were obviously not too welcome at the hotel. The loungers were clad in baggy black sweatsuits with round chest patches that bore silver lightning S.S. insignia four inches high.

"Hiya, Webster," one of them called.

"Whattayasay, Widman? What team are you on?"

It was my old replacement-system buddy from the 3rd Battalion. AWOL three weeks on a furlough to London, he had just returned to his company, told his captain his plane had been delayed by bad weather, and the day after his return, had abandoned guard and details for the boxing team, the captain of which, a friend of his, had arranged for his employment as official timekeeper. "You ought to get yourself a racket too," Widman said.

"I tried, but I couldn't make it."

We started in the door when another acquaintance from the replacement depots stopped and said hello. He reported that he had gone AWOL from his company in Saalfelden to visit a girl in Berchtesgaden. General Higgins, the assistant division commander, had shaken him out of his love nest after ten days and as punishment had ordered his transfer to Service Company. Now he drove a jeep for the officers in regimental headquarters. "They screw the countesses, I screw the maids," he leered. "I'm being punished." He went out to his jeep. "Gotta run down to Salzburg. Shopping, shopping, always shopping. See you, buddy."

"We're in the wrong town," I remarked to Chris. "Think the boxing team needs a waterboy?"

"Make it two waterboys."

The interior of the hotel had the fresh, cool, pinewood smell of summer hotels in the mountains. The furniture in the lobby, which was big and high, was semirustic, while the floor was covered with cool reed rugs. A huge fieldstone fireplace stood at one end of the lobby. In the sunny, pale-green dining room to the left, uniformed waitresses were setting tables for lunch with silver and linen, while athletes laughed and talked and played billiards and Ping-Pong in a game room on the right. A cigar-smoking room clerk in an S.S. sweatsuit who was pushing the day's mail into letter boxes paused as we went by and asked where we were going.

"V.D.'s room, 405," I replied.

"O.K., buddy, just checking. Guys have been coming in and swiping stuff while the boys are out training. Long as you know somebody, it's O.K."

"Thanks," Chris said sarcastically.

The clerk puffed at him and went back to his mail. We started up the stairs.

Two athletes passed us coming down. "I got 89 points," one of them said. "Eighty-five points and you're out of the Army." His friend laughed. "We got it made."

"Sonsofbitches," Chris muttered. He had 83 points. "They'll sit on their ass here while we're going through basic training, then they'll go home. We'll keep on training."

I nodded and kept my peace. Supposed to have 87 points, I was waiting for confirmation of the last five.

Jack Matthews was waiting for us in the hall when we reached the fourth floor. "Come down to the room, meatheads," he said. "We're all in training."

Sholty, Lyall, O'Keefe, Garcia, and two newer men, Hickman and McBreen, were playing cards or kibitzing. Matthews picked up his hand and went on with the game.

"How are things at the Company?" he inquired.

"Lousy. Training program has started. There's a rumor they're going to take away our vehicles soon."

"Oh?" Matthews was making conversation. It was obvious that he was no longer interested in the Company. "How's Mick?"

"He's doing all right. Got some gal in town."

"Best we all get laid, but the chambermaids are wise to us. Why don't you guys come down here? It's a cinch: no reveille, no retreat, no formations, no saluting in sweatsuits. Maids clean the rooms and make up the beds, waitresses serve the chow, Kraut soldiers do the K.P. Can't beat it, mates."

"Boy, I'll say," I murmured, studying the cool, clean room, with its twin beds and big windows looking over the steep roofs of Zell to the lake. "You guys really have it made." What irked me, and I knew it also irked Christenson, because we had often discussed the matter together, was that only Matthews was an old man; the others had all come in after Normandy. Half of them had seen no action at all. "What event are you out for, Matt?" I inquired.

"No event. Me buddy's captain of the track team, so I'm the official starter. Train on doughnuts and mud at the Criss Cross. Sholty's out for pole vault, McBreen's a boxer, O'Keefe and Lyall are drifting through the track team, Hickman and Garcia are running too. Everybody's using their muscles but me; I'm using me brain."

"Chow, chow!" somebody shouted in the hall.

The gamblers threw down their cards, and we started downstairs together. Christenson and I hung back with Matthews and let the others go ahead.

"Look," I said, "we're serious, we want to get on up here. Can't you or V.D. fix us up? Think you can work a deal with Winters to get us transferred to one of these teams? If Winters goes through Regiment and sends Speirs a direct order to put us on detached service with the athletes, then he can't stop us and we can get out from under Hale. On the other hand, if we ask Speirs for a transfer in person, he'll laugh at us. He's lost too many noncoms to this deal already, and he doesn't like it. He wants the whole Company back where he can train the hell out of us and impress the colonel, so he can go Regular Army. See my point?"

"Oh sure, sure, I see your point. But there's talk of weeding out goldbricks like Lyall and McBreen and O'Keefe, and the point system's about to start, so maybe you're too late."

"We could start a swimming team."

"I'll see what I can do."

"We have to get out of the Company. The war's over; I can't train anymore."

"You're crazy to stick with it."

"Put in a real strong plug for us, will you?"

Matthews nodded. "I'm not sure about V.D., though. He's cozy as hell about his job. Doesn't want anybody cutting in on it. And without his help, no meathead gets through to Major Winters."

"Work on him," Chris suggested. "Basic training is for the replacements. We want to be athletes."

DENIED THE LUXURY of living in Zell am See, I hitchhiked there as often as possible and spent most of my time on the beach. I left Saalfelden after breakfast, thumbed ten miles south to the beach club, swam across the lake, sunbathed, ate lunch at any available mess hall, swam some more, bummed supper, and went to the nightly movie in the regimental theater. Best of all was the lake.

I loved to swim in its clear waters, so cool and invigorating that I always felt reborn as I moved across it in a steady crawl that brought me a view of the mountains, the sky, and the deep, deep water every time I swung my head around in time with the stroke of my arms. Although the other side was off-limits, McBreen, who had quit the boxing team when they had started to make daily runs ("Be damned if I'll run; I went out for boxing, not track"), and I would row across, then I'd swim back while he accompanied me in the boat. Days when he couldn't come along I swam across and back by myself. It was almost two miles, but I never enjoyed swimming so much as in Zell. The beauty of the lake and its countryside made me forget all distance and weariness.

I returned from my swim one day, ate supper, and went for a walk with McCreary along the banks of the stream behind the barn. His points were coming through, he said, and soon he and the others with 85 and over would go to the 501 in Berchtesgaden to wait for transportation home. We discussed the change that was coming over the outfit—the tightening up on private cars, the rapidly expanding training program, the mounting discipline—and agreed that it was time for us to leave. Too many noncoms were new or political or both, too few officers had seen any action. With the replacements in charge, we no longer felt at home.

Trapuzzano rushed up to us when we came back in the hotel. "Jesus, where've you been, Web?" he asked excitedly. "We've been looking all over for you."

"Went for a walk. What's wrong?" I could tell that something terrible had happened.

"Janovec's hurt bad. Marsh took him to the aid station in Zell am See. He fell out of the truck and hit his head on a log."

"Oh my God. Where'd you say he was?"

"Regimental aid station."

"I'm going there. Tell Hale; he'll understand."

I ran outside and headed for the roadblock at a fast jog. The twilight air was crisp and cooling fast. Smiling at the wonderful smells of the open country—the grass, the hay, the wood fires, a touch of pine—I unbuttoned my fatigue jacket and swung my arms back and forth in long arcs. There was a rifle inspection for guard in half an hour, but that could wait. I was the sergeant of the guard for the next relief, but that could wait too. Janovec, the only person I had been close to in Holland and had known well since then, was badly hurt. He and I shared a negative attitude toward the Army, and when I had been made an acting squad leader in Marsh's absence, he had been the most cooperative man in the squad. With encouragement and understanding, he had been a good soldier. In fact, he was the one man in the squad, other than Marsh, that I could really count on. I did not want to lose him as a friend or a soldier.

I jogged through the intersection and began to walk toward Zell, thumbing the few vehicles that passed. Finally a G.I. truck stopped and gave me a lift into town.

The regimental medics occupied a large private home on the highway in the northern outskirts. Since the door was open, I walked in and looked for someone to help me. Major Kent, the chief medical officer, glanced up from his chair in a room that opened in the front hall. "Can I help you?" he inquired, coming out.

"Yessir," I said, smiling at him. I had always admired him for his work on the jumpfields and in combat and had never regarded him as an officer but as a doctor and friend of all men regardless of rank. "I'm looking for a friend of mine who got hurt in an accident. His name's Janovec."

"Oh yes." Major Kent frowned. "Are you a buddy of his?"

"Yes, I am."

"Come with me."

The Major led me into the dining room, where half a dozen enlisted men were laughing and joking and playing cards around a mahogany table six feet in diameter. They looked up at us quickly, then went on with their game. Major Kent opened the pantry door, turned on the light, and stepped aside.

"There he is," he said quietly.

"Oh my God." I stared down at a long figure lying still under a G.I. blanket on the floor. "He's dead, he's dead." My eyes filled with tears.

Major Kent shut the door. "Didn't they tell you?" he said.

"No, they didn't. They said he was hurt bad."

"Skull fracture. He was dead when they brought him in."

The medics in the other room burst into laughter and threw down their cards. "Almost time for the movie," one of them said.

I wiped my eyes and stared down at Janovec, at the peak where his face was and the twin peaks of his jump boots. They always throw a blanket over the face, I thought. That's the first thing they do, if they have time, so nobody will recognize him and he'll be just another dead soldier to his friends going by. If they don't have a blanket, they use a field jacket, a rag, a piece of parachute, anything to hide his face.

"Do you want to look at him?" the major said.

"No sir, I don't. I've seen enough dead men in this war to last me the rest of my life. I don't want to look at another one, ever."

Major Kent stepped over to the sideboard, picked up a brown envelope, and handed it to me. I continued to stare at Janovec. I wanted to bend over and shake him back to life, to curse him for sleeping so soundly.

"These are his personal effects." He emptied the envelope. "A parachute scarf, a Purple Heart, his wings, the E.T.O. ribbon, the Combat Infantry Badge, and his wallet. He had no money on him."

"I'll mail them home."

The major put everything back and handed me the envelope, then opened the door.

Before I went out, I looked at Janovec again, hoping that he would move or cry out, but the blanket was still. Grant shot and Janovec dead and the war over: It made no sense. The Army was death. Let's be done with it and go home. We should have gone home on V.E. Day, then Grant would be the same and Janovec would be alive, but no, we have to stay on and on and on. Come on, Janovec, get up, you're the slowest, stubbornest man in the squad. We both left Rader for Marsh in Mourmelon. Stick with me; I'll put you on a good detail.

Major Kent held the door open for me, and I thanked him and walked through the medics in the dining room, hating them for their indifference. I went out the front door and up the highway.

Winding Down

"Do you hear me, goddammit? We're leaving in ten minutes. Get your goddamn squad out front!"

I turned and frowned at Christenson, who was watching from the door with his gear on and Thompson in hand. It was about ten in the morning, and I was drunk already, because we were leaving Saalfelden for Kaprun, where we would start training in earnest. "Always in a rush," I muttered. "We have to finish the gin before we go. Here, have a drink."

He shook his head. "Second squad's outside already."

"Piss on the second squad."

"You're drunk," Winn said, slapping my back, "day and night." He laughed. One of the first athletes returned from Zell, he had helped mix and consume a pitcher of iced tea and gin while we prepared to move out. "That's the kind of squad leader I like." He lifted a tumbler and drank it down.

"Have a drink, Chris," I said. I poured the mixture into another glass until it spilled over onto the frayed reed rug. "I don't drink myself," I remarked as I lifted the pitcher, put its side lip against my mouth, and wet my face, "but I like to see other people having a good time."

"Better lay off," Chris warned. "Captain's forming the Company already."

"The hell with it. Party's over. I got 87 points, but I'm still in this goddamn outfit, still have to train with the replacements."

"Yeah, yeah, yeah. Now get going! Get your men out front with the rest of the platoon."

"O.K., O.K." I downed the full glass that I had poured for him, emptied the pitcher, and threw it out the window. "Geronimo, look out below!"

"Check the rooms for weapons and ammo," Chris said. "Step on it!" He left.

"Winn, you'd better go outside," I muttered, feeling very dizzy and barely able to separate him from his image. "I'll be along in a little while."

I went to the tall white wardrobe and got my M-1, which was standing in a corner, loosened the sling, and slipped it over my shoulder. Putting on my helmet, I staggered into the hall.

The building was empty. Feeling very much alone, I hurriedly checked the other rooms. Winn met me in Sholty's, and we both paused and looked out the window at the railroad station, where Kesselring's train had been. The rest of the Company had already left in their vehicles; only two remained. Christenson, who was standing by one, yelled for us to hurry.

Shouting and laughing, we went from room to room, kicking open the doors, slamming them shut, yanking dresser drawers to the floor, knocking over tables and chairs. All we found was a box of machine-gun ammunition. At work early, the men had tidied the area very well. The extra gin had been carefully packed, the ammunition crated. Liebgott had even taken the C.P.'s curtains and bedclothes.

"That's it," I said, slamming the last door. "We've had it. The party's over."

The trucks honked for us.

By now, the whole world was atilt. The hall rocked back and forth with tentative whirls, and it took all my self-control to keep from sinking to the floor and going to sleep. I started for the stairs and hit the wall. "Who moved the stairs?" I inquired. "They were there before. I was walking straight at them."

Winn helped me in the right direction, and we started down together, careening from side to side.

A captain and a sergeant from the 3rd Battalion passed us on the way up. "What's going on?" the captain asked.

"We're moving out, sir," I replied. "Always moving out. The hotel's all yours—what's left of it."

Only one vehicle remained when we got outside. An Opel Blitz with its tailgate down, it held half the first squad.

"My squad," I said to the grinning men who were watching us. "Best goddamn squad in the Regiment." I lunged for the tailgate and fell in the street.

Kohler and Trapuzzano jumped out and pushed me in beside Winn. The truck drove off.

We arrived half an hour behind the rest of E Company, in full view of Captain Speirs. Unable to rise, I was carried indoors and put to bed. The party was indeed over.

"RETREAT?" I said, opening my eyes and looking around in bewilderment. I could not recall moving into this strange, pine-smelling alcove under the eaves.

Sholty nodded. Having shaken me awake, he now stood over me to make sure I didn't go back to sleep.

"Retreat in O.D.s? I'll be goddamned. We haven't stood retreat in O.D.s since Mourmelon."

I raised myself on an elbow, wincing at the pain of a violent hangover.

"We've had it," Sholty said.

"What day is it?"

"Same day."

"Oh God. I hoped I'd slept through till tomorrow. Why did I have to wake up for retreat?"

"Camera Killer's orders: Every man stands retreat. Class A uniform, ribbons, and patches. Put on your jump wings, your Chevrolet badge, your Hershey bars, Spam ribbon, and hash marks."

"You make me sick." I jumped off the bed, ran downstairs to the toilet, and vomited.

"Retreat!" the C.Q. shouted. "Everybody outside in five minutes."

I ran back upstairs and told Sholty that I hadn't even pressed my blouse yet.

"You've had it," he said as he cocked his cap over his eye and adjusted his tie.

"Retreat! Everybody out! Let's go."

Sholty left the room, and I jerked on my pants, which had been rolled up in my barracks bag, and shouted for the squad to fall out. "I'll be along in a minute."

We fell in on the road out front, facing the slope of the mountain on the west. Captain Speirs and the Camera Killer waited till everybody was in place, then the captain called us to attention, took a count, and told the platoon leaders to inspect their men. Since our officer had been transferred after leading a posse to catch an S.S. colonel in hiding and taking him for a ride, the Camera Killer took his place. He came over to me, the first man in line, and stopped. Christenson halted behind him, while Hale, as platoon sergeant, took up a position on his left, pencil poised over a paper pad to note each man's demerits.

I snapped my left hand across my stomach, grabbed the top of my M-1, and brought it up smartly across my chest at a 45-degree angle. Holding the weapon in my right hand, I banged the bolt handle back hard, leaving the chamber open for inspection, and then brought my left hand back up to support the gun.

The Camera Killer shot a left jab at the middle of the stock. I let go as soon as the motion started and slapped my hands at my sides. The Camera Killer glared at me; he had just caught it in time.

I ignored him and stared at the grassy slope beyond. They certainly have green grass in the Alps, I thought. Next time I'll move a little faster, I'll make him drop it for sure.

"Too oily, soldier. Gotta keep it dry. Wipe it off and bring it to me after supper."

"Yessir."

He returned the gun and told Hale to write it down. I dropped the butt to the ground with an angry bang.

"Don't bang it, soldier! Ease it down. Let's see you do it again."

"Yessir."

I bit my lip and studied the grass. Must be the heavy rain up here, you sonofabitch. I jerked the M-1 to port arms and lowered it more gently.

"That's better."

He looked me up and down as if I were an old and unsuccessful classmate who had approached him for a loan. "Just get out of bed, soldier?"

"Yessir."

"You must have slept in them O.D.s; you sure as hell didn't press 'em, did you, soldier?"

"No sir."

Green grass. A dead lieutenant would make it so much greener.

"How long you been in the Army, soldier?"

"Three years."

"Three years what?"

"Three years, *sir.*"

"And you fall out for retreat in O.D.s with a barracks bag press?"

"Yessir."

"Don't let it happen again!" He turned to Hale, who was ready with his little pencil. "Sloppy uniform. He'll iron it and wear it after supper, when he brings his rifle back for inspection."

"Yessir."

"And put on them ribbons and medals, soldier. What the hell's the matter with you, you won't wear the Combat Infantry Badge?"

"Nothing, sir. I couldn't find it, sir." I never wear anything but my wings, Purple Heart, and the E.T.O. ribbon with three battle stars and the Invasion arrowhead. Sir.

"Find it and put it on, goddammit! If you can't act like a soldier, at least you can look like one."

My mouth curled. I wanted to kill him on the spot. And they wondered why nobody wanted to stay in the Army.

"And shine them boots!"

"Yessir." I'll chop him up and mix him with chickenshit, because that's what the Army is made of, and then spread him out on the hillside. That'll make the grass even greener.

"And take off that goddamn suntan shirt and put on an O.D. shirt like the rest of the men!"

"Yessir."

Hale wrote it all down and then turned to a fresh page for the next offender, while the Camera Killer moved on, inspecting the squad's scouts without comment. I wondered whether it was better to have a rotten, familiar, foulmouthed, noncombatant lieutenant for a platoon leader or to have no platoon leader and the Camera Killer as a substitute till a new one was found.

The rest of the platoon passed inspection with a few minor complaints and then the trio returned to the front. Hale put away his book and pencil, while the captain gave the Company at ease and checked his watch. When it was 5:15, he told Luz to blow retreat.

As the sweet notes of twilight sounded that had ended so many days for us in so many places, from the sandy mountains of Georgia to the rolling Wiltshire Downs and the great Bavarian Alps, we stood at parade rest, then at attention, and finally presented arms. Luz played the trumpet very well. It was a new trumpet that he had found in a music shop along the Rhine, and the clean, cool sharpness of the notes mellowed me temporarily and reconciled me to the inspection that I had just failed so completely. A retreat properly done was a very moving ceremony—as I knew from standing them at the 10th Replacement Depot in the winter, a place, strictly run, where several guardhouse prisoners were said to have been beaten to death.

The 506th had never stood a Regular Army retreat like the 10th Replacement, on a big, open parade ground with a post band and an officer lowering the flag slowly on a white pole seventy feet high, but we had occasionally caught the spirit of retreat in improvised, wartime ways of our own on muddy company streets in a dozen different places across half the world.

As the last notes died out among the mountains, Captain Speirs, who had been saluting with his hand, took a breath and shouted, "Order arms!" The Company lowered its weapons to the ground with a solid thump.

"Parade rest!"

We thrust our rifle muzzles out at arm's length, put our feet twelve inches apart, snapped our left arm behind our back.

"At ease!"

Audibly relaxing, we shifted our feet and wondered what he would say, for this was the regular time for directives, announcements, and proclamations.

"The party's over," the captain said. "It ended the night Grant got shot. We're not in a summer resort anymore but a training camp. From now on, we'll stand reveille every morning and retreat every night. The training schedule starts full force tomorrow—train in the morning and compulsory athletics in the afternoon. I'm going to make soldiers out of you men again."

A groan rose from the ranks.

"Platoon sergeants will collect all pistols after supper. They'll be tagged with the owner's name and locked up in a strongbox in the company C.P. Any man caught with a pistol after tonight loses it.

"All Kraut vehicles will be turned in to the 1st sergeant the same time as the pistols. That's a Division order. There have been seventy-four car wrecks in the Division in the past month. Sixteen men and five officers have been killed and God knows how many men injured, and the general doesn't want to lose any more. Bad enough to get killed in combat;

it doesn't make any sense to be killed in a car wreck now. We're allowed to keep two trucks per platoon with Kraut drivers, but these will all operate out of a company motor pool. Rest of the jalopies'll go to Military Government at Saalfelden.

"There will be no more drinking in duty hours. If I catch another man drunk in public, it'll be his ass."

He paused, and I winced. They had told me that he was standing six feet away when I was carried dead drunk into my billet this morning.

"We have to have discipline, we have to earn the respect of the goddamn Krauts and act like soldiers. There's still a war on in the Pacific, and I'm going to get you ready for it. Fall out for chow!"

While the rest of the men whooped and ran for their mess kits, Christenson hurried over to me. "Looks like we've had it but good," he commented. "Speirs is really going G.I."

"Everything's changing," I agreed.

We exchanged complaints and were about to go indoors when a familiar, slightly hunched-over figure with a long stride came down the street from company headquarters.

It was Lieutenant Peacock.

THE 10TH ARMY AND two Marine divisions continued to wage a close, bitter battle with the Japanese for possession of Okinawa, while Air Corps' B-29s bombed the mainland of Japan, burning thousands of civilians to death with incidental damage to military targets. The point system was officially announced, and the 1st Armored Division moved into Berlin and its black market to earn themselves the title of the "Million-Dollar Division." Sitting on the banks of the Elbe, the 82nd Airborne heard the Russians shoot and rape the Germans and watched the dead women float by in the morning. The 86th Infantry and 13th Airborne Divisions started for the invasion of Japan by way of the States. In Austria and Bavaria, the 36th Division organized a traveling rodeo to entertain the men, while the British 8th Army sent sightseeing convoys from Italy to the Alps and Berchtesgaden.

The 101st started a training schedule. Day after day, we did close-order drill and calisthenics, as if we had just come in the Army. Organized athletics were the order of the afternoon. And late in June, the general announced that an eight-hour training schedule would go into effect July 9th, in preparation for the Division's move to Japan via America in January, 1946.

I had to go along with the general—and Peacock, who had returned from his furlough home more fresh and eager than ever and raring to get us in shape again—because my last five points hadn't come through yet. Marsh, McCreary, Luz, Liebgott, V.D., Matthews, and all the other high-point men left for the 501 in Berchtesgaden, where they slept, swam, sunbathed, shot craps, fornicated, and rode horseback all day, while we drilled, studied nomenclature and functioning, marched up and down, practiced arm and hand signals, skirmished by squads, held mess-kit inspections, and learned to read maps. Triangulation occupied a solid week before we went on the range, a week that was one of the most maddening I had ever spent, with Peacock constantly breathing down my elbow.

A squad leader with 87 points, I was so fed up that I began to miss formations and avoid retreat by going for afternoon swims at Zell. In a short time, Peacock transferred Henderson from the mortar squad to lead mine and demoted me to his assistant. A quiet, freckle-faced boy from New Mexico, Henderson was apologetic about the shift, but I no longer cared, because my heart wasn't in garrison duty and I wasn't a noncom anyway. The highest I ever got was P.F.C. I would have liked to have been a squad leader or platoon sergeant in combat, which I understood, but I didn't have the patience for this garrison business of make-work, which I hated more than anything else in the Army. I could never scold Winn too severely for missing close-order drill, because I knew he was a good soldier in combat who had fought every day at Bastogne. What if he missed a formation or two? He was still a good man in the place where it counted—combat—and I thoroughly sympathized with his bored disgust.

And so I waited in Kaprun for my last five points to come through. These were the three-mission, or Bronze Star, points, which General Taylor had decreed should go to the old men to help them get home before the outfit fought the Japanese. Everybody got a meritorious service Bronze Star medal who had made Normandy, Holland, and Bastogne or who had made two and missed the third because of wounds. The idea was good, but like all the other medals in the Army, this one soon found its way onto the blouses of personnel clerks and others in rear echelon who had never seen an angry German. Captain Speirs was a freethinker who believed in just deserts to all, however, and so there was no abuse of the Bronze Star in E Company. He refused to give it to the cooks, claiming that it was intended solely for fighting men.

The point system was as confused and unfair as the Army's system of awarding medals for bravery, a system subject to the whim of every division commander. The Air Corps discharged flying personnel regardless of points and released men in the States who had been in the service a few months, while the infantry held everybody down. The Army claimed that first release would be given to men who had seen the most arduous service, but refused to give points for the Combat Infantry Badge. Thus, the Air Corps, which was never quite in the service or even with it but always in a private world of its own, discharged men regardless of points, while the infantry stayed behind to occupy Germany.

All in all, it was a pretty sorry situation that made me feel sorrier for myself than usual, but I tried to make the best of it as June slipped into July. I found a farmer a couple of miles down the road by the ruined castle beyond Kaprun who gave me five gallons of ice-cold milk for a pack of cigarettes whenever I came by, and I swam at Zell and borrowed horses from Headquarters Company for afternoon rides. In idle moments, I listened to the radio, played solitaire, and went for short walks.

The rains began in the middle of July. My milkman, der Oberschweiser, told me that the summers were very short in the Alps. May was nice, *ja*, and June and the first half of July, but from then on, cool weather brought heavy rainstorms that flooded the roads and swelled the creeks. Then came winter. In our valley, the air turned chilly in the rainy spells, and the wind bore the sweet smell of Alpine flowers, wood fires, pine needles, and new-mown hay. Although it ended my swims, the rain was not without its rewards, for it canceled altogether the outdoors training program and forced us to conduct sleepy, apathetic indoor classes on the mortar, B.A.R., and other weapons. These classes quickly degenerated into poker and pinochle games or a session with the radio.

To top off a general feeling of disgust, food began to get short, due, we were told, to the French shortstopping ration trains in their zone of occupation. The 2nd Battalion promptly declared open war on cattle.

Bands of riflemen went forth at night in German vehicles (for the program had the approval of our officers) and rustled calves and yearlings from pastures for miles around; no herd was safe. If a farmer protested, the livestock was taken at the point of a gun. Shot in the head, they were butchered in our basements in a crude, messy operation that left the floor slippery with blood and crawling with biting black flies. Most of the meat was wasted, because we were amateur butchers and had no means of preserving what we did not immediately consume.

Chickens were less plentiful but more amusing. On one foray into a large chicken farm, the men broke open the coops, grabbed their inhabitants by the neck, and whirled them around in the air until the neck broke and the chicken went limp. It was a wild scene from the old days of armies living off the land: The farmer pleading, shouting, cursing; his wife weeping and wringing her hands; the liberators whooping and hollering and thoroughly enjoying themselves; and the chickens squawking, fluttering, beating their wings, and filling the air with feathers. Sixty carcasses were brought back to the Company, where the cooks, following their ancient procedure, half plucked them, chopped them up with cleavers, and boiled them in a gray paste of flour and water.

This was the last organized raid in our area, for the farmers finally revolted and filed strong complaints with Military Government. A division order soon appeared forbidding all such expeditions—the 2nd Battalion alone had accounted for some seventy-five head of cattle, plus untold scores of chickens—and so Captain Speirs, vowing that no man of his would go hungry, sent his riflemen into the mountains in search of deer. A few were shot, but most of the hunters, who had taken the job primarily to get out of training, tramped through the woods so carelessly that they scared all game away.

Since I was the worst shot in the Company and Captain Speirs knew it, I couldn't even work this hunter routine to escape from the platoon. The weeks went by, more and more old men left, and still I stayed with Peacock, going nowhere and hating everything, but most of all the Army.

THE 2ND BATTALION was assembled under a black sky on a polo field half a mile west of Kaprun in O.D.s and overseas caps to practice for the weekly parade that took place every Saturday morning under the new training program. Though flat to the eye, the field was actually so rutted and pitted and bumpy underfoot that it was impossible for a company, much less a battalion, to stay in step more than a few paces. The aggravation of trying to hold a line and march properly without stumbling had reduced officers and men to a seething, sweating, hateful mass.

The storm burst on us with a density that reduced visibility to five hundred yards, but Colonel Strayer ignored it. Apparently determined to get us all in step before we left the field, he made us march by once again in a column of companies.

The rain soaked through our shirts, took the crease out of our pants, chilled our backs and hands, turned the dusty earth to slippery mud. We cursed and muttered as the water poured down our rifle barrels and the company commanders frowned at Colonel Strayer and audibly wondered why he didn't send us home. Finally he gave in to nature and ordered a retreat from the field. By the time E Company arrived at its billets, which were farthest away, every man was soaking wet from head to foot.

"Clean your weapons and stand by indoors!" Captain Speirs shouted. "Fall out."

Henderson and I rushed up to our room, changed into dry fatigues, and broke down our weapons and cleaned them with care. A rusty gun was harder to keep clean than one dirtied in firing.

"Goddamn Army," I muttered, shaking the water out of my trigger group. "Keep you in the rain till you're wet through, then send you home. I could have told Strayer it was going to rain, but he wouldn't have listened to me. Who the hell am I? Just a goddamn dogface. Could a dogface ever tell an officer anything? Hell no. They make you miserable just to show their power. And to think of Marsh and McCreary and Matthews lying around in Berchtesgaden!"

Henderson, who was very quiet and not given to complaining, nodded and left the room. The rain had stopped, I noticed, but a threat still hung in the air.

Henderson returned in a few minutes and bade the squad assemble for an hour's discussion of map-reading and the use of the lensatic compass. As soon as we were comfortably settled around a map of Salzburg province, Christenson popped in and shouted, "Everybody outside for rifle inspection!"

Livid at the thought, I jumped up, cursing Peacock, got my rifle, and went outdoors.

The air was cold and overcast, with a heavy wetness hanging overhead, waiting to fall. Thunder rumbled and banged in the mountains, and water dripped off the roofs and ran down the street in wild, muddy little streams.

"It's going to rain any minute now," I remarked to Chris, who was waiting for Peacock to appear. "We're the only platoon outside. Why not hold it indoors?"

"Peacock's orders."

"He should have stayed home. Why did the one guy who got a furlough to the States come back more G.I. than ever? We've been wet enough for one day."

The thunder rumbled closer and closer, sending gusts of cold wind before it. A drop of rain fell on my cheek. I frowned and held up my palm. Another drop splashed into it, then another and another.

"It's raining, Chris. We'll ruin our weapons again."

"Platoon, 'tenSHUN!"

Christenson spun around and saluted Peacock, who had just come up the road. "Firstplatoonallpresentandaccountedforsir."

The storm burst overhead with a clap of thunder that made us cringe. A sheet of rain fell into the valley.

Peacock fidgeted for a moment, then dismissed us to our houses. I almost fainted with astonishment.

Sensing that Peacock was in a good mood, I went to the platoon C.P. later to ask a favor of Christenson. He was reading the *Stars and Stripes* and appeared to be paying no attention as I outlined a plan to go to regimental headquarters in search of my missing five points.

"I'll think it over," he said finally. "You're still restricted for goofing off the other day, you know. . . . Say, did you see this one? A hell of a story. G.I.s found a murder factory still running just a few miles away from here. Krauts were killing off a bunch of crippled kids in a hospital."

"Vicious bastards."

"Killing little kids—a hospital full of them. Story says they were kids the S.S. wanted eliminated to improve the breed: lame, blind, deaf, and dumb. Imagine killing little kids."

"I'm glad I fought those people, Chris. I didn't believe in the war till I got to Germany and saw what they were up to with their lagers and their concentration camps. I only killed one Kraut for sure, but knowing what I do now, I'm sorry it wasn't more."

"Little kids," Chris mused. "Those cold-blooded sonsofbitches. Paper says the nurses knew the war was over, but they kept on killing 'em because those were their orders and they didn't think we'd have any use for kids like that either. Imagine that."

"Yeah, well, I hope they hang the nurses over a slow fire. . . . Look, it's raining too hard for athletics. Will you ask Peacock if I can go to Zell am See and see about my points? They were supposed to come through a couple of weeks ago."

Chris nodded and continued to read the paper, with verbal comments on the more interesting stories.

I shivered and stood up, buttoning my raincoat tightly around my neck. "Cold in here. That rain's made everything cold. Summer's over, it's time to go home. Let's close the Army and go home, Chris."

"I'll see what I can do for you, Web. Come back in about fifteen minutes."

In a cheerful mood, I strolled back to my billet and killed time drying my rifle. Chris smiled when I came back to the C.P. I removed my helmet liner, walked into the lieutenant's room, and stood at attention as I requested permission to go to Zell.

"Why?"

"To see about my points, sir. I've got five points due for that Bronze Star, but they haven't come through yet. I'd like to go to regimental personnel and see what's happened to them, sir."

"In the rain? It looks like more rain."

"Yessir. There's nothing much else to do this afternoon."

"Rain's slowed everything down, hasn't it? We can't follow the training schedule, go for a hike, take a run, or do anything outdoors anymore, can we? I'll be glad when we go back to France, where we can really train again. . . . All right, go to Zell am See, if you want to, but be sure you're back for rifle inspection at 5:15."

"Yessir."

I saluted and went outside in my heavy, sticky G.I. raincoat, airless and hot even in winter, and walked downhill to Kaprun with my head bent forward against the driving rain. Fast, gray clouds moved across the sky only a few hundred feet above my head and hung smoking against the mountainsides. The smell of pine trees and wet earth and smoke from the farmers' fireplaces made the day seem quite autumnal.

A truck shifted gears with a dry scraping behind me on the castle hill, and I stopped and thumbed a ride. An Opel Blitz in the Company motor pool, it was driven by a cheerful P.W. who had chauffered a German staff car in one of the panzer divisions that had overrun the British 1st Airborne at Arnhem. We rehashed the war on the way into Zell, and he went out of his way to let me off at regimental headquarters.

The lakefront hotel where it was located was warm and brightly lit. Entering with the humility of a muddy hind at the lord's castle, I took off my helmet liner and ran my fingers through my hair.

"Looking for somebody?" a guard asked. He was dressed in crisp O.D.s and white gloves.

I stared down at my soaking-wet fatigues and muddy boots while I beat my helmet liner against my raincoat. "Where's Personnel?"

"Right-hand corridor, third door on the left. Look for the S-4 sign."

"Thanks."

Leaving watery footprints behind me, I squished down the hall and knocked at the S-4 door.

"Come in."

A T-5 stared up from a desk behind a counter.

"This Personnel?"

"That's right. What can we do for you?"

"I have a meritorious-service Bronze Star coming. The damn thing was due several weeks ago, but I haven't gotten it yet. Five more points and I'll be out of the Army."

The corporal grinned. "I know how you feel, buddy. Everybody wants out. We have at least fifty guys in the Regiment hung up on those last five points."

"I have to have 'em. Do you know when they'll come through?"

"Nope. The whole Army's balled up on that point system. All you can do is sweat it out."

"Could you check for me? I want to make sure I was put in for those points."

"O.K., buddy, give me your name, rank, and serial number."

I gave him the information, and he sighed and rose from his desk. "Have a seat on the bench outside," he suggested. "This is going to take a long time."

I nodded, and crossing the hall to a wooden bench, took off my raincoat and sat down.

Regimental headquarters, I mused, staring around with mingled envy and contempt, they really have it made—as always. Every clerk and dog-robber up here is living high and wearing all kinds of medals. I leaned back and closed my eyes.

"What company are you from, soldier?"

I blinked and sat upright. The colonel! Speechless with fright, I jumped to my feet and saluted.

"I said, what company are you from?"

The colonel studied me without warmth. I could read his thoughts: wet fatigues, muddy jump boots, pants not bloused, face unshaven.

"E Company, sir."

"Don't you know you're not supposed to be in regimental headquarters in fatigues?"

"No sir."

"See that it doesn't happen again."

"Yessir."

"And don't salute indoors. You only salute indoors when you report to an officer in the orderly room."

"Yessir."

The colonel went down the hall, leaving me wilted on the bench, utterly crestfallen. What are they running around here, I wondered, a formal dance? No fatigues in regimental headquarters! Jesus Christ.

And the colonel. I always liked him. All the time I've been in this outfit, I hoped I would meet him someday and tell him how much we thought of him. Then what happens? The one time he speaks to me personally, he gives me hell for wearing fatigues in regimental headquarters.

I bounced to my feet and ran across the hall. "Any way you can speed up those points?" I inquired.

The T-5, who was pushing and pulling at a filing cabinet, grinned and shook his head.

"I can't wait another minute to get out of this goddamn outfit."

"MOVING OUT, goddammit, moving out."

Christenson kicked the bed and grinned. "Let's hope this is the last time. Next time we go home, huh?"

A whistle shrieked in the street out front, and the C.Q. opened the door and shouted, "Drop your cocks and grab your socks and fall out for France! Everybody outside! This is it. Moving out, moving out, moving out!"

The house quaked and shook with the sudden rush of men from every room.

Christenson hurried out, and I paused for a last look from the back window. It was a clear day, with big, white clouds moving slowly across the green meadows and jagged mountains. The rainy weather had brought the countryside to its greatest beauty, and I looked at it with a wrenching in my heart, hating to leave it behind. If only it were raining, I thought, then I wouldn't mind going away.

"Shake a leg, Web!" Henderson called from below. "Platoon's already assembled."

"I'm coming."

I ran downstairs two at a time and trotted out the front door.

The Company was already formed, every man with his weapon and helmet and ammunition and a horseshoe roll lashed to his musette bag. In a jovial mood, officers and noncoms stood before each platoon as they waited for Captain Speirs and the 1st sergeant to start them back to the country where they had first landed in Europe a little more than a year before.

Captain Speirs came out, took the count, then gave us at ease and briefed us on our destination.

"We're going back to France," he said, "and it isn't going to be nice, because the French don't love us anymore. They're tired of us already. They're sick of soldiers, and they don't want to be reminded of the war by seeing more of them. We're not going into France as liberators this time, men, we're going in as G.I.s who've worn out their welcome. We're going to be on our good behavior. The general doesn't want any friction with the civilians, and he's promised to throw the book at anybody who raises hell down there. 'TenSHUN!"

The Company snapped their rifles to their sides and clicked their heels together with a solid thump.

"Rightshoulder . . . HARMS!"

Captain Speirs looked up and down the green mass of men with their slanting forest of shouldered weapons and smiled with satisfaction.

"Right . . . FACE! Forwarrrrd . . . MARCH!"

We marched off, counting cadence, while an advance detail from the

42nd Division stood by their jeep and watched us go. The Kaprun Valley was changing hands. The 42nd was taking over our area, German P.W.s had moved into the slave-labor lager below us to work on the completion of the hydroelectric station; the D.P.s had all gone home.

A convoy of G.I. trucks was waiting for us in the village square. Half a platoon in each, we scrambled aboard and moved off, "to that crummy goddamn France," as someone said.

I lifted my eyes to the great, snowcapped mountains behind the upper valley to the south and rested them on a black dot in the snow of the Kitzsteinhorn, which was the tallest peak, a jagged white shark's tooth against the blue, blue sky. The black dot was a ski hut that parties of men had been going to on two-day passes the last couple of weeks. It would have been my turn soon, I thought. Now it's too late.

We crossed the river in the center of the valley, turned right, went east about two miles, and stopped at a country railroad station.

"Everybody out!" the 1st sergeant shouted, coming to our truck and unhitching the tailgate.

A long line of boxcars with an electric locomotive at their head stood at the station. Men were already jammed in most of the cars; a bale of hay stood beside each of the empties. Colonel Sink was walking up and down the platform, talking with the men.

"Nobody on the roofs," the colonel said as Captain Speirs saluted him. "No shooting at trees and cows along the right-of-way. Break up the straw and spread it around, so the men will have something to lie on."

Captain Speirs passed the word along and bade us climb aboard. In ten minutes we were under way. Standing nearby in the door of the car and clinging to the frame for support, Christenson sighed. "It was great, wasn't it?"

"The prettiest country in the world. I wouldn't have missed it for anything."

The Kitzsteinhorn disappeared behind nearer mountains, and the land whipped past with mounting speed.

"Yes," I continued, "it was the only time I enjoyed the Army. Berchtesgaden and Austria were worth everything that went before."

WE HAD SLEPT IN OUR CLOTHES four days and three nights, and we were hot and dusty and sooty and itchy and irritable and unshaven. We tramped carelessly through the empty streets of the little French village of Joigny in a surly, resentful silence, hating the apathy of the shuttered houses, the tedious roughness of the cobblestone paving, the air of death and defeat and decay that lay over the whole country.

A very old village, founded in Roman times, Joigny sloped up steeply from a slow, brown river. Its narrow, winding streets and half-timbered houses lacked, in a way that we could all sense, the life and vitality found even in similar medieval villages in England. Nothing moved in the afternoon heat; nobody waved to us or said hello or came out to watch us pass.

"France," the men muttered, wiping the soot from the corners of their eyes, rubbing the itches on their bodies, remembering the change that had come over the train as soon as it had crossed the border. In Germany, the train had traveled fast, with no delays. In France, it slowed down to a walk, with endless, mysterious stops in open fields, a wait of hours at every railroad yard and river crossing. "France," they said. It was not a country but a swear word.

We topped the hill and marched out on a plateau through the last houses of town to the high, white walls of an old garrison that looked like a Foreign Legion post in the movies. The walls, about thirty feet high, were topped with vicious rolls of concertina barbed wire. A rifleman in a striped sentry box beside a pair of open iron gates saluted Captain Speirs as we marched into the compound, a glaring, dusty place surrounded by old, two-story stucco barracks. A company of the 1st Battalion was drilling in the compound. Their shouts and the hot, dusty air, coupled with the barracks' smell and sounds, roused in us a terrible sense of anticlimax. "France," the men grumbled. "Take me back to Germany."

A small band of men lounging in the shade got to their feet and came forward to meet us. The advance detail, they saluted the captain, chatted awhile with gloomy head-shakings, and then went to their respective platoons and guided us to our billets.

The second and third platoons filed into a two-story barracks, while we circled around this to a long shed with a high roof, where Peacock left Christenson in charge. He bade us go inside and pick out our bunks.

Old and stale, the air smelled musty and unhealthy, and the bunks were crude, rickety contraptions, obviously homemade, with straw sacks for mattresses. We threw our gear under them and began to curse

France without restraint. One of the men from the advance detail moved among us, slapping backs and joking. Finally he stopped by Henderson and me.

"Welcome to France," he leered. "Civil War barracks, built in 1870, and for the first platoon, a goddamn stable with straw sacks. We've had it, mates, we've had it."

He sat down, and the rest of the squad gathered around to hear what he had to say about our new home.

"Krauts used this trap for a prison in the war," he continued, raising his voice for the benefit of latecomers. "Barbed wire still on the walls. There's only one gate, and nobody's allowed out without a pass."

I groaned and threw a boot at the floor.

"The latrine's a stone wall and a hole in the floor that hasn't been cleaned for seventy-five years. There's no hot water, and you can't drink the tap water, because it'll give you cholera, dysentery, and the bubolic plague. Have to get your drinking water from Lister bags. It's all souped up with Halazone tablets; tastes like a swimming pool."

He grinned at the circle of men around him.

"Germany's the best country in Europe," someone remarked.

"Goddamn right," another replied. "Krauts are really on the ball. No wonder they whipped the Frogs. We never lived like this in Germany."

The lecturer continued. "But that's only the beginning. There's nothing in town either. Red Cross girl that was shacking up with that sergeant took one look at this place and asked for a transfer back to Austria. She's leaving tomorrow.

"Yessir, it's a dead town. A couple of beer joints without beer, cognac, or calvados. Nothing but wine. The Frogs won't even say hello to you on the street or nod to you the way the Krauts would, and there's no women or hard liquor for miles around. No cathouses either, and no whores on the street. If you proposition a gal, she spits at you. Can't even buy a lardy cake here, Web."

He slapped my leg and smiled, and I shook my head in reply, for the atmosphere was very depressing. "This is worse than the Frying Pan," I muttered.

"Goddamn right. At least we had Columbus and Phenix City handy down there. Here we got nothing. Can't get drunk or laid or anything. Paris is ninety miles away, but the trains don't stop here, so what the hell good is Paris?"

"How about that river?" I inquired. "Can you swim in that river?"

"You know these Frogs: every river an open sewer. I dove in that thing yesterday and came up covered with turds."

He burst out laughing.

"The Frogs hate us here. They hate us everywhere in France. Save their country for 'em, and they hate you for it. But you can do business with 'em. Frog K.P.s are in the black market. Sell 'em your spare jump boots and fatigues and cigarettes. They'll give you a thousand francs— that's $20—for a pair of jump boots, five hundred francs for a carton of weeds or a fatigue jacket. Chow's on the blink already because the goddamn cooks are selling the good stuff to the K.P.s. Anybody who doesn't think Germany is the best country in Europe has rocks in his head."

"Holland's better," I said quietly. "They're Germans without the viciousness."

He ignored me and was about to continue his dissertation when someone on the edge of the group shouted for attention.

The men opened a path for him, and Peacock pushed through them angrily.

"What's going on here?" he asked. "You men are supposed to be cleaning up the barracks. We have a lot of work to do before retreat and just one hour to do it in.

"Sweep this place out! Get those cobwebs off the walls! Make up your bunks! Wash and shave and fall out for retreat in an hour in clean fatigues and helmet liners! This is the place where we're really going to soldier."

He spun around and stalked away with his long stride. Turning at the door, he called back, "These are dirty old barracks; God knows how many diseases are floating around in them. Bunks are jammed together too closely for proper circulation. Get back here after chow and stretch shelter halves between 'em! You'll have plenty of time, because there won't be any passes for several days."

He slammed the door, and Christenson, who had come near us, shrugged his shoulders and sighed. "That's the program, men. You have to take the program. Retreat comes first, then the rest of that crap."

We began to clean our M-1s. A murmur of complaint filled the air.

"I never did like the French," a man remarked who had jumped in Normandy. "Them and their goddamn Underground. When we jumped in Normandy, no Underground came out to help us, like in Holland.

There was us and there were the Krauts, and the Frogs only came out of their cellars to loot the Kraut supply rooms when it was all over. Hell, they were on the Krauts' side in Normandy. Beat up a couple of guys who landed in St. Marie du Mont. A French broad killed over a dozen troopers in St. Come du Mont before the 1st Bat finally cornered her. She was a sniper, shacking up with the Krauts. You can have them goddamn Frogs."

I blinked at him in disgust. "They're not all bad," I said. "They're nowhere near as good as the Dutch, but they're not all bad by any means. I met a good French trooper once, in Le Havre. And maybe there *was* an Underground outside of Normandy, in the rest of France. I don't know. There must be something to all that talk."

I pulled a rag through my rifle bore and squinted down the barrel. It was good enough to pass.

Irritated by the general—in fact, almost unanimous—attitude that the Germans were better than the French, I continued. "I met another good Frenchman once—in Normandy, of all places. I was in Headquarters Company then, on my way down the Carentan causeway to outpost a sandbank on the Douve River overnight. It was sundown, and there was a stinking dead Kraut every five yards. Dead Krauts, dead horses, the houses shelled to pieces, telephone wires all over the road, the sun going down white in a gray mist. It was goddamn scary, walking down that causeway with miles of water on both sides, not knowing where the Krauts were, and wondering when you'd get shot at and where you'd find cover if an 88 came in.

"Then an old man in rags and wooden shoes came out of a shelled house with a jug in his hand and gave us a drink of cider. His house was knocked down around his ears, he had nothing left in the world, but he thought enough of us to give us his last jug of cider and to thank us for killing those goddamn Krauts."

"Oh hell, one man."

"That's a country to me: one man. How do you judge a place? By the way people treat you, man to man, right? I hate to hear anybody say the Krauts are good because they have running water and kiss the conqueror's ass. Wait'll they get strong again and come back for thirds. Then you'll see who's on our side and who isn't."

The other man humphed and walked away, and I put my rifle together and began to polish my boots. When this was done, I washed and shaved and put on clean fatigues. With fifteen minutes left for retreat, I sat on my bunk and stared at the stables and the men, the dirty brick floor and the dusty white compound outside.

I'm right back where I started, I thought, suddenly overwhelmed by a feeling of futility and failure, just a lonely private sitting in a drab barracks in a hot, dead country like Georgia. I have accomplished nothing: won no medals, achieved no rank, seen almost no action. All I ever wanted to be in the Army was out.

Three years have gone by, and everything is the same, nothing has changed. Retreat at 5:15, supper at 5:30, no passes tonight; spread shelter halves between the bunks instead. Tomorrow there'll be an hour of calisthenics, two hours of close-order drill, an hour with the manual of arms. The afternoon will be devoted to squad tactics. Then retreat again at 5:15 and supper at 5:30. It'll take more than a war to change the Army. Nobody ever used a rifle sling in combat, and the Army knows it, but they will go on teaching the use of the rifle sling for the next thousand years, because that's the way it's been in the past, and the past is the safest guide to the future.

I thought of the Army, of all the wasted lives spent in stale barracks doing over and over again things proved utterly useless in war after war. Maybe they did them because there was nothing else to do. It was all make-work in the Army, putting in your time, trying to find something to do for thirty years. No matter what the outfit, the Army was always the same. It was not for me.

I WAS STILL WAITING for my points a week later when Christenson thundered into the stable in the lull between breakfast and the first formation, rushed to my bunk, grabbed my hand, and pumped it up and down.

"You're in!" he exclaimed. "They finally came through."

"No kidding? Wahoo!"

I sprang from my bunk, hooked my elbow in his, and whirled him around the aisle with shrieks of delight.

"Pack your bags and stand by."

"No more pencils, no more books, no more looeys' dirty looks."

He slapped my back and left the stable.

"Peace." I sighed, reclining on my mattress. "Isn't it wonderful?" I didn't know what I was going to do in civilian life, but I didn't care, because I was going back to freedom, to the place where all men were equal and there was no sirring or saluting. "Listen to those whistles. Listen to that goddamn C.Q."

"Everybody outside! O.D.s and helmet liners. Practice parade."

"Up your ass!" I yelled. I rolled onto my side to watch the others fall out. "Have a good parade, men."

"You go to hell." Winn grinned.

I looked forward to a last, delicious morning in the sack, a lazy, sleepy morning that I would sniff and sip and savor to the final minute, when I would rise and leave the Army forever. It would be like a day on Quarters, only instead of returning to duty tomorrow, I would remain on Quarters, doing nothing, traveling to the 501 and loafing with them. Tomorrow and tomorrow and tomorrow, on Quarters till I reached the States. Moaning with warm contentment, I closed my eyes and tried not to hear the loathsome sound of drilling.

"Webster!" someone yelled.

I cringed. It was my master's voice.

Peacock hurried to my bunk with a set face.

"Yessir?" I said, bewildered.

"Why aren't you out with the rest of the men?"

"My points came through, sir. I'm leaving today. They told me to stand by."

"They did, did they? Well, get out there with the rest of the men! As long as you're in my platoon, you're going to soldier. Everybody in the Company has to fall out for this practice parade, including you. On the double!"

"Yessir."

What a finale! I thought, as I started for the door. If chickenshit was money, the 506th would be millionaires.

I fell in with the platoon and marched off in the dust under a glaring August sun in a prickly wool uniform and a helmet liner that itched unbearably and spent a last, bitter morning marching back and forth before Colonel Sink and Colonel Strayer on a flat, brown field near the river. For three hours, we wheeled and turned, marked time in place, stood at parade rest, presented arms, passed in review by companies and battalions. By the time it was over, I was in a mood to bayonet babies and roast both colonels over small fires. What I planned for Peacock was unprintable.

Christenson came to me after lunch and told me to report to the supply room with my bags and bedroll for a final equipment check. The supply sergeant tried to take away a pair of new jump boots but settled for some old combat boots; otherwise everything was all right. When we were through arguing, he went into the bins and returned with an armful of new fatigues and jumpsuits and handed them to me.

"Take 'em," he said. "We have a lot of extras. Good work clothes for civilian life."

I gaped at him. "A uniform in *civilian* life? Jesus Christ!" Lifting the bundle of clothes high overhead, I smashed them down on the counter. "Shove these rags up the Army's ass. I'll never wear another uniform as long as I live."

I hoisted my duffel bag on my shoulder and went out the door, with the supply sergeant shaking his head behind me.

Since there were still a few minutes before departure time, I went into company headquarters to say goodbye to Captain Speirs, whom I had always liked.

"I want to thank you, Captain," I said.

He frowned. "For what?"

"For giving me a break. You're the only company commander who ever gave me a break, sir, the only one who ever made me a noncom."

"Well, hell, Webster, I tried to make a soldier out of you."

"It couldn't be done, sir." I grinned.

We shook hands and said goodbye and wished each other luck. I saluted him for the last time and went outside, where the other high-point men were waiting.

In the company area, whistles started to blow, the C.Q. ran from door to door like some medieval alarmist alerting a city, the men fell out noisily for squad tactics, and I felt a temporary rush of nostalgia for the outfit and the life that it led. It was my outfit, the 506th, the only outfit I had ever been in. I had cursed it steadily for three years, had avoided duty whenever possible, had prayed for light wounds every day in combat, and yet now that I was finally leaving, I was almost sorry to say goodbye. Nothing I had ever done before could compare with the feeling of belonging that I had had with the 506th. A job was a job, usually at somebody else's price, and school and college were prolonged adolescence. Only an adolescent could get excited about anything as juvenile and exclusive as a fraternity. The issues were petty and the people childish snobs.

The paratroops were life itself, life and death and the thrill of conquering yourself by jumping from an airplane. I would miss the din and clamor, the foulmouthed good humor, the wonderful sound of marching men, the wild excitement as I went out the door and fell a hundred feet before my chute opened.

But these were minor things, now that the war was over and all purpose had been lost. The 506th was just another training camp now, and I hated training almost as much as guard duty.

The men stirred as a noncom checked them off. I snapped out of my musings and prepared to go. All thoughts were on the future: What will the 501 be like? I wonder if I'll see Marsh and McCreary up there. When will we arrive in the States?

Captain Speirs said a fast goodbye and shook each man's hand, then the Camera Killer, who was also going home and who had charge of us, led us at a jovial route step to an open space near the main gate, where Colonel Sink was waiting in a jeep surrounded by several dozen men from other companies who were also leaving.

On the far side of the gate, in a barbed-wire enclosure set against the high wall, inmates of the regimental guardhouse stood listlessly in the shimmering heat and watched as the colonel mounted the hood of his jeep and began to make his farewell speech.

He sounded mechanical and uninspired, as if he had made this speech before and was losing interest, as if he knew that none of us cared for the outfit anymore but were thinking only of getting away from it, and soon my mind began to wander from his words to the guardhouse. I studied the faces of the men clutching the wire. One of them waved and called my name. I started in surprise, not hearing the colonel, and waved back.

The deserter, I thought. God, he has almost nineteen years to go.

He was an older man, with a wife and two children and no interest in war or the Army whatsoever, and why he had joined the paratroops was a mystery that even he couldn't explain. A replacement fresh from the

States, he had arrived several weeks before the Holland jump. When we went up the hill to Membury Airdrome, he had been so strongly affected by the tension that he had swallowed a large dose of sodium amytal pills. Thoroughly drugged, he had stumbled about the muddy tents in a blind haze, muttering, "I can't stand it, I can't stand it." But when the time came, he jumped with the rest of us. He went through seventy-two days in Holland and then he was through. "War," he had said, "is a game for vicious children. How could a mature man be a soldier?" When the outfit returned to base camp in Mourmelon, he walked out one day and never came back. The M.P.s picked him up in civilian clothes in Paris at the height of the Bulge and shipped him back to the Regiment, where he was given the usual sentence for desertion: twenty years at hard labor.

Of course, it won't be twenty years, I thought, studying him closely to see if he had changed, it never is. They give them three or four years in a detention training center and then turn them loose. They're alive when it's all over, while the good men, the fine, brave men like Mather and Hoobler, who stuck with the outfit till they were killed, are dead forever. The modern deserter is lucky, and he knows it. In the old days, he would have been shot.

But I wouldn't trade places for a minute. He ruined his whole life because he wouldn't (or couldn't; not everybody could) take what we had taken before and had to go on taking until it was all over. I'm glad I made it, and I'm glad I'm getting out with a clean record and a clear conscience. I couldn't sleep with myself if I were a deserter.

"Good luck and God bless you, God bless you all," the colonel concluded.

A noncom called us to attention, and we saluted, then gave three cheers for the colonel. He got down and drove off, waving goodbye as he went.

I climbed into the back of one of the G.I. trucks that were waiting for us and took a seat where I could look into the guardhouse. I'd kill myself if I had to put in any more time in the Army, I thought. The Army is prison with passes. Who wants to spend their life in prison?

The truck moved out of the compound, and my friend, whom I had liked and often felt sorry for, as one is sorry for a man in a totally unsuitable job from which he cannot escape, waved to me.

"Take it easy, buddy!" he shouted. "Give my love to the States."

"So long! Good luck!"

The truck bounced out the gate, and I raised my eyes and smiled at the concertina barbed wire. It could hold me no longer.

They had me for three years, I thought, three years with barbed wire and armed guards and sealed transports and marshaling areas where I couldn't even cross a hedge to the next company, and they'll never have me again.

We went downhill to the river. The walls grew smaller, and I could no longer see the barbed wire. Then we rounded a corner and left the Regiment forever.

Letters Home

Co. F, 506 Para.-Inf.
A.P.O. #472
Postmaster, New York, N.Y.
Enroute to England

Dear Cam,

If you ever sail on a troopship—and I pray God you won't—I suggest that you buy yourself several cakes of salt water soap, a dozen sets of underwear, a solid aluminum mess kit, and some interesting books. You will then be in a position to enjoy the trip and live in comparative comfort.

You see, since there are so many of us on this ex-second-rate liner there is not enough fresh water to go around. Fresh water, indeed, can be used for drinking from 6:45 to 7:15, 11:45 to 12, 12:45 to 1, 4:45 to 5, 5:45 to 6, and 6:45 to 7. If you think this is bad, consider the beards of my fellow travelers, who can get fresh water only from 7:15 to 8 in the morning and from 6:45 to 7:30 at night. Salt water, however, is always running in the showers, and so you will find that you will need several cakes of salt water soap; if you want to remain tolerably clean. That soap may not be too good, but at least it lathers a little. I have rubbed ordinary soap on my hands for five minutes at a time and produced nothing but wet slime. No lather. Salt water will leave you sticky, but you'll be clean, and that's what counts.

You will need the dozen sets of underwear because you will be sleeping with your clothes on and you will want to change often; my undershirt, worn only three days now, is black already. On account of the submarine menace all ranks must wear their life jackets (ours, the British type, are two little pillows fastened together with strings) and their cartridge belts with canteens attached and must sleep with their clothes on. People who have been raised on pajamas will find this uncomfortable. It's also rough and dirty on underwear. Incidentally, it's a smart idea, though discouraged by your officers, to buy an extra pair of fatigues so that you can change on board. Your outer garments will get dirty from sleeping in corridors and on the crummy deck.

You will find yourself a wiser and happier soldier too if you beg, borrow, buy or steal a solid aluminum mess kit, for you will be washing the utensils in salt water. Salt water corrodes and rusts; my spoon was so rusty yesterday I cut my lips when I ate with it. You will eat twice a day—in the morning and at night—in a crowded, stuffy, noisy mess hall on a lower deck where the soldiers fetch the food in tin buckets and clean the tables with black dishrags, the same tables you so blithely lay your bread on to butter it. The food, if it's like ours, will be good, the diet balanced, the grabbing at the table unbelievably ferocious (sometimes this ship resembles a floating madhouse). If you have an aluminum mess kit, the coffee won't corrode your cup and the salt water won't rust and spot the pans and knife, fork, and spoon.

This salt water is set out in three dishpans. About 130 men use these pans; if you're on the end of the line you feel you might as well wash your mess kit in a garbage pail—the water's so full of floating debris, bread, fish, vegetables, debris, corn flakes, etc.

Also, take along some Brillo to clean your kit and hold on to the latter as hard as you can, for you'll be living so intimately with your brothers in arms that you'll find anything you leave loose will be stolen; two blankets and a shelterhalf were taken from me; a sleeping man was robbed of his life jacket and first aid pack; a good mess kit is coveted by everybody on board so hold on to yours.

As for the interesting books, they will be a godsend to a man like you with so much time on your hands. Take only daily interruptions such as breakfast and supper, lifeboat drill (at noon), and a rifle inspection (at one). The rest of the time you lean on the rail and watch the convoy, or you walk around the deck or you sleep, or you shoot craps (Haney of the second platoon started with five dollars, worked up to twenty-two hundred, lost that trying to get twenty-eight more dollars, and came out with two hundred odd), or you read. Eventually you'll be so bored you'll wish you had some good book to read. If you are smart you'll bring several along in your barracks bag.

In some ways this trip has been rough, but I have enjoyed it, for it's a new, illuminating experience, an insight into the convoy system and into the army at sea. We are so crowded we sleep two men to a bunk; twenty-four hours inside, twenty-four outside on the deck. On your off night you hunt out a warm corridor or a spot down below or you sleep in the aisle next to your bunk. The decks are so overrun; calisthenics take only ten minutes a day. At night you have to stake out a sleeping place early if you want to lie in a sheltered spot away from the wind, rain and fog. Still, for most of the boys it's a thrilling new experience, this trip at sea, and they all take the misery with a jovial spirit. People talk about morale, but all we in the army ask is good food, a warm bed, and fair treatment.

Our weather, thank God, has been smooth all the way. Once the sea was so rough I whooped and whooped and ate no food, but that lasted only a day. This ocean isn't living up to its reputation.

I have been thinking of the training and the trials to come. What I fear most is that first jump into combat, when you float down into the darkness and hope a German doesn't get you with a bayonet while you're taking off your chute. I feel that once I get my rifle into my hands I shall take the fight to the enemy to the best of my ability. I hope that my small part may help to keep you from fighting in another war. My operation permitting, I'll do my best, so don't worry.

Love to your Mother and Father and Ann and Jim,

> from,
> Your loving uncle,
> Ken

> Co. F, 506 Para.*Inf.
> A.P.O. #472 New York, N.Y.
> November 1, 1943
> England

Dear Mother and Father,

Three cheers for our team. Thrown together from privates, sergeants, a couple of lieutenants and the colonel of the third battalion, with a private as captain, they smashed the Air Corps "E. J. O. Champs" 40 to nothing. The 506th team had to steal minutes from the field for practice, while our friends in the Air Corps lived on gravy and glory. The game started Sunday at 2:30. We traveled there by truck and train and walked a mile and a half through the city where we had a glass of stout, an apple, and a look at a German iron cross, which a British sergeant picked up in the last war.

When we reached the stadium, we found an atmosphere resembling that of a football crowd at home. Of course, most of the spectators were dressed in khaki, not coonskin, and the planes flying overhead were not skywriting "I.J. Fox, 5th Avenue" or "Come to the Hotel Commander After the Game," but were Mustang Spitfires and Army reconnaissance Taylor cubs on their way to work, but the spirit was the same as in the Ivy League—terrific cheering, catcalls, wisecracks, stamping feet. One solid part of the stands, filled with paratroopers, was especially raucous. I think our team knew they had the regiment behind them.

The Air Corps was so confident of victory that one of their coaches started the game by asking for bets, even giving odds. After a few minutes of play, however, he changed his tune, when a 506th man got the ball and ran 80 yards for a touchdown. Who says that all our running hasn't done us good? A little later it happened again, but the umpire ruled it out because our team was off sides. Nothing daunted, our boys kept plugging, making one lovely touchdown after another. Cries of "Nothing can stop the Army Air Corps. Yeh Yeh!" swelled up from the stands. Although the glamor boys fought hard, they were no match for the 506th, and the game ended in a drizzle, the score 40 to 0. I heard somebody say, "There are only two things that can stop the Air Corps, the weather and the 506th!"

Sunday was indeed a busy day. In addition to the football game there was an exhibition by the British judo experts and a formation for church. Church, judo, and football, who could go wrong?

Speaking of church, the chaplain has become so desperate that we have orders to go to church every Sunday if we are not otherwise occupied. Out of a regiment of about 1500 men, all he can get in two Sunday services is fifty-odd men. I understand the divisional chaplain has told ours that unless he increases church attendance he will be sent elsewhere. This is too bad, for Chaplain McGee is a good, sincere, pleasant man who makes all the jumps and goes on all the hikes (not one of those oily, boring chaplains who pass out tracts and bibles), but I'm afraid that paratroopers would rather raise hell and sleep it off than go to church on Sunday. In the army Sunday is a day when the barracks get dirty, when beds lie unmade all day, when fellows sleep through the morning, when one does the week's washing and catches up on the mail. Chaplain McGee is a still small voice shouting in the wilderness.

You asked about my health. Although the sun seems to have given place to fog and a persistent, penetrating drizzle (censored)—dirty beer/glasses, unwashed girls and a three-day problem on which they: 1. marched 25 miles; 2. slept in raincoats in the pouring rain, 3. returned to camp thoroughly chilled, wet, and hungry. Now they are learning that this climate is not good for very hard training. Some day they will learn to clean the latrines and go easy on the field problems.

Increasing rumors about a second front "before March" are beginning to make me think hard. I wish we could jump and get it over with, but I don't want to die for some politician who thinks the Allies should beat the Russians to Berlin.

Be that as it may, please father, make a tour of the 3rd Ave. and other pawnshops and see whether you can buy a .45-CALIBER, 6-SHOT REVOLVER with a shiny clean bore, an unbroken firing pin, and a trigger that works; and a holster. Perhaps Bannerman on lower Broadway—or is it 5th Ave.? can get you such a weapon. It is most essential for the first few minutes when we land and *are trying to get out of our chutes. I want a weapon that I can whip out and use immediately. It may mean the difference between life and death. I can load it with sub-Thompson ammunition, and will gladly pay for it out of what's left of the Gramatan fund. Please notify me by V-mail of the success of your mission. Incidentally, maybe the N.Y. police can help you: they dump thousands of pistols in the Atlantic every year. Seeing Frank Saturday.*

> *Your loving son,*
> *Kenyon*

P.S. Wrote a note to Mrs. Nininger. Really a terrible blow. He was a fine interesting man.

P.S. 2. Do you have any spare good Sun Maid raisins over there?

> *Headquarters Co., 2nd Bn.*
> *506 Parachute Infantry*
> *A.P.O. 472, Postmaster, N.Y.*
> *May 14, 1944*
> *England*

Dear Father:

I have received three letters from you in the past week, all interesting, all welcome. Bob Hamill was a very decent sort of fellow. When such a person dies suddenly, violently, and without any reason, you wonder what kind of a world we live in. People who are killed in a war at least die with the excuse that they are doing it for their country. When boys and girls like Bob Hamill and Joanny die, however, it's hard to find the reason and it's even harder to believe in a God.

Censorship, as you know, has clamped down over this island, so I'm afraid my letters will be considerably shorter and less mutilated than usual. I'm allowed to say, however, that I am well, that the English spring, though at times chilly, is as beautiful as the poets claim, that life is as dull and as easy as ever, and that I do not want to come home until I can get out of this ———— Army altogether.

I've just finished reading in Time about the federal seizure of Montgomery Ward, truly the most dictatorial, outrageous, inexcusable thing Roosevelt has ever done. Montgomery Ward didn't have any connection with the war, but our

President didn't hesitate the way he hesitated to squelch John L. Lewis' treacherous defiance of the war effort. When I read of such a thing, I feel I might as well be fighting in the German army.

The Red Cross has gotten a large number of new books now—cardboard-covered, excellent reprints about six inches by four, of bestsellers for which the public usually pays about $3.00. That they can make decent reading matter available to so many people when they print it so cheaply shows what can be done in wartime. If only good books were so cheaply made for civilians, more people might read. Who wants to pay $2.50 or $3.00 for a book they will only read once and give away? Publishers might argue that cheapening the price would ruin them, but the great sales and good profit of the Pocket Books in America and the Penguin series over here seems to belie them.

Two of the best books I found in the Red Cross were McSorley's Wonderful Saloon, a collection of short stories and articles written for The New Yorker by some clever Irishman, McNulty or O'Hara, I've forgotten which, about McSorley's bar (ever been there?) and various bars in general; and Delilah by Marcus Goodrich, a very long yarn about a destroyer in the Philippines in 1916. You would probably enjoy both books, especially the latter, which is so full of local color and tales of the islands.

I wish I could think of more to say, but, as I said before, censorship prevents describing training and, since I haven't had a long pass in two months, I cannot tell you about London or the world outside camp.

Your loving son,
Kenyon

Headquarters Co., 2nd Bn.
506 Parachute Infantry
A.P.O. 472, Postmaster, N.Y.
July 23, 1944
England

Dear John:

Since you ask for it, I'll try to give you as complete a description of my excursion abroad as possible. Any gaps will be the holes cut by the censor.

We must have reached the French coast at about 10:50 D-Day. We were stood up and hooked up twenty minutes before we jumped and during that time *you could hear the pilot gunning, then slacking the motor and you could see the tracers and flares outside. I was scared almost speechless. About 1:10 the green light came on. Somebody got stuck in the door; I thought I'd never get out of that damned plane, but when I did I regretted it, for all I could see was water, water, everywhere. I came down so fast, I didn't have time to take off my reserve and landed on my face in about three feet of water. Scared? I was shaking all over.*

Once I got out of my chute I assembled my M-1 (I am ammunition carrier in the M.G. platoon) and lay down in the water to await developments. All I could hear now was German machine-gun and sniper fire. I felt very much alone. Another battalion flew over a little later. I could see the tracers going into their chutes as they came down. Then I heard the slow swish-swish of somebody sneaking through the water. When he got near enough I signaled him and was delighted—to put it mildly—to find it was one of the men from my plane.

That night was like a nightmare. We wandered around in the water from 1:15 to about 8:00, circling, staggering, going over our heads in the deep, ten-foot-wide drainage ditches that bordered the flooded fields, picking up men from almost every regiment that jumped. Since none of us knew where we were, and since our cheap pocket compasses were waterlogged, we just tried to reach high ground. We kept as low as possible and avoided obvious thoroughfares—slightly flooded roads. Some of our boys were machine-gunned on these roads, dry plateaus, etc. Whenever they shot a flare, we stood stock-still; even our shivering stopped. Just as the sun came up we stopped to watch a large group of B-26s bomb the beach defenses, laying a string of bombs, almost a mile long. A lovely sight. I passed the bodies of two paratroopers cold and white and very still in the shallow water who had either been drowned or machine-gunned, but I didn't stop to see who they were. I just didn't have the stomach to roll them over.

Finally we hit dry land. As luck would have it, we immediately met D Company. We passed huge craters, thirty feet deep, made by our naval bombardment, went through an old deserted, undamaged village, where we helped ourselves to wine (the infantry coming in later complained that the paratroopers had taken all the wine in France wherever they went), which warmed me considerably. Incidentally, I never did dry out thoroughly. About an hour later, we met Headquarters Company. Then things got dull, for Headquarters just tags along behind the other companies.

By now the dead Germans were getting thicker. Killed by paratroopers during the night, they looked like wax figures you see in a museum. I felt no emotion

toward them. They were lying about in the little villages our boys had seized during the night, but the French paid no more attention to them than we did, although they were a little afraid of the black-faced, wild-eyed paratroopers who
had killed their rulers.

We kept on marching. The days are blurred, because they were so much alike.
About the third day, however, some German paratroopers almost caught us in a
trap. We were stopped on the edge of a small town. A sniper opened up on us
from the church steeple. When a bullet kicked up the dust next to my face, I decided to move across the road behind a stone wall. Meanwhile the lads in Headquarters Company, bored with a secondary role, were crowding around to shoot
at the sniper. They blasted him with M-1s, M-3s, tommy guns, bazookas, and
rifle grenades. Just as our intelligence sergeant jumped around the corner to
blast him with a tommy gun, all hell cut loose. He was killed instantly by a machine gun. We looked behind us. Smoke was coming down the road. We looked
to our left. Germans were pouring into the woods and sneaking around our
front. Headquarters Company started to sweat. We fired through all the open-
ings in the hedgerow. I got up behind a tree and blasted away at two hundred
yards at the woods. Probably never touched a German, but it was fun trying.
Things were sticky, however.

What saved us there were the tanks. A column of tanks had just passed
through us on the road several minutes before. The colonel sent a man down after them, got back three, and ordered them to fire at the enemy. They did. They
mowed the fields and hedgerows with their machine guns and threw 75s into
likely spots. Fifteen minutes or so of this and the Germans waved the white flag.
It might be well to add that we were on the high ground, they bunched up on the
low. We continued firing until ordered to cease. Thanks to the armored corps, we
had won.

It turned out that there was about a battalion of German paratroopers opposing us, that they had bicycled some forty miles into battle, that most of them
had not yet jumped in combat, that the tanks' shells had piled them up dead two
and three deep, that they had only about 125 men left alive out of about 500.
These figures are all hearsay, but most stories agree on them. Our boys had a
merry time picking up Lugers and German jump knives.

After this, the line companies met scattered opposition from snipers and machine guns, but Headquarters just tagged along. One night opposite (censored)
I had the scare of my life when an 88 millimeter cannon worked over us on outpost.

It was a gray, drizzling night. We went down a causeway littered with stinking dead Germans who had been caught by our artillery. It was the colonel's wish that we establish an outpost on the other side of a twenty-yard-wide, deep sluggish river. Since the bridge was blown out, we had to cross three at a time in a leaky rowboat paddling with old boards. No sooner were we all lying on the sandbar, surrounded by flooded fields and water, than BLAM, a shell lands on the opposite bank. I've never dug a hole so fast in all my life. One of the fellows scraped a slit trench with his mess-kit cup. Then they decided to bring us back and set up an outpost on the side nearer our own lines. I wasn't sorry. We scattered out and dug in. Once again the 88 fired. From then on that goddamned gun worked over the bank. I kept my head down all night. Every shell sounded as though it would blow me to pieces. When daylight came we returned to our Company. I was so jittery that my hands were shaking all that day. Luckily none of us was hurt.

Several nights later the Regiment moved out across that causeway, over a makeshift bridge built by our engineers one night, through some wild woods, and into the city of (censored). It was on the outskirts of that place that a mortar shell landed about six feet behind me, blew off my helmet (don't button your chin strap), and knocked me flat. When I got up, my right arm was bleeding a little, so I went into the nearby aid station, thinking it would only take five minutes to get fixed up. The next thing I knew, I was being evacuated to England. Although it meant a good rest, in a way I was sorry to leave, because I wanted to see a little close fighting.

If you ever go into combat, don't let the noise scare you and never get so terrified that you lie in your foxhole or refuse to move. Always keep going, always keep alert, and don't rely too much on the men around you. If you go out on an outpost or a patrol or flank guard, make sure that somebody else besides your squad leader knows where you are. Everybody forgets, occasionally with tragic results; the more people who know where you are, the less chance of your being forgotten. You won't have to be told to keep your gun and ammunition clean, to dig deep, to get all the rest you safely can, or to keep spread out. As a matter of fact, you can learn far more from the intelligence bulletins (orderly room) and the "Infantry Journal" than I could possibly tell you from my meagre week's experience.

> Your loving brother,
> Ken

P.S. Saw Frank about two weeks ago. He is now in France, I believe, but his job is a comparatively safe one. He's fine as ever.

Co. E, 506 Parachute Infantry
A.P.O. 472, Postmaster, N.Y.
July 29, 1944
England

Dear Mother:

English summer: rain, rain, gray skies, more rain. I go wild when the sun comes out. Will I ever get back to the land of milk (fresh), bars (always open), and hot sunshine? Sometimes, I wonder.

This is really just a note to say that I have once again changed companies; I am now a straight rifleman in E Company and am relieved of the burden of ammunition boxes and an irritable corporal. A rifleman is not too safe, but he is almost independent. He also gets close to the enemy, a dubious pleasure which I did not enjoy in Headquarters Company. My new Company, however, did well in France.

A box of yours, containing Sherry candy and some dates, mailed May 12th, has finally arrived. Many thanks. Fruit is always welcome. Thinking of you.

Your loving son,
Kenyon

Co. E, 506 Parachute Infantry
A.P.O. 472, Postmaster, N.Y.
July 30, 1944
England

Dear Mother and Father:

Sitting in the Red Cross, listening to a radio program entitled "Mail Call," I am reminded of the good job the Army is doing in the radio line. From seven o'clock in the morning until eleven at night, the A.F.N. (American Forces Network) provides an almost uninterrupted flow of swing music, with B.B.C. news every hour and an occasional interlude for a rebroadcast of the Bob Hope show, etc. The air is seldom dull. I might even venture to say that, with the exception of "Music While You Work," the B.B.C. cannot equal the U.S. Army. Although there are rare blurbs which advise us to keep clean, salute more often, or refrain from fighting ("Remember, men, if you're looking for a fight, wait till you meet the Germans"), the air is remarkably and most welcomely free from commercials.

In addition to the radio, we have the movies—twice a week—and the U.S.O. shows—maybe every two weeks. The former range all the way from cowboy thrillers to rare hits. I don't know why we get so few latest releases, but then I never go to the movies anyway so it doesn't worry me at all. As for the U.S.O. shows, they tell me they are almost all very good. The only one I saw was given at the regimental party we had recently. Al Banks, some former Boston radio actor, the master of ceremonies, had a fine line of patter that kept us roaring: appropriate jokes about Piccadilly, the British pubs, conditions in the States, girls, etc. He introduced two cute songstresses, a Boston comedian dressed in kilts who played very well on a miniature saxophone and who reminded me of an Old Howard comedian, and a drummer and pianist who accompanied the rest. The show lasted about an hour. Just to see American civilians was a treat enough; to be entertained by them was very gratifying. The States seemed closer for that one hour. Some of these U.S.O. shows are staffed with British talent, but they are almost all good. We have never seen any big-name comedians, however.

The Red Cross provides recreation of a sort in the big cities away from camp. Meals cost about thirty cents each and are uniformly terrible, but you can eat at a snack bar in between and buy Coca-Colas. Beds are two shillings a night— sheets changed every day. Through the Red Cross you can get tickets to shows, visit local citizens, go on tours, or find friends. The only things free are individual cigarettes. Even when you are in the hospital, red tape so constricts the A.R.C. that you have a hell of a time getting anything free. To promote a tiny ten-shilling loan you must fill out in triplicate a form as large as this paper. It's nice to have a place to go, but the Red Cross could be better and more economically run than it is at present. No complaints about our camp one, though. The Air Force seems to have priority on the Red Cross as it does on many other things.

I sometimes wonder what good will come of this war. Will those poor fellows sprawled in the Normandy lanes and hanging so calmly in the trees have died for nothing? The impression I get over here is that the news at home concentrates on the big pushes, the drives, the victories and forgets the boys who died to make those things possible. When the final drive is over, will the people think, "Well, that wasn't as bad as we thought it would be. We can let up on the Germans a little. They didn't kill too many of our boys." Will the politicians heave a sigh of relief and take up their old senseless partisanship? Will the war become just another fad, as quickly dropped as it was embraced? For the sake of the fellows who will never come back, I hope not.

Things are so damned dull, there is really nothing to say. I'm reading Tom Jones—*not as good as I had heard, but amusing in spots. Also working on* Wind, Sand and Stars. Yankee from Olympus, *although apparently good, is annoying in the sections where the authoress gives us Holmes' thoughts, which, as* The New Yorker *said, is taking a lot of liberties with a supposedly nonfiction book. I'd like to get hold of* We Jumped to Fight. *Can you arrange it?*

England, though a pretty country, has a climate which ruins it for me. The roses are beautiful, every house has a lovely garden; the hills, so green and gentle, are soothing to the eye, but the sun just won't come out. It's very aggravating to think that this is the second summer ruined for me: last year in the hospital, this year in the rain. I wouldn't live in the British Isles for anything in the world.

I, for one, never realized what a fine place America was until I came over here. America is richer, cleaner, healthier, more progressive, and more stimulating. People here are overcivilized, too set in their ways. They lack the fluidity, the spontaneity of Americans who, though acting like semi-savages at times, are much more alive than the English. Here you can leave a package in a small railroad station and nobody will take it—unless one of your fellow G.I.s comes along. Turn your back in the good old U.S.A. and your package is gone. It's more fun that way; keeps you on your toes. We do more for our soldiers than the English do, mainly because our people are more wide-awake, less contented. You can say all you want for the English, but I'll take the Americans any day. America has a future; England has a past.

The Scotch, though, are more like Americans than the quiet reserved English. They're cleaner, talk more, are more friendly, and will buy you drinks. You can't help liking a Scotchman.

Still, England hasn't been a bad place; I prefer it to one of those vast Southern training camps. Living in a village is more civilized than living in five square miles of tar-paper buildings inhabited by nothing but men, and located eight or ten miles from the nearest shabby town.

My new Company promises to be good. The officers came out of combat with medals, shrapnel, and the confidence of their men, and that's what counts in an outfit like this whose sole purpose is to fight. Some surprising things happened in other companies.

> *Your loving son,*
> *Kenyon*

Co. E, 506 Parachute Infantry
A.P.O. 472, Postmaster, N.Y.
August 6, 1944
England

Dear Mother and Father:

A succession of beautifully clear warm days that have left me with a tan and a feeling that I am not in England. The thunderbirds—yesterday Mosquitoes and Lancasters, today Thunderbolts, and always the boring C-47s—have been out in such strength that there is never a moment when the air is quiet. Fine weather.

I have been enjoying myself in the sun ever since Friday morning, when the medics gave me a "no duty" slip enabling me to sunbathe all day without interference. Saturday I spent an hour on detail, then returned to the sunlight. Today ditto. It's almost like summer at home.

Your letters, arriving almost daily, leave me with a mixture of emotions. I am glad to hear that you had a pleasant holiday, but I am amazed that you should consider the Purple Heart as an award of merit or anything but a mere indication that the recipient was wounded in action. Lest you think too highly of it, please remember that a dog has received it and that Wacs in London who were injured by a flying bomb also are wearing little purple ribbons. At one time you had to do something outstanding to get the Purple Heart, but nowadays it is given out in vast numbers for everything ranging from a finger cut by a mortar fragment to terrible wounds that result in death. It's a pretty ribbon, but I'm ashamed to wear it for my infinitesimal cut.

This subject reminds me of the attitude a lot of civilians seem to have: namely, that our advances are wonderful and very cheap. People forget that even though ten men only are killed to gain five miles, those ten men are something priceless, something which can never be bought, created, or equaled. And those wounded men who will never walk or never see again, will they be remembered? Will the public, so used to optimistic headlines, be able to face these lads and help them? I wonder.

Now you say you are still not reconciled to my joining the paratroopers. Would you prefer for somebody else's son to die in the mud? You want us to win the war, but you apparently don't want to have your sons involved in the actual bloodshed. That's a strangely contradictory attitude.

Somebody has to get in and kill the enemy. Somebody has to be in the infantry and the paratroops. If the country all had your attitude, nobody would fight, everybody would be in the Quartermaster and the ground crew. And what kind of a country would that be?

No, thanks, I'll stay in this outfit, even if it's the death of me. I am not interested in the Navy. I can't get into the Air Corps or the Marines, a job in the service forces would drive me crazy, so I'm staying right here. You can't find a better bunch of men; the Air Corps is looking for glamour, the Navy (speaking of officers) for social success, but the paratroopers just don't give a damn. The Germans realized this when they had to fight the "big pockets" and credited the paratroops with the best fighting ability of the Americans they had to face. I'll stay in the paratroops, so you may as well dry your tears.

The political situation, as I gather from Time, seems to resolve into a fight between Roosevelt and Dewey. Although Roosevelt is aging, is flippant, is at times indecisive, I trust him more than Dewey, who is too noncommittal to make the great leader necessary for these times. And, in spite of what you say, Roosevelt has done more for the average man than the Republicans thought of doing. And don't forget, it's the average man who is fighting in France, not the executives. You complained about the cost of the W.P.A., but you say nothing about the colossal waste involved in the war. I trust Roosevelt more than those Republicans who criticize F.D.R. without advancing any constructive program.

Yes, I finally got a pistol, a .45 automatic, at the cost of ten pounds. A number of boys were bayoneted and had their throats cut because they had no pistol handy to defend themselves with. I'd like to tell that in person to the gentleman who signed that letter to you, saying that pistols were not necessary. Ten pounds is a cheap price to pay for life.

I wish there was something pleasant to write about. Of course, the countryside is extremely beautiful. These English roses—every house has a garden full of them—make traveling a pleasure. All the way down through Kent the gardens were in bloom and north of London the road was lined with beauty. Even our little three-day problem out in the wheat-covered ridges was enjoyable. England is all right when the sun shines.

As you can see by my address, and as I have told you before, I am now a resident member of E Company, a rifleman and a squad scout. It's a good company.

The reason I left Headquarters was that I was tired of tagging along and doing nothing. I was second ammunition carrier and fired the machine gun only once in six months. No future in that.

Last night some fellow thought he was a humpy, whatever that is. About mid-night I woke up hearing shrieks of laughter followed by "I'm a humpy, I'm a goddamned humpy! Ha ha ha." This lasted almost half an hour, much to every-body's amusement. Almost as funny as the time Polecat Lachute, an amusing lit-tle fellow from New Orleans in Headquarters Company, got plastered and thought he was a beaver. "I'm a beaver, I'm a beaver." Then he started chewing on the bedposts. This Army would be the greatest show on earth if it wasn't for the tragic undertones.

I sent Sister a full description of my week abroad and told her to pass it on to you, hoping thereby to quiet forever any questions about Normandy. Please read it, because I'm bored to death writing about what was dull, nasty, dirty, ter-rifying, and exciting all at the same time.

Your loving son,
Kenyon

Co. E, 506 Parachute Infantry
A.P.O. 472, Postmaster, N.Y.
August 28, 1944
England

Dear Mother and Father:

Today was the second time I have attended a religious ceremony since I came into this regiment. The first was a year ago Easter in Charlotte. This Sunday was more worthwhile, however, because it included a memorial service for the lads who were killed in France.

When it was announced that we should give up our Sunday morning in order to honor the dead, there was terrific moaning and groaning; one individual averred that he would honor the dead on Saturday morning or all day Monday, but he'd be damned if he'd honor the dead on his own time. However, he piled into the buses with the rest of us at 9:30 and went down to regimental head-quarters, where we formed into companies and marched off to an open field nearby.

A parachute artillery band played the dead march in such a slow cadence that we got all out of step. Once we were formed and the services began (see the P.S. for the regimental prayer), things improved a bit. The sky was clear and blue, the sun hot—several men fainted—and the scene was quite inspiring.

Chaplain McGee gave an excellent address in which he tried to prove that the dead were really heroic, that America was worth dying for, that those who gave their lives had not died in vain, etc. He was followed by General Taylor, the division commander, but just then a flight of C-47s circled overhead and drowned him out, so we had to be content with the roster of dead and missing. I was surprised at the number of boys who had been killed. Every time a familiar name was read off, I thought of that poor fellow and of his family sitting quietly in a home that will never be full again. I certainly hope that they have not died in vain. We marched off the field to the tune of "Onward, Christian Soldiers."

Time alone can tell what has been accomplished by the death of so many genial brave souls. There's a lot of talk about what to do with Germany, but no action, even when the end is so near. The Germans should certainly be roughed up a little, because this is one war you can almost completely blame on that country.

The more I think about it, the less I am inclined to believe all the anti-German propaganda we've been fed so long. People forget, when they speak of atrocities, that war is a brutal, demoralizing business, that even our own American fighters are capable of great cruelty, that the Germans, as an army, cannot afford to have their supply lines and organization interfered with by skulking civilians. After all, international law says that anybody caught fighting without a recognized uniform is automatically a spy and therefore subject to the death penalty. As for the French hating the Germans who lived among them, I don't imagine their antipathy was any greater than that you occasionally notice among the Englishmen who have had American troops billeted on them. Nobody likes to share his home with a soldier. Germany should be punished, but watch out for our own propaganda, which would distort the German soldier into a bloodthirsty monster.

We were all sorry we didn't jump in southern France. From what I heard that was an excellent show—little flak, little ground opposition, not too many Dutchmen nearby. As it was, the High Command had a considerably rougher job planned for us then, but called it off. Next time, we all know, will be rugged.

There was a time once when only the paratroopers wore boots. In those dear dead days we had a certain pride, a certain distinctiveness, a certain feeling that as volunteers for a slightly dangerous job, we were a little better than the average soldier. But now things are different. Now everybody wears boots and we wear the infantry uniform to battle. Our glider troops were issued jump boots (we can't even get them) and are allowed to wear their pants bloused over them. In the last marshaling area, they were equipped with jump boots, while we had to wear those ugly combat boots. But the gliders aren't the only ones: the Rangers, the engineer beach battalions, and many elements of the S.O.S. are wearing boots now. It's a hell of a note.

To top it off, we are being punished for going to France, or so it seems, judging by the training schedule. On the pretext of bringing the replacements up to par, we go on night problems without getting any time off the next morning, and we work seven days a week, a disaster unparalleled in regimental history. Then they have the gall to wonder why men goldbrick and avoid formations. This outfit has the best men in the Army, but apparently the men who run the show don't know that they are killing a lot of enthusiasm by lowering the paratroops to the level of the rest of the Army, then running them ragged.

Gripe, gripe, gripe. There's really not much else to do or write. Today a couple of lads had a fight around the mess hall. Lots of fun and no blood. It all ended when the little corporal slugged his opponent in the belly.

Oh yes, I hitchhiked into London and back yesterday and saw Aunt Dora and Gilbert. Although a buzz bomb had only recently taken a penthouse off an apartment building down the street, they were both looking fine. With them was a callow lieutenant, in the Tank Destroyers, I believe, who turned out to be Leila Burton's husband. Since they were all going out to dinner, I only stayed five minutes.

Your loving son,
Kenyon

P.S. The following struck me as a splendid example of the Gott mit Uns school of religious thought:

The 506th Parachute Infantry Prayer

Almighty God, we kneel to thee and ask to be the instrument of Thy fury in smiting the evil forces that have visited death, misery, and debasement on the people of the earth. We humbly face Thee with true penitence for all our sins for which we do most earnestly seek Thy forgiveness. Help us to dedicate ourselves completely to Thee. Be with us, God, when we leap from our planes into the dread abyss and descend in parachutes into the midst of enemy fire. Give us iron will and stark courage as we spring from the harnesses of our parachutes to seize arms for battle. The legions of evil are many, Father; grace our arms to meet and defeat them

*in Thy name and in the name of freedom and dignity of man. Keep us firm
in our faith and resolution, and guide us that we may not dishonor our
high mission or fail in our sacred duties. Let our enemies who have lived
by the sword turn from their violence lest they perish by the sword. Help
us to serve Thee gallantly and to be humble in victory.*

—*Written by Lt. James G. Morton*

Co. E, 506 Parachute Infantry
A.P.O. 472, Postmaster, N.Y.
September 7, 1944
Holland

Dear Mother and Father:

Red-hot jazz coming over the public address system, while a motorcycle
stolen in France barks and roars outside. Our four-man horse stall is warm and
cozy and comfortably sloppy. It's good to be in out of the cold.

I've been putting off this letter until I had something interesting or amusing
to write about, but since that day will never come as long as we remain in this
country, I guess I'll just have to ramble on with the usual dull notes. I have been
nowhere and done nothing lately; our life is so damned monotonous, I sometimes feel like shooting myself—anything for a change.

By now you, too, will have read the plans for discharge and may even have
noticed the emphasis placed upon the coming shortage of transportation from
the E.T.O. to the States and the implication therein. As you can see, I shall not
be home for several years; the future contains no hope but a trip via Suez to the
Asiatic Theater, where I wouldn't mind being in on an attack on the Chinese
coast or an invasion of the Philippines. An outfit like ours will never get home
until all wars are thoroughly finished. They certainly would never use valuable
ships to give us a furlough in the Promised Land. What the hell, as long as we
leave England and see some sunshine I won't be too sorry.

The hardest thing to bear is the thought of enduring this repetitious monotony two or three more years. I'd almost rather be dead.

Unfortunately, we couldn't get in on the Paris deal, which must have been fun
for the G.I.s involved, mostly the tankers and the 4th Division. The latter, in
battle since D-Day, has really worked its way to Paris.

Although you do not seem to like it, Johnny got a break when he joined the paratroops. The infantry, as I have said before, goes into battle and stays forever; look at the 4th Division. You shouldn't take an ostrich attitude by wishing John in some safer branch of the Army, because nowadays a soldier in the infantry has no choice but the paratroops. It's not like it was several years ago, when a man could apply for O.C.S. or the Air Corps and get out of the infantry. If I should be killed, don't hold it against the paratroops and beg Johnny to get out, because his chances are still better as a jumper than as a doughboy in the line.

William L. Shirer's article amused me no end. He sits on his ivory throne and criticizes some obscure lieutenant—no doubt a victim of circumstances—who, like any sensible man, cannot see how our government could so propagandize German prisoners in a year's time that they will be converted to easygoing tolerant citizens of the world. The only way to treat those lads is to be fair, impartial, and very strict; treat them the way some of our boys treated their prisoners who got wise or refused to obey orders—shoot them. I hope we fight all the way through Germany, just to teach those people the true horror of war. Impress them with the Allied might and maybe they won't start another war. Shirer's a little off the track.

Although it's easy to criticize the confusion in the Army, you should remember that it's a rather large organization and does an amazingly good job for all its incoherency and red tape. The German army is probably just as seemingly balled-up as ours. In combat it's the same way—all confusion; nobody knows anything; plans go wrong; orders come too late. Still, battles are won and that's what counts.

I dread the thought of another winter in this country, of chills and rains, of dried eggs and watery beer, of $16 Scotch and dirty women. What I miss most of anything—more even than fresh fruit and fresh milk—is sunshine and blue skies. If I ever get out of this Army, I'm going to spend the rest of my life in Florida or California. And I'm never coming back to England.

> *Your loving son,*
> *Kenyon*

Det. of Patients, 4153 U.S.A. Hosp.
A.P.O. 350, Postmaster, N.Y.
October 8, 1944—England

Dear Mother and Father:

After a beautiful jump and approximately eighteen lively days in Holland, I am back in the land of mild-and-bitter, largely through the courtesy of a Wehrmacht bullet which whipped through the calf of my right leg. I was lucky to get out with my life.

Holland, all Germans there notwithstanding, is an excellent country. Although the Dutch Underground hasn't gotten a tenth the publicity accorded the French-F.F.S., which, incidentally, I never once saw in Normandy, we got more help than we ever got from the French. A resistance leader met us on the jump-field and is still with us; almost every line company has at least two Dutch volunteers who joined us to kill Germans and who have shared every firefight.

As for the average people, they gave us everything. When we filed through a village, the local citizens handed us hot coffee, cool beer, fresh milk, and all the apples, pears, and peaches we could eat. Old farmers unbidden helped us dig our slit trenches. A wonderful people.

The country itself impressed me as very rich, very progressive, very modern, and very clean. The good black soil seemed able to grow anything, there was plenty of fresh milk (we milked the local cows whenever possible); the cities were all new and beautifully designed for low-cost, healthful living; and everything, including the people, was so spick-and-span and better than England, it took my breath away. Holland is years ahead of Great Britain.

Our combat experience in that delightful country started out very easy, but got worse and worse as it went along, until finally on the day I was hit, the Germans counterattacked with vicious artillery support and raised six kinds of hell with us. I was wounded just in time to escape the worst of it.

Now I am back in the same hospital I enjoyed after France. The doctor tells me I'll be all right and back with the outfit in two weeks.

Your loving son,
Kenyon

Detachments of Patients
4153 U.S.A. Hospital Plant
A.P.O. 350, Postmaster, N.Y.
October 12, 1944
England

Dear Mother and Father:

Perhaps you are wondering how I got back to England and what process a soldier goes through before he is evacuated from the battle zone. A short letter on this subject may prove of interest to you.

I was hit at about 11:30 A.M., October 5th. At the time our Company was operating as an isolated unit sent over a dike onto some low, flat ground intersected by drainage ditches and directly below the artillery-infested hills occupied by the Germans. Since our object was to cut off some enemy who had broken through the night before, we moved off at dawn, walking silently and speedily through the cold ground mist. We had no transport with us, no stretchers or jeeps. Each platoon was followed by an aid man with his bandages, sulfa pills, morphine syrettes, and tags. In case of injury, every man had on his person a parachutists' first-aid kit—made, ironically enough, by Yardley's of Bond Street—a compact bundle approximately four inches square and six inches long which he either taped to his trench knife on his leg or tied to his helmet and which contained a morphine syrette, some sulfa powder, and a bandage. He also had a shell dressing, a similar package without the sulfa powder. These came in handy later.

After various skirmishes and some amusing sharpshooting at odd Germans, I ran up to a hedgerow junction with two other lads who also hoped to get a close shot at some Jerry. Two of our boys were firing like mad and shouting happily, "I got one, goddammit, I got one!" when suddenly an enemy machine gun spat out of the bushes.

I was knocked down and spun around by the force of the blow against my right leg, which felt as though it had been hit with a baseball bat. I immediately picked myself up, went back to the hedgerow, and found the aid man. Rolling up my right pants leg, he discovered a quantity of blood and two holes through my calf. He wiped away the blood, sprinkled some sulfa powder on the wound, wrapped a bandage around my leg, and asked me what I wanted to do. Noticing that the German artillery was beginning to range in on us, I said I was going to get the hell out of there. My leg throbbed and I limped, but I had no *intention of lying still on* that *target range. I decided to head for the battalion aid station, some two miles in our rear.*

When I was about 150 yards away from the Company and heading for a drainage ditch, the German artillery spotter, a man with an odd sense of humor, must have seen me and notified his 88s, because I suddenly heard the dry whirr and the sharp metallic blam of five or six shells, all meant for me and all within ten yards. Scared? I felt both terrified and self-conscious. I got behind a small mound and crawled through mud and cow dung for fifty yards. By that time the enemy had more worthwhile targets in the two machine guns we had set up on the dike, and so I was able to limp furiously over an open field, up the dike, and down the other side. I decided to head away from that area until I hit a road which would take me to the rear, because I knew the Germans had broken through on both sides; I had no intention of being ambushed just when I was assured a couple of weeks in a clean hospital.

After a mile and a half staggering through cornfields, over plowed land, over fences, and in wet drainage ditches, I arrived at a large farmhouse, where I was taken in, given hot milk, coffee, and delicious German pancakes with jam, and told that someone was fetching the American soldiers up the road. My appearance was enough to inspire various Dutch exclamations of pity. I hadn't shaved in eighteen days, my combat suit, unwashed in that time, was covered with dirt and dung, my right pants leg below the knee was rather bloody. While I was sitting in this farmhouse, I remembered to take my eight sulfa pills and lots of water. Half an hour and three pancakes later I was amazed to be greeted by two boys from F Company, then in reserve, who told me the Dutch had said there was an English soldier up here dying of his wounds! Americans aren't the only people who exaggerate.

They sat me on a bicycle, wheeled me up to a crossroads where I waited for the medical jeep, and left me in the sun and quiet with some bazookamen, to one of whom I gave my rifle which I had held on to until then. When the jeep finally came, covered with red crosses and driven by one of my old sick-call acquaintances, I was put across the engine hood, informed that we would go fast because the man on the rear stretcher was badly wounded, and told to relax.

The jeep delivered me to the regimental aid station. Here were assembled the major in charge of the 506th medics, the dentist—to give morphine and plasma, etc.—and some enlisted medics from Regimental Headquarters Company. This is the first place where completely adequate aid treatment can be given and it is usually set up in a civilian hospital or, as in our case, in a local schoolhouse. In the American chain of combat medical stations this is about the only place where men die. If you can live until you are treated here, you will not die along the route. Here I was completely tagged, was given water, and finally put in a jeep, covered with blankets, and driven to a former civilian hospital in a large city twelve miles away. I was never so relieved to depart from a place.

At this large hospital we were reclassified and given tetanus shots. Those with very minor wounds and those whose injuries were so severe they demanded immediate attention were kept behind, but I was tagged "evacuation" and put in an ambulance. We rode way down near the Dutch border to an American evacuation hospital, a tent city. Here I spent the night, slept on a cot, and ate some good meals. They also marked me "evacuation."

Next day about four we were taken to a British evacuation hospital and went through the same process of examination, change of dressing, and tagging. We were also given tea. The only reason I can see for this duplication was the tea. The rest didn't make sense. Another ambulance took us away—a boxlike British vehicle—far away to Brussels. On the road we stopped for a quick beer (two and a half apiece for me and the other fellow from my Company), arriving in that lovely city about twilight. Here we were put up at another British hospital. They had taken it over so recently that the German army notices were still on the bulletin boards! We were given tea and stew and white bread, that greatest of luxuries in wartime Europe. More tagging. The nurses wore quaint uniforms and were called "Sister," an anachronism that struck me as totally unnecessary, the enlisted men ward boys acted a little self-importantly, and the doctors were stuffy. I missed that breezy informality and that efficient cleanliness so native to American hospitals, but I enjoyed my deep hot bath. That, incidentally, was the first time I washed myself all over with hot water since I had jumped. One night I had stripped and taken an icy bath at a farmhouse pump, but that didn't count really, because it had failed to loosen up the dirt ingrained in my skin.

Unfortunately, I had no time to enjoy myself in Brussels because next morning I was taken to another tent hospital near an airport, checked again, put in a C-47, and, together with about twenty-five other walking wounded, English, Canadians, and American airborne, flown through a thick fog to England. When we came down out of the clouds and saw the familiar rolling hills, the hedgerows, the gray stone houses, I could have shouted with joy. I never felt relaxed on the Continent; twice when we were riding in trucks in what we thought was comparative safety we were shelled by the Germans. In England you know you're safe.

From this R.A.F. airdrome we were taken to an American general hospital where we were given all we could eat and retagged. American food tasted good *after more than two weeks on a British diet of tea, beef stew, meat and vegetable stew, beefsteak and kidney stew, and fruit pudding. Nobody complained about the tea, however, for it was a mixture of dehydrated tea, concentrated sugar, and dried milk all mixed together which, when poured into boiling water, made a stimulating drink of which we have no equal.*

We only stayed at that hospital long enough to have our data investigated and our stomachs filled. Then we rode an ambulance to our present home.

When I stepped out, I was amazed to find myself at the same hospital I stayed in after France. At first I was depressed, because that hospital was run like a concentration camp—patients not allowed in the kitchen, patients not allowed passes (we sneaked out over the fences), etc. But the hospital is under new management—snacks served at 4:00 and after supper, passes to town from 1:30 to 11:00, a newer, more tolerant attitude on the part of the doctors and nurses, and more efficient medical care. It's a pleasure to live here now. I am looking forward to several weeks' rest.

I wish I could tell you how well our medics have looked after us, how much care they take all along the line, from the brave, unarmed company aid men to the efficient medical staff of these general hospitals in England. You can rest assured that American wounded really do get the best care possible.

Your loving son,
Kenyon

Detachments of Patients
4153 U.S.A. Hospital Plant
A.P.O. 350, Postmaster, N.Y.
October 14, 1944
England

Dear Mother and Father:

It has been said that old soldiers never die. Although an airburst or a stray shot occasionally kills an old soldier, the casualty rate among the veterans is noticeably lower than among green troops or replacements. There are several reasons for this.

The longer a man is in action the more cautious he becomes. The old soldier leaves very little to chance. At one village in Holland, our convoy was fired upon and two-thirds of our Company had to dig in in an orchard and spend thirty-six hours under continuous shell fire. Every time there would be a letup, we would dig our slit trenches deeper; in six hours another fellow and I had made a hole four and a half feet deep, about fifteen inches wide, and six feet long. When at last we were able to march north to rejoin the undamaged third of our Company which had gotten through to the next town, we were appalled to find that they hadn't even dug in. We immediately started digging and didn't stop until we were at least four feet down. We had learned our lesson. Even though there were no 88s in the vicinity, we dug in. Old soldiers don't take chances.

You will find that the old soldiers noticeably (censored); they know better. One infantry replacement in one ward told us that the veterans in his outfit made him (censored) as soon as he was assigned to a squad. In our Battalion the old men prefer to be ammunition bearers and riflemen, leaving the scouting and bazooka activity to the (censored).

Old soldiers, too, have learned by bitter experience to be independent and to make their own decisions. Once our lieutenant told my squad leader to take his eight men and knock out some antiaircraft guns that were firing on a flight of gliders that was passing overhead. Nine men with rifles fighting dual-purpose 88s and 40 millimeters! The sergeant said yes (censored). By using his own judgment he saved our lives in a situation where a new man would have rushed in blindly. This same lieutenant later ordered two scouts into a German position, but they, knowing better, got (censored).

These hard-learned lessons are revealed nowhere better, however, than when a man is wounded. The veteran rushes to the aid man as fast as possible and gets off the battlefield with all the speed left him. He doesn't wait to be told what to do, because he wants to make damned sure he is evacuated from that hell which we all hate.

Perhaps I have made the veterans sound a little cynical. I have omitted some of the positive facts we have learned as we go along. We have learned not to let the artillery and mortars pin us down so badly that we cannot fire at the attacking enemy. We have learned not to be afraid of the sound of German small-arms fire but to keep our heads up and our rifles ready to pick off their operators. A small-arms fight is fun. Artillery, however, takes the joy out of life!! A few of us have even acquired a surface calm under fire which is the envy of the replacements. I am not one of those few, but I have learned to look at the noise and confusions a little more objectively.

Thus the old soldier, unshaven, dirty, quiet, cautious, cool, always prompted *by the motive of self-preservation, (censored) keeps alive as long as possible. Old soldiers die, but they die hard.*

> *Your loving son,*
> *Kenyon*

P.S. Better write to hospital address for a couple of weeks.

> *Detachment of Patients*
> *4153 U.S.A. Hospital Plant*
> *A.P.O. 350, Postmaster, N.Y.*
> *October 21, 1944*
> *England*

Dear Mother and Father:

The morning has been so like that when we went out to cut off "some" Germans—misty, cold, and quiet—that it brings back disturbing memories.

The big news is not the weather, however, but the invasion of the Philippines. I am sure that you were as thrilled as all of us in the ward when we heard the news, first as a Japanese report, then as an official M.D. announcement. Until I looked at a map today I had not realized how close Leyte was to Cebu; did we pass this island by chance on our way to or from Zamboanga? MacArthur must be a happy man indeed.

If and when all the islands are taken and we are shipped to the Pacific as soon as this phase of the war is over, I wouldn't mind jumping on a big beach-head in China. A beachhead is more appealing than the kind of maneuver we pulled in Holland, where there was no immediate certainty of reinforcements or supplies or the comforting appearance of American doughfeet. In the invasion of France we knew all that materiel was only a couple of miles away and hurry-ing in our direction.

But enough of that. If I had my choice, I'd never fight again. having no choice, I'll go back in a week or so and prepare for another jump. If I die, I hope it'll be fast.

Your letter of September 27th, describing the visit to the Ossorios', where there was "just homemade ice cream" (we have had ice cream once in thirteen months), and the affairs of Franklin and John Fitzell, arrived yesterday. When I say it was welcome, I understate the case, for it was the first letter in more than two weeks. You will be interested to hear that Gilbert Nicol is still fighting the battle of London at Grosvenor Square and sends his best. How is Jim Hawley? or Mots Lacozette? Hawley was wearing Marine sergeant's stripes as a weather observer at Quantico the last I knew, but I have a feeling he has been shipped abroad by now.

Your writing of the complacency at home comes as no great shock. Some people blame the untraveled Americans for enjoying themselves while they are fighting, but this doesn't worry me, because I had a good time while men were dying on Corregidor and landing on Guadalcanal. What irritates me are those American news analysts who read in the siege of Aachen the immediate defeat of Germany, who describe minor gains in the Siegfried Line as stabs in the back of Hitler, who make the war seem so easy and clean. Dealing in speculation and prediction as contrasted with facts, they compare very unfavorably with the calm, matter-of-fact, realistic B.B.C. announcers. The British, no matter what anybody says, understand war.

Christmas seems to be approaching fast. Please take as much of my savings as you need and use it for: 1) aunts and uncles, 2) the Trowbridges, 3) John and Frank, 4) Mrs. Loewenstein (some flowers), 5) Father and Mother (say $10 fancy Christmas basket of candied fruit, rich chocolates, salted nuts, etc., if that meets with your approval). Don't spare the cash; at times I doubt whether I'll ever get back to enjoy it.

Meanwhile, happy Thanksgiving and a Merry Christmas!

Your loving son,
Kenyon

Detachment of Patients
4153 U.S. Army Hospital Plant
A.P.O. 63, Postmaster N.Y.
December 8, 1944
England

Dear Mother and Father:

Your letter of October 30th, describing your trip to Taft and your reactions to Mrs. Eliot, arrived tonight. Many thanks. Having received my first message from Frank yesterday, I now feel that my correspondence is complete. Frank, *incidentally, is suffering from that epidemic of cynicism which has seized so many Americans abroad when they learn how the "occupied" peoples really lived under the Germans.*

After two delightful months in the hospital, I am scheduled to leave Monday or Tuesday. Although I dread battling in the cold worse than death itself, I am prepared to meet my doom in the Regiment. Perhaps I shall see Frank while I am still in garrison over there.

One of the most enjoyable features of my stay in the hospital has been the meeting with new and genial American soldiers. These friendly, happy-go-lucky G.I.s keep things humorous no matter what happens; the more I see of my fellow citizens the more I am convinced of the fact that America is really a wonderful country. You would be proud of the United States if you could see how well the American soldiers take their wounds and pain, not quietly and grimly like the British, or childishly whining like the Germans, but jokingly and humorously.

While I was in the hospital I had a chance to catch up on Somerset Maugham, now my favorite modern author. I liked "Rain" the best, Cakes and Ale *second,* Ashenden *third, and* Of Human Bondage *least. He seems in his medium when he is writing a short story. The Armed Forces Edition, pocket-sized reprints of all the best and popular books on the market, and no gift of that overrated organization, the Red Cross, led me to Maugham and to several other excellent authors.*

The optimism about the Philippines seems to have disappeared and left in its place that grim statement: "American troops on Leyte are holding their own!" Now Eisenhower warns us of an impending rubber shortage and the Germans prepare to fight bitterly for every inch of their soil. The government, always the first to condemn optimism, still does not print pictures of dead American soldiers, of burning British tanks—a common sight in Holland—or of bombers going down in flames, the victims of the fiercest antiaircraft fire these pilots claim they've ever seen. I think our whole propaganda machine is rotten clear through.

I wonder if the civilians at home realize, for instance, what an airborne operation in Germany will mean? It means trench foot and frostbite; it means ground so hard the shells go off quicker with more damaging effect and foxholes cannot be dug. It means more tanks and artillery than in Normandy or Holland. It means civilian snipers and boy cutthroats. I can see no glamour or glory in such an affair, but that's all the newspapers in the States will feature, that and the heroes. War is the nastiest business on earth; apparently our government considers that truth a military secret.

*December already. December, though it contains Christmas, does not bring
back sweet memories. I cannot forget Joanny and Moeyer.*

*The British are shooting the Greeks, the Belgians are rebelling, and the
French are protesting joining the Regular Army (the only good Frenchmen are
those fighting in Alsace-Lorraine); the rest of them strike me as selfish hyp-
ocrites, summer soldiers and sunshine patriots. Is this what we are fighting for?
Did our fine boys die in Normandy and Holland for the sake of British power
politics or unappreciative Frenchmen and Belgians? Sometimes I think we
should have left that diseased European continent in the hands of the Germans
and let them worry about it.*

*If I should die in this next jump, however, please do not think that I died
without hope or a belief in our cause. I hope that we can help the world to be a
better place and I believe that we, as a strong nation, were justified in going
to help the oppressed peoples of Europe. America in itself is a nation worth
dying for.*

> *Your loving son,*
> *Kenyon*

> *Detachment of Patients*
> *4153 U.S. Army Hospital Plant*
> *A.P.O. 63, Postmaster, N.Y.*
> *December 12, 1944*
> *England*

Dear Mother and Father,

*Until I came overseas I did not know the first thing about Army censorship.
I was under the vague impression that our mail was inspected and stamped by
an officer in a large office in London, a mysterious individual given to making
wisecracks—this was before Eisenhower made that a court-martial offense—
and blithely snipping out whole pages of correspondence. Since you seem to be
under this impression and since there is nothing else to write about, perhaps
you would be interested in hearing how censorship works.*

*Back in camp the vast majority of our mail is given to the company executive
officer to censor. In his absence the job is taken over by some other officer, generally a 1st lieutenant. The mail is taken from the letter box every morning and
censored immediately. If the officer finds something particularly objectionable,*

he may save a letter and read the offending part to the Company, warning them against writing similar. If the letter seems to violate all the rules of security (i.e., contains information giving aid or comfort to the enemy), it is returned to the writer.

This clause "giving aid or comfort to the enemy" can be very freely interpreted, as I have found out several times, because every officer has his own ideas about security. Frank could write, for instance, that he thought his old outfit stank and get away with it, because he had an easygoing censor, but when I once described my Regiment as amateurish, I was given a five-minute lecture in which I was called every name it's permissible for an officer to call an enlisted man and told never again to discuss military affairs; my censor had gotten up out of the wrong side of his bed. On the whole, this Company censorship works out as well as is possible under the circumstances.

Letters containing very personal matters, however, are enclosed in a blue envelope, sealed, and sent to the base censor. The unit censor has nothing whatsoever to do with this mail.

In the hospital our mail is censored by the wounded officers in their own wards. Since they must have some understanding of what the men are writing about who have just been evacuated from the front and since they have no other work or details to occupy their time, these men are given this chore. I imagine that certain officers are given certain wards to take care of.

Thus you will see that our mail is censored by combat men and not, as you imply, by certain rear-echelon individuals who live in ivory castles in London. Although it's an annoying thing, our censorship on the whole is both necessary and bearable.

> Your loving son,
> Kenyon

Co. E, 506 Parachute-Infantry
A.P.O. 472, Postmaster
New York, N.Y.
February 9, 1945
France

Dear Mother and Father,

After two months in the hospital and two months in replacement depots being shunted through half of England and all France, a very quiet, dead country
right now, incidentally, in trucks and boxcars, I am finally home again. Of
course, I am sleeping with my boots on and a pistol in my pocket and am sere-
naded by occasional mortar shells, but on the whole our life in cellars is relatively calm and secure. We have two excellent stoves and are living quite well.

I was amazed in passing through France at how deserted the countryside was.
A heavy snow lay over everything, making driving precarious and emphasizing
the bitter cold. All the houses had their windows closed tightly and nobody was
out on the street; it was as though all France were in mourning. Cognac, however, was plentiful—a thimbleful for thirty francs, but the beer was very watery.
We could buy no food at all. The people, it seemed to me, were neither friendly
nor resentful, accepting the Americans as a necessary evil. It wasn't the France
we had read about in geography books.

Coming back to the platoon after it has been through something rough like
the Bastogne affair is always a sad experience. So few (censored) that I wonder
how long it will be before I, too, disappear. I guess the only thing to do is to expect the worse, hope for the best, grab all the liquor and food left behind by the
civilians, and live as comfortably as possible. Life has become strictly a day-to-
day and hour-to-hour affair.

My God, Cobb has just brought in my first mail in two months. A Time, a
letter from Mrs. Smith—which I have no stomach for—two letters from Ann,
and two bundles of clippings from you. Please do not send me these military
commentators or other trash unless it concerns the paratroops; or this Division;
or a friend. I appreciate your thoughtfulness, but I do not have the inclination
to read the armchair strategists. As far as the manpower shortage, the infantry
shortage, and the nurse shortage is concerned, it seems to me from my limited
experience that it's not a question of getting more people in the Army but of using what they have properly. There's an awful lot of wasted labor in this Army.

The fellows in the platoon tell me that Frank kept coming to base camp

looking for me. Owing to the amazing inefficiency of the (censored), I was de-
layed so long I have never yet seen him. Now I do not know if I ever will. Please
tell him I'm very sorry I missed connections. And how is John? I still do not
know his address.

Blam! Blam! Blam! Life is never dull. There go the mortars. Sometimes up
here it sounds like a summer thunderstorm. There goes another one. Time for me
to sign off.

Your loving son,
Kenyon

Co. E, 506 Parachute Infantry
A.P.O. 472, Postmaster, N.Y.
April 14, 1945
Germany

Dear Mother and Father:

When we received the news yesterday morning of the President's death, I
found it hard to believe that another familiar landmark had disappeared. I had
come to take Roosevelt for granted, like spring and Easter lilies, and now that
he is gone, I feel a little lost.

If there wasn't a war going on, it wouldn't have been so hard to lose Mr.
Roosevelt. Granted that he had a flippant way, ignored the monetary facts of
life, and gathered about him a group of dreamers and swamis, still he prepared
this country for a war which he and other thinking people saw would soon in-
volve the United States. Without his leadership, I doubt if Congress would have
extended the draft service beyond a year or appropriated enough money to en-
large our navy. The senseless bickering of petty backbiters—many of them so
antagonistic to the President's personality they would have risked everything,
including the fate of America, in order to destroy him—almost lost the war for
us in 1941 if it hadn't been for Mr. Roosevelt's firm, guiding hand. Of course,
his politics at home were not perfect, but war is more important than politics.

I think that his death will be felt more strongly overseas both in Army areas
and in the Allied nations than it will at home, because Roosevelt's personality
was the strong adhesive which kept America, Britain, and Russia together. Al-
though no man is indispensable, the loss of such a popular leader is going to

mean a great deal abroad, especially in these critical times, when the peace can be won or lost so easily. The soldiers felt that Roosevelt could present America's case for international cooperation most efficiently. His ideals and hopes for a better world, combined with his pleasing personality, could have given the United States a high position in Europe. Now that he is dead, I do not have much confidence in the coming peace.

It seems a long time since that rainy winter day in 1932 when Frank and I stood in the tree before the Capitol and watched Mr. Roosevelt take his inaugural oath. When I think back that far, I feel like an old man, so much has happened. First there was repeal, then the N.R.A., then our trip to the Philippines, then the W.P.A., then Hitler's Anschluss in Austria and the death of King Albert, the war in Spain and Abyssinia, Joanny's death, and Pearl Harbor. When I joined the Army, something died inside me. That something disappeared altogether when we stood up and hooked up in Normandy and I saw the fantastic lights of the German tracer bullets ripping the sky. Seeing all the dead paratroopers and Germans, I was impressed with one fact—life isn't worth living if you don't try to make the most of every minute of it. I don't mean being virtuous or successful necessarily, but happy. I'd hate like hell to die and feel that I had missed any pleasure.

Now I read in the papers that General Marshall has announced that all possible men will be shipped to the Pacific straight from this theater. Although I am on the States' list, standing one chance in twenty-five, I do not think that I'll ever get home again. General Marshall phrased his proclamation in such a way that he made it sound as though every G.I. was so anxious to get the war with Japan over with that he was willing to sacrifice his hopes of getting home as soon as Germany was defeated. Does General Marshall realize that the soldiers in combat outfits who have lived through these campaigns, living only to get home even for just a furlough, may be killed in the Asiatic theater? The war will end sooner there, but over the dead bodies of men who fought over here, who saw their friends die and their companies reduced to half strength, men who were rewarded for long, hard service by being told they would never get home.

For the first time since I entered the Army, I was mad enough to write a letter to some high officer. I wrote General Marshall just how I and the seven other Normandy men left in the platoon felt about his statement. My letter was returned by the battalion commander.

Which is one thing I hate about the Army. You are helpless. Not only do you lose all identity but also all those rights which, as a civilian, you took for *granted, especially the privilege of telling off anybody who tries to cheat you. I am sick and tired of this whole Army. When they pull a stunt like that—giving you one chance in a million to get home alive—I figure it's time to start hoping to get shot again.*

We are, as I have said in other letters, in Germany. Ever since we entered this country, we have been living in private houses complete with electricity and hot and cold running water. The owners of our billets evacuated on two hours' notice, so we sleep on good beds (you can't get much out of a house in two hours) and cook with the proper utensils. Physically speaking, it's just like home.

The Germans I have seen so far have impressed me as clean, efficient, law-abiding people. I do not believe them when they say they never did like Hitler or that war is no good (their pictures, letters, postcards, calendars, and newspapers emphasize too much the glory of battle), but I will say that our propaganda has lied again, just as it did in France. Among other things, we have been told that Hitler destroyed all religion. If this is true, then why do we find crosses and crucifixes in every German home we occupy or examine? Why do the Germans continue going to church, making of it as great a ceremony as do the good citizens of Bronxville? In Germany everybody goes out and works in the fields and, unlike the French, who do not seem inclined to lift a finger to help themselves, the Germans fill up the trenches soldiers have dug in their fields. They are cleaner, more progressive, and more ambitious than either the English or the French.

But the same Germans have a queer twist to their characters which leads them to glorify war. They did not complain when Hitler shouted, "Heute gehort uns Deutschland, morgen die ganze Welt." These same people, misled by a propaganda as strong as ours, invaded Czechoslovakia, Poland, and France and wallowed in it. What I cannot forgive the Germans, however, is their enslaving the people of Europe. This is not propaganda but truth, because we were at one time near a slave-labor stalag and saw these people who were torn from their homes in Russia, Poland, Holland, France, and Belgium, and shipped to Germany to spend the rest of their lives behind barbed wire working for the Germans. I was walking guard one dark rainy night around a hut when I was seized with curiosity and peeped behind a shutter. There, seated knitting on double-deck bunks, were two women at least seventy years old. Several baby girls played on the floor near them. Here was Germany. Here was the new order; innocent lives ripped up from their homes and forced to labor for the Master Race. When somebody damages property, you can forgive them, but when they tamper with life, that great and only irreplaceable, you cannot help but wish them in hell. I hope these Germans are shipped off to Russia.

Your loving son,

Kenyon

Co. E, 506 Parachute Infantry

A.P.O. 472, Postmaster, N.Y.

May 13, 1945

Germany

Dear Mother and Father:

While recovering from a hangover, I shall take time out to write you a brief note. My life has been so pleasant—as a matter of fact, this period in Germany is the only time I enjoyed in the Army—that I have not had the urge to correspond. Although we are not allowed to fraternize with the women, we can, and I for one do, sunbathe or tour the countryside all day when not on guard, swimming, climbing over the hills, etc. Our living conditions have been superb and the food very plentiful, but what I like best of all is the sunny warm climate. No rain in the last ten days. If I had to live in Europe, I would live in Germany.

What have we been doing here? No action, but rounding up and guarding the thousands of German soldiers who have come down from the mountains to surrender. Every road you travel is lined with men loaded with packs and looking for somebody to surrender to. We have picked up and looted individuals from the Wehrmacht, the S.S.—very snappy, thoroughly hated soldiers—and the Luftwaffe, officers, noncoms, and privates. From them we have obtained pistols, knives, watches, fur-lined coats, camouflaged jump jackets (from a Luftwaffe officer who did not appreciate the fact that I was relieving him of excess weight). Most of these soldiers have taken it in pretty good spirit, but once in a while we get an individual who does not like to lose his watch. A pistol flashed in his face, however, can persuade anybody. I now have a Luger, two P-38s (similar to Lugers), a Schmeisser machine pistol, two jump smocks, one camouflaged winter jacket, several flags about three feet by two, and a watch. If they ever let us, I'll mail some of this back.

One of the best things we have appropriated is liquor—good French champagne and better brandy. While in Berchtesgaden I went up the hill to Hitler's bombed hideout and grabbed two cases of excellent champagne from the wine cellar. Now we can get drunk every night for nothing. What a life!

For a while we were allowed to take one German truck per squad. The captain found a beautiful Mercedes Benz, belonging to some S.S. general, but lost it to the regimental commander while we kept our Volkswagens, Schwimmwagens, staff cars, pickup trucks, fire engines, ambulances, and big troop carriers. When we went down the road, we looked like a column of gypsies. The big trouble with these vehicles was the fact that they had been driven so hard and so long that most of them broke down shortly after we got them. Whenever we needed gas, we just drove into a service station and helped ourselves. I wouldn't trade Germany for England and France put together.

Now we are resting and waiting for something to break, something about furloughs home. According to the point system, my score is 74. I hope I never visit the C.B.I.

You asked about this man Guzowsky from Brooklyn. He was in the 4th Infantry Division, was wounded in the right leg on his way into the Siegfried Line, and lives in that section of Brooklyn which overlooks the Narrows. Walter Guzowsky.

Would you do a favor for me? A friend of mine from Hartsdale and Taft was killed in an airplane accident in England in the fall. He was a very happy-go-lucky fellow, always full of good spirits and horseplay. I brought him up to the house several times. His name was Charlie Mead and, although I have already written his mother, I would appreciate it if you would go up and see her at 5 Walworth Avenue, first street off the Hartsdale station on the right-hand side of the tracks going toward White Plains, and tell her that I'll really miss Charlie and that I'm very sorry I am not able to see her myself.

The shirts and trunks arrived recently. Most welcome. Pictures also. Ann is really growing up.

We have now seen England, Scotland, France, Belgium, Holland, Luxembourg, and Germany. I haven't lived in a slit trench since October 5th and very glad of it too.

Your loving son,
Kenyon

P.S. Please thank Mrs. Fitzell for her letter and tell her I'm too busy to write. Squad leader's come back. Am now assistant.

Co. E, 506 Parachute Infantry
A.P.O. 472, Postmaster, N.Y.
May 28, 1945
Germany

Dear Mother and Father:

I don't want to be in Germany this winter. Already you can see signs of impending trouble in the mass of children who hang around our mess hall begging for food, in the surly soldiers tramping the roads, in the ordinary citizens who will do almost anything for a bite to eat, because already the food supply is getting low. What food reserves the Germans had have largely been appropriated by the Wehrmacht or the U.S. Army. The railroads have been bombed so hard that shipment of foodstuffs from areas of plenty to areas of scarcity is almost impossible. The net result will be a very rough winter for everybody.

These discharged soldiers whose endless columns marching down the side roads and the Autobahns give Germany the appearance of a nation of bums. The men are mostly city men, men from Berlin, Ludwigshafen, Cologne, Aachen, Duesseldorf, Hamburg, Bremen, and a dozen others, men who will go home to nothing with nothing. Although General Eisenhower has told them to work on the land, most of them intend to return to their old homes. When they get there, they will find nothing but ruins. There will be no factories left to work in and no houses in which to live. Food will be almost impossible to get. By late fall, the situation will be so bad that these men, now desperate, will get together in gangs and steal food, killing anybody who gets in their way. They will be very hard to control. Already one parachute regiment from the 82nd Division is having trouble in Essen. No, I don't want to be in Germany this winter.

Right now, however, Germany, or I should say, Austria, is very pleasant. Although we are being treated to great quantities of mountain rain, the weather on the whole is so sunny that I have acquired a deep tan and have been able to go swimming almost every day I'm not on guard. The food has been excellent, the beds are soft, and there are still forty-eight bottles of gin. It's the soldier's dream life.

The only thing that mars our paradise is the large number of accidents. I suppose a certain percentage of the men must suffer injuries and death, but it seems such a tragedy that a man will live through several campaigns only to die in a car wreck or be shot through the head by some drunken coward. The combination of liquor, pistols, and captured vehicles is very bad. It's heart-breaking to lose a friend this late in the game. In fact, the only casualties we have suffered since we left base camp at Mourmelon have been caused by accidents.

Your packages, letters, and magazines are appreciated as much as ever.

Your loving son,

Kenyon

Co. E, 506 Para;-Inf.
A.P.O. 472, Postmaster
New York, N.Y.
June 5, 1945
Austria

Dear Sister,

Tonight at ten o'clock we start celebrating the jump on Normandy, for then it will be exactly a year to the day and hour since we went to the airport loaded with equipment and ammunition (just a belt and a bandoleer per rifleman) and sat under the plane wings, listening to the pilots warm up the motors. The summer nights in England are so long that it was still light when we took our seasick pills and boarded the C-47s at eleven. My heart was beating like Gene Krupa's drum and my stomach was tied up and very empty. I figured I'd never live through that jump. Then we took off.

Two hours flying in the pitch black until we were stood up and hooked up over the Channel Islands, waiting for the coast of Normandy. Nobody had to tell us when we reached hostile territory. The sky lit up like a burning ammunition dump. Sweat? There were twenty-one men in the plane and I was number eighteen. The plane gasped and heaved as the pilot alternately gunned and slowed his motor to foil antiaircraft sound detectors. Green light. Rattle-rattle-bam-crash the boys went out the door. When I left that death trap, I looked down and all I could see was water. From now on, I thought, I'm here to stay. Might as well make the best of it. Splash!

Patches of the moonlight. Minutes of darkness. Water three feet deep. Drainage ditches six feet deep. German machine-gun fire spraying the next battalion as they jumped. Sniper fire cracking over the flood area. Cold, cold water. Day-

break; still in the swamp. Dead paratroopers floating on their stomachs, their chutes swaying back and forth gently in the front of them. B-26s bombing the beach. D-Day.

Now I am sitting in a cozy house in the Austrian Alps. I have a tall glass of iced tea and gin in one hand, my pen in the other. A lot of boys who took off from that Devonshire airport are dead, buried in lovely cemeteries in St. Mere Eglise, Zon, and in Belgium, but I'm still here and very thankful for it and to-night I shall remember them in the way they would have thought most fitting— by having a wild, noisy party.

Your loving brother,
Kenyon

ABOUT THE AUTHOR

DAVID KENYON WEBSTER worked as a reporter and writer after the war. *The Saturday Evening Post* published a portion of his memoir, but book publishers rejected his manuscript, seeking sensationalized novels of the war rather than authentic memoirs. He died in 1961 in a boating accident while shark fishing.